THE FA

The Fall of Tsarism contains a series of gripping, plain-spoken testimonies from some of the leading participants of the Russian Revolution of February 1917, including the future revolutionary premier Alexander Kerenskii.

Recorded in the spring of 1917, months before the Bolsheviks seized power, these interviews represent the earliest first-hand testimonies on the overthrow of the Tsarist regime known to historians. Hidden away and presumed lost for the better part of a century, they are now revealed to the world for the first time.

Semion Lyandres is Professor of Modern Russian History, University of Notre Dame, and author of *The Bolshevik's German Gold Revisited: An Inquiry into the 1917 Accusations* (1995). He is also co-editor, with Dietmar Wulff, of the diaries of Petr P. Vologodskii (2002, 2007).

THE FALL OF TSARISM

UNTOLD STORIES OF THE FEBRUARY 1917 REVOLUTION

SEMION LYANDRES

OXFORD
UNIVERSITY PRESS

OXFORD
UNIVERSITY PRESS

Great Clarendon Street, Oxford, OX2 6DP,
United Kingdom

Oxford University Press is a department of the University of Oxford.
It furthers the University's objective of excellence in research, scholarship,
and education by publishing worldwide. Oxford is a registered trade mark of
Oxford University Press in the UK and in certain other countries

First published 2013
First published in paperback 2014

Impression: 1

British Library Cataloguing in Publication Data

Data available

ISBN 978–0–19–923575–9 (Hbk.)
ISBN 978–0–19–871348–7 (Pbk.)

Preface

The Russian Revolution of February 1917 was a defining event of the twentieth century, shaping much of what has followed. In nine short days, the centuries-old tsarist regime was overthrown, and a chain of events was set in motion that led to the disintegration of the Russian empire and the rise of the Soviet regime that would come to dominate the world stage. Yet even today, as we approach the centennial of the February Revolution—and twenty years after the opening of the previously inaccessible Russian archives—historians still lack firsthand contemporary accounts of what happened during those nine fateful days. This volume presents for the first time the earliest known oral histories (interviews) of the February Revolution as told by ten of its leading participants shortly after the events, at a time when the outcome of the revolution was far from certain.

The book is divided into two parts and consists of thirteen chapters. The first part (Chapters 1–2) traces the history of the interviews—from our efforts to resurrect these long-lost documents to the individuals and institutions who were responsible for recording and preserving them. The second part (Chapters 3–12) presents the interview transcripts. Each is prefaced by an introduction that includes a biographical note on the interviewee and the specific circumstances and significance of the interview, with textual and contextual annotations. The volume closes with an interpretive chapter that discusses the historical significance of the interviews and their broad implications for our understanding of the February Revolution.

Acknowledgments

Many people and institutions have contributed to the realization of this project in countless ways over the course of two decades. I owe the greatest debt of gratitude to Pavel Aleksandrovich Tribunskii who has been a source of constant assistance and encouragement at nearly every step of this long and challenging undertaking. I am most grateful to Samuel C. Ramer, who read the whole manuscript and made invaluable suggestions. I am also grateful to the following colleagues and friends for their support, advice, expertise, research, careful reading of various drafts, and other important assistance: Ilya Fine, Gary M. Hamburg, Mike Westrate, Louis E. Jordan, George Rugg, A. B. Nikolaev, Terence Emmons, James Turner, Rev. Wilson D. (Bill) Miscamble, CSC., Doris L. Bergen, Thomas J. Sanders, Richard Robbins, B. M. Witenberg, A. V. Smolin, Sabine MacCormack (1941–2012), Rex Wade, Robert Service, Maria Rogacheva, Sean Brennan, Jeanette Torok, Norman. M. Naimark, Michael S. Bernstam, David Hisle, Thomas Kselman, Jeffrey C. Kantor, A. James McAdams, E. A. Rostovtsev, Molly Molloy, Patricia Polansky, Nadia Zilper, Carol Leadenham, and Kenneth Kinslow.

I wish to thank the four anonymous readers who reviewed the typescript at different stages and offered helpful criticism which have greatly enhanced the quality of the final product. Finally, special thanks are due to Christopher Wheeler, Matthew Cotton, and Emma Barber of the Oxford University Press and to Mary Worthington for their patience, flexibility, careful reading of the typescript, good counsel, and unfailing cooperation.

Generous support for research and publication of this book was provided by several institutions, including the Earhart Foundation, the National Endowment for the Humanities (research fellowship FAA5513410), Notre Dame's Institute for the Scholarship in the Liberal Arts, Office of Research (Faculty Research Program), the Helen Kellogg Institute for International Studies, and the Nanovic Institute for European Studies.

In pursuing this project I have been sustained by the memory of the late Professor S. V. Utechin (1921–2004) who would have been very pleased with the publication of this book, which I gratefully dedicate to his blessed memory.

Contents

List of Illustrations

Textual Figure

List of Maps

List of Abbreviations

BLPES	British Library of Political and Economic Science
CHAG	Central Historical Archive of Georgia (formerly Central State Historical Archive of the Georgian Soviet Socialist Republic)
CWIC	Central War Industry Committee
EC	Executive Committee
FA	Family Archive
GARF	State Archive of the Russian Federation
GARO	State Archive of Riazan' oblast'
HIA	Hoover Institution Archives
HIC	Higher Investigative Commission
JMRHH	*Journal of Modern Russian History and Historiography*
IKPZh	*Izvestiia Komiteta Petrogradskikh zhurnalistov*
KA	*Krasnyi arkhiv*
MAA	Main Artillery Administration
MAGS	Main Administration of the General Staff
MAPP	M. A. Polievktov Papers
MC	Military Commission
MMA	Military Medical Academy
NIA SPb II RAN	Nauchno-istoricheskii arkhiv Sankt-Peterburgskogo Instituta istorii Rossiiskoi Akademii nauk (Scientific-Historical Archive of the St. Petersburg Institute of History of the Russian Academy of Sciences)
OGPU	Joint State Political Directorate, a successor to Cheka (Soviet secret political police)
ONO	Order Number One
OR RNB	Manuscript Department of the Russian National Library

RBD	Biographical Dictionary of the Imperial Russian Historical Society
RGVIA	Russian State Military History Archive
RGIA	Russian State Historical Archive
RPG	*The Russian Provisional Government, 1917: Documents,* 3 vols. Selected and ed. Robert Paul Browder, and Alexander F. Kerensky (Stanford: Stanford University Press, 1961)
SR	Socialist Revolutionary
SSR	Society for the Study of the [Russian] Revolution
Stavka	General Headquarters
TsGIA SPB	Central State Historical Archive of St. Petersburg
WPI	Women's Pedagogical Institute

ABBREVIATIONS USED IN ARCHIVE REFERENCES

d.	*delo* (file)
f.	fond
l./ll.	*list/listy* (folio[s])
ob.	verso
op.	*opis'* (finding aid)

A Note to the Reader

This is a translation of the Russian-language transcripts of interviews with ten leading participants in the events of the February Revolution in Petrograd: B. A. Engel'gardt, A. A. Chikolini, P. V. Gerasimov, M. V. Rodzianko, L. S. Tugan-Baranovskii, N. V. Nekrasov, N. S. Chkheidze, M. I. Skobelev, A. F. Kerenskii, and M. I. Tereshchenko. The interviews were conducted and recorded from May 4 to June 7, 1917 by the Interview Commission, which was organized and directed by the Petrograd historian M. A. Polievktov. The Commission was part of a broader effort by the Society for the Study of the Russian Revolution, headed by Polievktov's colleague A. E. Presniakov, to document the overthrow of Russia's old regime. The manuscripts are presently located in the Department of Rare Books and Special Collections of the Hesburgh Libraries, University of Notre Dame, Notre Dame, Indiana.

The original handwritten transcripts have been transcribed and translated specifically for this publication and are made available here for the first time. The interviews appear in their entirety: nothing has been omitted, embellished, or paraphrased. In translating the documents, the author sought to preserve the particularities of conversational Russian and, wherever possible, to use English idiomatic expressions that are equivalent and still maintain the interviews' format and style.

Names of people and institutions mentioned in the interviews are given as they appear in the original, either in full or abbreviated form. For example: "Kerenskii" or "Aleksandr Fedorovich Kerenskii"; "the Petrograd Soviet of Workers' Deputies" or "the Petrograd Soviet," or "the Petrograd Soviet of Workers' and Soldiers' Deputies"; "the Duma Committee" or "the Temporary Committee," or "the Temporary Duma Committee." Full names and definitions are provided in the notes.

Words and dates enclosed in square brackets have been inserted by the author for ease of comprehension. For example: "at around eight-thirty [in the evening]" or "commander of the [Baltic] fleet." *Italics* are used to indicate text written by members of the Interview Commission. Unless the authorship is identified in the original transcript or in the author's note, the italicized text belongs to Polievktov, who edited most of the interviews. Underlining in the original is noted in the translation. Transliterated Russian words in *italics*, which are inserted in square brackets after the English translation, are meant to offer the linguistically equipped reader an opportunity to see the original word or phrase when the English rendering is approximate or ambiguous.

Russian names of people, places, and institutions have been transliterated following the Library of Congress system (including diacritical marks) for the modern Russian orthography even though the transcripts are written in the old orthography, which was in use in Russia until 1918. The same rule has been followed for commonly known names. For example: Trotskii instead of Trotsky; Kerenskii instead of Kerensky; Aleksandra instead of Alexandra—all except for Nicholas II and Alexis. Names of streets, bridges, palaces, squares, rivers, churches, factories, and regimental barracks have been translated if they are well known in anglicized form or unambiguous (Winter Palace, Palace Embankment, Tauride Palace, or semicircular hall) but not otherwise (Povarskoi Lane, Mariinskii Palace, Sadovaia Street, Znamenskii Square, Nevskii Avenue).

The transcripts' original headings have been preserved; they are preceded by biographical information on the interviewee and highlights of the interview. Endnotes include textual annotations, cross-references, and bibliographic references, as well as biographical and historical information related to the period described in the interview. Notes on individuals are provided at first mention in the interviews only. The interviews are presented in chronological order. A Petrograd city map, a map of Nicholas II's train route (February 28–March 1, 1917), a diagram of the Tauride Palace, and a Chronology of Main Events are included. These supplementary materials are intended to be used with the text of the interviews and the notes for ease of reference.

All dates before February 1, 1918, in both the interviews and the notes, are given according to the "old style" or Julian calendar, which was thirteen days behind the "new style" or Gregorian calendar in the twentieth century. All dates after February 1, 1918, when Russia switched from the "old style" to the "new style," are given in accordance with the current calendar.

Chronology of Main Events Mentioned in the Interviews

Outbreak of First World War (August 1, 1914)

EVENTS OF 1917

January

27   Police arrest nine members of the Labor Group of the Central War Industry Committee (CWIC), including K. A. Gvozdev

February

9–22   Strikes escalate in Petrograd

14   Resumption of the Duma session

22   Nicholas II leaves for General Headquarters (Stavka) in Mogilev

23   International Women's Day; demonstrations begin in Vyborg District

24   Strikes and demonstrations increase and spread to all districts of the city, including Nevskii Avenue; meeting of Left "organizational bureau" at N. D. Sokolov's residence

25   Armed clashes between troops and demonstrators; Putilov workers join general strike; a few soldiers become insurgents; last meeting of the fourth State Duma before the prorogation; meeting of Kadet faction; meeting of Left "organizational bureau" at Maksim Gor'kii's residence; City Duma meets; police station chiefs killed by insurgents; Nicholas II orders Khabalov, by telegram, to subdue demonstrations; police arrest opposition leaders, including remaining members of the Labor Group of the CWIC

26   Armed clashes between troops and demonstrators; mutiny of the 4th Company of the Pavlovskii Guards Regiment's reserve battalion; commander of the Pavlovskii reserve battalion murdered by

demonstrators; Khabalov issues an order, following Nicholas II's instructions, to unit commanders in his district to use all necessary force to disperse demonstrating crowds; Khabalov also posts a proclamation to the population banning demonstrations and warning striking workers that they would be conscripted and sent to the front if they did not return to work by February 28; Rodzianko telegrams General Headquarters and the front commanders, but appeal to Nicholas II goes unanswered; meeting of Left "organizational bureau" at Kerenskii's residence; prorogation decree delivered to Rodzianko (retroactively dated Feb. 25, Rodzianko does not inform Duma until the morning of the 27th).

27   Soldiers' uprising is begun by Volynskii Regiment and spreads quickly to Preobrazhenskii, Pavlovskii, Litovskii, and Finliandskii Regiments, others join in later in the day, and by day's end there is widespread mutiny; insurgent troops begin arriving at Tauride Palace (continues over the next several days); striking workers seize weapons; most prisons overrun and prisoners released; Rodzianko sends second telegram to tsar; private meeting of the Duma deputies in the semicircular hall; formation of the Military Commission; formation of the Duma Committee; formation of the Soviet of Workers' Deputies; formation of the joint Food Supply Commission; establishment of Committee of Petrograd Journalists; first issue of Izvestiia of Petrograd Journalists published, which includes Soviet Executive Committee's appeal to the population; former tsarist ministers and high-ranking officials arrested on Kerenskii's orders; positive replies from Generals Ruzskii and Brusilov to Rodzianko's telegrams of Feb. 26; 1st Reserve Infantry Regiment arrives at Duma; Guchkov convinces General Zankevich to cease active operations against the insurgents; Nicholas II orders punitive expedition, led by General Ivanov; Duma delegation headed by Rodzianko negotiates with Grand Duke Mikhail Aleksandrovich in the Mariinskii Palace; Nicholas II refuses Mikhail's recommendation to appoint him temporary dictator; government resigns; Preobrazhenskii Regiment declares its support for the Duma Committee.

28   Soldiers from Strel'na, including the 2nd Machine-Gun Regiment, as well as soldiers from the Oranienbaum and Petergof garrisons, reach Petrograd and join the insurgents; insurgents accidentally fire upon Duma; insurgents take over Admiralty; Okhta gunpowder

plants seized by workers; insurgents seize Ministry of Transportation, including telegraph station; Military Commission issues "Rodzianko's Order" and Soviet denounces it; St. Peter and Paul Fortress comes under control of the Duma Military Commission; Khabalov arrested; Protopopov surrenders; negotiations regarding the Provisional Government begin between representatives of the Soviet Executive Committee and the Duma Committee overnight from Feb. 28–March 1 and continue, with interruptions, until March 2; Nicholas II leaves Mogilev for Tsarskoe Selo

March

1   Order Number One; Soviet Executive Committee presents their "program" to the Duma Committee; military officers in Petrograd meet and pass a resolution to support the Duma Committee; Grand Duke Kirill brings the naval Guards Equipage to the Duma to pledge allegiance to the Duma Committee; Grekov telegrams station chiefs along tsar's train route that imperial trains should be prevented from proceeding to Tsarskoe Selo; the tsar's train passes twice through Bologoe while trying to get through to Tsarskoe Selo, then turns west to Dno before finally arriving at Pskov; General Ivanov with part of his punitive expedition arrives at Tsarskoe Selo late at night, but Duma leaders had already convinced General Headquarters to abort Ivanov's mission, and he withdraws; Nicholas II refuses advice from Grand Dukes Kirill and Pavel to grant responsible ministry

2   Mutiny by naval crews stationed in Helsingfors harbor; Kerenskii appeals to his Petrograd Soviet colleagues to approve his participation in the cabinet; Steklov decries "Rodzianko's Order" of February 28 in a speech to the Petrograd Soviet; Duma Committee sends Guchkov and Shul'gin to Pskov to secure abdication, Nicholas II abdicates after meeting with them; Miliukov announces the formation of the Provisional Government and mentions the necessity of preserving the monarchical form of government under the regency of Grand Duke Mikhail Aleksandrovich

3   8-point declaration of the Provisional Government is published; delegation sent from Soviet to Sveaborg Fortress; Grand Duke Mikhail Aleksandrovich abdicates after meeting with members of the Duma Committee and the newly appointed Provisional Government; Nicholas II travels from Pskov to General Headquarters in Mogilev

8	Nicholas departs General Headquarters for Tsarskoe Selo under arrest
9	Nicholas arrives in Tsarskoe Selo accompanied by the Duma Committee and Petrograd Soviet commissars; Provisional Government bows to Soviet pressure and does not allow the former tsar and his family to leave Tsarskoe Selo without the explicit agreement of the Soviet Executive Committee
14	Soviet "Appeal to the People of the World" published
19	Exiled deputies of the Second Duma return to Petrograd from Siberia (including Tsereteli); Provisional Government abolishes discrimination based on nationality or religion; massive women's demonstration for equal rights held in front of Duma
23	Miliukov gives interview to the press in which he confirms that Constantinople and the Straits should remain part of war aims
29–April 3	(First) All-Russian Conference of Soviets of Workers' and Soldiers' Deputies
31	Plekhanov returns to Russia from exile

April

3	Lenin returns to Petrograd
4	Lenin's April Theses announced
7–17	(First) Congress of the Western Front in Minsk
18	Miliukov sends his "Note" to the Allies, reiterating Russia's old war aims and provoking what came to be known as the April Crisis (April 18–21)
20	Demonstrations against the Provisional Government
21	Demonstrations continue; leaders of Provisional Government visit General Headquarters
27	Meeting of members of all pre-revolutionary Dumas
29	First Congress of Delegates from the Front
30	Guchkov resigns from Provisional Government

May

2	Miliukov resigns from Provisional Government
2–5	Reorganization of government into coalition cabinet, which now includes Soviet leaders

7–12   (First) All-Russian Menshevik Conference meets in Petrograd
9   Aksel'rod, Martov, and Martynov return to Russia from exile
10   Provisional Government dissolves Military Commission
30   Kropotkin returns to Russia from exile

June

3–5   (First) All-Russian Congress of Soviets of Workers' and Soldiers' Deputies

July

3–5   July Days
8   Kerenskii becomes minister-president
21–3   Reorganization of government into second coalition cabinet

August

27–30 Kornilov Affair

September

25   Reorganization of government into third coalition cabinet

October

25–6   Bolsheviks overthrow the Provisional Government and seize power in Petrograd

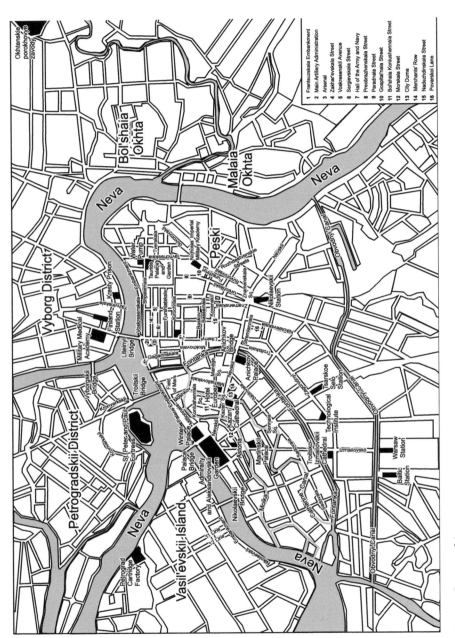

Map 1 Petrograd in 1917

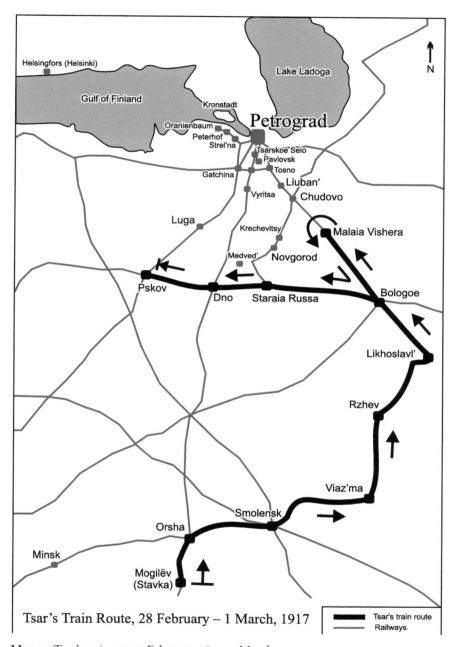

Tsar's Train Route, 28 February – 1 March, 1917

Tsar's train route
Railways

Map 2 Tsar's train route, February 28 to 1 March, 1917

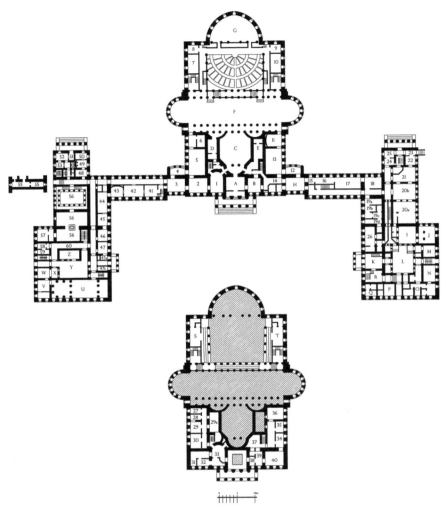

Map 3 Plan of the Tauride Palace

LEGEND TO THE TAURIDE PALACE PLAN

Lower (main) Level:

A – Main Entrance and Vestibule
B – Cloakroom
C – Round Hall (*Kruglyi zal*)
F – Katherine Hall
G – Semicircular Hall (*Polutsirkul'nyi zal*)
H and 14 – Post and telegraph

  1 – Room for sorting printed materials for the Duma Deputies
  2 – Room of the Duma Marshals
  4 – Office of the Duma President Deputies
  5 – Office of the Duma President
11 – Room of the Finance Commission
12 – Room of chairmen of the Budget and Finance Commissions
13 – Room occupied by the Petrograd Soviet of Workers' and Soldiers' Deputies (formerly of the Budget Commission)
48-49 – Rooms occupied by the Temporary Duma Committee
41 – Office of the commandant (occupied by the Military Commission during the first days of the revolution)
42 – Office of the Duma Secretary (occupied by the Military Commission during the first days of the revolution)
43 – Office used by N.V. Nekrasov during February 27-March 3, 1917
44 – Room occupied by the Military Commission during February 27-March 1, 1917
22 – Room occupied by the Military Commission after March 1, 1917
45 – Chancellery of the Duma

Higher (second) Level:

S – Cafeteria (Buffet)
T – Soldiers' section (of the Petrograd Soviet)
34-36 – Meeting rooms

PART I

The Story of the Interviews

I

The Quest for the Lost Oral Histories of the February Revolution

IN THE SUMMER of 1992, the first summer since the failed putsch of August 1991, hundreds of researchers from all over the world descended on Russia's archives to explore previously classified or restricted materials. Despite the summer heat and the dust of over-polluted cities, reading rooms in all the central archives were literally packed. The fervor to examine documents that had been inaccessible to preceding generations was such that researchers waited for long stretches outside of overcrowded depositories in order to spend a few more hours inside the suffocating, under-ventilated reading rooms. For a country where an opening of archives required a change of political regimes, this situation was unprecedented.

I too went to Moscow that June. I had just completed my research on the accusations that the Provisional Government had leveled against the Bolshevik leaders in July of 1917, charging them with receiving financial support from the German government. I was eager to confirm the main lines of my argument by examining the twenty-five-volume case of previously classified materials that the Provisional Government had assembled against Lenin and his associates. But I also wanted to see other materials that directly or indirectly touched on the July accusations and the period of the February Revolution more generally. My "wish list" was long. Compiled over several years from references in the secondary literature and archival guides, it included records of late tsarist legislative institutions, ministries, and judicial commissions of the Provisional Government, as well as the personal papers of government officials and public figures.

In the middle of my list—toward the top, but admittedly still in the middle—I had written a reminder to look for an interview project with major figures of the February Revolution, which apparently included interviews with A. F. Kerenskii, M. V. Rodzianko, N. V. Nekrasov, and M. I. Tereshchenko. I knew from reading the works of Tsuyoshi Hasegawa and the Soviet historian E. N. Burdzhalov that the project was part of an "historical commission to study the process of revolution," which was organized "immediately after the February Revolution" by a group of young Petrograd historians under the direction of their senior colleagues and mentors A. E. Presniakov and M. A. Polievktov.[1] I also knew that at least some of the interview transcripts collected for this project had "come into the personal collection of Professor M. A. Polievktov" and as of the late 1970s were still "preserved by his widow, Professor R. N. Nikoladze," presumably in Soviet Georgia.[2]

No other information about the interviews (size, dates, number, or the circumstances under which they had been conducted and recorded) was available to me at the time. I did not know when or how the transcripts ended up in Georgia or what had happened to them between the late 1970s and 1992. Hasegawa wrote that he had attempted to gain access to these documents, but was unable to do so. As far as he knew, Burdzhalov was the only recent historian who had actually seen them.[3]

Finally, I knew from reading the correspondence of the great Menshevik historian and archivist Boris Ivanovich Nikolaevskii, whose enormous personal archive is preserved at Stanford's Hoover Institution, that there had been a number of attempts in Moscow and Petrograd in 1917–18 to organize a revolutionary archive (he himself was involved in some of them). The archive would have served as the main depository for materials pertaining to the history of the revolutionary movement and the February Revolution, including those collected by the Presniakov–Polievktov historical commission. But at the onset of the civil war the plans to create such an archive fell apart, while the documents either remained with those who had

---

[1] E. N. Burdzhalov, *Vtoraia russkaia revoliutsiia. Vosstanie v Petrograde* (Moscow: Nauka, 1967), 79; Burdzhalov, "Istochniki i literatura po istorii vtoroi russkoi revoliutsii," in I. I. Mints et al., *Sverzhenie samoderzhaviia. Sb. statei* (Moscow: Nauka, 1970), 254–5; Tsuyoshi Hasegawa, *The February Revolution, Petrograd, 1917* (Seattle and London: University of Washington Press, 1981), 349 n. 5.

[2] Hasegawa, *The February Revolution*, 349 n. 5.

[3] Ibid.; Donald J. Raleigh, who knew Burdzhalov and translated and edited his famous monograph into English, confirmed that he was "the only historian" who had cited the interviews. See Raleigh's note 108 on p. 358 in E. N. Burdzhalov, *Russia's Second Revolution. The February 1917 Uprising in Petrograd* (Bloomington and Indianapolis: Indiana University Press, 1987).

collected them or were deposited in various state archives. This was the extent of what I knew in 1992.

What attracted my interest and sustained it over the years was an understanding that the interviews likely constituted a uniquely valuable body of sources on the February Revolution. They were the only such body of documents containing testimonies by major participants recorded by an historical commission (rather than a political, criminal, or judicial investigation) shortly *after* the overthrow of the old regime and *before* the Bolshevik takeover. Accordingly, they would be less susceptible to subsequent embellishments or distortions, and were of course completely free of the post-1917 hindsight inevitably conditioned by the drastically new political circumstances both inside and outside of Soviet Russia. The interviews also stood in sharp contrast to the only other known 1917 testimonies, assembled by the Provisional Government's Extraordinary Judicial Commission. Here the depositions were extracted under extreme psychological pressure from high-ranking officials of the old regime who were essentially forced to implicate themselves. Admittedly, what also attracted me to the documents was an element of naiveté by a budding historian who hoped to find the "smoking gun" of the Russian Revolution.

The will to discovery was there; reliable clues that would lead to such a discovery were not. Of the few possible leads, the most obvious was to follow in the footsteps of Polievktov, whose figure loomed large in the interview project and whose heirs were reportedly in possession of at least some of the transcripts as late as the 1970s. Polievktov had been a recognized specialist in the history of nineteenth-century Russian political institutions and had written a survey of Nicholas I's reign, but his life and scholarly interests after 1917 were unknown to me. There was little useful or reliable information about him in available reference sources. The memory of his days at Petrograd University, where he taught for some time before and during the revolution, faded after his apparent relocation to Soviet Georgia in the 1920s. According to an official archival guide published in the 1960s, his papers had been deposited in the main historical archive in Tbilisi. Following the available clues, I should have taken my search to Tbilisi, but this was not a viable option in the early 1990s.

The once prosperous, hospitable, and beautiful Soviet Republic of Georgia was now a newly independent nation. It had just plunged into a protracted period of civil war and inter-ethnic conflicts, aggravated by economic collapse and driven by political and military infighting among competing regional warlords and rival clans. Traveling to Georgia during the "lost decade" of the 1990s was not only extremely dangerous, but could well be futile, for the chances of finding the right contacts or gaining access to the mostly defunct state archive were far from certain. Thus, I set the Georgian lead aside and waited for more stable and calmer times.

In the meantime, to keep the project alive, I decided to pursue another clue—less promising to be sure, but easier and safer to accomplish. I set out to uncover what happened to the documents collected by the Presniakov–Polievktov historical commission that had supposedly been deposited in the Russian archives, mostly in Petrograd (now St. Petersburg). If I could find them, they might lead to copies—or even originals—of the transcripts, which, according to some sources, must have remained in the former capital. And so, for the rest of the 1990s, during almost annual trips to the Moscow and St. Petersburg archives, I spent some time trying to track down these documents. In 1999, after several years and a few false leads I had some luck in the State Archive of the Russian Federation.

In the papers of a revolutionary veterans' organization with the long and cumbersome name of the Society of the House-Museum for Preserving the Memory of Freedom Fighters,[4] which I soon learned had absorbed the Presniakov–Polievktov historical commission in the early fall of 1917, I discovered important evidence that would soon alter the direction of my search. According to the protocol of an early 1918 meeting recorded by B. I. Nikolaevskii, who as it turned out had served as a member of the Society of the House-Museum board and its secretary, Polievktov delivered a report on the activities of his interviewing team during the spring of 1917. He listed the names of the interviewees and identified those who had conducted the interviews. He also proposed resuming the work of the historical commission. Polievktov wanted to expand the list of potential interviewees, even though the year that had passed since February 1917 had been tumultuous, and also sought to involve his younger Petrograd University colleagues (and future prominent historians) B. A. Romanov and S. N. Valk in the process. Nothing came of the initiative, but the reasons for that are not difficult to guess, considering the political and economic circumstances of the soon-to-be-launched war communism and the ensuing civil war. As to

---

[4] GARF [State Archive of the Russian Federation], fond 6685 (Obshchestvo Doma-muzeia pamiati bortsov za svobodu), opis' 1, 11 archival files.

the 1917 interviews, Polievktov disclosed that the transcripts had long since been taken out of Russia for safekeeping, to Kutaisi province in Georgia.[5]

This was a revelation to me and very important to my quest. Here Polievktov implied that the originals had never been deposited in a Russian state archive, and this contradicted previous assumptions. His report further suggested that what later ended up in the hands of his heirs were the same transcripts that had been in Georgia since before early 1918. To me, this meant that any additional searches in Russia were unlikely to bear fruit. From then on, my efforts would focus on finding Polievktov's descendants in Georgia.

This turn of events was very timely and opportune. The political situation in Georgia was beginning to show signs of stabilizing. In 2000–1, I began looking for a reliable contact in Tbilisi who could comb through the Polievktov papers in the Georgian Historical Archive (just in case the interview transcripts had been added to the collection since the 1970s) and who could look for the historian's heirs (who might still be in possession of the documents).

Finding the right contact, however, presented a challenge. I had no personal or professional connections in Georgia, so I began inquiries with various friends and colleagues. After a few miscues and mishaps, a Russian colleague took an active part in my quest and eventually helped me to identify a promising contact. For many years, this Russian colleague has been a source of great help with finding contacts, identifying archival collections, and accessing all kinds of important information mostly inaccessible from the other side of the Atlantic. It was also through him that between 2001 and 2006, I maintained most of my communications with various contacts, whether in Russia or in Georgia. This mode of communication was terribly inconvenient but necessary considering how unsettling and financially devastating the times had been for scholars and archivists since the fall of the Soviet Union. Any disclosure that a foreign researcher was behind this or that inquiry would potentially have invited demands for excessive compensation without guarantee of reliable information in return.

In 2001, this colleague helped me to find a Georgian archivist who introduced himself as "Rezo." This is how he wanted us to address him in our telephone and e-mail communications; we never met him in person.

---

[5] GARF, f. 6685, op. 1, d. 5, l. 1; Ibid., d. 1, l. 34.

In contrast to some of his predecessors, Rezo took the assignments to
heart, and after an extended period of silence, he resurfaced with some
results. The Georgian Historical Archive had survived the civil war and so
had the Polievktov papers. Yet they contained no information about the
interviews and no apparent clues that might have indicated their location.[6] Years later, I had the opportunity to work with this collection and
to confirm Rezo's findings firsthand. I realized then how difficult his task
must have been, considering the truly sorry state of the former Georgian
state archives during the first decade and a half of the country's independence. Even though I had seen the terrible situation of the Russian federal
archives in the early 1990s, what I saw in Tbilisi as late as 2006 was incom-
parably worse. The nation's main historical archive had hardly any hard-
wood floors left in its long hallways. A local archivist told me that the
wood had been chiseled away and used for heating and cooking by the
inhabitants of central Tbilisi during the warlike conditions of the previous
decade. Researchers had to advance along the archive's hallways by literally jumping from one island of bare concrete and iron armature to another
to avoid sinking their feet in pools of sludge that were composed of leak-
age from sewer pipes, decades of accumulated dust, and all sorts of other
hazardous elements.

By braving such challenges, Rezo acquired a second piece of information that was just as significant as the first. He told us that Polievktov's
widow, Professor R. N. Nikoladze, had published her memoirs in Georgian
in 1975. In her memoirs, she devoted seven pages to the February Revolution
and disclosed some previously unknown details on the history of the interviews, including her active involvement in the project, together with her
sister, as well as the circumstances of some of the interview sessions.[7] She
also clarified the organization of the project. The interviews had been conducted and recorded by what was called the Interview Commission, under
the direction of her late husband, and its work had been part of a larger
effort undertaken by the Society for the Study of the Revolution to document the history of the February Revolution, led by Presniakov. As I was to
discover two years later, this was actually a second edition of her memoirs.

---

[6] Central Historical Archive of Georgia (CHAG), formerly Central State Historical Archive of
the Georgian Soviet Socialist Republic, fond 1505 [M. A. Polievktov], 222 archival files.

[7] R. N. Nikoladze, *Na bol'shom zhiznennom puti* (in Georgian; title in Russian and Georgian)
(Tbilisi, 1975), 264–71.

The first edition, which contained additional details about the interview project, had been published in Russian in a literary journal in 1970.[8]

Finally, in 2004, Rezo provided the name of Polievktov's relative and presumed heir (the exact relationship was not clear at that time). He identified her as Zinaida Leonidovna Polievktova-Nikoladze, and supplied her telephone number. Her surname implied a connection with both the historian and his wife. I could now initiate a direct contact and, presumably, arrange for access to the materials. It seemed that the search was over. The documents were within reach, separated from me only by geographic distance. Unknown to us at the time, however, there were other distances which my colleague and I would have to cover in order to obtain access to the transcripts.

In weighing the various options of establishing contact with Zinaida Leonidovna, I had to consider a few precautionary measures. First, it was not immediately obvious to me whether I should contact her directly or continue to act through an intermediary. I wanted to avoid any gaffs. I was well aware that any mistakes could end this quest just as it was nearing completion. But how should one approach an unfamiliar person who might or might not want to talk to a complete stranger, let alone an American academic who had been born and raised in the Soviet Union (obvious from my accent-free Russian)? I had no idea whether she was Georgian or ethnically Russian and how—especially given the already tense relationship between the two countries—she would react to my telephone call with a request to see documents the existence of which she might not even want to admit.

After careful consideration—and here my Russian colleague was again a source of wisdom and goodwill—we decided that he would make the first phone call to Zinaida Leonidovna. As much as our plan may appear naive or shortsighted in retrospect, it seemed a sensible precaution to us at the time. Even the slightest possibility that Zinaida Leonidovna might harbor antiforeign or ethnic prejudice could turn out to be a deal breaker (I hasten to add that, in reality, she was completely free of such prejudice). Her ethnicity, unknown to us at the time, also seemed important. An ethnic Georgian would possibly be more open to a conversation with a fellow Georgian; the same might be true if she were Russian.

---

[8] R. Nikoladze, "Nezabyvaemye dni i mgnoveniia. Na beregakh Nevy," *Literaturnaia Gruziia* 3 (1970): 69–74; "Nezabyvaemye dni i mgnoveniia," *Literaturnaia Gruziia* 4 (1970): 24–31.

With these considerations in mind, my Russian colleague made the first contact during the winter of 2004. He introduced himself as a Russian historian interested in the work of the Society for the Study of the Revolution—indeed, this was his true area of interest and what had attracted him to my quest in the first place. The conversation did not go well. Zinaida Leonidovna was understandably cautious in talking to a stranger, and would neither confirm nor deny the existence of the documents. After a few months of persistent phone calls, she acknowledged the possession of historical documents, but she still refused to provide any specifics. She likewise refused to send my colleague a sample excerpt from an interview or to allow a visit.

At some point in their "negotiations," my colleague described to Zinaida Leonidovna the significance of the documents and proposed a joint publication. She refused, but did not deny having the documents. The telephone conversations, with my colleague talking and Zinaida Leonidovna listening, continued with some regularity, and by early 2005 we were fairly certain that she had in her possession handwritten transcripts of some testimonies pertaining to the February Revolution. Although she never sent my Russian colleague a sample, a few months into 2005 she did fax him a list of the interviews, which mostly corresponded to the list given in Polievktov's 1918 report. Her list also had the dates of the interviews—all but one of them conducted in May of 1917. There was no longer any doubt that she had the interviews. All that we needed now was to secure Zinaida Leonidovna's permission to examine them *de visu*.

This, however, proved to be exceedingly difficult. Over the next year, Zinaida Leonidovna repeatedly refused to provide any further information concerning the interviews. In addition, she denied all requests for a visit. She also rejected all requests to make the documents available by any other means (such as photocopying or scanning). All appeals based on the scholarly significance of the documents, the necessity of making them broadly available, and other similarly abstract arguments were met with silence. She offered no explanation for her decision. Yet while avoiding contact, she apparently was not ready to shut down the line of communication completely. The increasingly rare conversations by telephone became more difficult and frustrating, and by the middle of February 2006, my Russian colleague's patience had reached its limit. He informed me of his decision to discontinue any further contacts with this "unreasonable" and "obstinate" person. Thus, fourteen years after my search began, and after exhausting all reasonable enticements, it seemed that my quest was at an end.

I saw no workable solution, and could not think of what else might persuade Zinaida Leonidovna to change her mind. The situation was disheartening. Then, one evening at the end of February 2006, as I was mulling over possible next steps, I received a call from a close friend of many years. He had grown up in Soviet Georgia in the 1960s and had been educated at Tbilisi University, but he had long since lived in Israel where he had become a successful and well-known biophysicist. The caller ID on my telephone displayed a "Georgia Call," which of course meant the state in the American south, not the independent country toward which all my recent thoughts had been directed. He was calling from Atlanta, where he was attending a professional conference and had a few minutes in between various activities to chat.

We had not seen each other in over a year, but we occasionally talked on the phone and exchanged emails. In retrospect, I cannot comprehend why during all those years I never told him—despite his keen interest in history—about my quest for the "Georgian treasure." Although most of his family left Georgia in the 1970s, he might have resumed some old connections after the breakup of the Soviet empire and could have helped with advice or in recommending a reliable contact at an earlier stage in my search. But, for whatever reason, I had not thought to include him.

Even so, such things are better late than never. Consumed by my recent failure, I decided to share with him the story of my search. He listened attentively and after I finished, asked for the names of the main personages. I thought to myself, "What is the point of telling a historian's name to a biophysicist?" I hesitated; he insisted. Then I told him about Polievktov and his wife R. N. Nikoladze. His reaction was most unexpected. It turned out that my friend, while studying physics at Tbilisi University in the mid-1970s, had once heard a substitute lecture by a noted nuclear physicist who made such a lasting impression on him that more than thirty years later he still remembered both the lecture and the lecturer. His delivery style, his anything but standard approach to the topic of the lecture, his erudition, his old-fashioned manners, and his beautifully spoken Russian were as unusual for a late Soviet-era academic as his hyphenated surname was uncommon. That name was Nikolai Mikhailovich Polievktov-Nikoladze.

The connection was obvious—Nikolai Mikhailovich was almost certainly the son of the historian M. A. Polievktov and the chemist Rusudana Nikolaevna Nikoladze. After all, how many Polievktov-Nikoladzes could have lived in Tbilisi in the 1970s? Following the same logic, we decided that

Zinaida Leonidovna Polievktova-Nikoladze must have been Nikolai Mikhailovich's wife or, perhaps, his child.

The story of the search made an impression on my friend. The possibility of finding unique historical documents whetted his appetite and prodded his "hunting" instincts. His prudent advice was to approach Zinaida Leonidovna through an insider, someone local whom she would be more likely to trust. More importantly, my friend took it upon himself to find a suitable candidate among his former classmates and students of Nikolai Mikhailovich's, someone who was still living in Georgia. This was not an easy task, because many of them had left the country during the turmoil of the 1990s and continued to live abroad. Hardly a month later, however, my friend sent me the name of a friend and former classmate in Tbilisi who agreed to approach Zinaida Leonidovna. We corresponded, and in early April, I supplied my new Tbilisi contact with a list of questions for Zinaida Leonidovna. I also requested that he ask to examine the transcripts. Things were beginning to look promising again.

To this day, I do not know all of the details of his first conversation with Zinaida Leonidovna, nor do I know exactly how he introduced himself to her, but the ice melted. She invited him to come to her flat. Zinaida Leonidovna introduced herself as the widow of Nikolai Mikhailovich Polievktov-Nikoladze, and explained that she had been his former student. My contact claimed the same educational pedigree, which was apparently enough to inspire initial trust and encourage a good conversation. Though of different generations, they reminisced about their student days at the university. They talked about history and a shared interest in mathematics. Zinaida Leonidovna told him that Polievktov and his wife had one child and heir, Nikolai (Nika) Mikhailovich, who in turn had no children of his own. After Nika had passed away in 1989, the family archive, including the interviews, had been inherited by Zinaida Leonidovna.

Even more surprising (and encouraging), during that same first visit, Zinaida Leonidovna opened part of her treasure trove, the transcripts of the 1917 interviews, for my contact. He promptly informed her that he was acting on my behalf and was kindly allowed to write down some of their details and pass them on to me. The next day I received a detailed report that both confirmed and far exceeded what I had known about the interviews. There followed a couple of smaller requests to confirm this or that detail, but the overall picture left no doubt as to the documents' origins, authorship, and present location.

Encouraged by these developments, I asked my contact to inquire about the possibility of a short visit to examine the documents *de visu*. The next day, a phone call from Tbilisi confirmed that my request had been well received, and that I should contact Zinaida Leonidovna directly to make the arrangements. With a mixture of excitement and apprehension, I dialed her telephone number. The voice on the other end of the line was that of an older female which betrayed a slight accent in her otherwise perfect Russian (Zinaida Leonidovna was half Russian and half Mingrelian, as I was to discover a bit later). We had a friendly conversation, and agreed that I would travel halfway around the globe to visit her as soon as I could arrange for tickets and accommodations.

On Monday, May 8, 2006, two planes landed in the early morning fog at Tbilisi's hopelessly outdated Soviet-era airport. For some reason, in those days a foreign airline could only take off and land there between 2:00 and 5:00 in the morning. I came on a flight via Vienna. My friend the biophysicist, whom I asked to join me and act as host in his native land (and as an expert on Georgian cuisine), flew in from Tel Aviv. A few hours later, we paid our first visit to Zinaida Leonidovna. Standing in front of the entrance to her rundown building, fourteen years and seven thousand miles behind me, I reviewed in my mind all that I had learned about Polievktov and his 1917 Interview Commission, as well as the early stages of my pursuit for the documents he had collected and preserved during such trying times.

We were greeted by Zinaida Leonidovna and led through a long open terrace into a dining room decorated with faded wall and ceiling frescos (reportedly painted by Sergei Sudeikin during his short stay in Tiflis in 1919), early twentieth-century paintings, shelves of old books, a marble fireplace, and an old-fashioned space heater. Several doors leading to adjacent rooms radiated from where were sitting. We had a friendly conversation, mostly about Zinaida Leonidovna's late husband, the physicist, and about the previous custodians of the family papers. Soon Zinaida Leonidovna disappeared into one of those doors and returned carrying a thick folder with the materials of the Interview Commission. Over the next week, I copied and scanned the entire folder, along with many additional papers that had been preserved in the family's archives.

As I read through the precious manuscripts—some barely legible, others much better preserved—both in Tbilisi and during the months after my return home, I began to realize that finding the interviews was only the beginning of what would become a long and painstaking process of researching their history. While many characters and events mentioned in the interviews were familiar to every student of the Russian Revolution, I knew very little about the circumstances or the individuals who had created this unique body of historical sources. I spent much of the intervening time researching their lives and the historical context in which they carried out the interview project. They were the Petrograd historian M. A. Polievktov, the main intellectual and organizational force behind the project; his wife, Rusudana Nikolaevna Nikoladze; her sister Tamara; and their friends, colleagues, and classmates. Together, they conducted, recorded, and preserved these testimonies about the fall of tsarim, one of the most profound upheavals of modern times. It is to them that we owe the deepest debt. It is to their histories that we shall now turn.

2
M. A. Polievktov and the First Oral Histories of the February Revolution

O N DECEMBER 21, 1942, a mild winter day, Mikhail Aleksandrovich Polievktov, one of the last remaining representatives of the great St. Petersburg school of Russian historians, died in the old Tbilisi neighborhood of Sololaki. As the besieged empire struggled for survival in the Second World War, his death went largely unnoticed outside of his immediate family and a small circle of Georgian students and colleagues. Most of his old Russian friends had already departed this world. Those few remaining—cut off in Nazi-occupied Prague or in blockaded Leningrad—could not be notified. Only thirty years later, on the hundredth anniversary of Polievktov's birth, was his death officially lamented, when the Soviet Georgian Academy of Sciences acknowledged and celebrated his contribution to Georgian historical scholarship in a series of ceremonial meetings and laudatory publications. The entrance to the run-down Sololaki building where he had lived and died was adorned with a memorial plaque in Russian and Georgian. Though the Russian words were chipped away by Georgian thugs during the nationalistic frenzy of the early 1990s, Polievktov is still revered in that far-off land via a succession of his former students (and their students) for his central role in founding the discipline of early Russian-Georgian studies.[1]

---

[1] See, for example, "Pamiati vidnogo istorika," *Zaria Vostoka*, April 8, 1972, 3; "Vashe imia vpishetsia zolotymi bukvami," *Vechernii Tbilisi*, April 18, 1972, 4. For more recent examples of Polievktov's high standing among Georgian historians of Russia, see Iu. S. Sulaberidze, "M. A. Polievktov i ego lichnyi fond v Tsentral'nom gosudarstvennom arkhive Gruzii," *Otechestvennaia istoriia i istoricheskaia mysl' v Rossii XIX–XX vekov. Sbornik statei k 75-letiiu Alekseia Nikolaevicha Tsamutali*, ed. R. Sh. Ganelin (St Petersburg: "Nestor-Istoriia," 2006), 69–74; G. D. Zhuzhunashvili, "Istorik—ne… bezdarnyi memuarist," *Istorik i ego epokha. Vtorye Danilovskie chteniia (20–22 aprelia 2009 g., g. Tiumen')*, ed. A. G. Emanov (Tiumen': Mandr i K, 2009), 49–50.

A scion of the famous Maikov family, whose members included distinguished poets, painters, linguists, and art connoisseurs, Polievktov was
himself a student of the eminent St. Petersburg historians Sergei Fedorovich
Platonov, Georgii Vasil'evich Forsten, and Aleksandr Sergeevich Lappo-
Danilevskii. A peer and a lifelong friend of Russian historian Aleksandr
Evgen'evich Presniakov, Polievktov belonged to the generation of prerevolutionary historians that was educated during the 1880s and the early 1890s,
a generation which—in the words of Terence Emmons—"produced more
first-rate historical scholarship than any before or since."[2] For more than
twenty years Polievktov taught in various institutions of higher learning in
the imperial capital, and produced two major monographs. By the time he
was elected professor of Petrograd University in November 1918, he had
established a reputation as a leading specialist on the history of Russian
foreign relations in the early eighteenth century and an authority on the
political institutions of the first half of the nineteenth century.[3] His unusually thoughtful and balanced study of Nicholas I's reign is still considered
the essential scholarly treatment of the subject.[4] Yet his intense professional
(as well as personal) interest in the history of the Russian Revolution—to

[2] Terence Emmons, "Got'e and His Diary," in *Time of Troubles. The Diary of Iurii Vladimirovich
Got'e. Moscow. July 8, 1917 to July 23, 1922,* trans., ed. and intr. Terence Emmons (Princeton: Princeton
University Press, 1988), 12.

[3] In June 1918, on Platonov's recommendation, and with the support of an overwhelming
majority of his colleagues, Polievktov was elected *dozent* of the Department (*kafedra*) of Russian
history (TsGIA SPB [Central State Historical Archive of St. Petersburg], fond (f.) 14 [St. Petersburg
University], opis' (op.) 2, delo (d.) 909, listy (ll.) 1000b., 101, 102.). In November of that year, after
a Sovnarkom decree abolishing "old" scholarly degrees and ranks and allowing all *privatdozenty*
who served in that rank for more than three years to be promoted to professorship, Polievktov,
A. S. Lappo-Danilevskii, V. N. Stroev, and A. I. Zaozerskii were elected professors of the historico-
philological faculty in the department of Russian history (V. S. Brachev, A. Iu. Dvornichenko,
Kafedra russkoi istorii Sankt-Peterburgskogo universiteta (1834–2004) [St. Petersburg: Izdatel'stvo
S.-Peterburgskogo universiteta, 2004], 170).

[4] See M. Polievktov's main monographs: *Baltiiskii vopros v Russkoi politike posle Nishtadskogo mira
(1721–1725)* (St. Petersburg: Tipografiia M. A. Aleksandrova, 1907) and his *Nikolai I: biografiia i obzor
tsarstvovaniia* (Moscow: Izdatel'stvo M. i S. Sabashnikovykh, 1918), which was recently republished in
Moscow: M.A. Polievktov, *Nikolai I: biografiia i obzor tsarstvovaniia* (reprint, Moscow: Mir knigi, 2008).
It is also worth recalling here a recommendation put forward by the scholarly council of the
department of Russian history of Petrograd University (Professors S. F. Platonov, S. V. Rozhdestvenskii,
A. E. Presniakov, and M. D. Priselkov) in support of Polievktov's election to *dozent* in June 1918,
stating that in the areas of his specialty (modern history, especially nineteenth century and the history
of foreign relations), "M. A. Polievktov is unquestionably the best among the university faculty," and
that his seminars on the era of Nicholas I and topics of Russian foreign policy during the eighteenth
and nineteenth centuries "became an organic part of the Russian history curriculum at the [histor-
ico-philological] faculty." TsGIA SPB, f. 14, op. 2, d. 909, ll. 1000b.

which he made an important and original contribution—remains essentially unknown to historians of modern Russia.[5] This chapter, which evaluates that contribution, begins with a review of his family background and education, the professional and personal milieus in which he lived, and his political views in the period leading up to the February Revolution.

Early Life, the Polievktovs and Maikovs

Although Polievktov spent the last twenty odd years of his life in Georgia and most of the first eighteen in the sleepy Kaluga province of central Russia, in his heart as well as in his memory, he always considered himself an old Petersburger (*staryi peterburzhets*). Or, at any rate, this is what he wrote in a short autobiographical sketch in 1927, which was commissioned (but later censored) by the Tbilisi Communist paper *Zaria Vostoka*.[6] Petersburg was his native city. He was born there, attended the University during 1890–4, and spent the next thirty years there that included the most active part of his life and career. By his own admission, he "was entwined into the fabric of that magnificent city (*srossia s etim chudnym gorodom*)," embracing Petersburg's unique spirit and soul.[7]

His father, Aleksandr Nikolaevich Polievktov—whose short but colorful life included stormy periods of student activism in the early 1860s and service as a deacon of the Russian ambassadorial church in Constantinople—was a justice of the peace at the time of Mikhail Aleksandrovich's birth and by all accounts was a charming, cheerful, and generous man of liberal views. Polievktov's grandfather was a prominent and urbane Petersburg priest (*shikarnyi stolichnyi pop*) who, as Polievktov nostalgically recalled in the early

---

[5] Except for brief and not always accurate references in the specialized works by E. N. Burdzhalov, *Vtoraia russkaia revoliutsiia. Vosstanie v Petrograde* (Moscow: Nauka, 1967), 79; Burdzhalov, "Istochniki i literatura po istorii vtoroi russkoi revoliutsii," in I. I. Mints et al., eds., *Sverzhenie samoderzhaviia. Sb. statei* (Moscow: Nauka, 1970), 254–5; A. B. Nikolaev, *Revoliutsiia i vlast': IV Gosudarstvennaia duma, 27 fevralia–3 marta 1917 goda* (St. Petersburg: RGPU, 2005), 114–15, 119; and Tsuyoshi Hasegawa, *The February Revolution, Petrograd, 1917* (Seattle and London: University of Washington Press, 1981), 349 n. 5.

[6] M. Polievktov, "Kak slozhilas' moia nauchnaia rabota," p. 1, manuscript; 12 pp., Tiflis, 1927, in M. A. Polievktov Papers (MAPP), unprocessed, Family Archive (FA), presently located in the Rare Books and Special Collections Department of the Hesburgh Libraries, University of Notre Dame. A typed and slightly shorter, typescript version of this autobiographical note under "Avtobiografiia Polievktova M.A. 1927 g." is also preserved among his papers (CHAG, f. 1505, op. 1, d. 1, ll. 1–10). Hereafter I will refer to the original manuscript of his autobiographical note from the FA; See also R. N. Nikoladze to A. K. Kharadze, August 28, 1943, 1. Handwritten letter, in MAPP, FA; and Sulaberidze, *Polievktov i ego lichnyi fond*, 71–2.

[7] Polievkotv, "Kak slozhilas' moia nauchnaia rabota," 1.

1920s, enjoyed a comfortable life and the privileges associated with the position of a well-paid priest at the Nativity of Our Lady Cathedral in the
imperial capital's affluent Peski district.[8] His was the comfortable milieu of
the educated clergy, defined not only by their more privileged position
among the brethren but also (and especially) by their more democratic, better educated, and generally tolerant *esprit de corps*. At least it seemed so to
Polievktov, from the distance of half a century and having observed firsthand
the not-so-democratic and far more doctrinaire "priests" of the new Soviet
religion.[9]

Aleksandr Nikolaevich died prematurely in 1880, when his son, the future
historian, was only 8 years old. Mikhail Aleksandrovich remembered little
about his father except that he was very kind and gentle to him and well
liked by his colleagues and neighbors (Mikhail Aleksandrovich was later
told that he inherited many of his father's traits of character, especially his
mild and pleasant manners). Nor could he remember much (or perhaps did
not care to) about his relatives on the paternal side, besides that they were
generally known for their passionate love affair with alcohol and untamed
behavior. And so it fell squarely on his strong-willed and domineering
mother, Natalia Mikhailovna (née Maikova) and her close relatives (her
sisters and cousins, the future historian's *tetushki* and *diadiushki*) to play the
formative role in her son's upbringing and early intellectual development.

It was Natalia Mikhailovna who—to the constant annoyance of
Polievktov's future wife and some of his closest friends—exercised the most
lasting influence over her only son's life and was the biggest claim on his
heart and time. According to Polievktov, he and his mother lived together
"for nearly fifty years," both before and after his marriage and the birth of

---

[8] Polievktov, "Moi vospominaniia," 57, MAPP, FA. A. N. Polievktov studied in a seminary and
later attended classes in St. Petersburg University. In 1861, he was expelled from the University
because of his participation in student protests. Arrested, he spent some time inside the Peter and
Paul Fortress, together with Niko Nikoladze, who was a law student at the time. Some fifty years
later, Nikoladze's oldest daughter would marry A. N. Polievktov's son (M. A. Polievktov, "Moi
vospominaniia," 59). Soon after his release, Aleksandr Nikolaevich took the position of
psalm-reader at the church of the Russian Embassy in Constantinople. He later studied at the
St. Petersburg Ecclesiastical Academy, completing his course work in 1869 and entering, in June
of that year, state service as chancellery clerk or staffer at the Petersburg District Court. In 1871
he was appointed judicial investigator in the Orenburg Province, then justice of the peace in
Vitebsk province (after his son's birth), and later at the Simbirsk District Court before his last
appointment as court investigator (*sudebnyi sledovatel'*) in the small town of Likhvin of the Kaluga
province, in 1877. He died on March 7, 1880, at the age of 41 (Ibid., 59–64. MAPP, FA; TsGIA
SPb, f. 14, op. 3, d. 27363 [*Studencheskoe delo M. A. Polievktova*], l. 7–90b.)

[9] Polievktov, "Moi vospominaniia," 54.

his own son, and for the most part got along quite well.[10] Polievktov was surely his mother's boy and a good son. He took care of her in her waning years, often at the expense of his own family. He was especially attentive after Natalia Mikhailovna fractured her hip and became permanently confined to her bed. She suffered terribly during the last two years of her life, which in Polievktov's view atoned for her overly demanding, capricious, and at times unbearable behavior.[11] During Natalia Mikhailovna's final illness, Polievktov remained in Petrograd to care for her, separated from his wife and son. He rejoined them only after her death in January 1920.

But Natalia Mikhailovna had another, more admirable side that her son appreciated and remembered well into his own declining years. After her husband's untimely passing, she was left without sufficient financial means. For a long time, until she received a modest inheritance, she had to support both herself and her son. She sacrificed her own personal life, never remarrying, and worked hard to teach her son music, the French language, and Russian literature.[12] She gave private lessons to pay for tutors to prepare Polievktov for the classical gymnasium in nearby Kaluga, which he was able to attend from 1884 to 1890 largely because of her selfless efforts. In his insightful, witty, and beautifully written memoirs, Polievktov recalled her with affection and admiration as a hardworking and religious woman, devout yet not dogmatic, decent and generous, socially and politically conservative yet open-minded and tolerant of other beliefs and views. The doors of their modest dwelling were open to political exiles and ethnically diverse local personages whom Polievktov remembered from growing up in the terribly parochial provincial town of Likhvin, not far from Kaluga. Polievktov especially credits his mother with instilling in him a strong, longlasting passion for music and art.[13]

---

[10] Polievktov, "Moi vospominaniia," 5–6. At the time of his birth, Natalia Mikhailovna (1839–1920) was almost 34 years old, an unusually mature age for a first child.

[11] Ibid.; Polievktov, "Kak slozhilas' moia nauchnaia rabota," 1. See also *Aleksandr Evgen'evich Presniakov. Pis'ma i dnevniki, 1889–1927*, ed. A. N. Tsamutali and T. N. Zhukovskaia (St. Petersburg: Dmitrii Bulanin, 2005), 625, 667.

[12] It was no coincidence that Polievktov dedicated his first monograph to his "dear mother" who instilled in him respect and dedication to scholarship and supported his gymnasium and university studies in a variety of ways (Polievktov, *Baltiiskii vopros v Russkoi politike posle Nishtadskogo mira*, xi).

[13] Polievktov, "Moi vospominaniia," 6–8, 108–13, 120. Following the death of her husband, Natalia Mikhailovna was not eligible for a state pension or any other type of state support. Throughout his student years in St. Petersburg, Polievktov regularly submitted applications to the education authorities for tuition wavers (*po bednosti*). TsGIA SPB, f. 14, op. 3, d. 27363, ll.4, 5, 8, 10, 19, 39.

Many of Natalia Mikhailovna's qualities were shared by other members of the Maikov family, about whom Polievktov had much to say in his memoirs. He remembered them as devoted monarchists and loyal servants of the crown. The Maikovs particularly cherished the military service their ancestors had rendered the state during the endless campaigns of the late eighteenth and early nineteenth centuries. The ethos of these ex-military men, the "veterans of the 1812 campaign and artillery generals," as Polievktov collectively (and bitingly) called them, loomed large in the family tradition and was carefully preserved.[14] The older Maikovs also prided themselves on their old if not particularly distinguished (*znatnyi*) ancestry and were in Polievktov's words the quintessential middle gentry (*srednee dvorianstvo*), thus fairly conservative both socially and politically.[15] Nevertheless, they did not blindly or uncritically accept every official tenet of the government, or agree with its most reactionary policies. Far from it. Polievktov recalled an occasion in March of 1881, when two of his reputedly arch-conservative aunts, while disapproving of revolutionaries in general and indignant over the tsar's assassination in particular, refused to turn a political fugitive in to the authorities.[16]

As to other aspects of the Maikovs' legacy, in his memoirs Polievktov is perhaps too quick to distance himself from the traditional socio-political conservatism of the family, but he is also a bit too self-serving in boasting of his supposedly inherent "predilection for the weaker half of humanity."[17] On a more substantive level, however, he readily acknowledges the Maikovs' defining role in his early intellectual development. In addition to his mother, he especially credits her two (second) cousins, the Moscow-based Slavonic scholar and linguist Apollon Aleksandrovich Maikov and his cousin Leonid

[14] Polievktov, "Moi vospominaniia," 54. In all likelihood, Polievktov refers here to his grandfather on the maternal side, Mikhail Apollonovich Maikov (1799–1881), a retired artillery general. During the 1840s, when he headed the Artillery Department, M. A. Maikov resided with his family, including his younger daughter Natalia Mikhailovna, in his own house on Furshtatskaia Street (no. 24). He later sold the house and, until his death on March 1, 1881, lived in a rental flat at 23 Furshtatskaia Street (unit 5). It was also on Furshtatskaia, not far from his grandfather's house, where Polievktov resided during most of his thirty years in Petersburg/Petrograd. See TsGIA SPb, f. 14, op. 3, d. 27363, l. 4; A. Dubin, *Furshtatskaia ulitsa* (Moscow and St. Petersburg: Tsentropoligraf, 2005), 87, 289.

[15] Polievktov, "Moi vospominaniia," 6. In his birth certificate and other official documents, Polievktov was identified as from "*ober-ofitserskikh detei*" (See TsGIA SPb, f. 14, op. 3, d. 27363, ll. 3–30b.), in accordance with his father's non-noble clergy social origin and low professional rank.

[16] Polievktov, "Moi vospominaniia," 108–13.

[17] Ibid., 6–8, 108–13, 120.

(the brother of the famous poet Apollon Nikolaevich Maikov), the noted Petersburg philologist, ethnographer, and Pushkin scholar, both of whom had great influence over their young nephew.[18] Uncle Leonid appealed to Polievktov because of his strict adherence to scientific methodology, which he ably combined with a friendly, benevolent disposition toward budding scholars. His cousin, Apollon Aleksandrovich, impressed the young Polievktov with a lively, creative, and independent mind and a rare ability to connect scholarship with daily life. It was also uncle Apollon, with his moderate Slavophile views, who first drew his nephew's attention to the so-called Eastern Question and more generally to the relationship between foreign and domestic affairs.[19] In short, during his last years in gymnasium and his time as a student at St. Petersburg University, young Polievktov found himself in the company of several leading cultural figures of the time. This would continue throughout his years in Petersburg–Petrograd.

The Maikovs' most lasting influence on Polievktov was probably in the area of art history. Uncle Leonid's father, Nikolai Apollonovich, was a well-known painter of his day and member of the Imperial Academy of Fine Arts. His son, "Uncle Apollon" the poet, himself started out as a painter but later abandoned his brushes for verses and rhymes. He not only sparked Polievktov's initial interest in fine arts, but also encouraged his nephew to embark on a serious study of the subject that soon enough developed into a real passion and a lifelong avocation. In his own words, Polievktov's interest in art history became his "second religion," a criterion in selecting friends, and an important component of his future teaching and scholarship.[20] By all indications, Polievktov's knowledge of Russian and Western European art was so deep, his interest in it so profound, that for years after his graduation from the historico–philological faculty he repeatedly considered abandoning Russian history and concentrating all his time and efforts on the history of art. He continued to write art reviews for the main liberal papers in Petersburg

---

[18] Ibid., 5–6, 10; Polievktov, "Kak slozhilas' moia nauchnaia rabota," 1–2. Their father, Nikolai Apollonovich Maikov, was a well-known painter; their mother, E. P. Maikova, was a noted writer. Their two other brothers, Valerian and Vladimir, were also well-known literary figures, historians of literature and translators.

[19] Polievktov, "Kak slozhilas' moia nauchnaia rabota," 2; Polievktov, "Moi vospominaniia," 20–3. See also the preface to his first book in which he especially recalls, "with deep gratitude," the early influence of the late Academician L. N. Maikov (*Baltiiskii vopros v Russkoi politike posle Nishtadskogo mira*, xi). Uncle Apollon Aleksandrovich died in 1902, before Polievktov completed his dissertation.

[20] Polievktov, "Moi vospominaniia," 6.

(*Rech'*) and Moscow (*Russkie vedomosti*), contributed half a dozen entries on Gothic, Renaissance, and Italian art and architecture to various encyclopedic dictionaries, and taught a series of successful courses on the history of art in some of the finest academic institutions in the capital, including the Countess Obolenskaia Gymnasium for women (1897–1907), the Women's Pedagogical Institute, and the Higher (Bestuzhevskie) Women's Courses (1906–16).[21]

Polievktov's Early Career; Political and Philosophical Views

In the end, Polievktov's commitment to Russian history proved the most enduring. His interest in history was first piqued during his last two years (seventh and eighth grades) at the Kaluga classical gymnasium by the young and enthusiastic teacher (and later, his friend of many years) Petr Alekseevich Treiter, who encouraged his pupil to continue his studies at the historico-philological faculty of St. Petersburg University.[22] There he took the courses on Russian history given by the great Professor Platonov, whom he considered his "primary mentor" and under whose direction he wrote his award-winning undergraduate thesis on Catherine II's Commission on the New Law Code (*Ekaterininskaia komissia dlia*

[21] In the fall of 1900, while collecting materials for his *Magister's* dissertation in Central Europe, Polievktov also took two university-level history courses in Berlin, one of which was in art history (OR RNB [Manuscript Department of the Russian National Library], St. Petersburg, f. 585 [S. F. Platonov], op. 1, d. 3884 [Polievktov to Platonov, 1900–7], l. 70b.) According to Presniakov, Polievktov was on the verge of changing his focus from Russian history to art history during the 1907–8 academic year and again during 1910–11. His wavering greatly annoyed one of his senior colleagues, Professor I. M. Grevs (*Presniakov. Pis'ma i dnevniki*, 546–7, 570, 714–15). On Polievktov's teaching at the Higher Women's Courses, the so-called Bestuzhevskie Courses, named after one of its founders, Count Bestuzhev-Riumin, and at the Women's Pedagogical Institute (both institutions were the equivalent of university education for women), see M. A. Polievktov, "Moi vospominaniia," 5–6, 143; A. S. Kan, *Istorik G. V. Forsten i nauka ego vremeni* (Moscow: Nauka, 1979), 92–4; O. B. Vakhromeeva, *Dukhovnoe prostranstvo Universiteta. Vysshie zhenskie (Bestuzhevskie) kursy 1878–1918 gg.: issledovaniia i materialy* (St. Petersburg: Diada-Spb, 2003), 120–1, 232; *Presniakov. Pis'ma i dnevniki*, 533. During 1906–8, Polievktov served as lecturer in art history, first at the Higher Women's Courses and then at the Women's Pedagogical Institute (Polievktov to Platonov, October 8, 1906, OR RNB, f. 585, op. 1, d. 1921, l. 34–340b.). A list of Polievktov's publications on topics of art and architecture can be found in I. Tsindadze, *Trudy Tbilisskogo gosudarstvennogo universiteta imeni Stalina*, 35 (1943): 251. Not long before his death, Polievktov published a brochure on the Muscovy painters in Georgia (M. Polievktov, *Novye dannye o Moskovskikh khudozhnikakh XVI–XVII vv. v Gruzii* [Tbilisi: Izdanie muzeia Metekhi, 1941]).

[22] Polievktov, "Kak slozhilas' moia nauchnaia rabota," 3; Polievktov, "Moi vospominaniia," 127, 143; See also P. A. Treiter's letters to his "dear friend" Polievktov covering the years of 1896–1902 and 1908–14, in MAPP, FA.

sochineniia novogo Ulozheniia).[23] Polievktov also studied ancient, Byzantine, and European history with Vasilii Grigor'evich Vasil'evskii, Forsten, Ivan Mikhailovich Grevs, and Nikolai Ivanovich Kareev.[24] Following his graduation, Platonov asked him to stay on at the University to work on his *Magister*'s (Master's) dissertation.[25]

Reflecting on his experience at St. Petersburg University decades later, Polievktov had good things to say about all his teachers, but he reserved special words for his second mentor (and his later colleague and friend), Professor Georgii Vasil'evich Forsten (1857–1910), a specialist on foreign relations, modern European and Scandinavian history, and a well-known art and music connoisseur. His engaging and gracious mentoring style, his affable personality and truly extraordinary erudition was of lasting significance not only to Polievktov but also to several generations of the most promising students and younger faculty.[26] Though formally Polievktov wrote his *Magister*'s dissertation with Platonov, whose scholarly advice—as well as assistance in obtaining financial support—he continually sought, it was Forsten who inspired his choice of topic (on Russia's foreign policy in the aftermath of the Northern War), helped identify archival repositories in Europe and Scandinavia, and guided his protégé through the vicissitudes of this long and demanding enterprise.[27]

[23] Polievktov, "Kak slozhilas' moia nauchnaia rabota," 5; Polievktov was awarded a gold medal for this work. TsGIA SPB, f. 14, op. 27, d. 616, ll. 36, 95.

[24] Polievktov, "Moi vospominaniia," 134–7. According to Polievktov's "student file" at the University, he took courses in general history from Kareev and Vasil'evskii, and Russian history with Platonov (TsGIA SPb, f. 14, op. 3, d. 27363, ll. 12, 13, 16, 200b., 21, 240b., 25, 290b., 30, 350b., 36, 400b., 41, 49, 50). However, in his memoirs he also mentions the courses taught by Forsten and Grevs. Shortly after Polievktov's graduation, Platonov confirmed that during 1890–4 Polievktov studied Russian history with him and general history (*vseobshchaia istoriia*) with Forsten and Vasil'evskii (TsGIA SPb, f. 14, op. 2, d. 909, l. 100). It appears therefore that his student file only reflects courses for which he officially registered (that is, paid for), but not all the courses he had either audited or participated in some way.

[25] Polievktov, "Kak slozhilas' moia nauchnaia rabota," 4–5; Polievktov, *Baltiiskii vopros v Russkoi politike posle Nishtadskogo mira*, p. x. Polievktov graduated with the first degree diploma. The request to keep him at the University was formally brought up before a meeting of the historico-philological faculty on September 10, 1894, and approved by the rector on November 12. See TsGIA SPb, f. 14, op. 3, d. 16049, ll. 19, 20, 28. See also ibid., f. 14, op. 27, d. 616, ll. 36, 95, 303; op. 3, d. 27363, l. 47; op. 2, d. 909, l. 4.

[26] Polievktov, "Kak slozhilas' moia nauchnaia rabota," 5–6; Kan, *Istorik Forsten*, 81–90. Forsten was a Finish-born Swede, who became a moderate Russian patriot, knew many languages and apparently felt at home in many cultures.

[27] See, for example, Polievktov's frequent letters to Platonov that also contain references to his correspondence with Forsten, written while he was working on his *Magister*'s dissertation in Europe and Russia: from Berlin (1900–1); Copenhagen and Dresden (1901); and from Moscow,

In 1895, Forsten organized and, for more than a decade, hosted a seminar for younger historians and humanists from the University and the Bestuzhevskie Courses. Participants of the Forsten Circle (*kruzhok Forstena*) met on Saturdays in Forsten's welcoming home to discuss each other's work and engage with more senior colleagues. These Saturday gatherings soon rivaled (as well as complemented) the better known and more established Wednesday meetings of the circle of Russian historians (*kruzhok russkikh istorikov*) that Platonov led. Polievktov attended both seminars; both contributed greatly to his development as a professional historian and shaped his views and scholarly interests for years to come.[28] But on a personal as well as an intellectual level, he identified himself more closely with the Forsten Circle and belonged to the original core group of twelve *forsteniat* (disciples or pupils of Forsten). During the second half of the 1890s, this group of eight men and four women participated in a stimulating laboratory of learning. It was a place that fostered the formation of lifelong personal as well as intellectual friendships.[29] In addition to Polievktov, the original *forsteniata* included such eminent future scholars as the historian Aleksandr Evgen'evich Presniakov, the neo-Kantian philosopher and logician Ivan Ivanovich Lapshin (aka John), the art historian and docent Vladimir Aleksandrovich Golovan', and the literary scholar, linguist, and journalist Sergei Aleksandrovich Adrianov—all close personal friends of Polievktov's.[30]

Polievktov's two known memoirs, both of which were written during the Soviet era, understandably say little about his political views, and so we are compelled to cull indirect evidence from a variety of sources. It appears that Polievktov and his friends from the Forsten Circle shared not only common intellectual and cultural pursuits but also had a similar political

St. Petersburg, and Gurzuf (in Crimea) during 1903–4 (OR RNB, f. 585, op. 1, d. 3884, ll. 1–260b.). See also his brief acknowledgment of Platonov's and Forsten's respective roles in his training and early career in the introduction to his first monograph, *Baltiiskii vopros v Russkoi politike posle Nishtadskogo mira*, p. x, and his "Kak slozhilas' moia nauchnaia rabota," 5–6.

[28] In a letter to Platonov, dated May 26, 1926, written from the academically provincial Tbilisi, Polievktov lamented how much he missed the scholarly atmosphere of his Moscow and Petrograd (*piterskikh*) colleagues and "your [Platonov's] Wednesdays." *Ne khvataet... Vashikh sred* (OR RNB, f. 585, op. 1, d. 3885, l. 330b.)

[29] Kan, *Istorik Forsten*, 81–90; Polievktov, "Moi vospominaniia," 143–7.

[30] Kan, *Istorik Forsten*, 85–6; Polievktov, "Moi vospominaniia," 143–5. All four—Presniakov, Golovan', Lapshin, and Adrianov—also studied with Platonov and continued to pay respects to their former teacher long after graduation (OR RNB, f. 585, op. 1, d. 2472, l. 1; d. 2057, l. 1.)

orientation. There is little doubt that along with his fellow *forsteniata*, he condemned repeated encroachments on the university's autonomy under Alexander III and his successor.[31] Like many of his educated contemporaries, who were brought up venerating the heritage of the Decembrists but not necessarily the revolutionary terrorists of the 1870s, Polievktov abhorred tyranny. At least initially, he may have believed in the prospects of a peaceful evolution of the existing political and social order in Russia. He also appears to have been a man of generally liberal views, though he nourished a number of romantic populist notions about the will of the people. That sentiment, despite subsequent political and social upheavals, would not diminish over time.[32]

His more specific political preferences are difficult to pinpoint. But if his close association with other members of the Forsten Circle is any indication of where he stood politically, it would be plausible to assume that he agreed with his friends. As Forsten's biographer points out, the *forsteniata* were not apolitical, but they generally refrained from making public anti-government statements and declarations. And unlike their more radical peers from other student-faculty circles—led by the more politicized and politically engaged Professors Kareev and Grevs—they preferred intellectual discussions and concerts to overt political activity and collective walks in parks and the countryside over mass demonstrations with the working class.[33] This disposition appears to have survived the turbulent months of 1905–6, although there is evidence that Polievktov associated briefly with the Constitutional Democrats (Kadets) during the summer and fall of 1905. His friends Presniakov and Lapshin had not only joined the Party's ranks, but

---

[31] See, for example, Polievktov, "Moi vospominaniia," 114, 138.

[32] See Iu. V. Got'e's perceptive, if somewhat harsh, remarks as recorded in his diary on December 18, 1918 (*Time of Troubles. The Diary of Iurii Vladimirovich Got'e*, 222) and especially Polievktov's *Afterword* to the 1918 edition of his monograph on Nicholas I, which he wrote on October 31, 1917 (*Nikolai I: biografiia i obzor tsarstvovaniia*, 378). See also his essay on the Decembrists, published in the Kadet-run series "Biblioteka svobodnogo grazhdanina," which he wrote shortly after the February Revolution (Prof. M. A. Polievktov, *Rodonachal'niki russkoi revoliutsii—dekabristy* (Petrograd: Izdanie N. N. Karabasnikova, 1917), 32 pp.).

[33] Kan, *Istorik Forsten*, 85–7. Very little is known about Forsten's politics, except that he was a Russian patriot who subscribed to generally liberal views, sympathized with moderate Kadets, but did not belong to a political party (A. S. Kan, e-mail communications to the author, December 26–7, 2010). During the revolutionary years of 1905–6, Forsten reportedly disapproved of students' radicalism and political involvement, especially to the detriment of their studies (see Platonov's testimony to OGPU, recorded on January 14, 1930, in *Akademicheskoe delo 1929–1931 gg. Delo po obvineniiu akademika S. F. Platonova.* Vyp. 1 (St. Petersburg: BAN, 1993), 30).

were elected to the Kadet Committee of the Liteinyi district in the center of Petersburg during the summer of 1906. On the other hand, their other best friend Golovan' ("*nash Golovanchik*" as they affectionately called their apolitical and genteel pal) could not wait for the revolution to be over with so he and others could "return to the atmosphere of scholarship, art, and serious music" of the Forsten Circle.[34] In the end, Golovan' got his wish. As soon as calm and order in the country were restored, the *forsteniata* resumed their "Saturdays" and the satisfying routine of teaching and research.

It remains open to conjecture whether Polievktov was "pulled into" politics by his two activist friends or if his brief flirtation with the Kadets was just a symptom of the prevalent radical mood. But in the first part of his memoirs, written in Tbilisi during the tumultuous spring of 1921, he admitted in passing that during 1904–5, he "accepted" the rationale for going to war with Japan without realizing its "full implications for the internal life of the people," that he was once a proponent of a strong imperial state, and that he forced himself to revisit many of his core beliefs only in the wake of the First World War and the Revolution.[35]

Much has been written recently about the degree to which the prerevolutionary historians who continued to practice history during the Soviet period embraced Marxism and whether this embrace was part of a genuine intellectual evolution, a continuation of their earlier, pre-1917 interest, or a readjustment of their worldview to the political-ideological constraints of the time and a pragmatic act of self-preservation.[36] In this respect, Polievktov's

---

[34] Kan, *Istorik Forsten*, 85–7, 127. Kan quotes Presniakov's letter to his wife, Iuliia Petrovna, dated September 11, 1905 (*Presniakov. Pis'ma i dnevniki*, 532). See also ibid., 530–1, 547. On V. A. Golovan', see the very brief but moving remarks by his Hermitage colleague during the 1930s (V. M. Glinka, in "Blokada. Fragmenty vospominanii, napisannykh letom 1979 goda," *Zvezda* 7 (2005): 177).

[35] Polievktov, "Moi vospominaniia," 23.

[36] See, for example, V. M. Paneiakh, *Tvorchestvo i sud'ba istorika: Boris Aleksandrovich Romanov* (St. Petersburg: Dmitrii Bulanin, 2000), 68–70; Boris S. Kaganovich, "A. E. Presniakov, peterburgskaia shkola i marksizm," *Cahiers du Monde russe* 42, 1 (January–March, 2001): 31–48; T. N. Zhukovskaia, "A. E. Presniakov i marksizm: opyt istoriograficheskoi demifologizatsii," *Rossiia v XIX–XX vv. Sbornik statei k 70-letiiu so dnia rozhdeniia Rafaila Sholomovicha Ganelina*, ed. A. A. Fursenko (St. Petersburg: Dm. Bulanin, 1998), 28–40; See also Alfred J. Rieber's insightful introduction to the English-language edition of A. E. Presniakov's *The Formation of the Great Russian State. A Study of Russian History in the Thirteenth to Fifteenth Centuries*, trans. A. E. Moorhouse (Chicago: Quadrangle Books, 1970), pp. xxiv, xxxiv, xxxviii; and A. Presniakov, "Historical Research in Russia During the Revolutionary Crisis," *The American Historical Review* 28, 2 (1923): 248–57. Useful in this context is also a recent discussion of Lidiia Iakovlevna Ginsburg's views by Andrei Zorin in "Lidiia Ginzburg: opyt 'primireniia s deistvitel'nost'iu,'" *Novoe literaturnoe obozrenie* 101 (2010): http://magazines.russ.ru/nlo/2010/101/zo3.html

case is an interesting one that might offer insights into this complex and intriguing question. Like many historians of his generation, Polievktov seems to have subscribed to a positivist notion of the scientifically objective nature of knowledge based on serious, preferably archival research. But though not completely indifferent to the sociological approach to history, he appears to have been less interested in this approach than many of his peers, especially the disciples of the Moscow school of Russian history. Unlike his friend Presniakov, whose allegedly longstanding interest in Marxism has recently become a subject of stimulating discussion, it seems Polievktov never developed a sustained fascination for this "most advanced" theory. His "Marxist education" was apparently limited to one introductory lecture "enthusiastically taught" by the economist Andrei Alekseevich Isaev, which he attended during his freshman year.[37] There is also little evidence that the Marxist approach ever influenced Polievktov's choice of research topics (diplomatic, political, or art history) or colored his interpretation of historical facts either before or after the revolution. This is not to say, however, that he did not acknowledge the importance of economic factors in foreign relations or that he did not agree, for example, with Marx's sharp analysis of the international situation on the eve of the Crimean War.[38] But on the whole, Marxism as a theory of economic and social development, or for that matter the sociological-schematic approach to history as practiced by the early Soviet Marxist historians of the Pokrovskii School (which he privately abhorred), found no place in Polievktov's rich methodological toolbox or his view of the world.[39]

---

[37] Polievktov, "Moi vospominaniia," 141.

[38] See, for example, Polievktov's approving comments on Marx's analysis of international affairs but also his criticism of the "[direct] translation of the ideology of Moscow Slavophiles into tonnage of the Black Sea merchant fleet and vice versa," as was said to have been argued by the early Marxist historian and Bolshevik N. Rozhkov in his 1915 article "Konstantinopol' i prolivy" (M. Polievktov, "Literatura po vneshnei Russkoi istorii XVII–XIX vv. za 1900–1915 gg.," *Istoricheskie izvestiia, izdaiushchiesia istoricheskim Obshchestvom pri Moskovskom universitete* 1, 3–4 [1916]: 55–7). See also his comments on M. N. Pokrovskii's early works in M. A. Polievktov, "Obzor nauchnoi literatury o tsarstvovanii Nikolaia I," *Istoricheskii zhurnal* 3–4 (1917): 242; M. Polievktov, "Pogranichnyi rubezh evropeiskoi Rossii v ego istoricheskom razvitii," *Mezhdunarodnaia politika i mirovoe khoziaistvo* 5 (1918): 15.

[39] Contrary to the claim by the Georgian historian Iu. Sulaberidze, I found no evidence of adaptation of the so-called M. N. Pokrovskii theory of commercial capitalism in Polievktov's works (Sulaberidze, "M.A. Polievktov i ego lichnyi fond," 73). Not only did he reject the Pokrovskii-led onslaught on traditional historical scholarship during the 1920s, he was also critical of some aspects of Pokrovskii's prerevolutionary explanation of Russian foreign relations during the nineteenth century (M. Polievktov, "Literatura po vneshnei Russkoi istorii XVII–XIX vv. za

His *Weltanschauung*—as he himself put it in a 1927 autobiographical note—was formed during his student years in St. Petersburg primarily under the influence of Aleksandr Ivanovich Vvedenskii's popular "introduction to philosophy" course, which also attracted many of Polievktov's friends and peers. Vvedenskii was a leading Russian neo-Kantian philosopher and logician, a rising star, and among the youngest professors at the University. During Polievktov's senior year, Vvedenskii also attended Platonov's Wednesday seminars on Russian history and in this way could have exerted additional influence on Polievktov's bright young mind. Moreover, Vvedenskii's most promising disciple at the time was Polievktov's close friend Ivan Ivanovich Lapshin, and there is little doubt that the two engaged in philosophical discussions related to the course and beyond. According to Polievktov, Vvedenskii's "introduction to philosophy" in reality amounted to a detailed exposition of the Kantian philosophy and was intended by its author as "an ideal preparation" for the newly fashionable neo-Kantianism.[40] But for Polievktov, with his "phenomenally anti-philosophical mind," the course represented the ultimate point beyond which his philosophical thinking did not evolve; it was a philosophical Rubicon which he dared not cross. As he unabashedly admitted nearly half a century later—writing in the year of the publication of Stalin's *Short Course*—he had been and remained a convinced Kantian (*kantianets*).[41] His qualified indifference to

1900–1915 gg.," 55–6). More to the point, Polievktov's *Konspekt lektsii po sotsial'no-ekonomicheskoi istorii Rossii XIX–XX vekov, chitannykh na 2 i 3 kursakh fakul'teta obshchestvennykh nauk v 1922–23 ak[ademicheskom] g[odu]* (Tiflisskii gosudarstvennyi Politekhnicheskii institut: Izdatel'stvo Sovstupreda TGPI, 1923) as well as preparatory notes and study plans for his lectures and seminars taught at Tbilisi State University during the 1929–30 academic year suggest that while Polievktov "adopted" official terminology ("The Epoch of the Commercial Capital in Russia (XVIII–beginning XIX centuries)" and similar course titles) and assigned some of the required Marxist literature, he continued to use many of the same readings from his prerevolutionary teaching. In the last part of his memoirs, written after May 1938, Polievktov admitted that in teaching a course on "Istochnikovedenie po istorii SSSR" at Tbilisi University during the 1930s, he used the historiographical and source analysis (*istochnikovednoe*) introduction to Platonov's famous lecture course on Russian history which he himself took in the early 1890s (Polievktov, "Moi vospominaniia," 127, 132).

[40] On Vvedenskii's participation in Platonov's "Wednesdays" during 1894, see *Presniakov. Pis'ma i dnevniki*, 130–1. In the early 1900s, Polievktov and Vvedenskii were part of the same socioprofessional circle that included Forsten, F. Zelinskii, Lapshin, Presniakov, Golovan', and Andrianov. See OR RNB, f. 585, op. 1, d. 2472, l. 1.

[41] Polievktov, "Moi vospominaniia," 131; Polievktov, "Kak slozhilas' moia nauchnaia rabota," 3; Presniakov also comments on Vvedenskii's course, which he took at the same time as Polievktov, and on the influence Vvedenskii's teaching and writing had on his philosophical development (*Presniakov. Pis'ma i dnevniki*, 26, 63). Of the three friends, Ivan Ivanovich Lapshin (1870–1952) was

Marxism alongside his lifelong interest in Kant thus suggests an enduring respect for intellectual freedom, human liberty, and dignity—those classic attributes of moderate liberalism that perhaps most accurately describe his *Weltanschauung*.

The Last Prerevolutionary Decade: Polievktov's Professional and Family Life

The relatively peaceful and prosperous decade between the convocation of the first Duma and the outbreak of the February Revolution was arguably the most productive and successful period of Polievktov's professional life. His scholarly productivity was on the rise despite his heavy teaching obligations at the University and a slew of additional teaching responsibilities at various institutions of higher education and gymnasia in the capital. In 1907 he published his first major monograph on the subject of Russian foreign policy in the Baltic Basin during the four years following the Neustadt Peace Treaty of 1721, which had ended the long Northern War between Russia and Sweden. In February 1908 he defended it as his *Magister's* dissertation.[42]

It can be argued that on one level Polievktov's work was a continuation of Forsten's two dissertations on the role of the Baltic question in Russia's foreign policy (Muscovy's *Drang nach Westen*) during the fifteenth and seventeenth centuries, which Forsten saw as prelude (*Vorgeschichte*) to the Northern War.[43] On another level, however, Polievktov took his investigation a step further by examining Peter I's gains vis-à-vis Sweden in the context of Russia's relations with major European powers, most prominently

---

probably the most successful. He defended his doctoral dissertation, bypassing the *Magister's* dissertation, in 1906. Between 1913 and the time of his expulsion from the Soviet Russia in 1922, he was Professor at St. Petersburg/Petrograd University. He subsequently lived in Prague where he was Professor at the Russian Juridical Faculty. Lapshin is mostly known for his works on the philosophy of science, music, and art. He was also a noted phenomenologist and published works on psychology and logic (*Noveishii filosofskii slovar'*, compiled by A. A. Gritsanov [Minsk: V. M. Skakun, 1998], 356–7; P. V. Alekseev, *Filosofy Rossii XIX–XX stoletii. Biografii, idei, trudy*, 3rd edn [Moscow: Akademicheskii proekt, 1999], 447).

[42] Polievktov, "Kak slozhilas' moia nauchnaia rabota," 6. M. Polievktov's *Baltiiskii vopros v Russkoi politike posle Nishtadskogo mira* was published in accordance with the May 17, 1907 decision of the historico-philological faculty of the University. The dissertation defense took place on Sunday, February 17, 1908, the official *opponenty* were Platonov and Forsten (TsGIA SPB, f. 14, op. 2, d. 909, l. 55).

[43] M. Polievktov, "Literatura po vneshnei Russkoi istorii XVII–XIX vv. za 1900–1915 gg.," 58; Polievktov, "Kak slozhilas' moia nauchnaia rabota," 6 (corrections on the margins).

Austria, Prussia, France, and England.[44] More broadly, Polievktov saw the Baltic episode, which in his view ended in 1725, not as an isolated moment in Russian foreign policy but rather as part of its long-term "Europeanization," a process that began with the conclusion of the so-called "eternal peace" treaty with Poland in 1686 and continued through the end of the eighteenth century.[45] This was a mature and novel interpretation that apparently did much to reinforce Platonov's already high opinion of his former student and protégé and prompted the senior scholar, in March of 1908, to recommend Polievktov—along with only one other young *Magister*, Moscow's Iurii Vladimirovich Got'e—to the recently vacated Russian history chair at Odessa's Novorossiiskii University.[46]

Over the next few years Polievktov continued his research on Russia's relations with Europe's major powers during the first half of the eighteenth century. He hoped to develop it into a doctoral dissertation, and he collected an enormous amount of archival material for this dissertation in Moscow, St. Petersburg, Berlin, Dresden, Vienna, Rome, Paris, London, Munich, and Stockholm.[47] Although he never defended the dissertation, he used this rich material in a dozen or so monographic encyclopedia articles, and biographical essays published in various places in 1911–16.[48]

---

[44] See Polievktov, *Baltiiskii vopros v russkoi politike posle Nishtadskogo mira*, pp. vii, 1–4, 298–301; Polievktov, "Literatura po vneshnei Russkoi istorii XVII–XIX vv. za 1900–1915 gg," 59.

[45] Polievktov, "Pogranichnyi rubezh evropeiskoi Rossii v ego istoricheskom razvitii," 6.

[46] S. F. Platonov to G. K. Ul'ianov, March [1908], written in response to Ul'ianov's request from March 13, [1908] to recommend persons with doctoral degrees for the Russian history chair at Novorossiiskii University (OR RNB, f. 585, op. 1, d. 1921, l. 1. Got'e defended his *Magister's* dissertation, *The Moscow Region in the Seventeenth Century. A Study of the History of Economic Conditions in Muscovite Rus*, in 1906 (See Emmons, "Got'e and His Diary," p. 11). The Russian history chair in Odessa, which in the end was not filled by either candidate, became vacant after Professor Georgii Ivanovich Peretiatkovich's (1840–August 1908) retirement in early 1908. In April 1905, two years before the completion of his *Magister's* dissertation, Platonov recommended Polievktov for a senior Russian history post at the Historico-philological Institute of Prince A. A. Bezborodko in Nezhin. But at that time, Polievktov considered moving to a culturally remote Ukrainian town undesirable. Besides, he did not think, or so he wrote to Platonov, thanking him for the recommendation, that he deserved to be put forward as senior candidate without first finishing his book (OR RNB, f. 585, op. 1, d. 3884 (Polievktov to Platonov, 1900–7), ll. 32–32ob.).

[47] In my estimation, between 1908 and 1914 Polievktov made at least six (annual) trips to European archives during which he was collecting documentation on Russia's relations with German states, France, and England (TsGIA SPB, f. 14, op. 2, d. 909, ll. 62–91ob., 100ob.).

[48] See, for example, his long biographical essay on A. I. Osterman in the *RBD* and his "Osterman Andrei Ivanovich. Iz perepiski barona A.I. Ostermana (pis'ma k kn. B. I. Kurakinu i gr. A. P. Golovkinu, 1727–1729)," *Chteniia v Obshchestve istorii i drevnostei Rossiiskikh* (1913). See also M. Polievktov, "Kak slozhilas' moia nauchnaia rabota," 7; and his essay, "Literatura po vneshnei russkoi istorii XVIII–XIX vv. za 1900–1915 gg.," 55–6.

With his growing maturity as a scholar, and with more research and teaching experience under his belt, he began to appreciate the benefits of incorporating his research findings into the more specialized courses of his wide-ranging teaching repertoire and vice versa. In this respect, some of the pertinent courses that he taught between the completion of his *Magister*'s dissertation and the academic year of 1916–17 included a survey of Russian political history during the first half of the nineteenth century, research seminars and proseminars on Russian political history during the reign of Alexander I, foreign policy during the imperial period, and memoir sources related to Nicholas I and his government during the first period of his reign.[49]

As Polievktov recalled in his autobiographical note, teaching to a well-informed and motivated audience was interesting and very useful. It stimulated his interest in the subject matter and opened up new vistas and "new scholarly horizons."[50] After a while he began to develop his own conception of Russian history that was reflected, in part, in his second and arguably most significant monograph on Nicholas I and his reign. The first, shorter version of this study focused on Nicholas's biography and presented a brief survey of his reign. Written originally in early 1914 for the *Biographical Dictionary of the Imperial Russian Historical Society* (RBD), the 165-page essay was left out of the intended eighth volume for a variety of last-minute editorial and technical reasons.[51] This, however, did not deter Polievktov. In September of that year he published his lengthy essay as a short book, titled *Emperor Nicholas I*, with attribution to *RBD*.[52]

---

[49] On Polievktov's teaching at the University, the Women's Higher Courses, and the Pedagogical Institute, Obolenskaia gymnasium, and the Nicholas' General Staff Academy see his correspondence with Platonov during 1908–15 (OR RNB, f. 585, op. 1, d. 3885, ll. 1–300b.) and "Kak slozhilas' moia nauchnaia rabota," 8. On Polievktov's teaching at the University, see his personnel file, in TsGIA SPB, f. 14, op. 2, d. 909, ll. 1000b., 1270b.–1310b. Polievktov was allowed to teach courses as *Privatdozent* of the University beginning on July 1, 1903 (TsGIA SPB, f. 14, op. 2, d. 909, l. 1250b.; Brachev and Dvornichenko, *Kafedra russkoi istorii Sankt-Peterburgskogo universiteta*, 162, 165, 167). See also [Polievktov], *Zapiski po politicheskoi istorii, sostavlennye po lektsiiam privat-dotsenta Mikhaila Aleksandrovicha Polievktova, chitannye v mladshem klasse Imperatorskoi Nikolaevskoi voennoi akademii*, part 2 (St. Petersburg: Tipo-litografiia I. Trofimova, 1910). Forsten taught this course for many years until the 1908–9 academic year. Polievktov took it over following his mentor's long mental illness and death in 1910.

[50] Polievktov, "Kak slozhilas' moia nauchnaia rabota," 9.

[51] M. P. Lepekhin, "Predislovie," *Russkii biograficheskii slovar', Nikolai I–Novikov* (Moscow: Aspekt Press, 1998), 3. Polievktov's entry on Nicholas I was published eighty-five years later in a supplemental volume of the *RBD*'s previously unpublished contributions (ibid., 5–158).

[52] M. Polievktov, *Imperator Nikolai I* (St. Petersburg: Tipografiia Glavnogo upravleniia udelov, 1914) came out in September 1914, with a limited print run. On the verso of the cover page it is

Over the next eighteen months, he significantly expanded his work to examine the most important policies and institutions of Nicholas's reign in the context of the tsar's personality as well as his personal and educational background. Polievktov first tested this new material, written as a year-long lecture course, on his students at the Petrograd Higher Women's Courses during the 1915–16 academic year.[53] However, more ambitious plans to add sections on educated society and the main currents of social thought did not come to fruition "because of curriculum changes" at the Higher Women's Courses. The originally proposed two-year sequence was reduced to one term; hence, Polievktov had to limit the scope of his work by concentrating on Nicholas and the political-administrative structures of his government. In its final form the monograph was based on both his *RBD* essay and the lectures at the Higher Women's Courses and more than doubled the size of the earlier publication. It was completed in May of 1916 but published only in the summer of 1918.[54] Notwithstanding the early Soviet denunciation of the book as an apology for Nicholas and his regime and its outright denigration as "utterly inadequate,"[55] it is still considered the standard work on the subject.

It may well be the case that Polievktov's initial curiosity about Nicholas I was inspired by the stories his maternal grandmother, Anna Petrovna née Meller-Zakomel'skaia, had told him in childhood. A lady-in-waiting at the court, Anna Petrovna spent the memorable day of December 14, 1825 in trepidation inside the imperial residence. Whatever the original impetus, his

stated that the publication was an offprint from the *RBD* (Lepekhin, "Predislovie," 3. The date of publication is established on the basis of Polievktov's handwritten inscription on the copy of the book in MAPP, FA). Polievktov's academic file at the University lists Nicholas's biography as a *RBD* publication (TsGIA SPB, f. 14, op. 2, d. 909, l. 1000b.). The outbreak of the war caught Polievktov in Switzerland with his mother, young wife, and her sister, penniless and unable to travel back to Russia across Central and Eastern Europe. He returned to St. Petersburg only in late September 1914, after a long detour via Marseilles, Constantinople, and Odessa (OR RNB, f. 585, op. 1, d. 4429, ll. 18–19; d. 3885, ll. 24–250b.; d. 1816, l. 12. His wife recalled that on the last leg of the journey they were on the same boat with the members of the renowned K. S. Stanislavskii theater company. See R. N. Polievktova-Nikoladze, *Diaries*, Notebook IV (Summer 1914), MAPP, FA). See also *Spisok russkikh poddannykh, zastignutykh za granitsei*, vypusk I (s 26 iiulia po 19 avgusta 1914 goda) (Petrograd: Tipografiia V. F. Kishbauma, 1914), 80; ibid., vypusk II (s 20 avgusta po 4 sentiabria 1914 goda), 97.

[53] Polievktov, "Preface," *Nikolai I. Biografiia i obzor tsarstvovaniia* (Moscow: Izdatel'stvo M. and S. Sabashnikovykh, 1918).

[54] The book came out in an impressive print run of 3,000 copies.

[55] *Nikuda negodnaia* ([D.], *Kniga i Revoliutsiia* 1 [1920]: 27–8 as cited in Lepekhin, "Predislovie," 4).

subsequent scholarly interest in the era of Nicholas I stemmed from his teaching of Russian political history and institutions, along with his growing dissatisfaction with the emerging historiographical tendency to treat Nicholas' reign as "enlightened absolutism." In Polievktov's view, such an interpretation fell short of grasping the all-pervasive nature of the despotic absolutist system created by Russia's last true autocrat.[56] Perhaps even more important, Polievktov's continued attention to Nicholas and his era may also have been motivated by the need to understand his own contemporary political reality. As someone who from his youth learned to appreciate the connection between scholarship and real life, Polievktov's turning to Nicholas I in order to learn more about Nicholas II was not an unfamiliar strategy.

It is true that any direct parallels between the two systems—Nicholas I's absolutism and Nicholas II's ramshackle autocracy—may be deemed superficial, even incongruous. But it is also probably true that the more deeply Polievktov immersed himself in the historical literature on Nicholas I's reign, the more he realized that the two periods shared more numerous features than was generally assumed. To a historian and concerned citizen like Polievktov, Russia on the eve of the Great War—with its resources stretched to the utmost and political and social stability hanging in the balance—might indeed have resembled Nicholas's empire on the eve of the Crimean War that would quickly expose the manifold inadequacies of a regime hitherto perceived as a bastion of power and stability. If we take Polievktov at his word, it was his work on Nicholas I that pressed him to conclude that the entire Russian political system, as long as it was based on some form of political absolutism, was in the long run doomed to fail. It mattered little how hard Nicholas's successors—far lesser figures ("pigmies," in Polievktov's designation), to be sure—tried to restore political absolutism or reform the system with half-measures. "There are no repressive or [for that matter] palliative measures," he wrote, that could ensure the system's survival much beyond the life of its creator.[57] Strange as it might have seemed to his contemporaries, it was this realization, as Polievktov confessed

[56] Polievktov, "Moi vospominaniia," 31–2. See also his comments on A. A. Kornilov's famous *Kurs istorii Rossii XIX veka (v trekh chastiakh)*, part 1 (Moscow, 1912), referring to p. 119, in Polievktov, *Nikolai I* (2008 reprint), 183.

[57] Polievktov, *Nikolai I* (1918 edn), 378; Polievktov, *Nikolai I* (2008 edn), 8, 182–4; Polievktov, "Protivorechiia absoliutizma," *Vestnik kul'tury i politiki* 3 (1918): 16–21.

in the afterword to his monograph—written, notably, one week after the Bolshevik takeover—that gave him confidence that the day would come when the "people's will" and "people's truth" would no longer be violated and Russia would have a constitutional regime based on popular sovereignty.[58]

Writing his survey of Nicholas I's reign precisely at the time of the regime's worst performance thus impelled Polievktov to realize much faster that the system had long since outlived itself, and that nothing short of a regime change was required to stave off Russia's collapse; no superficial fixes or change of personalities could stop its spiral of decline. That such a view was shared by most members of his largely liberal social and professional milieu is neither surprising nor new. What was new is that this radical realization was now supported (to his monarchist mother's dismay) by a new member of the family—his younger and notably more radical wife, the Georgian-born chemist Rusudana (Rusia) Nikolaevna Nikoladze (1884–1981).

Very little about their marriage, dating from the summer of 1913, can be gleaned from the surviving family papers. We know that they were acquainted as early as 1907, when Rusudana was a senior at the Women's Pedagogical Institute (which was headed by Platonov) and where Polievktov, as Platonov's protégé, taught history and art history courses at the time. Whether she was ever a student in his classes remains unknown. It is perhaps more likely that the two were introduced to each other by a mutual acquaintance, the chemist Vadim Nikandrovich Verkhovskii, who had known Polievktov for some time and who was Rusudana's principal mentor at the Institute. Be that as it may, the available evidence suggests that Polievktov's possessive mother was quite reluctant to share her 41-year-old bachelor Minia (endearment of Mikhail, Misha) with another strong-willed, educated, and very independent woman. His friends Golovan' and Presniakov were taken aback by the apparent lack of tenderness and mutual admiration between the young couple and even more so by the purported signs of Rusudana's selfish disposition. It should be noted that some of their misgivings would be borne out by future events, but that should not concern us at the moment. Whatever marital difficulties they had (and they certainly had

---

[58] Polievktov, *Nikolai I* (1918 edn), 378–80.

their share of trials and tribulations, separations and reunifications) the union survived for almost thirty years.[59]

The marriage substantially expanded Polievktov's social circle to include the younger and generally more radical friends of his spouse as well as members of her family, who proudly counted among their ranks such committed opponents of the old regime as Rusudana's exiled cousin Irakli (Kaki) Tsereteli, the famed Social Democratic deputy to the Second Duma and future leader of the Petrograd Soviet, and her father, Niko (Nikolai) Iakovlevich Nikoladze, a man of the "sixties generation," who was a Georgian democrat, an acquaintance of Karl Marx, a sometime associate of Alexander Herzen, and a friend and devoted follower of Nikolai Gavrilovich Chernyshevskii.[60]

---

[59] See various, mostly disapproving, comments on this marriage by Polievktov's friends, Presniakov and Golovan', in *Presniakov. Pis'ma i dnevniki*, 732, 738, 759, 761; Golovan's letters to Polievktov, dated December 8, 11, 1924, in MAPP, FA. It should be noted that Rusudana never got along with her mother-in-law. She often chastised her husband for not standing up to his mother, especially on matters concerning his own family (See Polievktov's "Moi vospominaniia," 5–6, and Rusudana's diary notes and letters to Polievktov during 1922–39, MAPP, FA). The longest and most serious split of their marriage took place in the spring of 1924. Polievktov moved out and traveled to Moscow and Leningrad. Upon his return to Tbilisi in November or December 1924 and for the next six years he lived separately from his family at 51 Kamo Street. Sometime in early 1926 the couple reconciled, but continued to live separately. All the while Polievktov maintained a very friendly and warm relationship with his father-in-law, Niko Nikoladze, who filled him in on family matters and more during Polievktov's frequent research trips to Moscow and Leningrad (See Rusudana Nikoladze to Polievktov, July 29, 1924, January 11, 29, 1929, MAPP, FA; Polievktov to Platonov, May 26, 1926 (from Tbilisi), OR RNB, f. 585, op. 1, d. 3885, l. 320b.). On Rusudana's work under the direction of Professor Vadim Nikandrovich Verkhovskii, see her *Diaries*, Notebook IV and her "Vospominaniia o Lebedeve," typescript [1934–8], MAPP, FA. On her education and other biographical details, see TsGIA SPb, f. 918 (Muzei Gosudarstvennogo pedagogicheskogo instituta), op. 1, d. 5673, l. 59.

[60] A well-known radical in his youth, in his more mature years Nikoladze became a moderate Georgian patriot and democrat, favoring a federation of all Caucasian peoples on the basis of economic equality. Instead of overt political activity, he channeled his enormous energies into strengthening the Georgian economy and its institutions of self-government. Politically, however, he remained an uncompromising opponent of the old regime. On Niko Nikoladze's remarkable life and early political involvement, see his interviews with B. I. Nikolaevskii, recorded on October 10 and 12, 1926, in Berlin (Nicolaevsky Collection, box 525, f. 3, notebook 1, ll. 122–7, Hoover Institution Archives [HIA]); Vano Shaduri, "Introduction," *Pis'ma russkikh literaturno-obshchestvennykh deiatelei k N. Ia. Nikoladze* (Tbilisi: Zaria Vostoka, 1949), 5–44; G. Dzhavakhishvili, *Iz perepiski N. Ia. Nikoladze s russkimi i zarubezhnymi literaturno obshchestvennymi deiateliami* (Tbilisi: TGU, 1980), 8-9-36; Ronald Grigor Suny, *The Making of the Georgian Nation*, 2nd edn (Indiana University Press: Bloomington and Indianapolis, 1994), 131, 134–5, 137; A. N. Bogoliubov, *Georgii Nikolaevich Nikoladze (1888–1931)* (Moscow: Nauka, 1973), 5–30, 107–16; and Stephen F. Jones, *Socialism in Georgian Colors. The European Road to Social Democracy, 1883–1917* (Cambridge, MA: Harvard University Press, 2005), 32–47, 127, 166, 199–203.

The February Revolution; the Creation of the Society for the Study of the Revolution and the Interviews Project

Given the prevailing political orientation of the recently formed Polievktov-Nikoladze clan, it is hardly surprising that they greeted the news of the February uprising with elation and great enthusiasm.[61] Rusudana recorded in her diary that her parents' reaction to the demise of the old order was more jubilant and euphoric than her own or that of her younger sister Tamara, a recent graduate of the Women's Pedagogical Institute.[62] As early as the morning of February 28, Niko Nikoladze went on foot to the editorial office of *Russkaia volia* (in 1916 he had joined the board of this leading patriotic daily along with a few other big names of the pro-war Left) and began composing editorials in support of the new Duma/Soviet authority.[63] Within days, the Nikoladze sisters offered their services to the newly formed Petrograd Soviet, and in the following weeks they worked eight-hour shifts every day inside the Tauride Palace as telephone operators on the lines designated for the Soviet's leaders.

Polievktov also plunged into civic activity. From the very first days of the revolution, he began working in the City Duma—a key observation point used by anti-government forces.[64] It should be noted that at the time of the February Revolution the two families, the Polievktovs (Natalia Mikhailovna, Mikhail Aleksandrovich, Rusudana, and their eighteenth-month-old son

[61] With the single exception of the ailing Natalia Mikhailovna Polievktova. According to her daughter-in-law, she remained a staunch monarchist (Rusudan [*sic!*] Nikoladze, "Nezabyvaemye dni i mgnoveniia. Na beregakh Nevy," *Literaturnaia Gruziia* 3 [1970]: 68).

[62] R. N. Nikoladze (Polievktova), *Diaries*, Notebook IV, 33–69, MAPP, FA. On Tamara's education, see TsGIA SPb, f. 918, op. 1, d. 5674, l. 23.

[63] Five years later, in a private letter to V. L. Voitinskii, Nikoladze recalled his long and distinguished journalistic career. He was especially proud of his work in the iconic populist "thick" journal *Otechestvennye zapiski* under M. E. Saltykov-Shchedrin and N. K. Mikhailovskii, but also in the patriotic *Russkaia volia* edited by his former protégé A. V. Amfiteatrov (N. Ia. Nikoladze to V. L. Voitinskii, December 3, 1922 in *Iz perepiski N. Ia. Nikoladze s russkimi i zarubezhnymi literaturno-obshchestvennymi deiateliami*, 217–19). On *Russkaia volia*, see Iu. G. Oksman, "'Russkaia volia.' Banki i burzhuaznaia literatura," *Literaturnoe nasledstvo* 2 (Moscow, 1932): 165–86. On March 4, the editorial staff of *Russkaia volia* voted overwhelmingly (with one dissenting vote by E. D. Grimm) to endorse a republican form of government (Rusudana N. Nikoladze-Polievktova, *Diaries*, Notebook IV, 69, MAPP, FA).

[64] Rusudana N. Nikoladze (Polievktova), *Diaries*, Notebook IV (entries from February 28, 1917; March 1–2, 1917; March 4–8, 1917): 29, 33, 39, 45, 89, 101 MAPP, FA; R. N. Nikoladze, "Uchitel'-drug. Vospominaniia o S.V. Lebedeve," 166, 179, MAPP, FA; R. Nikoladze, "Nezabyvaemye dni i mgnoveniia. Na beregakh Nevy," *Literaturnaia Gruziia* 3 (1970): 71.

Nika) and the Nikoladzes (Niko, his wife Olga Aleksandrovna née Guramishvili, and their younger daughter Tamara) lived in the same massive rental building on Furshtatskaia Street (no. 27), which was located on the corner of three streets—Furshtatskaia, Voskresenskii Avenue, and Kirochnaia—and only a short walk from the Duma itself.[65] The Polievktovs occupied a spacious apartment on the third floor; the Nikoladzes lived in an identical unit directly above.[66]

From their windows they could observe insurgents streaming in the direction of the Tauride Palace, which became the "headquarters of the revolution" by midday on February 27th. They could also watch what was transpiring in the nearby barracks of the Preobrazhenskii Regiment—one of the first units to revolt on the morning of February 27. Not far from their building, on Liteinyi Avenue, the Petrograd District Court was set on fire by insurgents during the first hours of the uprising and continued to burn for several days. According to Rusudana's diary, as soon as she and Polievktov saw smoke emanating from the Petrograd District Court, they decided to go there, hoping to salvage anything that survived the fire and looting. She claims that they managed to collect a few police documents, including censored leaflets from the days of the 1905 revolution. More importantly, she notes that upon witnessing this and other massive acts of destruction in the first revolutionary days, Polievktov wrote a letter on March 2 to Pavel Nikolaevich Miliukov, the newly appointed Minister of Foreign Affairs, urging him to organize immediate efforts to safeguard the records of imperial and public institutions.[67]

We have no reliable information on whether the letter actually reached Miliukov, or if any of the requested measures were ever taken by the noted historian-cum-politician. A number of attempts were made to preserve

---

[65] Because the building stood on the three corners, it carried three separate numbers, each in accordance with numeration of the pertinent street (Furshtatskaia, no. 27; Voskresenskii Avenue, no. 17; and Kirochnaia Street, no. 26). The building had close to 500 residents at the time. For more on this well-known building and some of its occupants, see Dubin, *Furshtatskaia ulitsa*, 104–21.

[66] R. Nikoladze, "Nezabyvaemye dni i mgnoveniia," 68. Polievktov's family resided at 27 Furshtatskaia, in unit 39 where Polievktov continued to store part of his library and other personal belongings even after his departure from Petrograd in the summer of 1920 (Letter from an unidentified neighbor, residing at 18 Furshtatskaia Street, unit 4, to Polievktov, dated May 10, 1923 and Natalia Shtakel'berg's letters to Polievktov, October 4, December 31, 1923, in MAPP, FA; TsGIA SPb, f. 14, op. 2, d. 909, ll. 36, 45, 105).

[67] Rusudana N. Nikoladze (Polievktova), *Diaries*, Notebook IV: 51, MAPP, FA. Throughout the first months of the revolution, Rusudana kept her diary uninterruptedly but with varying degrees of detail.

historical documents, especially the records of the notorious *Okhranka* (tsarist secret police), during the first days and weeks of the revolution, but these
were mostly the work of former revolutionaries such as Vladimir L'vovich
Burtsev and Sergei Grigor'evich Svatikov, sanctioned by the Ministry of
Justice under Aleksandr Fedorovich Kerenskii. It appears that Polievktov
acted independently of these structures when in early March he and his
friend Presniakov launched their own efforts to collect materials documenting the historic events of the February Days. At first they operated
from their residences—Presniakov at Nadezhdinskaia Street (no. 11) and
Polievktov at nearby Furshtatskaia—with the help of their family members.
Authorization from the Provisional Government came a few weeks later,
and by the end of April, a new Society for the Study of the Revolution
(SSR) was officially created.[68] Presniakov became its chairman (probably
because he held a higher status in Petrograd academic circles and was
better connected with political figures on the Center/Left). The classicist
Konstantin Vladimirovich Khilinskii, a colleague of his and Polievktov's
from the University and the Women's Pedagogical Courses, agreed to serve
as treasurer; and Presniakov's former student, the young historian Ol'ga
Konradovna Nedzvetskaia[69] became the Society's secretary.

The SSR cast its collection net very wide. An official announcement was
sent out to numerous local libraries and archival commissions urging citizens of the new Russia to collect any materials pertaining to the history of
the February Revolution—from official documents, memoirs, notes, diaries,

[68] Later that year the name changed to the Society for the Study of the Russian Revolution.
During 1918, SSR was more frequently referred to as the Society for the Study of the 1917
Revolution (R. N. Nikoladze-Polievktova, "Uchitel'-drug. Vospominaniia o S. V. Lebedeve," 181–4,
MAPP, FA; Nikoladze-Polievktova, "Nezabyvaemye dni i mgnoveniia," 72; See also A. Presniakov,
"Reforma arkhivnogo dela," *Russkii istoricheskii zhurnal* 5 (1918): 205, 209; Presniakov, "Obzory
perezhitogo," *Dela i dni. Istoricheskii zhurnal* 1 (1920): 347; GARF, f. 6685 [Dom-muzei bortsov za
svobodu], op. 1, d. 5, l. 1, 7.

[69] Ol'ga Konradovna Samarina (née Nedzvetskaia) (1887–1972), daughter of the prominent
Kadet lawyer Konrad Viktorovich Nedzvetskii, was a recent graduate of the Higher Women's
Courses where she studied with E. D. Grimm and A. E. Presniakov. After the revolution,
Nedzvetskaia taught history at Petrograd University and the Petrograd Archeological Institute's
Archival Courses, together with her former teachers A. E. Presniakov, M. A. Polievktov, and O. A.
Dobiash-Rozhdestvenskaia. In 1923 she was purged from the history faculty of Petrograd
University and for the rest of her working career taught foreign languages in various institutions
of Higher Education in Leningrad. See N. S. Shtakel'berg, "'Kruzhok molodykh istorikov' i
'Akademicheskoe delo,'" ed. B. V. Anan'ich and E. A. Pravilova, in *In Memoriam. Istoricheskii sbornik
pamiati F. F. Perchenka*, ed. A. I. Dobkin, M. Iu. Sorokina (Moscow and St. Petersburg: Feniks-
Atheneum, 1995), 33, 34, 74; *Dela i dni. Istoricheskii zhurnal* 1 (1920): 514.

and personal accounts to books, leaflets, songs and verses, drawings and photographs, advertisements, and records of meetings by political and social organizations—and send them to the SSR's temporary depository in the Manuscript Division of the Academy of Sciences Library in Petrograd.[70] It was also decided to divide the SSR into several sections, each collecting materials documenting the contribution of a particular social, occupational, or political group to the overthrow of the old regime. Hence the following sections were formed: soldiers, workers, students, political parties, and the so-called *Sektsiia po izucheniiu Tavricheskogo dvortsa* (Section on the Study of the Tauride Palace), soon renamed the Interview Commission of the Tauride Palace (*Komissiia oprosov Tavricheskogo dvortsa*).

According to a sample letter to prospective interviewees, the Commission sought "to interview those participants of the [February] coup who were active during the revolutionary days inside the Tauride Palace or were involved in forming the Temporary Committee of the State Duma, the Soviet of Workers' Deputies, and the other entities organized there."[71] The letter further stated that the SSR viewed the material it collected as having exceptional scholarly value and had no plans for its immediate publication. Individual interviewees could opt to keep their depositions barred from public release for a period of time.[72] The letter concluded by encouraging the addressees to share their recollections by contacting the chairman

---

[70] See copies of an announcement on the establishment of the SSR and of its appeal to donate historical documents, in GARO (State Archive of Riazan' oblast'), f. 869 (*Riazanskaia uchenaia arkhivnaia komissiia*), op. 1, d. 126, l. 89 and in GARF, f. 6685, op. 1, d. 10, l. 1. See also R. N. Nikoladze, *Na bol'shom zhiznennom puti* (in Georgian; title in Russian and Georgian) (Tbilisi, 1975), 271.

[71] Typescript of the original letter, signed by Presniakov and stamped with the official seal of the SSR, is preserved in MAPP, FA. The letter is not dated, but there is every reason to assume that it was written in late April, just in time for the first two interviews to take place on the first and second days of May. This, in turn, suggests that the SSR was created in April, not in May as stated in the SSR report from June 1918 and also recalled half a century later by Rusudana Nikoladze and accepted by historians (GARF, f. 6685, p. 1, d. 5, l. 7; Nikoladze, *Na bol'shom zhiznennom puti*, 263–4; Nikolaev, *Revoliutsiia i vlast'*, 114). Moreover, the organizational structure of the SSR, including the Section on the Study of the Tauride Palace (also known as the Polievktov Commission) had been outlined by Presniakov and Polievktov no later than mid-April 1917. See Presniakov's entry in his Notebook, dated April 16, 1917 (NIA SPb II RAN [Nauchno-istoricheskii arkhiv Sankt-Peterburgskogo Instituta istorii Rossiiskoi Akademii nauk], f. 193 (A. E. Presniakov), f. 193, op. 1, d. 159, l. 40b.).

[72] Typescript of Presniakov's sample letter is addressed to "M[ilostivyi]. G[osudar']." R. N. Nikoladze, "Uchitel'-drug. Vospominaniia o S. V. Lebedeve," 166, 179, in MAPP, FA; Nikoladze, "Nezabyvaemye dni i mgnoveniia," *Literaturnaia Gruziia* 3 (1970), 72; 4: 24–31. According to R. Nikoladze, that period was to last fifty years, but that number has not yet been corroborated.

of the Interview Commission, Mikhail Aleksandrovich Polievktov, at his Furshtatskaia address.

Exactly how many people responded to this appeal remains unknown, but in the end the Interview Commission produced transcripts of twelve complete interviews and several brief summaries of conversations with such active participants of the February Days as the Duma Chairman Mikhail Vladimirovich Rodzianko; the first Commandant of the revolutionary Tauride Palace and moderate Duma deputy Boris Aleksandrovich Engel'gardt; deputy chairman of the All-Russian Central War Industrial Committee Mikhail Ivanovich Tereshchenko; deputy Duma speaker and leading Left Kadet Nikolai Vissarionovich Nekrasov; Aleksandr Fedorovich Kerenskii; the Duma Social Democratic deputies and leaders of the Petrograd Soviet Matvei Ivanovich Skobelev and Nikolai Semenovich Chkheidze; the Kadet Duma deputy and the Temporary Committee's Commissar Petr Vasil'evich Gerasimov; Kerenskii's adjutant, Lt. Colonel Lev Stepanovich Tugan-Baranovskii; members of the Duma's Military Commission Staff-Captain Aleksandr Aleksandrovich Chikolini and Maksim Grigor'evich Kantor; and the Duma Chancellery's staffer Stepan Vasil'evich Sufshchinskii; the Nationalist Duma deputy and Temporary Committee member Vasilii Vital'evich Shul'gin; Petrograd historian and Popular Socialist Petr Borisovich Shaskol'skii; Irakli Tsereteli; and General Kornilov's one time aid Captain of the General Staff Nikolai Nikolaevich Krasnov.[73]

For political historians, this was by far the most important section of the SSR. Polievktov organized the Commission, oversaw the interviewing process, and reportedly took part in all but one of the interviews.[74] He also recruited his wife and Tamara Nikoladze as secretaries. Tamara's friend and

---

[73] The last four are summaries of conversations (with Shul'gin, on May 11, 1 page; with Shaskol'skii on May 25 at Presniakov's, 1 page; with Tsereteli at Niko Nikoladze's, on May 7, 1 page, May 25, 5 pages; and with Krasnov on June 5, 8 pages), recorded by Polievktov after the fact, and later placed by him in a separate folder and designated for summaries of conversations, "Iz razgovorov i rasskazov" (in MAPP, FA). On the Polievktov–Shaskol'skii connection, see Presniakov. Pi'ma i dnevniki, 569, 652. In her memoirs, written late in her life, Rusudana Nikoladze claimed that the Commission interviewed up to twenty people and that all the interviews were conducted during the month of May, before June 2 (R. N. Nikoladze, Na bol'shom zhiznennom puti, 264–71; Nikoladze, "Nezabyvaemye dni i mgnoveniia," Literaturnaia Gruziia 3: 72; 4: 24–31; Nikolaev, Revoliutsiia i vlast', 115). That number seems a bit high, even if one includes Polievktov's summaries of conversations. There is no evidence to suggest that any of the interviews recorded by the Commission have been lost or did not end up in the Family Archive.

[74] GARF, f. 6685, op. 1, d. 5, l. 7. Polievktov evidently was not present at the very first interview, on May 1, with Sufshchinskii. It was recorded by R. Nikoladze, her sister Tamara, and Ol'ga Nedzvetskaia who also conducted the interview.

colleague, the young zoologist Viktor Ivanovich Pavlov (the middle son of the physiologist Ivan Pavlov), became their record-keeper (*deloproizvoditel'*), and about half a dozen volunteers, mostly Tamara's friends and former classmates from the Women's Pedagogical Institute and the Higher Women's Courses, served as interviewers and stenographers.[75]

May 1917 was by far the Commission's busiest and most productive period. All but one interview was conducted during that month, beginning on the first day and ending on the last.[76] The interview sessions lasted anywhere from one to several hours and, with the exception of the Tereshchenko and Kantor interviews, took place either in the Tauride Palace or in government offices, depending on the interviewee's affiliation at the time.[77] The length of the interviews, which varied greatly, seemed to depend more on the interviewee's readiness to talk than on the prominence of his position. Some were recorded over the course of two or more sessions.

Each interviewee was asked about his participation in the revolutionary events of February 25–March 3, 1917, that is, from the outbreak of the popular uprising in Petrograd to the formation of the Provisional Government and the abdications of Nicholas II and Grand Duke Mikhail Aleksandrovich. Following this initial testimony, the interviewers posed more pointed questions. Though the specific questions were suppressed from the available transcripts, they could be surmised from the interview-

---

[75] According to the June 1918 Bulletin of the Society of the House-Museum for Preserving the Memory of Freedom Fighters (*Pervyi biuleten' Obshchestva Doma-muzeia pamiati bortsov za svobodu*)—which absorbed the SSR eight months earlier—in addition to the Nikoladze sisters, Ol'ga Nedzvetskaia and Viktor Pavlov, the most active "members of the [Interview] Commission, were Krupskaia, Mikeladze, Pokrovskaia, Polovinkina, Ropp, the 1st and the 2nd, and Iakubchik." (GARF, f. 6685, op. 1, d. 5, l. 7). However, the available interview transcripts indicate that the most active interviewers were Rusudana Nikoladze-Polievktova, her sister Tamara (1892–1939), Pavlov, and their peers and friends: Rusudana Solomonovna Mikeladze (1893–1993), a graduate of the Higher Women's Courses; the two Ropp sisters: Margarita (Margo) Feliksovna (1891–1971) and Maria (Mira) [1892–after 1960], both were graduates of the Women's Pedagogical Institute (WPI); Zoia Fedorovna Pokrovskaia (1892–after 1960) (Tamara's classmate at the WPI and the future radiologist who later assumed her husband's name Orlova); and Tat'iana Vsevolodovna Krupskaia. The direct involvement of the Polovinkina sisters: Maria Irinarkhovna, later Lopyreva (1895–after 1962) and Iuliia Irinarkhovna (1895–1974), both graduates of the WPI, and Anastasiia Osipovna (Iosifovna) Iakubchik (1894–1973), also a graduate of the WPI and a future prominent chemist, cannot be independently confirmed. On Polievktov's unsuccessful effort to revive the interview project in the spring of 1918, see GARF, f. 6685, op. 1, d. 1 [Protocol of the Board Meeting, March 19, 1918], l. 34.

[76] The interview with then Foreign Minister Tereshchenko took place on June 7.

[77] For example, Kerenskii and Tugan-Baranovskii were interviewed in their offices in the war ministry. Chkheidze's interview, on the other hand, took place in the Tauride Palace.

ees' answers. Recurring among these were queries on the soldiers' uprising; conspiracies against Nicholas II; the arrests and initial custody of the
most notorious of the tsarist ministers and other police, military and government officials; the formation of the Petrograd Soviet and the Provisional
Government; the origins of dual power and of Order Number One; and
the abdications. As May 1917 witnessed the breakup of the first revolutionary government and formation of the first coalition cabinet, some of
the more politically involved interviewees were also asked about the
events leading up to the most recent crisis, including Miliukov's diplomatic note to the Allies and the April demonstrations in Petrograd. By and
large, however, the interviews remained focused on the February Days,
and, as far as we can determine, the interviewees were not intentionally
drawn into making normative evaluations.

Convincing former participants, many of whom continued to be politically active under the transitional regime, to sit down for an interview session
was no easy task. The time and effort that went into arranging these sessions
varied from interview to interview and from one interviewee to another.
Rusudana Polievktova-Nikoladze recalled that those on the Left were far less
cooperative (many simply refused to be interviewed) than their more moderate colleagues. Chkheidze, for example, demanded the questions in advance,
had to be chased after, and in general proved difficult to accommodate.[78]
Kerenskii, on the other hand, was noted by the memoirist to be the only
representative of the Left genuinely excited about the project. He brought the
interviewing team to his office in his ministerial automobile and was quite
expansive (even if characteristically evasive) in his deposition.[79] Skobelev, too,
was cooperative and forthcoming, even talkative, though his willingness to be
interviewed was probably a result of personal connections with the Nikoladze
sisters, in particular with their cousin Kaki Tsereteli. In fact, Tsereteli was

[78] R. N. Nikoladze, *Na bol'shom zhiznennom puti*, 264. Chkheidze was apparently related to
Rusudana Mikeladze (via her mother Iuliia née Chkheidze) who at the time served as secretary
of the Executive Committee of the All-Russian Soviet of Peasant Deputies. This might have
played a role in convincing the reluctant Chairman of the Petrograd Soviet to agree to an interview. In his deposition to the Provisional Government's Investigative Commission on May 29,
1917, Chkheidze discussed events related to the activity of the Social Democratic faction in the
fourth Duma, but did not utter a word about the February Days. Deposition of N. S. Chkheidze,
May 29, 1917, *Padenie tsarskogo rezhima. Stenograficheskie otchety doprosov i pokazanii, dannykh v 1917
godu v Chrezvychainoi sledstvennoi komissii Vremennogo pravitel'stva*, ed. P. E. Shchegolev (Moscow and
Leningrad: Gosizdat, 1923–7), III: 485–506.

[79] R. N. Nikoladze, *Na bol'shom zhiznennom puti*, 264; interview with A. F. Kerenskii, May 31, 1917.

present during part of Skobelev's three-session-long interview and even inserted a qualifying remark concerning the origins of dual power.

Whatever their initial hesitation, almost all loosened up and began talking as soon as they sat down for the actual interview. It is important to note that only four of the interviewees—Kerenskii, Rodzianko, Engel'gardt, and Skobelev—later wrote memoirs or left behind additional testimonies, but these proved to be far less revealing than their May 1917 interviews.[80] For the rest of the interviewees, these depositions would become their only recorded testimonies.[81]

According to an SSR report, each interview (opros) was conducted by three or four members of the Interview Commission, one leading the conversation and everyone taking minutes.[82] All transcripts were then read and compared, corrected, and transcribed into an aggregate master version (obshchaia svodka).[83] This, depending on the circumstances of the moment, would normally be accomplished on the day of the interview or shortly thereafter.[84] In one or two cases, however, the process of compiling a master version, which fell on either Pavlov or the Nikoladze sisters, took days, even weeks. Yet a comparison of available draft transcripts with the pertinent

[80] B[oris]. E[ngel'gardt]., "Revoliutsionnye dni (Vospominaniia uchastnika fevral'skikh dnei 1917 g.)," *Obshchee delo* (Belgrade), March 16–17, 1921; Engel'gardt's deposition, April 12, 1921, in *Rossiiskii arkhiv*, vol. VIII: *N. A. Sokolov. Predvaritel'noe sledstvie, 1919–1922 gg.*, compiled by L. A. Lykov (Moscow: Trite, 1998), 280–1; Engel'gardt, "Vospominaniia kamer-pazha," *Dlia Vas* (Riga) (1939): 41–3 (1939); Engel'gardt, "Fevral'skaia Revoliutsiia," ed. and introduced A. B. Nikolaev, *Klio* 1, 20 (2003): 176–97; M.V. Rodzianko, "Gosudarstvennaia Duma i fevral'skaia 1917 goda revoliutsiia," *Arkhiv Russkoi Revoliutsii*, vol. IV (1922); Rodzianko, "Krushenie imperii," *Arkhiv Russkoi Revoliutsii*, vol. IX (1926); Alexander F. Kerensky, *The Catastrophe: Kerensky's Own Story of the Russian Revolution* (New York, 1927); Kerensky, *The Crucifixion of Liberty* (New York, 1943); Kerensky, *Russia and History's Turning Point* (New York, 1965); [M. I. Skobelev], "Gibel' tsarizma. Vospominaniia M. I. Skobeleva," *Ogonek* 11 (207), March 13, 1927; Skobelev, "25 fevralia–3 marta: (Vospominaniia b[yvshego] chlena Sotsial-demokraticheskoi fraktsii Gosudarstvennoi dumy M. Skobeleva)," *Vecherniaia Moskva*, March 11, 1927.

[81] With the possible exception of N. V. Nekrasov's interrogations, extracted from him under extreme psychological and possibly physical pressure by the Soviet political police in 1921, 1931, and 1939, in which he briefly touched upon the events of the February Revolution. See [N.V. Nekrasov], "Iz sledstvennykh del N. V. Nekrasova 1921, 1931 i 1939 godov," *Voprosy istorii* 11–12 (1998).

[82] GARF, f. 6685, op.1, d. 5, l. 7.

[83] Rusudana Nikoladze-Polievktova recalled that she, her sister, and Pavlov often did this work on a big desk inside the Tauride Palace in between their regular shifts of answering telephones for the Soviet leaders (R. N. Nikoladze, *Na bol'shom zhiznennom puti*, 268).

[84] GARF, f. 6685, op.1, d. 5, l. 7; R. N. Nikoladze, *Na bol'shom zhiznennom puti*, 264, 271–2; Rusudan[a] Nikoladze, "Nezabyvaemye dni i mgnoveniia," 71; Rusudana Mikeladze (in Petrograd) to Rusudana Nikoladze (in Didi-Dzhikhaishi), September 14, 1917 (received by the addressee on 25 September), MAPP, FA.

master versions does not reveal any substantive or content-altering changes. If anything, changes were limited to grammar and style.

The master versions would then be turned over to Polievktov for a final editing that—as far as we can establish—focused on matters of presentation and consistency, not historical accuracy. Wherever feasible, external details were added to the master copies: names of stenographers and the master copy compiler, time, location, and circumstances of the interview. We have no reliable information as to the exact timing of Polievktov's final edits, but the fact that not all transcripts bear the mark of his pen suggests that he did not complete this work. Still, there is good reason to believe that Polievktov did the bulk of the editing in fairly short order, not long after master versions were prepared by his assistants and handed over to him, and certainly no later than September 1917. This supposition is consistent with what we know about Polievktov's travels that summer and the whereabouts of the interview transcripts.

Shortly after the last interview was recorded on June 7, Polievktov, accompanied by his wife and their two-year old son, left Petrograd for a summer vacation in the southern city of Zheleznovodsk. It appears that they brought along draft transcripts and master versions of all of the interviews, except for the last two—with Kerenskii (recorded on May 31) and Tereshchenko (on June 7)—those drafts having been left with Pavlov to produce master versions. In the middle of June, Rusudana's parents also left the capital for their country estate of Didi-Dzhikhaishi in western Georgia.[85] Polievktov stayed in the South for about two weeks and then, on July 5, embarked on a Moscow-bound train and from there to Petrograd. He returned to the South (this time to neighboring Kislovodsk) to finish his vacation in late August or early September. But by then Rusudana had decided not to return to Petrograd. On September 5, she and her son Nika (Nikolai) departed for Didi-Dzhikhaishi.[86]

---

[85] See Rusudana Mikeladze (in Petrograd) to Rusia (R. N. Nikoladze-Polievktova), in Didi-Dzhikhaishi, September 14, 25, 1917; Nikoladze-Polievktova, "Uchitel'-drug. Vospominaniia o S. V. Lebedeve," [Tiflis, 1934–7]; unpublished typescript with handwritten corrections by the author, 192; Nikoladze-Polievktova, *Diaries*, Notebook IV: 142, MAPP, FA. Tamara left Petrograd around June 10, after taking part in the last two interviews. Later in the summer, on her way to Georgia, she planned to make a stop in Zheleznovodsk to see the Polievktovs, but could not get train tickets and instead traveled directly to Didi-Dzhikhaishi.

[86] Rusudana Nikoladze-Polievktova, *Diaries*, Notebook III: 25. The timing of Polievktov's return to Kislovodsk was determined by the inscription on the back of a photograph, picturing him and his Petrograd friends, the Povorinskiis and a female student of the WPI named Devel', in MAPP, FA.

Though we have no direct confirmation that Rusudana took with her to Georgia all the materials that she and her husband had brought from Petrograd in June, it seems likely that she did. For by the time Polievktov returned to Petrograd at the end of September or early October, all but the last two interviews' transcripts were already in Georgia. The latter two would reach Didi-Dzhikhaishi sometime between October 1917 and January 1918 via Rusudana Solomonovna Mikeladze, the Nikoladzes' old friend and member of the Interview Commission, and Kaki Tsereteli.[87]

The fate of any additional copies remains obscure. As far as we can tell, Polievktov never followed through on his earlier intention to deposit the interviews with the Manuscript Division of the Academy of Science Library in Petrograd; if he did, they are yet to be found.[88] Some of the draft transcripts and copies of the master versions could have remained with Viktor Pavlov before he fled from Bolshevik Petrograd in the second half of 1918, but his sudden death in January 1919, while on his way to the South, makes the survival of any transcripts unlikely. Rusudana Mikeladze (1893–1993), who would become the longest-lived member of the Polievktov Commission, apparently also held back one of several draft transcripts of the Kerenskii interview, which she published in early 1919 in an obscure Tbilisi Russian-language monthly in violation of the confidentiality pledge and against the better judgment of the Nikoladze sisters who implored her not to make public an unverified and incomplete text.[89] In short, there is every reason to believe that the Polievktov-Nikoladze transcripts are the only surviving records of the interviews collected by the Tauride Palace Section of the SSR during May–early June 1917.

[87] Rusudana Mikeladze to Rusudana Nikoladze-Polievktova, September 14, 1917, MAPP, FA; GARF, f. 6685, op. 1, d. 34. It is also possible, though unlikely, that Polievktov brought the remaining transcripts with him when he visited his wife and son in Georgia in late December 1917–January 1918. See his manuscript "Vospominaniia Polievktova o poezdke iz Petrograda v Tiflis," recorded in January 1918, in CHAG, f. 1505, op. 1, d. 9, ll. 1–12.

[88] For several relatively recent efforts to locate the interviews in various Russian archives, see Burdzhalov, "Istochniki i literatura po istorii vtoroi russkoi revoliutsii," 254–5; R. N. Nikoladze, *Na bol'shom zhiznennom puti*, 271; Nikolaev, *Revoliutsiia i vlast'*, 115.

[89] GARF, f. 6685, op. 1, d. 10, l. 1; d. 1, ll. 35, 35ob.; R. N. Nikoladze, *Na bol'shom zhiznennom puti*, 271–2. Viktor Pavlov (1892–1919) died from typhus near Khar'kov (Iu. A. Vinogradov, Iu. P. Grekov, T. I. Grekova, *I. P. Pavlov: Dostovernost' i polnota biografii* (St. Petersburg: Rostok, 2005), 11, 315. Recent inquires with Rusudana Mikeladze's descendants in Tbilisi have confirmed that the unverified, mistakenly dated (June 5 instead of May 31) and incomplete transcript of the Kerenskii interview that she gave to the editors of the Tbilisi monthly, *Orion*, in 1919 ("A. F. Kerenskii i Fevral'skaia revoliutsiia," *Orion. Literaturno-politicheskii ezhemesiachnik* 2 [1919]: 60–1) did not survive. Professor A. B. Nikolaev discovered this obscure publication and was the first historian to use

Polievktov in Soviet Georgia: The Last Twenty-Two Years...

In the summer of 1920, Polievktov's personal life and career took a decisive if not entirely unexpected turn. He left Petrograd and was reunited with his Georgian-born wife and their 5-year-old son, who had left the city three years earlier hoping to wait out the revolutionary turmoil in the safety of the family's estate in western Georgia. That fall, Polievktov was elected professor of General (*obshchei*) History (there was no separate Russian history chair at the time) at the recently founded Tiflis (later Tbilisi) University. For the better part of the next twenty-two years he lived and taught in Tbilisi (at the University, the Polytechnic Institute, and the Pedagogical Institute) and held successive research and low-level administrative positions at the Georgian branch of the Central State Archival Administration. During this time he continued to write, trained the occasional graduate student, and advised students and colleagues from across the Caucasus on matters of Russian and European history and archival organization.

To ease his isolation and escape the provincial world of the Georgian academy, but also to see his old prerevolutionary friends and colleagues, he organized his research around frequent, practically annual, visits to archives and libraries in Moscow and Leningrad. There he identified and subsequently published diplomatic and travelers' accounts of the European "discovery" of Georgia during the fifteenth century and early Russo-Georgian relations in the nineteenth century.[90] By the end of his life Polievktov had amassed an impressive record of publications that would lay the foundation of the new discipline of Caucasian studies (*kavkazovedenie*), and in

it. He also made it available to the broader scholarly community (A. B. Nikolaev, "A. F. Kerenskii o Fevral'skoi revoliutsii," *Klio* 3, 26 [2004]: 101–11). The 1919 publication provoked outrage from the Nikoladze sisters (at that time Polievktov was in faraway Petrograd), who contacted Mikeladze and also wrote a letter disclaiming any responsibility for publishing the Kerenskii interview and questioning its authenticity (Draft of the letter, "A. F. Kerenskii i Fevral'skaia revoliutsiia. Pis'mo v redaktsiiu [*sic*!]," [March 1919], written by R. N. Nikoladze and signed by her and Tamara as secretaries of the Tauride Palace Section of the SSR, in FA). The letter was sent to the editorial board of the Tbilisi newspaper *Novyi den'*, which also published the monthly *Orion*. The Kerenskii interview was conducted by Tamara Nikoladze shortly before her departure from Petrograd in early June 1917 (Zinaida Chichinadze to Tamara Nikoladze, June 9, 1917, autograph, MAPP, FA).

[90] See, for example, copies of his official *otchety* (reports) on research trips to Moscow and Leningrad during 1924, 1926–39, in CHAG, fond 1505, op. 1, dd. 96–7.

particular the important yet mostly unexplored subfield of Georgian-Russian relations.[91]

We should also recognize that it was this early "disappearance" from the vibrant academic scene of the two capitals at the height of his productivity and scholarly career, along with the subsequent readjustment of his research interests, which likely contributed to his near disappearance from the personal and institutional memory of his Russian colleagues. Neither his 1972 centennial nor any of the more recent anniversaries have generated a conference or a volume discussing his contributions to Russian historiography of the eighteenth and nineteenth centuries. No reliable biographical sketch, much less an informed discussion of his "life and works," appears in any of the reference or encyclopedic literature in Russian.[92]

His voluntarily "exile" in academically provincial Tbilisi did have its apparent advantages. It is quite plausible that Polievktov's isolation from the centers of academic life in Moscow and Leningrad allowed him to avoid the clutches of Stalin's secret police. As far as we know, he was never arrested, and emerged relatively unscarred from the purges of prerevolutionary historians during the infamous "Platonov affair" of 1929–31. This turn of fortune was remarkable, considering Polievktov's close and longstanding ties with some of the principle defendants in that case, including Professors Platonov, Sergei Vasil'evich Rozhdestvenskii, and Evgenii Viktorovich Tarle, as well as his former Petrograd University student and confidant Natalia Sergeevna Shtakel'berg.[93]

---

[91] For a preliminary, and far from complete, list of Polievktov's publications, compiled shortly after his death by one of his Georgian students and colleagues, I. Tsindadze, see *Trudy Tbilisskogo gosudarstvennogo universiteta imeni Stalina* 25 (1943): 250–4 and file "correspondence" in FA. Roughly half of Tsindadze's list of seventy-five titles relates to topics on the Caucasus and Russo-Georgian relations, which in and of itself is a testimony to Polievktov's scholarly productivity during the last twenty years of his career.

[92] Even the recent *Bio-bibliographical Dictionary of Russian Historians of the Twentieth Century* devotes only two short lines to Polievktov based exclusively on a short and outdated entry from the 1968 edition of the *Soviet Historical Encyclopedia*. See A. A. Chernobaev, *Istoriki Rossii XX veka. Biobibliograficheskii slovar'. Tom vtoroi M-Ia* (Saratov: SGSEU, 2005), 205, citing the entry (S. M. Troitskii, "Polievktov, Mikhail Aleksandrovich") in *Sovetskaia istoricheskaia entsiklopediia*, XI (Moscow: Sovetskaia entsiklopediia, 1968), 269. The year of Polievktov's death is often mistakenly given as 1925 (for a most recent example, see the reprinted edition of his 1918 monograph on Nicholas I).

[93] Shtakel'berg, "'Kruzhok molodykh istorikov' i 'Akademicheskoe delo'," 31–2, 46, 54–5. See also Shtakel'berg's very informative letters to Polievktov, dated February 27, October 4, December 27 and 31, 1923, MAPP, FA. Polievktov's last letter to Platonov is dated September 25, 1929, a few months before his mentor's arrest in January 1930. OR RNB, f. 585, op. 1, d. 3885, l. 35. See also

It is true that in May of 1931 he was smeared in a Tbilisi paper as a "right-ist professor" and temporarily lost his teaching positions at the University and the Pedagogical Institute. But he appealed to the Georgian Soviet Republic's Commissar of Enlightenment and was soon reinstated and allowed to continue with his teaching and research.[94] He subsequently published five short books and about a dozen articles. In 1938 he suffered a mild stroke, but recovered and continued to work. He completed his last publication and submitted it to a journal on May 15, 1942, shortly before suffering a second stroke that impaired his vision and speech and ultimately led to his death six months later.[95] Polievktov died in his own bed, surrounded by his son and wife and a few relatives from her side of the family. For a person of his generation and of his social and cultural background, dying in one's own bed was no small feat. To paraphrase Anna Akhmatova, by the cannibalistic standards of the time, he was a very lucky man indeed.

Polievktov's Heirs and the Fate of the Interviews

The subsequent history of the interviews is not difficult to reconstruct. Polievktov joined his family in Didi-Dzhikhaishi in the summer of 1920 and in early 1921 they, together with Rusudana's parents, her two aunts, and Tamara, moved into a spacious six-room flat in the old Sololaki section of Tbilisi. From then until May 2006—when this writer was allowed a visit and granted unlimited access to the documents—the interviews remained in the same flat, for most of that time in the same room occupied by the Polievktovs.

Polievktov's letters to Platonov, dated May 26, 1926, August 17, 1927 (ibid., ll. 32–4). During his interrogations by OGPU, Platonov mentioned Polievktov's name only once and as a representative of his counterrevolutionary "organization" in Tbilisi. However, the charges against Polievktov were not pressed and no case against him was apparently initiated. (See *Akademicheskoe delo 1929–1931 gg. Delo po obvineniiu akademika S. F. Platonova.* Vyp. 1 (St. Petersburg: BAN, 1993), 170.)

[94] See a draft of his appeal to the People's Commissar of Enlightenment of the Georgian Soviet Socialist Republic, n.d. [summer] 1931, autograph, 5 pages, MAPP, FA. It is not clear whether Polievktov's employment status at the University changed after his reinstatement. He continued to teach there (at least part-time), advised graduate students, and participated in doctoral (*kandidatskii*) examinations until as late as September 1940 (See order of the Tbilisi University's Rector, no. 2198, September 18, 1940, MAPP, FA).

[95] M. A. Polievktov, "Pervaia otechestvennaia voina (1812 god) v vospominaniiakh i pis'makh sovremennikov," in *Trudy Tbilisskogo gosudarstvennogo universiteta imeni Stalina,* vol. 23 (1941): 57–69. The volume was published at the very end of 1942.

Following the historian's death, his widow continued to keep the documents close at hand.[96] In 1961 Rusudana, by then a distinguished chemistry professor at the Tbilisi Polytechnic, was contacted by the Moscow historian and former Communist party functionary Eduard Nikolaevich Burdzhalov (1906–85), who was working on his second Doctoral dissertation on the February Revolution. After years of unsuccessful searches for the Interview Commission records in Moscow and Leningrad archives, he realized that the documents in question could still be in the possession of Polievktov's heirs. He located Rusudana and inquired about the possibility of examining them. It took a while before she agreed. Burdzhalov went to Tbilisi sometime between July 1963 and mid-1964, and spent about a week working with the interviews, seven of which he cited in his 1967 monograph.[97] All further attempts to see the documents, by Burdzhalov or others, were unsuccessful.

We may never know for sure what prompted Rusudana or her son, the physicist Nikolai Mikhailovich Polievktov-Nikoladze (1915–89), to refuse subsequent requests. Perhaps those seeking the interviews were simply less persuasive or persistent than Burdzhalov. It is also quite plausible that the mother and the son did not wish to compromise their self-imposed custodian rights and feared that any further exposure would eventually require them to deposit the documents in a state archive. For them, both the idea for the interviews project and its execution was very much a family affair. Writing in her late eighties, Rusudana maintained that her husband had long since deposited the interviews with the Academy of Sciences Library[98]

---

[96] On August 28, 1943, nine months after Polievktov's death, his widow gave part of his professional papers (covering the period 1928–42) to a family friend, prominent Georgian mathematician, Archil Kirillovich Kharadze (1895–1976) requesting that he deposit them in the archive of the Georgian Branch of the USSR Academy of Sciences. He apparently complied. Sometime in the 1950s these papers, supplemented by additional material from the family archives, were transferred to the Central State Historical Archive of the Georgian Soviet Socialist Republic in Tbilisi (now CHAG, f. 1505). See R. N. Nikoladze, Correspondence (unprocessed), MAPP, FA; Sulaberidze, *Polievktov i ego lichnyi fond*, 70–4. The "private" part of Polievktov's papers, including correspondence (beginning with the early 1880s) and official documents reflecting his life and work in Tbilisi academic institutions, remained with the family in their Sololaki flat.

[97] E. N. Burdzhalov to R. N. Nikoladze, January 17, 1963; Burdzhalov to [N. M.] Polievktov-Nikoladze, June 26, 1963; Burdzhalov to R. N. Nikoladze, March 4, 1966, November 8, 1966, MAPP, FA; R. N. Nikoladze, *Na bol'shom zhiznennom puti*, 271–2; Burdzhalov, *Vtoraia russkaia revoliutsiia*, 78–9, 158–9, 163, 204, 226, 234, 235, 291, 326, 376. During his visit to Tbilisi, Burdzhalov also met with Rusudana Mikeladze and more than likely discussed with her "*dela davno minuvshikh dnei.*"

[98] R. N. Nikoladze, *Na bol'shom zhiznennom puti*, 271.

(which of course he never did) and hence she might have treated the transcripts in her possession as the family's personal copy. This same belief, it seems, motivated the documents' last family custodian, Nikolai Mikhailovich's widow Zinaida Leonidovna Polievktova-Nikoladze (b. 1938), who in accordance with established tradition kept them inaccessible to scholars for seventeen more years following her husband's death.

On the other hand, Mikhail Aleksandrovich Polievktov's motivation in keeping the documents secret appears to have been different. In contrast to his heirs, he was almost certainly held back by the confidentiality pledge extended to the interviewees before they agreed to make their depositions. By the time of his departure from Petrograd, it became abundantly clear that his and Presniakov's initial plans to create a special revolutionary archive in which to deposit all materials collected by the SSR were not going to materialize. This may have led him to conclude that the documents—already in Georgia since the second half of 1917—would be safer with his family. By the end of the 1920s, when he might have reconsidered and entertained the possibility of depositing the documents in an archive, the political situation took a sharp turn for the worse. His mentor, the Academician Platonov, along with a number of other former colleagues and students, some of whom worked as archivists in Leningrad, were arrested and accused of participating in a plot to restore the monarchy. Under the circumstances, the divulging of such politically sensitive material as interviews with the officially declared "counterrevolutionary monarchists" and leaders of the best-forgotten bourgeois revolution would pose enormous personal risks.

And so the documents remained with the family, stored in a drawer of Polievktov's desk for nearly nine decades, having survived the revolution and civil war, the Stalinist purges, the Second World War, hunger and reconstruction, Khrushchev's Thaw and Brezhnev's Stagnation, the fall of the USSR, and a devastating civil war and unrest that lasted for almost ten years after Georgia regained its independence in 1991. Recorded during May 1–June 7, 1917, months *before* the Bolsheviks came to power and at a time when the outcome of the revolution was far from obvious, the interviews represent the most significant, contemporary, direct testimony on the February Revolution that we know of. As such they also represent Mikhail Aleksandrovich Polievktov's own most lasting contribution to historical scholarship.

PART II

The Interviews

3

Boris Aleksandrovich
Engel'gardt

B ORIS ALEKSANDROVICH ENGEL'GARDT (1877–1962) was a descendant of a
wealthy noble family (originally of Swiss extraction) from the southwestern
Mogilev province. A man of many talents, refined tastes, and high culture, he was
broadly educated and had pursued many careers throughout his long, difficult, but
colorful life. His first career was in the military. He studied in the prestigious (and
highly privileged) Corps des Pages and fought his first war against Japanese forces in
the Far East in 1904–5. But in 1908, soon after graduating from the General Staff
Academy, he resigned from military service with the rank of Lieutenant Colonel
(podpolkovnik) for health reasons and retired to his family estate in the Mogilev
province. There he developed a strong interest in farming, taught himself agronomy,
and devoted the bulk of his time to learning about new agricultural techniques and
improving productivity. He also became active in local organizations of the gentry
and the Zemstvo, from which he was elected to the (fourth) Duma in 1912. During
his first two years in the Duma he was a member of the small moderate Center
Faction; during the last two—after a personal invitation from the Duma President
M. V. Rodzianko—he joined the largest and somewhat more conservative Zemstvo-
Octobrist faction of the Octobrist party, of which Rodzianko was an unofficial
leader.

With the outbreak of the First World War, Engel'gardt, along with many former
officers, re-enlisted in the military service. During the first year of the war he served
as a senior staff officer in the headquarters of the Guards Corps but in July 1915
received his final discharge and retired with the rank of Colonel. He returned to his
Duma seat that fall even more determined to improve Russia's failing performance in
the war. He quickly distinguished himself as an active, hard-working parliamentarian,
serving on a number of important committees, including Military and Naval Affairs,
Budget, and Financial. He also joined the influential Special Council for the Discussion
and Consolidation of Measures for Defending the State (*Osoboe soveshchanie dlia obsu-
zhdeniia i ob'edineniia meropriiatii po oborone gosudarstva*), headed by the war minister
and whose membership included high-ranking state officials and leading Duma and
State Council deputies. In his interview with the Polievktov Commission, he dis-

cusses his work on the Special Council, most of which is not reflected in the official records. During April–June 1916, he was also a member of the Russian parliamentary delegation to the Allied and neutral European countries, and soon after his return from abroad, he joined the oppositionist Progressive Bloc. As one of only a handful of high-ranking military officers among the Duma deputies, he was considered an excellent candidate by various conspiratorial groups whose aim was to remove Nicholas II from the throne and replace him with his young son under the regency of Grand Duke Mikhail Aleksandrovich. It appears that he was well informed about the existence of such plots and was recruited to one of them in late 1916.

During the February Revolution Engel'gardt played a crucially important and widely acknowledged role in defeating the forces of the old regime. His contribution to the revolution's success can hardly be overestimated. He was simultaneously a member of the Duma Committee, the first revolutionary Commandant of the Tauride Palace and of Petrograd, and the first appointed chairman of the Military Commission.[a]

In this interview, Engel'gardt discusses his involvement in prerevolutionary plots against Nicholas II, his work as the commander of the revolutionary forces during February 28–March 3, 1917, and his short-lived tenure as the first minister of war in the Provisional Government in greater and more revealing detail than in any of his subsequent memoirs.[b] One of the more striking aspects of his testimony is how quickly—barely two months into the post-tsarist era—he had adopted the new revolutionary "speak" and a class-conscious way of thinking about his recent experience. He talks about the diverging democratic and bourgeois mindsets and the inability of those adhering to the latter to comprehend the aspirations of the former. This ostentatious and unprovoked self-flagellation may of course reflect his profound disillusionment with the old social and political order and perhaps even his attempt to embrace the revolution. But it may also indicate an unusual sensitivity to the new political realities or perhaps a naked opportunism driven by a relentless desire to march in step with the forces of history. Engel'gardt's personal qualities of

[a] The Military Commission (MC) of the Duma Committee was formed during the day on February 27, 1917, mainly on the initiative of Kerenskii and engineer P. I. Pal'chinskii. The Duma President, M. V. Rodzianko, appointed Engel'gardt to chair the MC in the early hours of February 28. A. I. Guchkov became the MC's formal chairman on March 1. He appointed Aleksei Stepanovich Potapov, major general of the General Staff, as his deputy, but at the same time asked Engel'gardt to continue on in his duties as chairman. Engel'gardt was replaced by General A. S. Potapov on March 4.

[b] See, for example, the protocol of his less revealing, though still very valuable, score-settling comments about his closest colleagues on the MC, General Potapov and the engineer Pal'chinskii, in his short April 12, 1921 testimony to N. Sokolov, investigating the circumstances of the murder of the imperial family, recorded in Paris, April 12, 1921, in *Rossiiskii arkhiv*, vol. VIII, *N. A. Sokolov. Predvaritel'noe sledstvie, 1919–1922 gg.*, ed. L. A. Lykov (Moscow: Trite, 1998), 281; B[oris]. E[ngel' gardt]., "Revoliutsionnye dni (Vospominaniia uchastnika fevral'skikh dnei 1917 g.)," *Obshchee delo* (Belgrade), March 16–17, 1921; Engel'gardt, "Vospominaniia kamer-pazha," *Dlia Vás* (Riga), 41–3 (1939); Engel'gardt, "Fevral'skaia Revoliutsiia," ed. A. B. Nikolaev, *Klio* 1, 20 (2003): 176–97.

character aside, one wonders how his remarkable adaptability might have influenced his subsequent interpretations of the February Revolution, an experience to which he repeatedly returned throughout his long life and under ever-changing circumstances.

And his circumstances were indeed drastically changing. A period of fascination with the revolution was soon replaced by disillusionment, and the recently castigated sense of "bourgeois" responsibility for the fate of a great nation soon steered him in a different direction. Not long after his interview to the Polievktov Commission, Engel'gardt joined the ranks of the semi-conspiratorial officers' organization known as the Republican Center, which supported General Kornilov and his efforts to restore order and authority. Then, following the Bolshevik takeover, he went to the South where he served under the White General A. I. Denikin in various staff positions, including chief of the propaganda and information office.

In February 1920 he left Russia. He first settled in Paris, where he drove a taxi and wrote his first post-1917 account of the February Revolution.[c] Two years later he relocated to Riga, received Latvian citizenship, and supported himself with agricultural work. He later started a horse racing business. He continued to write, and in 1939 published a new, fuller version of his memoirs.[d] But his story doesn't end there. In 1940, following the Soviet annexation of Latvia, Engel'gardt was arrested and exiled to Central Asia where, as an administrative exile, he did odd jobs, applying his many talents and skills, from painting to horse breeding and riding lessons. In 1945, he must have been deemed loyal enough by the Soviet authorities to receive USSR citizenship, and the following year was allowed to return to Riga. He spent the rest of his days working as a translator of European languages for the state meteorological service and writing and editing his memoirs, which he doggedly tried to publish in the Soviet press during the late 1950s and early 1960s, with very limited success.[e]

[c] "Revoliutsionnye dni (Vospominaniia uchastnika fevral'skikh dnei 1917 g.)," *Obshchee delo*, March 16–17, 1921; Engel'gardt's deposition, April 12, 1921, in *Rossiiskii arkhiv*, VIII: 280–1.

[d] B. Engel'gardt, "Vospominaniia kamer-pazha," *Dlia Vas* (Riga), nos. 41–3, 1939. B. Engel'gardt, "Vospominaniia kamer-pazha (v Tavricheskom dvortse v fevrale 1917 goda. [Part] XXV," *Dlia Vas* 41 (October 8, 1939): 14; this memoir was republished (verbatim) in *Novoe Russkoe slovo* on March 9, 1947, 2 ["Pochemu antirevoliutsionnaia Gosudarstvennaia duma vozglavila revoliutsionnoe dvizhenie v 1917 godu (Iz vospominanii byvsh[ego]. chlena Gos[udarstvennoi]. Dumy B. A. Engel'gardta)."]. See also A. D. Mal'tsev, "B. A. Engel'gardt. Vospominaniia: 1940–1941," *Istochnikovedcheskoe izuchenie pamiatnikov pis'mennoi kul'tury* (Leningrad: Nauka, 1990), 150.

[e] For the most complete and reliable short biography of Engel'gardt and bibliography of his memoirs, some of which still remain unpublished, see A. B. Nikolaev's entry in *Gosudarstvennaia Duma Rossiiskoi imperii, 1906–1917. Entsiklopediia*, ed. V. V. Shelokhaev et al. (Moscow: ROSSPEN, 2008), 715–16; and Nikolaev's publication of Engel'gardt's February Days memoirs: A. B. Nikolaev, "Vospominaniia predsedatelia Voennoi komissii Vremennogo komiteta Gosudarstvennoi Dumy o Fevral'skoi revoliutsii 1917 g.," *Klio* 1 (20) (2003): 176–97; A much-abridged version of Engel'gardt's memoirs on the first day of the revolution was, in the end, published in the USSR: B. A. Engel'gardt, "Krushenie imperii. Byvshii deputat Gosudarstvennoi dumy rasskazyvaet o padenii tsarizma," *Nedelia* 51 (December 13–19, 1964): 6.

The document below is reproduced on the basis of a master version of the inter-
view compiled by Rusudana Polievktova-Nikoladze with a few minor edits in
M. A. Polievktov's hand, as well as the draft transcript written in shorthand by
Tamara Nikoladze during the interview.

★ ★ ★ ★ ★ ★

An Account [rasskaz] by Duma Deputy Colonel Boris Aleksandrovich Engel'gardt. May 4, 1917.[1]

Until 1908 served in the military. Participated in the Japanese campaign.[2]
Wounded. Upon his discharge settled on his country estate and worked in
the zemstvo, but continued to maintain ties with St. Petersburg, where he
had been brought up; was elected to the IV Duma from the zemstvo.
From the war's very outset, without waiting for the opening of the Duma
session on 26 July,[3] he resigned his membership and went off to war. He
joined the general staff of the Guard Corps. [His] resignation from the
Duma was accepted, but an order from the tsar soon followed allowing
Duma deputies to participate in the war. Thus, after spending a year at war,
Engel'gardt returned to the Duma where he worked on military budget
matters for the remainder of the term as a member of a special commission whose work was secret, and my [Engel'gardt's] work on it was not
known to the public.

He was sent abroad as a part of a [parliamentary] delegation together
with Miliukov and Shingarev.[4] He brought back interesting data on military
affairs in France, which were very useful to the war effort. Upon his return
from abroad, he was elected to the special commission on defense, which
included, under the chairmanship of the minister of war, nine members of
the State Council and nine members of the State Duma.[5]

This commission dealt with all aspects of the national economy: foodstuffs, fuels, and so on. In all areas, there was a clear picture of complete
economic collapse. Engel'gardt, relying on exact data, pursued this line:"We
are fighting by our sweat and blood. We cannot continue like this. We should
change the way we fight." The authorities who were present when he made
this argument looked at him askance. It was becoming clearer than ever that,
without conspiracies, the country was moving toward revolution.

In October of 1916, Engel'gardt gave a report to the commission at which
only members of the State Council and Duma were present.[6] He offered

many statistics and drew a picture of the utter hopelessness of the state of defense. The commission entrusted him, Gurko,[7] Stishinskii,[8] and Shul'gin[9]—as representatives of the parties who sat on the commission—with compiling a letter to the sovereign. Engel'gardt took the letter to [General] Alekseev[10] and consulted with him. The letter, on the basis of irrefutable evidence, spoke about making an inventory of human resources available for the war effort. The letter reached its intended destination. It was reported that a reply was being prepared.

In the meantime, the complete collapse of the transportation system, food supplies, and coal became clear. The situation with fuel was particularly disastrous. There was no metal or fuel. All this led inexorably to revolution. The situation could not be contained by strikes alone. Guard regiments were turning to Engel'gardt with the question, "What can be done?" The idea of conspiracy was coalescing. Engel'gardt conducted talks with an officer from the 1st [Cavalry] Guards Division who lived on Furshtatskaia Street: with the squadron from the 1st Cavalry Guard Regiment, to march on Tsarskoe [Selo][11] and carry out a coup.[12] In the Mariinskii Palace,[13] at the Court, and in all circles close to the throne, the atmosphere and the conversation strongly and resolutely favored a palace coup. At the same time, the Guchkov plot[14] was ripening and came into contact with the Engel'gardt conspiracy within the ranks of the Guards. But there was still no reply to the October (or November) letter, even though more than two months had passed.

The commission on defense had sent a similar letter to the sovereign previously, but without results. Finally, in January [1917], the tsar replied to the letter of the four. However, his answer was a joke, and utterly ambiguous: You may be right, but what can be done? There isn't much—you've got it wrong, and We know better anyway. In other words, he was gently telling the commission to keep their noses out of it. After that, Gurko and Shingarev began calling for change.

Engel'gardt insisted on a plan to descend on Tsarskoe [Selo] by surprise. The inevitability of catastrophe was clear to all. Engel'gardt went to consult with Shingarev, who doubted whether things would get better if a conspiracy was carried out. In response to Engel'gardt's question, "Is there another way?" Shingarev proposed to lift the spirits of the people so that they could find the inner strength to overcome all hardship; he thought this preferable to encouraging riots [bunty], at least until order and the flow of military supplies had been restored.

At the end of January [1917], it was decided to adopt the most decisive measures. Gurko and Shingarev demanded that the sovereign take direct control of the commission, thereby better informing himself on the state of the economy and the rest of the situation on the home front.[15] Then, in the name of the sovereign, the reply came that he himself knew when to take matters into his own hands. At the reading of the letter Beliaev[16] was spouting banalities. Shcheglovitov[17] kept quiet and occasionally gave Beliaev a look of approval and confidence. It was decided to send the tsar another letter. This time, there was a split. Stishinskii opted out; Mosolov[18] too. Six people ended up writing the letter: Gurko, Engel'gardt, Meller-Zakomel'skii,[19] Guchkov, Shingarev, and Shul'gin.

Tensions grew. Engel'gardt conducted negotiations with Miliukov, Shingarev, etc. about what would be done if one day a wounded officer stuck three bullets in "His" or "Her" back as they were visiting a field hospital. Are we ready for that? Who then would stand at the helm of the state? On February 3, we sifted through suitable names and, guided by the idea of a palace coup, wrote down: L'vov, Guchkov, Miliukov, Polivanov,[20] Shingarev. The last-named winced and said, "All the same, this is blood. I don't like it." But Engel'gardt, as a military man, was willing to go for it, thinking that it was unavoidable and urgent for the sake of the country. It was decided to force the boy[21] to sign a document prepared in advance and to form a [ruling] council around him made up of Rodzianko[22] and Polivanov as well as the ministers Prince L'vov[23] (the Muscovite), Miliukov, and Guchkov.

Shingarev was asked: "And what about you?"

He replied: "I am a man of words, not deeds. This is not for me."

Later on in February, the Duma met for regular sessions. In the special council on defense, it was quite clear that rioting by workers—who were idle and starving—had become inevitable. Indeed, on the 23rd [February], strikes broke out.

On the 27th, the private meeting of the Duma[24] was held, but Engel'gardt could not attend because he was in the New Club on the Dvortsovaia Embankment,[25] wearing his military uniform, with his St. George Honor Saber that he would not give up to the crowd even if it had dared to disarm him. He sent for civilian clothes, and changed. There was shooting in the streets. In the evening, around 9:00, he made his way to the Duma. There wasn't enough room there to breathe. Deputies were in the lobbies; twelve members of the newly created Temporary Committee were meeting in Rodzianko's office.[26] The Military Commission was being formed.[27] There was a need to make swift decisions in answer to countless urgent requests from soldiers and officers. Iurevich, the newly appointed city police and administrative chief [*gradonachal'nik*], was the one responding.[28]

There was complete anarchy in the streets. Engel'gardt thinks it was imperative for the Duma to exercise authority. But the Temporary Committee wavered and Rodzianko hesitated to take power into his hands. Engel'gardt barged into the meeting of the Temporary Committee and insisted that the Duma assume leadership and not lose momentum. Some members supported him, but Rodzianko still wavered. At that moment, Shidlovskii entered and reported that the entire Preobrazhenskii Regiment had placed itself under the command of the Temporary Committee. This finally forced Rodzianko to make up his mind to assume power, but he had one condition—he demanded absolute obedience to himself. He turned to Kerenskii and said, "This especially refers to you, Aleksandr Fedorovich."[29]

"As for me, I am willing," he replied, "but I cannot afford to ignore what is boiling to the Left of me." Vladimir L'vov[30] demanded that Engel'gardt be attached to the Temporary Committee. Immediately after this co-optation, Engel'gardt was appointed chairman of the Military Commission. Rodzianko went out to introduce him to the Commission, but the attorney Nikolai Dmitrievich Sokolov[31] (from the Soviet of Workers' Deputies) raised objections, declaring that a collegial body such as this should elect its own chairman. Rodzianko categorically insisted, arguing that Engel'gardt was a competent man, so Engel'gardt stayed and was recognized as the chairman of the Military Commission. He then went to the Preobrazhenskii Regiment in order to consolidate its transfer of allegiance to the Temporary Committee.

A few minutes prior to Rodzianko's decision, disorders erupted in the street and Engel'gardt tried to convince Karaulov[32] to take power by assuming command of his Cossacks. But the latter refused, saying that he did not want to lead the Cossacks into anarchy.

Once Rodzianko made the decision, work really picked up. The restoration of order began. In the Preobrazhenskii Regiment, where Engel'gardt had gone, the officers vowed for themselves and for their soldiers that from now on they would recognize only one authority—the power of the Temporary Committee—and no one else's. Upon his return to the Military Commission, he found that it had been flooded with all sorts of urgent requests: to meet the troops that had been coming to the Duma; to obtain and distribute weapons (rifles and the like); to stop looting and anarchy. There was no time to give much thought to the answers.

Around 3:00 [on the morning of February 28], he flopped down on a chair and took a nap. But just after four he was awakened by Nekrasov[33] and, after changing into a military uniform, went back to work. He summoned officers of the General Staff: Iakubovich, Prince Tumanov, and Colonel Tugan-Baranovskii.[34] There was a massive number of different problems to address: the looting of small shops and kiosks; complaints from widows of murdered officers that their husbands were being dumped out of their caskets; arrests; clashes; and so on. February 28, generally speaking, represents the end of the first waves of revolution—the struggle against tsarism, accompanied by all sorts of excesses.

On the night from the 27th to the 28th, Rodzianko and Engel'gardt drew up an order to the troops that units should return to their barracks and submit to the authority of the Temporary Committee, and so on. In Engel'gardt's opinion, as he was writing the order, his "bourgeois" mindset had come to the fore: with the transfer of power into the hands of the Temporary Committee, the bourgeoisie had emerged victorious; now it had to secure its position and restore order. But "Democracy" saw the situation from a completely different perspective. They regarded Rodzianko's order as premature because tsarism was far from shaken to its core, and a counterrevolution was possible; besides, much had yet to be achieved. Engel'gardt understood this immediately and, accepting the risks, had the printing of the order stopped at once. Rodzianko was unhappy when he later learned of this, but Engel'gardt assumed responsibility.[35]

Already on the morning of February 28, it became clear to Engel'gardt that he was no longer restoring order, but had become a revolutionary. He believed that there was a need to give an order to attack the Admiralty and arrest the Council of Ministers who were under siege there.[36] However, if counterrevolution were to gain the upper hand, this order would put Engel'gardt two steps away from the gallows. He therefore went to show his order to Miliukov and Kerenskii. They approved it, and even put their signatures next to his. It was then sent to the Preobrazhenskii Regiment, but the soldiers' response was sluggish. And in any case, the Ministers soon ran away and were later brought to the Duma.

February 28 was spent in writing orders.

March 1: the struggle continued. Guchkov showed up. The question of new ministers emerged. Guchkov was proposed as minister of war. Engel'gardt considered withdrawing from the Military Commission and passing the chairmanship on to Guchkov. But he decided that this was not appropriate, and they shared power. Engel'gardt stayed in the Duma and Guchkov went to railway stations to meet troops (arriving from Tsarskoe Selo, etc.) and restore and preserve order. In the Duma, Engel'gardt talked to delegations of soldiers. In the Catherine Hall[37] there were speeches, "hurrahs," and celebrations of the victory over tsarism. It was impossible to get any rest. When things calmed down, Engel'gardt estimated that he had spent the first sixty-five hours of revolution on his feet. He was only able to have four glasses of tea and two sandwiches during this time, and even that was because some journalists insisted.

On March 1, a new wave arose; tsarism had been broken on the day before. Following that, they were destroying everything: old norms, structures, and ways of life. The banks were being attacked; they needed to be defended. A new movement was emerging with the firm goal to discredit officers. Weapons were being confiscated and various excesses were taking place. There was a need to find people to combat all this, but they were few and far between. From the mass of officers who were present in the Tauride Palace, Engel'gardt had to select people who looked alert enough ["*s bodroi rozhei*"]. He grabbed them without giving them the chance to figure out what was going on and sent them to where they were needed at the moment. All sorts of *quid pro quo*[38] arrangements resulted from this. One officer had the following complaint. As he arrived from the front, he was immediately disarmed by the soldiers in the street. When he entered the Tauride Palace looking for help, a colonel jumped on him, saying, "You are exactly who I need," grabbed someone else's saber, strapped it on the officer, and immediately sent him somewhere on an important assignment. It turned out that this colonel had been Engel'gardt.

To guard against this new wave, the Temporary Committee, through the Military Commission, took over the telephone and electrical stations as well as the water supply. The Soviet of Workers' Deputies took over the printing houses, where they began to issue leaflets of the most radical type. The relationship between the Soviet and the Temporary Committee was very sharp and bitter. The Temporary Committee was even expecting that they would all be finished off. Steklov[39] scolded Rodzianko for his order of February 27,[40] by which he had wanted to put a lid on the revolution. Rodzianko responded to Steklov that Engel'gardt had not actually issued the order. Steklov gave a long and eloquent speech about the incompatibility of interests between the bourgeoisie and democracy. It was possible to agree with most of the speech, except for its military aspects.[41]

Elections among troops. Soldiers came to the Military Commission with a demand for reform. Engel'gardt and these soldiers wrote up an order and he took it to the Temporary Committee for sanctioning. But there, the reaction to the order was one of horror—they said that it would result in the disintegration of the army, etc. There was a heated discussion with Guchkov, who was adamant, and all members of the Temporary Committee agreed with him. Engel'gardt went out to the soldiers who were waiting for him on behalf of the Soviet of Soldiers' and Workers' Deputies. Once they heard that the Temporary Committee disagreed, they replied, "In that case, we will write it ourselves!" and wrote Order Number One.[42]

Agitation against the Military Commission began. Steklov claimed that officers were locking soldiers up in the barracks and disarming them. Engel'gardt explained that these accusations were incorrect. They checked on several regiments, and indeed, the rumors proved to be false. Engel'gardt declared that if this were to happen anywhere, he would order that the guilty officers be shot immediately. Steklov asked that this statement be recorded, and Engel'gardt immediately, with his own hand, wrote it out in duplicate. He gave one copy to Steklov for publication by the Left, and the other to the newspapers on the Right. A few minutes later, an outraged Steklov came back to Engel'gardt and accused him of giving different texts to the Right and the Left. It turned out that without asking him, Engel'gardt's colleagues had changed, and somewhat softened, the text of the order which had been given to the newspapers on the Right by omitting the word "execution." The new version had been written in different handwriting, which immediately vindicated Engel'gardt, and he proceeded to rewrite the original text in its entirety. This, in Engel'gardt's opinion, ended the factual description of his work in the Military Commission. His closest associate was engineer Pal'chinskii.[43]

When they brought Sukhomlinov[44] in on the evening of March 1, Engel'gardt did not offer to shake his hand. Beliaev asked Engel'gardt to arrange house arrest for him. But Engel'gardt refused, pointing out that Beliaev's ties to Rasputin did not constitute a motive for leniency. Beliaev denied his connection to Rasputin. But Engel'gardt insisted because he knew it for certain.

Officers gathered in the Hall of the Army and Navy and called for Engel'gardt, but instead Iakubovich went and brought them to the Duma, where Engel'gardt met with them.[45]

On the night of March 1, Guchkov took over the Commission and went to the railway station to meet Ivanov.[46] At 5:00 in the morning on March 2, Engel'gardt clashed with Guchkov over the "execution" clause, resigned from the Commission, and went home.

In the afternoon of the 3rd, in the Duma, Nekrasov notified Engel'gardt that Guchkov had submitted his resignation because he had been arrested because of reports on the regency. Shingarev confirmed this, and even worse, as a monarchist Miliukov was also leaving. Engel'gardt was offered the war ministry. Guchkov was nowhere to be found. Urgent requests for directives, orders, and signatures poured in every minute, and from all directions. In Guchkov's absence, Deputy Minister Filat'ev[47] turned to Engel'gardt and asked for the transfer of twenty-two million rubles to the southern front. Engel'gardt risked this, and many other things, because there was no time to lose. Alekseev, for the third time, called for Guchkov on the telephone. Engel'gardt picked up the receiver and reported on the state of things, but then it became clear that Alekseev had just talked to Guchkov, and that he had not said a word about his resignation.[48] Engel'gardt called Guchkov, who most emphatically declared that no one had arrested him and that he had not resigned.

NOTES

1 The narration in this interview is mostly in the third person, which was probably the result of incomplete editing by Rusudana Polievktova-Nikoladze, who compiled this (amalgamated) master version of the interview on the basis of available draft transcripts. However, as far as we can establish, no substantive or contextual changes of any kind have been made to this text.

2 The reference is to the Russo-Japanese War of 1904–5.

3 The emergency one-day-long session of the fourth Duma took place on July 26, 1914. The deputies met, and with the exception of the Social Democrats, voted to authorize war credits. The next, third, session of this Duma took place only six months later on January 27, 1915, when the deputies were reconvened to vote on the state budget.

4 The Russian parliamentary delegation, consisting of ten Duma deputies and six members of the State Council and led by the moderate Octobrist deputy and senior deputy speaker A. D. Protopopov, visited the Allied and neutral countries in April–June 1916. The main goal was to reassure the Europeans of the Russian public's commitment to the Allied war effort. The delegation met with government and elected officials, members of parliaments, and had a personal audience with King George V. Pavel Nikolaevich Miliukov (1859–1943) was one of Russia's most influential historians before the revolution, a founder of the Kadet party, and the leader of the Kadet faction in the Duma and of the Progressive Bloc (1915–17). During the February Revolution he was by far the most influential liberal politician in the country, the de facto leader of the Duma Committee and the principal architect of the Provisional Government, in which he also served as minister of foreign affairs from March 2 to May 2, 1917. Andrei Ivanovich

Shingarev (1869–1918) was a prominent Kadet and deputy to the second (from Voronezh), third (from Voronezh province), and fourth (from St. Petersburg) Dumas. He was a member of the Bureau of the Progressive Bloc (1915–17), participated in the parliamentary delegation to the Allied countries in 1916, and represented the Duma on the Special Council starting in August 1915.

5 The reference is to the Special Council for the Discussion and Consolidation of Measures for Defending the State (hereafter Special Council), which met from May 1915 to November 1917 (formally dissolved in March 1918) and was presided over by the minister of war. The Special Council initially included four representatives from the State Duma, four from the State Council, and four from trade and industry groups, as well as selected officials from the ministries of navy, war, finances, railways, trade and industries, and the state comptrollers' office. In 1916, the membership was expanded to include up to ten representatives from the Duma and the State Council. However, the number of actual participants varied from meeting to meeting and in terms of permanency of membership. Engel'gardt participated in the meetings of the Special Council starting on June 22, 1916.

6 This information was not reflected in the available protocols of the Special Council's meetings for October 1916. Engel'gardt probably refers here to the Special Council's commission on procurement of labor force for the defense industry, which was chaired by the State Council member A. S. Stishinskii.

7 Vladimir Iosifovich Gurko (Romeiko-Gurko) (1862–1927) was a high-ranking official in the ministry of internal affairs until 1907, and was an elected member of the State Council (1912–17), where he belonged to the moderate Circle of Nonparty Associations (*Kruzhok vnepartiinogo ob'edineniia*). He took part in the Russian parliamentary delegation to the Allied countries in 1916. He was also a leader of the Progressive Bloc. In August 1915, he was elected to represent the State Council on the Special Council.

8 Aleksandr Semenovich Stishinskii (1851–1922) was a high-ranking official in the ministry of internal affairs, where he served as deputy minister (1899–1904) and head of the land administration in 1906, until forced to retire at P. A. Stolypin's request. He later served as an appointed member of the State Council (1904–17), where he belonged to the Rightist Group. Starting in August 1915, he also represented the State Council on the Special Council. He was arrested during the February Days and spent three months in the Peter and Paul Fortress (March 1–June 11, 1917). He later served in the Denikin and Wrangel administrations in the South. He died in Constantinople.

9 Vasilii Vital'evich Shul'gin (1878–1976) was a leading conservative deputy to the second, third, and fourth Dumas from Volyn' province, a jurist by training and a prolific political writer and journalist. In August 1915 he joined the leadership of the Progressive Bloc, representing the Progressive Nationalists faction, and was also elected to serve as a Duma representative on the Special Council. On February 27, 1917 he became a member of the Temporary Duma Committee.

10 Mikhail Vasil'evich Alekseev (1857–1918) was adjutant general (1916), and from August 18, 1915 to April 2, 1917 served as chief of staff of General Headquarters, the de facto commander of the Russian armed forces. He was appointed commander in chief on April 2 and remained in this post until May 22, 1917.

11 Tsarskoe Selo (now part of the city of Pushkin), a town and railway station 15 miles (24 km) south of St. Petersburg, was the main place of residence of the imperial family.

12 In his unpublished memoirs, Engel'gardt alluded to his involvement in a palace coup but not specifically in the Guchkov plot (see n. 14), and he never named the officer in question: the cavalry captain Dmitrii Vladimirovich Kossikovskii. See B. A. Engel'gardt, "Potonuvshii mir. Vospominaniia." Typescript. Chapter XII, l. 95 (308), Manuscript Department of the Russian National Library (OR RNB), f. 218, folder 306-3, and n. 46 to the M. I. Tereshchenko interview (Chapter 12).

13 Mariinskii Palace was the seat of the Russian imperial government and of the State Council, the upper chamber of the legislative assembly. The Provisional Government "inherited" the Palace, and turned it into its main seat from March 7 until the middle of July 1917.

14 The name of the plot refers to its main organizer, Aleksandr Ivanovich Guchkov (1862–1936). It was formed no later than October 1916 and was led by a group of five: the first two participants were Guchkov and his long-time acquaintance Prince D. L. Viazemskii; soon thereafter Kossikovskii joined them, followed by Nekrasov and Tereshchenko. The plotters planned to seize the tsar's train while it was traveling from General Headquarters (in Mogilev) to Tsarskoe Selo, somewhere in Novgorod province, and force Nicholas II to abdicate in favor of his son, Alexis (still a minor), with Grand Duke Mikhail serving as regent. Guchkov was a founder and leading figure of the Union of October 17 (or Octobrist party) throughout its existence. During the years 1915–17, he was a member of the State Council and chairman of the Central War Industry Committee (CWIC). Guchkov served as minister of war and navy in the first Provisional Government until April 30, 1917.

15 According to the protocols of the Special Council, this question was indeed brought up by several members (Gurko, the Duma President Rodzianko, and others) during the February 1, 1917 meeting, and then reiterated by the more moderate and liberal members representing the Duma and State Council at the next meeting on February 4. See *Zhurnaly Osobogo soveshchaniia po oborone gosudarstva, 1917 god* (Moscow: Institut istorii AK SSSR, 1978), 159–76.

16 Mikhail Alekseevich Beliaev (1863–1918) was a career army officer, a general in the infantry (starting in 1914), acting commander of the General Staff and deputy minister of war (June 1915–August 1916). He was the last tsarist minister of war from January 3 to February 27, 1917. He also presided over the Special Council in his capacity as minister of war. Beliaev was arrested on March 1, 1917 and imprisoned in the Peter and Paul Fortress. He was later executed by the Bolsheviks.

17 Ivan Grigor'evich Shcheglovitov (1861–1918) was a conservative jurist and state official. He served as minister of justice (1906–15). He was also a member of the State Council (1906–17), and he served as its president starting on January 1, 1917. He was arrested on February 27, 1917, kept in the Ministerial Pavilion until March 1, and then moved to the Peter and Paul Fortress. He was shot by the Bolsheviks in Moscow on September 5, 1918.

18 Aleksei Ivanovich Mosolov (1863–1943) was an elected member of the State Council from the nobility associations (1906–17) and a leading member of the Council's Rightist Group. Starting in July 1915, he represented the State Council on the Special Council.

19 Vladimir Vladimirovich Meller-Zakomel'skii (1863–1920) was a prominent Octobrist and an elected member of the State Council (1912–17) from the St. Petersburg zemstvo provincial assembly; he belonged to the moderate Center Group. In the summer of 1915 he was one of the organizers of the Progressive Bloc and starting in August 1915, he represented the State Council on the Special Council.

20 Aleksei Andreevich Polivanov (1855–1920) was a general in the infantry, an appointed member of the State Council (1912–17), and minister of war (1915–16). He had a reputation as a liberal bureaucrat.

21 The reference is to Aleksei Nikolaevich (1904–18), the tsarevich or caesarevich, the only son of Nicholas II and Aleksandra, and heir to the throne.

22 Mikhail Vladimirovich Rodzianko was a leading Octobrist and President of the last Duma. See his interview in this volume.

23 Prince Georgii Evgen'evich L'vov (1861–1925) was deputy to the first Duma from Tula and a prominent Moscow-based zemstvo liberal. From July 1915 to March 1917, he was the chairman of the Main Committee for the Supply of the Army of the United All-Russian Zemstvo Union for Relief to Wounded and Sick Soldiers and Union of Towns (Zemgor) and as such was considered by most opposition groups to be a leading candidate for premiership in a

post-Nicholas II government. From March 2 to July 7, 1917, he served as minister president (prime minister) in the first two cabinets of the Provisional Government.

24 The reference is to the private meeting of the Duma deputies held between approximately 2:30 and 5 in the afternoon on February 27, in the semicircular hall. The meeting ended with the decision, in defiance of the prorogation decree, to establish the Temporary Committee of the Members of the State Duma for the Restoration of Order in the Capital and for the Establishment of Relations with Public Organizations and Institutions (the Duma Committee), which despite its misleadingly cumbersome name became the first de facto revolutionary government. For more on the circumstances and participants in this pivotal meeting, see Semion Lyandres, "On the Problem of 'Indecisiveness' among the Duma Leaders during the February Revolution: The Imperial Decree of Prorogation and Decision to Convene the Private Meeting of February 27, 1917," *The Soviet and Post-Soviet Review* 24, 1–2 (1997): 115–27; A. B. Nikolaev, *Revoliutsiia i vlast': IV Gosudarstvennaia duma, 27 fevralia–3 marta 1917 goda* (St. Petersburg: RGPU, 2005), 137–45.

25 New Club or *Novyi klub* was one of the two aristocratic clubs (the New and the English), located next to each other on Dvortsovaia (Palace) Embankment (nos. 12 and 14), just around the corner from the Winter Palace. The New Club was presided over by Feliks Iusupov, one of the principle organizers of Rasputin's murder.

26 Rodzianko agreed to preside over the Temporary Committee of the Duma (also known as the Duma Committee) that was formed between 4:00 and 5:00 in the afternoon of February 27 and included: Rodzianko, I. I. Dmitriukov, S. I. Shidlovskii (Octobrists); N. S. Chkheidze (Social Democrat); M. A. Karaulov (Independent); Kerenskii (Laborite); A. I. Konovalov and V. A. Rzhevskii (Progressists); V. N. L'vov (Center); Miliukov and N. V. Nekrasov (Kadets); and Shul'gin (Progressive Nationalist). Engel'gardt joined this group shortly after Rodzianko's midnight announcement that the Duma Committee was taking over government responsibilities.

27 According to Maksim Grigor'evich Kantor, a Petrograd sworn attorney and Kerenskii's confidant, who served as the MC's secretary throughout its existence, the Commission was created around 1:00 in the afternoon on February 27 to organize the insurgent units of the Petrograd garrison and coordinate efforts against the forces of the old regime. During the first hours following its formation, the MC was still being referred to inside the Tauride Palace as "the Kerenskii Headquarters," and included V. N. Filippovskii, P. I. Pal'chinskii, N. E. Parshin, and Kantor in addition to Kerenskii and Skobelev. See the transcript of Kantor's interview with the Polievktov Commission, May 2, 1917, in MAPP, FA; and Nikolaev, *Revoliutsiia i vlast'*, 227–311, 593–609; By March 3, the MC had sixteen departments and more than one hundred members, and included representatives from the Petrograd Soviet, the Duma Committee, and the war ministry. However, the MC soon became a source of continuous friction between the Duma Committee and the Soviet leadership, and was dissolved by the Provisional Government. Some of its members were transferred to the war ministry; others were placed under the command of the Petrograd Military District. On the composition and activities of the MC, see also the interview with A. A. Chikolini in this volume (Chapter 4).

28 Vadim Aleksandrovich Iurevich (1872–1963) was a doctor of medicine, professor and head of the department of infectious deceases in Petrograd's Military Medical Academy (MMA) from 1910 to 1918. On the evening of February 27 (and until he was replaced by Engel'gardt in the early hours of the 28th) he acted as the first chairman of the Military Commission (MC) of the Duma Committee. During February 28–March 2, 1917 he was commander of the MMA, and on March 2 he was appointed the first public chief of the city administration and police. He left Russia in 1920, lived in Constantinople in 1921 and Prague in 1922, and was then appointed head of the Saigon branch of the Pasteur Institute. He died in New York City.

29 This famous episode has often been described in the literature, in both memoirs and scholarly histories. Yet the exact details vary and often contradict each other (see, for example, the interview with Nekrasov in this volume, Chapter 8; Tsuyoshi Hasegawa, *The February Revolution, Petrograd, 1917* (Seattle and London: University of Washington Press, 1981), 358–9; and Nikolaev, *Revoliutsiia i vlast'*, 313–14). Although most historians accept Engel'gardt's account (repeated in his later memoirs), many questions remain. One such question is about the timing and the actual impact of Shidlovskii's announcement on Rodzianko's decision to assume power. Another unanswered question concerns the precise nature of the information conveyed to Shidlovskii and, in turn, by him to the Duma Committee: was it the "entire Preobrazhenskii Regiment" that declared support for the Duma, or just a group of officers who decided to subordinate themselves to the command of the Duma Committee?

30 Vladimir Nikolaevich L'vov (1872–1934) was a deputy to the fourth Duma from Samara province and leader of the moderately nationalist Center Faction, which he also represented in the Progressive Bloc. On February 27, 1917 he was elected to the Duma Committee, and from March 2 to July 21, 1917 served as Procurator of the Holy Synod in the Provisional Government.

31 Nikolai Dmitrievich Sokolov (1870–1928) was a veteran non-factional Social Democrat and well-known defense attorney specializing in political cases. He had extensive connections with different revolutionary and oppositional groups in Petrograd and Moscow. During the February Days, he was one of the founders and leaders of the Petrograd Soviet, a member of its executive committee, and principal negotiator with the Duma Committee for the formation of the Provisional Government. He is considered to be the author of Order Number One.

32 Mikhail Aleksandrovich Karaulov (1878–1917) was a moderate deputy to the fourth Duma from the Cossacks of the Tersk region and belonged to the Independents faction (*gruppa nezavisimykh deputatov*), which he also represented on the Council of Elders. During the February Days, he was elected to the Duma Committee (from which he resigned on March 8, 1917); during March 1–4 he served as the commandant of the Tauride Palace.

33 The reference is to Nikolai Vissarionovich Nekrasov. See his interview in this volume.

34 In his later memoirs, Engel'gardt claimed that the three officers came to the Duma around 10:00 in the morning on February 28 (Nikolaev, *Revoliutsiia i vlast'*, 295). Grigorii Andrianovich Iakubovich (1880–1926) was a career army officer and a graduate of the General Staff Academy (1910); starting in September 1915 he served in the Main Administration of the General Staff (MAGS), he was promoted to colonel in December 1915 and then to department head in October 1916. After the February Days he returned to his position at the MAGS and beginning on May 9, 1917, along with his peers and fellow General Staff officers Tugan-Baranovskii and Tumanov, he served as special assistant to minister of war Kerenskii. On August 30, 1917 he was promoted to major general. He later emigrated, and lived and died in Paris. Prince Georgii Nikolaevich Tumanov (1880–1917) was another colonel of the General Staff (starting in June 1915) and a friend of Iakubovich's and Tugan-Baranovskii's. Tumanov graduated from the General Staff Academy in 1909 and starting in April 1914, he served in the MAGS as acting deputy head of the 3rd division of the mobilization department and later as the division head. On February 28, 1917 Tumanov and his two friends were summoned by Engel'gardt to join the Military Commission under his command. On May 9 Tumanov was appointed special assistant "to the minister of war [Kerenskii] for the duration of the war." On August 30 he was promoted to the rank of major general. He was murdered by the Volynskii Regiment soldiers in Petrograd, on October 26, 1917, during the Bolshevik takeover. On Tugan-Baranovskii, see the preface to his interview in this volume (Chapter 7).

35 The reference is to the order known as "Rodzianko's Order," issued by the Military Commission in Rodzianko's name on February 28, which instructed officers and soldiers to return to their barracks and to obey military discipline. It is said to have provoked such a strong reaction from the insurgent soldiers, who viewed the order as an attempt to restore the old authority, that they sent representatives to the meeting of the Petrograd Soviet demanding that "Rodzianko's Order" be counteracted by issuing in the name of the Soviet what came to be known as Order Number One. See Hasegawa, *The February Revolution*, 375–6, 390–2. In his later memoirs, Engel'gardt claimed that he and his moderate Duma colleague the Progressist A. A. Bublikov actually wrote the order, but issued it in Rodzianko's name on February 28 (Hasegawa, *The February Revolution*, 390). However, Bublikov's authorship is questionable because he was not involved in the work of the MC and spent February 28–March 2 in the ministry of transport, monitoring the movement of the tsar's train.

36 The admiralty was seized by insurgent forces between 4:00 and 5:00 in the afternoon on February 28. Until then the building had been occupied by three companies of the Izmailovskii Regiment as well as some cavalry and mounted artillery units. They left on their own just before the insurgents came, however, and the remaining ministers of the old government left with them.

37 The reference is to the large oval-shaped colonnade hall that preceded four entrances to the main assembly (or White) hall of the Tauride Palace.

38 *Quid pro quo* (*Latin*), literally: "something for something" (or "favour in return") but in this case it is used to define a misunderstanding or blunder made by the substituting of one thing for another.

39 Iurii Mikhailovich Steklov (real name Nakhamkis or more accurately: Nakhamkes, Ovshii Moiseevich) (1873–1941) was a veteran revolutionary, prolific publicist, and non-factional Social Democrat sometimes associated with the Bolsheviks. During the February Revolution, he was one of the organizers and leaders of the Petrograd Soviet and a member of the Executive Committee; together with N. D. Sokolov and N. N. Sukhanov he represented the Executive Committee in the negotiations with Miliukov and the Duma Committee on the formation of the Provisional Government. He joined the Bolshevik party in early fall of 1917.

40 The reference is probably to the order known as "Rodzianko's Order," which was issued on February 28 (see n. 35 above).

41 Steklov's speech, in which he actually mentioned Engel'gardt by name, was delivered to the session of the Petrograd Soviet in the afternoon of March 2 and is reproduced in a recent edition of the Soviet's documents (*Petrogradskii Sovet rabochikh i soldatskikh deputatov v 1917 g. Protokoly, stenogrammy sektsii, zasedanii Ispolnitel'nogo komiteta i fraktsii*. Vol. I: *27 fevralia–31 marta 1917 g.* [Leningrad: Nauka, 1991], 61–6). This same speech was described by a colleague of Steklov's from the Petrograd Soviet, the moderate SR V. M. Zenzinov, not as "eloquent and long" but rather as "characteristically [for Steklov] verbose and boring." (V. Zenzinov, "Fevral'skie dni," *Novoe russkoe slovo*, March 26, 1947: 2).

42 Order Number One (ONO), issued on March 1 in the name of the Petrograd Soviet under pressure from the insurgent soldiers' delegates, was in part a reaction against the order known as "Rodzianko's order" of February 28, which asked soldiers and officers in Petrograd to return to their barracks and obey military discipline. This was viewed by the insurgent soldiers as an attempt to restore the old authority that many were now determined to destroy. ONO freed soldiers from traditional military discipline, authorized elections of soldiers' committees, and granted them control over all aspects of life in a military unit. Formally, ONO pertained only to the Petrograd garrison but it quickly spread to all military units, including at the front. The impact of the Order on the integrity of the Russian armed forces is impossible to overestimate: it irreparably undermined traditional military authority and contributed to the rapidly growing alienation between soldiers and their commanding officers.

43 Interestingly, in his later testimony, Engel'gardt described his "closest associate" Pal'chinskii as "a smart and cunning careerist." See Engel'gardt's April 12, 1921 deposition in *Rossiiskii arkhiv*, 281. Petr Ioakimovich Pal'chinskii (1875–1929), a prominent mining engineer, was a veteran non-factional revolutionary, sympathetic to P. A. Kropotkin's anarchism and to the Socialist Revolutionaries. During the war years, he was a leading figure in CWIC, Guchkov's trusted aide and co-conspirator, and chairman of the influential Committee for Military-Technical Assistance. His role in organizing anti-government forces from the very first day of the February Revolution is difficult to overestimate. Together with Kerenskii he set up the ubiquitous MC and became its first manager of affairs. On March 1 he was named assistant chairman of the MC under Guchkov, a position that concentrated in his hands most human and material resources at the disposal of the MC. After the February Revolution, he joined the Petrograd Soviet Executive Committee and continued to occupy many important posts in the Provisional Government, including organizing the defense of the Winter Palace in October 1917.

44 General Vladimir Aleksandrovich Sukhomlinov (1848–1926) was a disreputable minister of war during 1909–15. See n. 1 to the Tugan-Baranovskii interview.

45 The Officers' Assembly Hall of the Army and Navy (*Zdanie ofitserskogo sobraniia armii i flota*), or "Officers' Club," was located on the corner of Liteinyi Avenue and Kirochnaia Street, within walking distance from the Tauride Palace. This reference is to the gathering of "officers of the Petrograd garrison and all officers who are currently in Petrograd" in the Officers' Club on the morning of March 1, 1917, which was requested by the MC on the previous night. The officers were asked to come to the Club in order to register and receive assignments from the MC. Around 1:00 in the afternoon on March 1, they passed a resolution recognizing the authority of the Duma Committee and confirming their solidarity with the people. See *RPG*, I: 63; *Fevral'skaia Revoliutsiia 1917 g. Sbornik dokumentov i materialov*, 123.

46 Nikolai Iudovich Ivanov (1851–1919) was adjutant general and commander of the southwestern front (July 1914 to March 1916). He was subsequently dismissed and attached to the emperor in General Headquarters. Late at night on February 27, Nicholas II appointed him military dictator of Petrograd and sent him to the capital on a punitive expedition to put down the uprising and restore order. On March 1, Guchkov had indeed expressed interest in meeting with Ivanov, whom he had known for a long time, in order to convince the general to halt his punitive expedition. They agreed to meet either in Vyritsa (a railway station 12 miles or 20 km southeast of Gatchina) or in Gatchina on Guchkov's way back from Pskov. However, the meeting did not take place; after receiving the abdication late at night on March 2, Guchkov proceeded directly to Petrograd. In Pskov he also learned that Ivanov's mission had been halted and hence had no obvious reason to see the general.

47 Dmitrii Vladimirovich Filat'ev (1866–1932) was a lieutenant general (1916) in the Russian imperial army and professor of the General Staff Academy (1912–17). Starting in January 1917, he served as chief of the war ministry chancellery. On March 3, 1917 he was appointed by Guchkov as one of his three deputies (in charge of military justice, education, and medical affairs) and concurrently continued to serve as chief of the war ministry chancellery until Guchkov's resignation two months later. On May 9, 1917 Filat'ev was replaced by L. S. Tugan-Baranovskii and returned to his teaching position at the Academy.

48 A transcript of this March 3 conversation between General Alekseev and Engel'gardt, which corroborates his testimony, is reproduced in "Fevral'skaia revoliutsiia 1917 goda (dokumenty stavki verkhovnogo glavnokomanduiushchego i shtaba glavnokomanduiushchego armiiami severnogo fronta)", *Krasnyi arkhiv* 22, 3 (1927): 39.

4

Aleksandr Aleksandrovich Chikolini

ALEKSANDR ALEKSANDROVICH CHIKOLINI (1872–after November 1917) was one of those little-known characters whose meteoric rise to prominence and almost equally swift fade into oblivion could only have been possible in the whirlwind of the revolution. Born in Moscow to the family of a middle-ranking civil servant (state councilor) of Italian descent, Chikolini studied law at Moscow University. Following graduation, he served his year in the military and then returned to Moscow where he worked as a sworn attorney until the outbreak of the First World War. As an ensign in the infantry reserves, Chikolini was recalled for active duty in August 1914 and deployed as a noncommissioned officer to the 86th Vologodskii Reserve Infantry Detachment. In August 1916 he was promoted to First Lieutenant but, given the acute shortage of trained and physically fit officers, was assigned to fill in for the higher position of Acting Captain.

At the time of the February Revolution, his unit was deployed in the capital, patrolling parts of the city center, including the vicinity of the Tauride Palace. On 27 February, sheer chance brought him into the ranks of the powerful Military Commission (MC). In the early afternoon hours, as he was being chased by a gang of revolutionary soldiers, Chikolini accidentally burst into the semicircular hall of the Tauride Palace, where the famous private meeting of the Duma members had just commenced, and asked for protection.[a] Rodzianko led him away to the opposite end of the Palace, near his office and just across from rooms 41 and 42, where at that very hour the MC was being organized. What happened next was somewhat more predictable. Chikolini quickly oriented himself to the new situation and gladly offered to apply his clerical skills to the revolutionary cause.

Having joined the ranks of the MC at such an early, formative stage, he thus found himself among the small core group of military officers and civilians who led the effort to organize anti-government forces and to capture key military and

---

[a] See *Volia Rossii*, March 15, 1921: 4; Semion Lyandres, "Zur Errichtung der revolutionaren Macht in Petrograd: Neue Dokumente über die inoffizielle Beratung von Mitgliedern der Staatsduma am 27.2.1917," *Berliner Jahrbuch für osteuropaische Geschichte* (1997): 35, 319.

government installations. The MC's records reveal that over the course of the next few days he issued hundreds of orders to revolutionary troops on behalf of the MC's chairman and on a few occasions (after March 4) even as the deputy war minister.[b] After the formation of the Provisional Government, Chikolini showed no intention of returning to his military unit, from which he was retroactively (effective February 27) discharged on March 18 and on the same day formally assigned to the MC. He stayed on until the MC was dissolved on May 10, 1917.[c]

Chikolini's subsequent whereabouts remain obscure. Later in the year he resurfaced in his native Moscow as an aide to the city Bolshevik military commissar and Soviet leader N. I. Muralov.[d] There were also unconfirmed reports that during 1918–19 he was a Cheka operative and an especially cruel interrogator. Otherwise he seems to have disappeared from the pages of history.

Chikolini's May 5, 1917 interview with the Polievktov Commission remains his only recorded testimony. The interview offers a rare insider's account of the MC's structure, composition, and its multitude of tasks by an intelligent, perceptive, well-informed, and generally talkative participant with no particular political affiliation. Yet as a leading staffer who was about to become at least temporary unemployed—the MC was to be dissolved less than a week after the interview, as he and others on the Commission were well aware—he would have been eager to emphasize the MC's unparalleled contribution to the overthrow of the old regime. On the whole, Chikolini is quite reliable in offering the information of which he had personal first-hand knowledge. He is not always dependable, however, when he relates the information provided to him by others.

The interview is reproduced on the basis of a master copy compiled by an unidentified hand,[e] with stylistic edits and corrections written between the lines in Tamara Nikoladze's hand, as well as the draft transcript in shorthand by Tamara Nikoladze, which was likely jotted down at the time of the interview.

★ ★ ★ ★ ★ ★

[b] RGVIA [Russian State Military History Archive], f. 8366 (*86-ia peshaia Vologodskaia druzhina gosudarstvennogo opolcheniia*), op. 1, d. 16; f. 1343, op. 10, d. 7176 (lichnoe delo A. A. Chikolini), l. 1–5; f. 8366, op. 1, d. 153 (*posluzhnye spiski ofitserov*), l. 7, 8, 9. According to A. B. Nikolaev, Chikolini joined the MC on February 28, but his information is based on the first orders of the MC signed by Chikolini, whereas he actually began his work with the MC on the afternoon of February 27 (A. B. Nikolaev, *Revoliutsiia i vlast': IV Gosudarstvennaia duma, 27 fevralia–3 marta 1917 goda* (St. Petersburg: RGPU, 2005), 599). For all practical purposes, both before and for some time after the formation of the Provisional Government, the MC was generally viewed by the population and the garrison as a temporary war ministry.

[c] RGVIA, f. 8366, op. 1, d. 16; f. 1343, op. 10, d. 7176, l. 1–5; ibid., op. 1, d. 153, l. 7, 8, 9.

[d] F. F. Raskol'nikov, *Na boevykh postakh* (Moscow: Voennoe izdatel'stvo, 1964), 234. He was among Muralov's assistants for special tasks, along with the old Bolshevik Mandel'shtam and the young officer Left SR Vladimirskii.

[e] Most likely by V. Pavlov, as only he and the Nikoladze sisters are known to have been compiling master versions of all interviews.

Sworn Attorney A. A. Chikolini, Captain of the 86th Vologodskii Reserve Detachment [*druzhina*], Manager of Affairs of the Military Commission. May 5, 1917

I will start from the moment when I first heard, on the street, the Bolshevik slogan, "Down with the War!" This was on the morning of 23 February when, in my capacity as the Guard officer on duty, I was touring the city. I was driving around all of the factories that were on strike, and I ran into a crowd of workers that was moving along Vyborg Side. The procession was fairly peaceful in nature. I stopped my car and started asking around. I was told that the workers were striking because of the shortage of bread (one pound per day). Just then, some hostile crowds shouting "Down with the War!" began coming towards me. Someone from the second group even shouted, referring to me:

"What's the point of talking with him?!" Even so, they let me through. The first signs of what would become commonplace later were already taking shape. Five Cossacks and a precinct policeman were following the more peaceful crowd. It moved towards the Cartridge Factory.[1] The factory director[2] told me that this crowd—his workers—had not wanted to go on strike because they had adequate food supplies. The commander of the factory's equipment department complained to me about the authorities, from whom he had been unable to secure assistance. He had started calling the police precinct in the morning, asking for help. They had advised him to turn to the city police chief. The city police chief had directed him to the commander of the Guard—who in turn referred him to the chief of staff of the Guards' Corps. Only in the evening, when everything was already over, did he receive a company from the Moskovskii Regiment. Had it arrived in time, the workers would not have joined the strike. This was the factory director's opinion. The hostile crowd, which engaged in looting, had many provocateurs: new peaked student caps and well-fed mugs. Apparently, the factories were unguarded. I did not see a single policeman. The picture was the same on February 24 and 25.

On February 26, the movement intensified. No one, except officers, was allowed to cross bridges from the Petrograd Side. That day, I passed from the Petrograd Side into Nevskii [Avenue]. In the city center, the policemen were replaced with soldiers. On Nikolaevskaia Street, soldiers were imposing order by dispersing everyone from the streets and lanes. They stood in lines on both sides of the street, with their officers by their sides. Their complete obedience to the officers, and their openly hostile attitude toward the crowds and disorders, was noticeable. On my way back, I was not allowed to take Nevskii Prospekt. Shots were being fired there. Nevskii Prospekt was empty. On the corner of Nikolaevskaia and Nevskii, officers and policemen acted in accord. I formed the impression that disorders were being suppressed by soldiers. All the same, starting with Miliukov's speech, the officers had been convinced that the troops would not fire at the people. At the beginning of November [1916], according to the order of the [reserve] battalion commander of the Finland Guard Regiment,[3] a hand-written text of Miliukov's speech had been placed on the table at the officer's club.[4] The officers were conspiring with each other. A revolutionary attitude permeated the officers' mood. When I asked what would happen if revolution broke out, the battalion commander replied that they would all take to the streets. Even the old monarchist colonel, who had been in the trenches since 1914, became an ardent revolutionary after Miliukov's speech in the fall of 1916.

On February 26, I still thought the movement was not a revolution, but only a Protopopov-instigated[5] provocation [protopopovshchina].

On the morning of February 27, I rode a horse to the bookstore Pravo.[6] There, I was told that the same training unit of the Volynskii Regiment—which on the evening before had been calling on soldiers by name to shoot into the crowd ("Ivanov, Fire!")—had killed its commander[7] and had taken to the streets. They were joined by the Preobrazhenskii soldiers. (There is an amusing anecdote: I noted that lentils had played a certain role in the psychology of the Preobrazhenskii soldiers, in their decision to join the revolutionary movement. Later, in Moscow, I spoke with a noncommissioned officer of this regiment, and he told me that they probably would not have taken to the streets if the government had fed them better.)

Soon, music and single blank shots were heard. This was the Volynskii Regiment taking to the streets with their band. I left the shop and went to my orderly, who had been waiting downstairs with my horse. Someone had told him that if he was with an officer, it would be better for him to leave. I rode to Nevskii. In the streets which faced Liteinyi Avenue, ambushes had been placed, manned by soldiers from the Semenovskii and other regiments. They made an uninterrupted line, standing deep inside the adjoining streets with their heads facing Liteinyi. I saw an ensign with a platoon, and asked him if he knew about an uprising. He said, "Of course, that's why we're here." I moved on. Machine-gun and infantry companies were moving in the opposite direction. I got the impression that all of them were on the side of the government, and that the uprising would be suppressed. I asked myself again, "What is it, a revolution or a *protopopovshchina*?" I continued on to Nevskii. Everything was quiet there. The normal businesslike routine reigned. Life was going on as always. There were no policemen. They had been replaced by soldiers. I stopped by headquarters and there I heard the same talk about shooting

I was very worried about my company, which was guarding the Tauride Palace. I had just heard a report that sporadic shooting had begun there. I went to the palace. On my way there, I was warned about the danger to officers: that they were being disarmed. One ensign near the Finland [Railway] Station, who was leading a guard patrol, was disarmed and almost killed. They demanded that he side with the people. He did not know how to react, but the crowd insisted. Then someone said, "He is only an ensign, it's not worth killing him," and he was left alone. Evidently, the idea of killing high-ranking officers was not alien to them.

In the Tauride Palace (it was at 1:00 in the afternoon), Deputy Karaulov conveyed Rodzianko's request not to shed blood to the Commander of the Guard, Ensign Medvedev.[8] Medvedev said that the soldiers would not shoot, that they would remain neutral. I headed to the Volynskii soldiers who were on guard across from the Tauride Palace, near the Water Pump. I gave them the same request, in Rodzianko's name. They gave their word. As I was talking to them, a crowd of people dressed in soldiers' coats was moving toward the palace in small groups of ten to twenty people each. They were armed: some with sabers and others with rifles. But these were not soldiers. This was an unruly crowd pushing ahead in total disorder. I walked into the guardroom, which had two entrances. There, some shameless, suspicious characters smelling strongly of alcohol began to emerge through the back door. Right then, an automobile drove up to the entrance. I walked out onto the front stoop, in order to talk with the new arrivals. They turned out to be civilians. We agreed that they would not shoot. Suddenly, at that moment, from the direction of the guardroom, a shot rang out and screams were heard: "Why? What for?" The wounded ensign, Medvedev, was the one shouting; his hand was splintered. The crowd had taken him to the guardroom, but he had run towards the stoop, following me. But near the threshold, two soldiers caught up with him, and one of them shot him with a revolver, sending a bullet through his hand. The other cut his chest with a saber. Someone shouted that Medvedev was shooting back, and the crowd apparently wanted to finish him off; but we managed to rescue him and send him to an infirmary. Still, his right hand had to be amputated.

Back at the palace, I found myself thoroughly bewildered. I did not know how to interpret what was going on. Karaulov's report, that the Duma was prorogued, confirmed my impression that this was a *protopopovshchina* rather than a revolution; I never believed that a revolution could happen in Russia. I did not see any organized leadership—I saw only panic. Once I learned about the Temporary Committee, I began to support it. The ambulance carrying the wounded Medvedev had not yet departed when a group of *intelligenty* came to the guardroom. One of them turned to me and said, "Are you for the government, or for the people?"

I replied: "I am not for the government, but I do not see 'the people.'"

Someone from the crowd said, "Arrest him," but for some reason, no one arrested me. Then I (not being a fool) quickly distanced myself from them and went to the Catherine Hall, proceeding to the semicircular hall, where I turned to Rodzianko for protection. Rodzianko grandly calmed me down, and sent me to his office, "guaranteeing my safety."[9]

At about 7:00 in the evening, the deputies dispersed. Only members of the Temporary Committee remained in the Tauride Palace. In a sense, by electing the Committee the Duma dissolved itself. The mood of most of the Committee members was pretty sour. At about 4:00 in the afternoon, Guchkov showed up. Rodzianko, Guchkov, and Miliukov left to conduct negotiations with Grand Duke Mikhail Aleksandrovich.[10] We discussed what could become of it. I insisted that the Temporary Committee should take power. I said that all of the officers would follow the Committee if it declared itself the government. Engel'gardt was ready for battle, and demanded decisively that the Temporary Committee waste no time in forming a provisional government. He was called to the Preobrazhenskii Regiment, and returned with a report that the entire regiment had subordinated itself to the new authority.[11]

Soon after 10:00 in the evening, the last decisive meeting of the Temporary Committee began. The majority of them were vacillating, but in the end they decided to take power into their hands. Only Rodzianko continued to waver. Finally, he came out and announced that they had decided. Vladimir L'vov turned to me and said, "Now you can join the people." At that meeting, Engel'gardt and Guchkov were appointed to the Temporary Committee.[12] I went over to Engel'gardt, and he told me that the general mood of the meeting's participants had been indecisive. Hopes for Mikhail Aleksandrovich had not materialized; only three—Guchkov, L'vov, and Engel'gardt—had been ready to take decisive action. Engel'gardt had been appointed to head the Military Commission, and I was introduced to him.

While waiting for the results of the Temporary Committee's meeting, I walked into room number 4 of the Tauride Palace. There, I saw Steklov, Gvozdev, and maybe Sukhanov.[13] They were sitting and writing something. It looked like they were composing some kind of proclamation.[14] But something was not working out for them, some phrase. They were soon joined by N. D. Sokolov, a master of writing, who helped them. Upon noticing a stranger, they stood up and five or six people went to another room. This is how the Soviet of Workers' and Soldiers' Deputies was born. Engel'gardt and I went to another room as well, where we found Pal'chinskii, Filippovskii, Kantor, N. D. Sokolov, and a languid gentleman with a bored look on his face. This was the Military Commission. A few minutes later, Rodzianko came to us and introduced Engel'gardt as Chairman of the Military Commission. Sokolov protested, insisting that a chairman should be elected, not appointed by the Temporary Committee. Rodzianko replied, "If you want to elect your own leader, I will quit the Temporary Committee." Sokolov had to acquiesce, and recognized Engel'gardt.

I did not know that the Soviet of Workers' and Soldiers' Deputies had already been formed, but Sokolov demanded that the Military Commission admit eighteen people from some kind of organization, evidently from the Soviet of Workers' Deputies. They were admitted, but did not do any work and very soon they melted away. In the beginning, five or six of them attended; in the end, only one worker—Grinevich.[15]

The first decision by the Military Commission was the division of the city into districts, and the restoration of order. Reports of looting and drunkenness in the city were coming in. It was not yet clear which of the units had joined the revolutionary movement. Toward the evening [of the 27th], it became clear that about 25,000 had joined.[16] The city was divided into military districts; commandants were appointed from among the military officers of the Commission. These assignments went to those who wanted them. Various kinds of military work had begun: giving orders; making arrests; removing ambushes; taking over railway stations; establishing lines of communication with the railways; protecting shops; liaising with troops; and defending the revolution from provocation. Every half an hour, we received fresh updates about everything.

During the night of February 28–March 1, we received information about the tsar. An order for his arrest was immediately sent to Dno Station.[17] (During February 27 and 28, orders were issued only by the Military Commission. On March 2, Order Number One appeared, and this already pointed to the Soviet of Workers' and Soldiers' Deputies.) Arrangements were made to meet the tsar at Dno Station. All telegrams from Alice[18] to the tsar were held up. The organization of communications as a means of defense—post, telegraph, radio-telegraph, telephones, communication with the railroads—was in the hands of the Military Commission. This is how we learned about troops approaching Petrograd by foot and by train, and about their mood. We dispatched fifty people to control telephone conversations. The defense of Petrograd was organized. The trains carrying troops coming to Petrograd to pacify the uprising were stopped 50 *versts*[19] away from the city. The mobilization of soldiers was organized. Trucks carrying officers crisscrossed the city, collecting soldiers and establishing assembly points. In the beginning, the Military Commission also carried out food-related tasks, and it supplied material for bandages. Later on, a separate food commission split off.[20] The main goal of the Military Commission was to give some organization to the revolution, turning the Tauride Palace into its center. We accommodated the "homeless" soldiers who had left their barracks in the first days and who were afraid to return.

On the 27th, Shcheglovitov was arrested. The Admiralty was seized.[21] The question of the St. Peter and Paul Fortress was raised. At first, they wanted to capture it by a night assault, even though an unnamed officer was turning the soldiers against the revolution and swearing that the fortress would go over to the side of the people. In the end, they decided not to launch an assault at night, because that could do damage to the city. Towards the morning of the 28th, Shul'gin went over to the St. Peter and Paul Fortress to conduct negotiations with the commandant. In the morning, the fortress surrendered, and the status of the revolution became clear.[22]

During the night of the 27th–28th, it was impossible to say for certain whether the revolution had won. On the morning of the 28th, the reports about the approaching echelons were no longer considered so threatening. Everything in Petrograd had been settled. Ministers were arrested and were brought in. Balk[23] arrived first, along with his aide and adjutant. Balk handled himself quite well. He was asked who had given the order to strafe the crowds with machine-guns. He replied that the order had come from Khabalov.[24] "Then give the order to have it stopped," he was told. But he replied: "They trust you more than they trust me, why don't you give the order?"

Balk asked to be placed in the same room as his aide and adjutant. He looked fresh; apparently he had not been beaten. After him, Shtiurmer[25] was brought in, and he looked really desperate and oppressed. He complained that he had been hit in the cheekbone. An ensign brought him in at the point of a cocked gun. His appearance awakened the fighting spirit of the crowd, which was literally snapping its teeth. After that, Pitirim[26] came in—a small, green person. He was completely at a loss, and turned to the members of the Military Commission and said, "If you wish to take my life from me, then what can I do? I will die. But if you were to grant it to me, I would immediately retire."

One of the specific tasks of the Military Commission was to save officers from danger; to safeguard them from abuses. When the need to defend against possible counterrevolution dissipated, the militant heat of passion evaporated and work began to return to normal. As a consequence, the purpose of the Military Commission narrowed.

The revolution triumphed toward the evening of the 28th, certainly by March 1st. At that same time, however, provocation and the threat of anarchy from the Left began to loom large. On the 1st—no, on the morning of the 28th—no, actually, on the evening of the 28th—Guchkov became the head of the Military Commission and Engel'gardt was appointed Commandant of Petrograd and of the Tauride Palace. On the night of February 28–March 1, members of the Military Commission—colonels of the General Staff and other "unemployed" officers—held a meeting in order to divide tasks among themselves.[27] They divvied up the assignments in accordance with a plan that had been worked out in advance of the meeting. At 4:00 in the morning Pal'chinskii completed the flow chart, which is attached. (All this was functioning, but there was a slight departure from the flow chart.)[28] A series of departments was created: a department of assignments (Parshin[29]), which was in charge of the guard of the Petrograd Garrison and of all institutions (banks, treasuries, and the like); a department of inquiries; a department of armaments; and a quartermaster department (armories were looted and everything was brought into the Duma: machine-guns, cartridge belts, and so on); a department of railways; a department of counter-intelligence (spies had been released from prison and had left for Finland, where we were catching them); a department of information; a department for gauging the spirit of the troops (and, in connection with that, agitation); a radio-telegraph department; a department of automobiles; and so on.

Generally speaking, the Military Commission performed all of the functions of a war ministry. On March 1, the Military Commission moved from room number 44 into number 22 on the second floor, where it is now. Downstairs, party politics were immediately imposed. Troops only came into contact with the Soviet of Workers' and Soldiers' Deputies (I even suspected that we were deliberately relocated upstairs, further away from the soldiers).

On March 1, Order Number One was composed. This is how it happened, as I was told by Engel'gardt himself. Soldiers came to the Tauride Palace and went to Engel'gardt with a request to issue an order. With those soldiers, Engel'gardt (who saw the order in terms of daily tasks [*v khoziaistvennykh funktsiiakh*] rather than its political implications) sketched out a proclamation, which he showed to Rodzianko and Guchkov. They objected categorically. Guchkov declared: "If this is so necessary, it would be better if such an order came from them instead of us." Engel'gardt went back to the soldiers with that refusal and they replied, "There is no need; we will issue it ourselves." And the Soviet of Workers' and Soldiers' [Deputies] issued Order Number One.

On the afternoon of March 1, Grand Duke Kirill Vladimirovich[30] arrived and went to the Military Commission, where he recounted how he, along with Grand Duke Pavel Aleksandrovich,[31] had warned the tsar and tsarina. Their reply had been: "So what if the gentry and everyone else is lined up against us; the peasants and soldiers are for us." (Sworn attorney Pis'mennyi.[32] Home-made draft abdication [*domashnee otrechenie*] and sworn attorney Kantor about the Baltic Railway Station.)[33]

Resentment against officers deepened. The Military Commission was swelling because of the arrival of new officers. Rumors were spreading that our commission was only admitting officers as members; indeed, their number was multiplying. The Military Commission became a shelter for officers who had been left without living quarters. Because of that, soldiers looked askance at us. On March 1 and 2, it became clear that there was no need for a new tsar—that all the "i"s were dotted, and that a regency should be rejected. Rumors were going around that officers opposed a democratic form of government. Serious talks were conducted on the subject of a provisional government. Because of the fear of anarchy, this question was dealt with expeditiously. It was thought imperative to select ministers at once, because the Executive Committee of the Soviet of Soldiers' and Workers' Deputies had already been formed.

At about 1 or 2 in the afternoon, on March 2, Petr Struve and Rodichev arrived.[34] In the name of the officers, I asked Petr Struve to go to the Temporary Committee and demand, also on behalf of the officers, that the Committee immediately enter negotiations with the Executive Committee of the Soviet of Workers' and Soldiers' Deputies, and form a provisional government. The officers had the impression that the Temporary Committee was dragging its feet. They even decided to come out with a printed proclamation that they stood for a democratic form of government and against regency. The Temporary Committee was forced to hurry up. On March 2, the crisis intensified so much that it could be expected that soldiers would burst into the Military Commission and hack everyone to death. From downstairs, information came up to us that the soldiers were against the officers and wanted to kill them. Some characters were coming in and attempting to call on members of the Military Commission to come down, but we did not comply.

On February 27, a whole regiment of soldiers showed up without their officers, even without noncommissioned officers.[35] On the 28th, regiments without officers were pouring in, but noncommissioned officers were coming to the Commission separately. On March 1, a large group of officers arrived, and in the evening Potapov, the first revolutionary general, showed up.[36] When Guchkov became minister (on the morning of March 3), I received an order to transfer to the war ministry, and to dissolve the Military Commission. But after a series of negotiations between the Commission and the Executive Committee and between Pal'chinskii and Guchkov, it was decided that the Military Commission should remain in the Tauride Palace. (Kantor and I kissed.) Its continued existence was recognized as necessary because it would serve as a buffer between the Provisional Government and the Executive Committee.

The significance of the Military Commission:

1. To serve as a buffer.

2. As long as the War Ministry did not democratize its personnel, which would be impossible to accomplish fully, the Military Commission should keep some powerful responsibilities.

3. It directed the attitudes of the Petrograd garrison and of the army.

4. To clear up misunderstandings between officers and soldiers.

5. To put pressure on the War Ministry with respect to removing undesir-ables, *en masse*, from the officer corps.

6. To discuss different organizational questions and the smoothing of frictions.

The Military Commission's organizational work consisted of dispatching marching companies to the front.

From the creation of the Military Commission, we had to contact the Soviet on all of these points. Not infrequently, there were disagreements about tactics. Here is an example: a case involving the Kronstadt sailors. A sailor came from Kronstadt[37] and demanded that the Military Commission put officers—as "traitors" to the new government—along with their fam-ilies, on the rations of enlisted soldiers. The Military Commission convened a meeting to discuss the issue with this sailor, and members of the Commis-sion argued that this should not be done. Until they had been indicted by a court, they could not legally be punished in this way. There were laws, and they should be obeyed. According to the laws, officers were entitled, before trial, to receive one half of their allowance, part of which went to their wives. Therefore, they could not be put on enlisted soldiers' rations. After three or four hours of fruitless debate, the sailor went to the Executive Committee. There he was told: "The people's voice is God's voice. There is no need for old laws." Thus there were two different answers.

The Military Commission replaced a number of dissipated old military institutions. Today, the Military Commission is truly a conciliatory commis-sion, which includes, on the one hand, eighteen members from the Soviet of Soldiers' and Workers' Deputies, as well as republican officers; and on the other hand, a bureau. At one time, when representatives of the Soviet of Soldiers' and Workers' Deputies were joining the ranks of the Commission, there was a tendency to subordinate the Military Commission to the Soviet. But we defended its non-party character and conciliatory functions because the main aspiration of the Military Commission was to be a non-party organ.

NOTES

1 The Petrograd Cartridge Factory was one of the larger state-owned munitions factories on the Vyborg Side (district). It was located on Tikhvinskaia Street behind the Finland Railway Station, and next to the Petrograd Metal Factory, Promet, and Phoenix. In early 1917, the Cartridge Factory employed about 8,300 workers. The demonstrations in question had indeed started on

February 23. By 4:00 in the afternoon, a group of about 8,000 workers from several nearby munitions factories broke into the factory, making sure that work was disrupted in all of its shops. The police were called in and arrested nineteen of the demonstrators, but three days later, on February 26, the police station on Tikhvinskaia Street was taken over by workers and other insurgents. By early morning on February 27, the police had virtually disappeared from the Vyborg district, and by the late morning, workers from nearby factories occupied the Cartridge Factory and seized a large amount of ammunition that had been stocked inside.

2 The reference is to Major General Aleksandr Vladimirovich Rostovshchikov (1863–1918?), who was the commander of the Petrograd Cartridge Factory from July 1915 to February 27, 1917. On February 28, the MC replaced him with Staff Captain V. D. Meshcherinov.

3 This may have been Colonel Aleksandr Stakhievich Sadovskii (1872–1920), who commanded the reserve battalion of the Finland Life Guards Regiment at that time.

4 This is a reference to Miliukov's famous "stupidity or treason" speech, delivered at the opening session of the Duma on November 1, 1916, in which the Kadet leader accused the imperial government of utter incompetence and pro-German policies. The text of the speech was distributed across the empire in hundreds of thousands of hectographed copies and had a revolutionizing effect on many among the educated public, moving ever greater numbers to oppose the old regime. The speech has often been referred to as "a storm signal of Revolution," and is considered by many to have marked the beginning of the Russian Revolution.

5 Aleksandr Dmitrievich Protopopov (1866–1918) was a notorious and ineffectual minister of internal affairs from September 1916 to February 28, 1917.

6 Pravo (in this case Law) was a well-known bookstore, warehouse, and publishing house of juridical literature, located at 28 Liteinyi Avenue, and owned by the lawyer Iakov Matveevich Gessen (1869–1942), a relative of several prominent Kadet lawyers and publishers.

7 The reference is to the Staff Captain Ivan Stepanovich Lashkevich (1891–1917) who commanded the training unit of the Volynskii Life Guards Regiment's reserve battalion from August 1916 to February 27, 1917.

8 Mikhail Konstantinovich Medvedev (1876–after July 1918) was a comptroller in the Petrograd branch of the State Bank and an ensign in the reserves. He was called to active duty in April 1916, and joined the 86th Vologodskii Reserve Detachment. In February 1917, he served under the direct command of Chikolini, whose description of this episode is consistent with the "official" version recorded in Medvedev's service record. (RGVIA, f. 408, op. 1, P/s 154–770, 1917). Following his injury, sustained at 1:30 in the afternoon on February 27, Medvedev was hospitalized at the Physiotherapeutic Institute, and on the 28th he was transferred to the Nicholas Military Hospital. After his arm was amputated, Medvedev received a one-time compensation from the Duma (1,000 rubles) as a "victim of revolution," but was not discharged from military service until July 1918. (Ibid., doc. 3; Nikolaev, *Revoliutsiia i vlast'*, 184; RGIA, f. 1278, op. 10, d. 17, l. 24, 38, 315).

9 This famous episode, variously described in many memoir accounts, took place between 2:30 and 3:00 in the afternoon, shortly after the start of the private meting of the Duma deputies in the semicircular hall. According to the meeting's minutes, Chikolini burst into the hall and asked the deputies "to hide him from the crowd and soldiers" (*Volia Rossii*, March 15, 1921, 4; Lyandres, "Zur Errichtung der revolutionaren Macht," 35, 319).

10 Here Chikolini's reporting is inaccurate and likely based on information received secondhand. In actuality, Rodzianko was joined not by Guchkov and Miliukov, who strongly objected to negotiating with the grand duke at that time, but by his deputy N.V. Nekrasov, his confidant and Octobrist deputy N.V. Savich, and the Duma Secretary I. I. Dmitriukov. They left the Tauride Palace for a meeting with the grand duke in the Mariinskii Palace between 5:30 and 6:00 that evening. Mikhail Aleksandrovich (1878–1918) was Nicholas II's younger brother and heir to the throne from 1899 to 1904 (until the birth of tsarevich Aleksei). By the time of the

February Revolution, he was inspector general of the cavalry. Various opposition groups and plotters considered him the leading candidate to assume regency for Aleksei after Nicholas's abdication.

11 Engel'gardt visited the Preobrazhenskii barracks on Millionnaia Street in the early morning hours of February 28, *after* the Duma Committee received an earlier report from the Preobrazhenskii officers pledging their support to the Duma authority. See n. 29 to the Engel'gardt interview (Chapter 3).

12 Guchkov was not formally a member of the Temporary Duma Committee because he was not a Duma deputy at the time. He was, however, closely involved with the Committee's activities. On the night of 1–2 March, the Duma Committee sent Guchkov and the nationalist deputy V. V. Shul'gin to obtain Nicholas II's abdication.

13 Kuz'ma Antonovich Gvozdev (1883–after April 1956) was a prominent Menshevik worker, chairman of the labor group of the CWIC (1915–17), and one of the organizers and leaders of the Petrograd Soviet; he later served as minister of labor in the Provisional Government during September–October 1917. Nikolai Nikolaevich Sukhanov (real name Gimmer) (1882–1940) was a prominent non-factional Social Democrat and publicist; he was a founding member of the Petrograd Soviet and initially an ardent proponent of the "dual power" arrangement with the Provisional Government. After joining the Menshevik-Internationalist group in late May 1917, he became a fierce critic of the Soviet's moderate socialist leadership and of the Provisional Government. He is the author of the seven-part *Zapiski o revoliutsii* (Notes on the Revolution), which is probably the single most influential memoir account of the February Revolution. Nik.[olai] Sukhanov, *Zapiski o revoliutsii*, 7 parts (Berlin, Petersburg and Moscow: Izdatel'stvo Z. I. Grzhebina, 1922–3). Room no. 4, officially designated as the office of the Duma president's deputies, was located next to Rodzianko's office (room no. 5).

14 Rodzianko led Chikolini from the semicircular hall to his office between 2:00 and 3:00 in the afternoon. Chikolini apparently stayed there (or in close proximity) for some time before joining the MC later that day. At that time, the MC occupied rooms 41–2, almost directly across from room no. 4. In his *Notes*, Sukhanov described how he and his Socialist colleagues, including Steklov, had worked on the proclamation announcing the formation of the Petrograd Soviet later that night in the office of the president's deputies (room no. 4), and how their work had been constantly interrupted, forcing them to move from room to room. (N. N. Sukhanov, *Zapiski o revoliutsii* (Moscow: Izdatel'stvo politicheskoi literatury, 1991), I, 1–2: 94–7).

15 Two unrelated Grineviches represented the Petrograd Soviet on the MC. The first was Konstantin Sergeevich Grinevich (real name Shekhter, 1879–after 1926), who was a prominent Petrograd Menshevik and one of the founding members and leaders of the Petrograd Soviet. He joined the MC as a representative of the Executive Committee on March 1, 1917. The second was A. G. Grinevich, a member of the Petrograd Soviet, who was sent to the MC after March 1 "for a more permanent participation" in its work. The "worker Grinevich" to whom Chikolini referred here was probably A. G. Grinevich.

16 That number was known to the MC even earlier, when the first mass of 25,000–30,000 insurgent soldiers showed up at the Duma to pledge their support, between 1:00 and 2:00 in the afternoon.

17 The reference is probably to the order requesting that imperial trains be prevented from proceeding to Tsarskoe Selo (Dno railway station was located 124 miles [200 km] south of Tsarskoe Selo) and instead rerouted directly to Petrograd, issued by first lieutenant K. F. Grekov (signed as commandant of the Nikolaevskii Station in Petrograd) in the early hours of March 1 and sent to station chiefs along the Nikolaevskii Line. It was feared that by reaching Tsarskoe Selo, the tsar might have joined with General N. I. Ivanov's troops and launched a successful military operation against the Duma forces. However, the Grekov order was issued *before* the imperial trains reached Bologoe (not Dno), just before 7:00 in the morning of March 1. The

tsar did reach Dno later that day and then turned toward Pskov. Chikolini's testimony that Grekov's order was also about arresting the tsar adds credence to the suggestion that it was actually issued in full agreement with the MC.

18 The reference is to Aleksandra Fedorovna Romanova (1872–1918), born Princess Alix of Hesse and by blood a granddaughter of Queen Victoria, the spouse of Nicholas II and the last Empress of Russia. Upon conversion to Russian Orthodoxy, she changed her name to Aleksandra Fedorovna.

19 *Versta* (singular) is a pre-revolutionary Russian unit of distance equal to 3,500 feet (0.66 mile) or 1.067 kilometers (50 versts = approx. 33 miles/53 km).

20 A reference to various food supply initiatives organized by the MC and the Petrograd Soviet on the evening of February 27 and closely coordinated with the Duma Committee. This resulted in the creation of the joint Food Supply Commission during the late evening–early night hours of February 27–8. The commission had nine members: six from the Soviet and three from the Duma. Vladimir Gustavovich Groman (1874–1932), the veteran Menshevik economist and statistician, was chairman of this joint commission, while Shingarev was the leading member on the Duma side.

21 The Admiralty was taken over by the insurgents around 4:00 in the afternoon on February 28.

22 Shul'gin was asked to negotiate with the commandant of the Fortress, general of the artillery Vladimir Nikolaevich Nikitin (1848–1922), because the general was an old personal acquaintance of his and (so it was thought) might therefore be able to negotiate a quicker and peaceful resolution of the standoff. He succeeded in persuading Nikitin to recognize the authority of the Duma Committee and to refrain from engaging in hostile actions against its forces. In the afternoon of February 28, Nikitin was replaced by a temporary commandant of the Fortress, SR officer S. D. Maslovskii, who was sent by the MC. The next day the MC appointed artillery Staff Captain F. E. Kravtsov as the permanent commandant of the Fortress, who, in turn, was replaced on June 1.

23 Aleksandr Pavlovich Balk (1866–1957) was a senior police official with the military rank of major general; he was the police and administrative chief of Petrograd from November 10, 1916 to February 27, 1917.

24 Sergei Semenovich Khabalov (1855–1924) was lieutenant general of the Russian imperial army and commander of the Petrograd military district during February 5–28, 1917. Khabalov was arrested in the afternoon of February 28 and brought to the Duma. But he escaped later that night only to be detained the next morning. On March 1, he was transferred from the Ministerial Pavilion in the Duma to the Peter and Paul Fortress as part of the first group of eleven former ministers and high-ranking officials.

25 Boris Vladimirovich Shtiurmer (1848–1917) was prime minister between January and November 1916 and concurrently minister of internal (March–July) and foreign (July–November) affairs. On March 1, 1917 he was transferred to the Peter and Paul Fortress, where he died in August in the prison hospital.

26 Pitirim [Pavel Vasil'evich Oknov] (1858–1920) was Metropolitan of Petrograd and Ladoga and Archbishop of the Holy Trinity Aleksandr Nevskii Monastery. He was appointed to this post in November 1915, reportedly on the insistence of the Empress Aleksandra Fedorovna and G. E. Rasputin. Pitirim lobbied for the appointment of B. V. Stiurmer to the post of prime minister in January 1916. Arrested on February 28, 1917 and brought to the Ministerial Pavilion of the Tauride Palace, Pitirim was released after promising to retire. A few days later he left Petrograd and went to Piatigorsk. He died in Ekaterinodar on February 21, 1920.

27 The core military leadership group of the MC included eight colonels of the General Staff (Engel'gardt, F. I. Balabin, V. L. Baranovskii, L. S. Tugan-Baranovskii, V. P. Gil'bikh, P. A. Polovtsov, G. N. Tumanov, and G. A. Iakubovich) and about a dozen lower-ranking officers (captains,

lieutenants, and ensigns) who had left their units in the first hours and days of the uprising and came to the Duma to offer their services to the MC.

28 The reference is to the handwritten note, signed by Chikolini, which is attached to the interview: "At 4:00 in the morning on March 1, a meeting took place of the members of the Military Commission, including Pal'chinskii and Chikolini. The flow chart depicting the organization of the Military Commission was sketched out. A. Chikolini." A copy of the chart is preserved in the papers of the Interview Commission in MAPP, FA. An identical chart can also be found among the papers of the Military Commission in RGIA, f. 1278, op. 10, d. 19.

29 Nikolai Evgrafovich Parshin (1879–after November 1930) was a prominent mining engineer; during 1915–17 he worked with Pal'chinskii in the CWIC in Petrograd. In the MC he was in charge of the Department of Troop Assignments. He stayed in the MC until it was dissolved in May 1917. After 1917 he worked in the Soviet mining industry administration but was subjected to constant arrests and prosecutions.

30 Grand Duke Kirill Vladimirovich (1876–1938) was Nicholas II's first cousin, rear admiral in the imperial suite and commander of the naval Guards Equipage, which he brought to the Duma on March 1 to pledge allegiance to the Duma Committee—more than 24 hours prior to his cousin's abdication.

31 Pavel Aleksandrovich (1860–1919) was the youngest son of Alexander II, general of the cavalry (1913), and inspector-general of the Cavalry Guards (since November 1916). After the February Revolution, he was discharged from military service.

32 Iakov Konstantinovich Pis'mennyi (1887–1938) was, at the time of the February Revolution, a wartime clerk of the 1st order in the First Railway Labor Battalion stationed in Petrograd. Prior to his conscription in September 1916, he worked as an assistant sworn attorney in Petrograd. On February 27, 1917, he was reportedly recruited by Kerenskii to serve as an officer on call and later as a secretary in the MC. He was discharged from military service in June. After October 1917, Pis'mennyi moved to Moscow where he held various legal and administrative positions in the Soviet defense and aircraft industry. He was arrested and executed during the Great Terror (e-mail communication from Vladimir Pis'mennyi, Iakov Konstantinovich's great grandson, to Lyandres, February 8, 2009; RGVIA, f. 16074, op. 1, d. 244, ll 2–13, 18–24).

33 We are unable to identify the meaning or the precise context of this sentence. One possibility is that either Pis'mennyi or Kantor, who knew each other before the revolution and now worked together in the MC, were asked to draft an abdication document that Rodzianko (on March 1) or the Duma delegates Guchkov and Shul'gin (on March 2) would present to the tsar. See S. P. Mel'gunov, *Martovskie dni 1917 goda* (Paris: Éditeurs réunis, 1961), 57–8.

34 Petr Berngardovich Struve (1870–1944) was a prominent Russian political thinker and economist. Together with V. A. Maklakov, he represented the leading voice of the moderate Right in the Kadet party. He was ill on February 26, 1917 and apparently did not come to the Duma until the 28th, the day he performed an undisclosed task at the request of the MC for which he was provided with an automobile. Struve did not participate in direct negotiations on the formation of the Provisional Government, but considering his extensive connections inside the broad Center/Left camp, he might have contributed to the task behind the scenes. Fedor Izmailovich Rodichev (1854–1932) was a leading Kadet figure of centrist orientation, and was a deputy to all four Dumas. He came to the Duma on February 27 and the MC often dispatched him to pacify soldiers in different units of the Petrograd garrison. During March 1–3, 1917, he served as Commissar of the Duma Committee for the office of the state secretary for the Great Principality of Finland.

35 The reference is probably to the 1st Reserve Infantry Regiment of about 12,000 men that came to the Duma in the early evening hours (but before 7:00) on February 27.

36 Aleksei Stepanovich Potapov (1872–after 1924) was a major general (1912) of the Russian imperial army. He retired from service the same year that he was promoted to major general, but was recalled to duty after the outbreak of the First World War. He served as a brigade commander in the 64th infantry division between January 1916 and January 1917 on the western front, and was assigned to the staff reserves of the Kiev military district in mid-January 1917. Potapov joined the MC on March 1, 1917 as deputy to Guchkov. He replaced Guchkov as chairman of the MC on March 4 and kept the post until April 14. A month later, he was transferred to the war ministry and became "general for [various] tasks," or special assistant under the war minister, and retired from military service in June 1917. He later served as a Soviet intelligence agent and a liaison with Chinese Communists.

37 Kronstadt, a town and fortress located on Kotlin Island in the Gulf of Finland, 19 miles (31 km) west of Petrograd, was the main base of the Russian Baltic Fleet.

5

Petr Vasil'evich Gerasimov

P ETR VASIL'EVICH GERASIMOV (1877–1919) was a leading Kadet deputy in the third and fourth Dumas from Kostroma province. He came from a family of prominent entrepreneurs (and hereditary honorary citizens), and was groomed from an early age to take over the family business. His parents sent him to a commercial school, which he duly completed, but in the upper grades he developed a strong interest in social and political questions. Following graduation in 1898, Gerasimov passed his external examinations at the Kostroma classical gymnasium and went on to study law at Moscow University. After two years, he was expelled for participating in student protests but was later able to complete his training at Yaroslavl's Demidov Juridical Lyceum. In 1903, he returned to his native Kostroma to practice law and to become a leading liberal activist, publisher, and publicist. In October 1907, he was elected to the (third) Duma, where his good writing and organizational skills were quickly put to use. He served as secretary of the Kadet faction and authored or co-authored a number of important pieces of legislation on local courts, peasants' bankruptcy protection, and on the property and family status of married women. One of his signature legislative initiatives in the next (fourth) Duma was the new and much more liberal law on the press (*zakon o pechati*), which he both helped to write and lobbied for its passage.

Like most of his Duma colleagues, Gerasimov greeted the news of the outbreak of the First World War with patriotic enthusiasm, which he promptly translated into action. He would spend most of the next two and a half years at the front, organizing medical and food supply detachments under the auspices of the All-Russian Zemstvo Union and other wartime voluntary organizations.

The February uprising caught him in the capital. By early morning on February 27 he was already in the Duma, witnessing firsthand what was transpiring in the office of the Duma President, Rodzianko's last-minute appeal to Nicholas II to grant political concessions, and some of the most important developments that led to the formation of the first revolutionary authority. That afternoon Gerasimov participated in the pivotal private meeting of the Duma deputies and, as soon as the Duma Committee was formed, readily placed himself at its service. On February 28, he was appointed the Duma Committee commissar in charge of the Petrograd city police and administration. Over the course of the next several days, he and his fellow commissars helped maintain order and discipline by touring the barracks of the rebellious units in Petrograd, Tsarskoe Selo, and the Kronstadt Naval Base. His other important assignment was to greet and deploy the revolutionary troops arriving in the capital from the nearby garrisons.

Gerasimov described his actions and impressions during the February Days in his interview with the Polievktov Commission; and he did so in an unassuming and dignified manner, without exaggerating his own role or diminishing that of his former Socialist allies now turned political rivals. Perhaps one of the more striking aspects of Gerasimov's testimony is his admission of his authorship of the minutes of the private meeting of February 27. Considered until now anonymous, the circumstances and timing of their compilation have often been called into question. Gerasimov's testimony should lay all doubts to rest and provide a more complete and accurate context of when and how this single most important source on the formation of the Duma Committee was created.

During the spring and summer months of 1917, he continued to play a leading role in the Kadet party and the Duma Committee. In early March, he replaced Miliukov as the Kadet representative on the still-functioning Duma Council of Elders. In May, he was elected to the Kadet Central Committee, and in August was nominated for the party's list of candidates to stand for elections to the Constituent Assembly. At the same time, Gerasimov kept up with his work in the Duma Committee. He chaired the important Liaison Department with the Troops, Population, and the Provinces. One of the most significant tasks of this department was to publish and distribute massive amounts of pro-war patriotic literature to the armed forces and across the country. As always, Gerasimov approached this duty with his usual energy, skill, and dedication. Yet by the end of July, after realizing that all the efforts to restore order and fighting morale in the army were failing to achieve tangible results, his patience ran out. He soon found himself among the strong supporters of a temporary military dictatorship.

Gerasimov was profoundly anti-Bolshevik. Following the October takeover, he joined the leadership of the Petrograd branch of the anti-Bolshevik All-Russian National Center and until his arrest in the summer of 1919 remained very active in the anti-Bolshevik underground. He lived under false names and was responsible for coordinating contacts between various anti-Bolshevik organizations in and around Petrograd with General N. N. Iudenich's forces in the northwest. After his arrest and initial interrogations, Gerasimov (under the alias "Grekov") was transferred to Moscow and executed by a Cheka firing squad, along with sixty-six other members of the so-called Tactical Center, on September 23, 1919.

The interview—his only known testimony—is reproduced on the basis of a master copy compiled by Rusudana Polievktova-Nikoladze and three draft transcripts: the first transcript is in an unidentified hand, with comments and stylistic edits by Tamara Nikoladze; the second is in Rusudana Polievktova-Nikoladze's hand, with abbreviated words and sentences; the final draft transcript was written by Tamara Nikoladze.

★ ★ ★ ★ ★ ★

Petr Vasil'evich Gerasimov, Deputy of the Third and Fourth State Duma, member of the Party of People's Freedom, member of the Agitation Commission of the Temporary Committee. May 9, [1917]

My contact with the Tauride Palace during the days of the coup manifested itself in that I was at the disposal of the Temporary Committee and of the Provisional Government. From the beginning of the revolution I was asked by the Temporary Committee to meet the incoming troops; I performed the responsibilities of the city police chief around the clock on the first two days. In that capacity, on the nights of February 28 and March 1, I imposed order. Later I was in charge of the liaison department to the troops, the distribution of literature, the publishing department, and the liaison department to the provinces.

I am a deputy of the third and fourth Duma from Kostroma province, and have resided in Petrograd since the time I became a deputy ten years ago. With the outbreak of the war, I went to the front and stayed there the whole time until just before the revolution, when I returned to Petrograd. I participated in the work of the Progressive Bloc. Over Christmas [1916], I was finally convinced that the reports about the mood of the opposition in the army were quite objective, and that the army had actually been revolutionized. Even common soldiers clearly understood where the danger was. The officer corps (officers, commanders of divisions, and so on)—who before that had been mostly fervent nationalists—opened their eyes. I was able to organize several open meetings in different units. The conversations showed me that everyone had a similar mindset.

The mood of the army today is completely different from what it was three months ago, before the revolution. During the three years of war before the revolution, even though there was a war-weariness and one could not detect a will to fight, there was also a feeling that people had gotten used to it. The trenches had been dug carefully and diligently, and they were getting warmer and more comfortable; the food was getting better, and so on. Today, soldiers have absolutely no desire to fight. They could not care less about annexations and contributions. They are being guided by one desire only—to be discharged as soon as possible. It is very difficult to understand such a complete change in the mood of the army and the shift in popular psychology that occurred after the revolution.

I arrived in Petersburg [*sic*!] a few days before the opening of the Duma. I could not adjust to local life right away, or immerse myself in the local mood, which was so different from the psychological mindset of a person at the front. I have many recollections about what was going on in the streets during four days, February the 23rd to the 27th.

On the 23rd, the disorders erupted. From the very first days, it was clear that, thanks to the conduct of the troops (Cossacks and dragoons), the mood was drastically different from all previous occurrences of this kind, and that the events had taken on a very different character. Two episodes can serve as an illustration of the conduct of the troops: at the corner of Fontanka Embankment and Nevskii Prospekt, the dragoons were dispersing a crowd. An officer menacingly commanded, "Crush them!" However, the smiling soldiers used their horses' heads to push not the workers in the street, but the public walking on the sidewalk. Right then, an exchange took place between the officer and a civilian lady. The officer yelled at the public, "Keep moving!" The lady shouted back, "It is easy for you to say keep moving—you're on a horse!" and a laugh erupted all around her. In this instance, the appearance of the soldiers did not cause panic at all. The [Duma] deputy Stepanov[1] and I were on Nevskii. As we approached Znamenskii Square, we learned from the crowd that a clash between the Cossacks and precinct policemen had just occurred there. The Cossacks used force to disperse the policemen. All this was quite unlike anything that had happened in similar situations before.

On the 27th, I spent my day on the streets. On the evening of the 26th, we in the Duma knew about the disorders in the 4th Company of the Pavlovskii Regiment and about the murder of Eksten,[2] the company commander. On the 27th, at eight in the morning, I was already in the Duma. There, I happened to be present at a telephone conversation between Maklakov and Pokrovskii.[3] The latter did not know anything about what was happening among the troops, and got very concerned. At 12:00, again in my presence, a very interesting conversation took place between Rodzianko and the war minister Beliaev. Judging by Rodzianko's reply, it was clear that Beliaev was asking the Duma for help. Rodzianko raised his voice and very sharply replied: "You are destroying the country by yourselves; we cannot help you."[4] With this answer, Rodzianko in part predetermined the outcome of the four-hour-long meeting of the State Duma. The Council of Elders [*senioren convent*] was in an ongoing session from 11:00 in the morning until 4:00 in the afternoon.[5] So, with the exception of the conversation with Beliaev, we were cut off from the outside world. Our only sources of information about what was happening on the streets were reports to Shingarev from the medical-sanitary station of the City Duma. But these were sporadic reports, and 50 percent of them turned out to be incorrect.

Around 11:00, I went out into the streets: soldiers were still shooting at random. I walked to Kirochnaia Street. There, the Volynskii and Preobrazhenskii Regiments were approaching the Arsenal.[6] This took place between 11:00 and 12:00. They were attempting to get into formation. From somewhere appeared a young, mounted officer. He assumed command over the soldiers. It was the same officer who was described in Lukash's brochure and was later killed near the Moskovskii [Regiment's] barracks.[7]

When I came back to the Duma, the atmosphere was dominated by a mood of impatience. The deputies demanded immediate convocation of the meeting, but the representatives of the factions were not so eager and were waiting until events played themselves out. Around 3:00, a small crowd of about 50–60 people came to the Duma: 40 workers, 30 soldiers, and 2–3 students. Those in the Duma got nervous. Rodzianko, worrying about a clash between the newcomers and the Duma guard, wanted to send the guards away. The commander of the guard, Chikolini, objected, saying that it was his duty not to let anyone into the Duma. This further increased the already widespread anxiety. Kerenskii, Chkheidze, and five or six more deputies were the first ones to go out and greet the people. Kerenskii delivered a very successful, well-constructed speech, and prevented the possibility of a clash between the crowd and the guards by asking the latter to become the first honorary guard of the Duma. Chkheidze spoke after Kerenskii. Someone unknown opened the small middle gate [*kalitka*]. When I went out to the crowd, the big gates were already open.

At 4:00, the meeting of the State Duma in the semicircular hall began.[8] It was interrupted when a frightened Chikolini suddenly burst in and exclaimed in horror that he was about to be killed. Rodzianko sent him to his office. The meeting ended with the decision to form the Temporary Committee and transfer all power to it. All factions agreed, and the Temporary Committee was formed. I was immediately assigned to the Committee, and this assignment was cleared with the factions. From that moment on, I have been considered on assignment to the Temporary Committee. Rodzianko did not invite stenographers, so there are no minutes of that historic meeting. For my own purposes, I sketched the whole meeting into my notebook, but so far I have not had time to transcribe it.[9]

On the night of the 27th, Kerenskii and Nekrasov were asked by the Temporary Committee to organize a military commission to maintain connections with the troops. On the morning of the 28th, the leadership of that commission was transferred to Engel'gardt.

The first person from the outside whom I met in the Duma was Charnolusskii.[10] On the evening of the 27th, he sneaked into the Duma with others who had been released from prison, among whom, by the way, were Gvozdev and Khrustalev-Nosar'.[11] On the night of the 27th, the Soviet of Workers' Deputies was formed. Their first document was issued on March 1st. In the beginning, they were situated in the vestibule, and later also occupied rooms. Only late in the evening and during the night of the 27th did the crowd find its way to the rooms of the Tauride Palace. However, from the moment when Charnolusskii showed up in the Duma, soldiers also appeared—at first as guards, and later as part of ever-growing crowds. On the evening of the 27th, Nikolai Dmitrievich Sokolov, who later organized the Soviet of Workers' Deputies, also arrived. On the second or the third day, Khrustalev-Nosar' disappeared somewhere from the Soviet of Workers' Deputies. In the beginning, the membership of the Soviet appeared to be random and scanty.

On the morning of the 28th, a general came to the Duma and reported that the Hotel Astoria, where he resided, had been ransacked by a mob. I was sent to the rescue at once. Somewhere in the vicinity, a police machine-gun could be heard. The mob, which consisted of some riff-raff made up of soldiers and sailors, was shooting at the windows of the Astoria, thinking that the machine-gun was firing from the roof. I went into the hotel. The lower level was completely ransacked. I was approached by second lieutenant Orel[12] and a sailor, who whispered to me, "Appoint sailors to be the guard." He was thinking that sailors are better disciplined than infantry soldiers. I did as he said, and set a guard from among the sailors. Later, I ordered that about twenty officers from the Allied armies, who happened to be staying at the Astoria, be taken to the Duma. I also transferred women and children to nearby buildings. After that, we went to search the hotel. On the lower level, we found a murdered general[13] and a wounded woman.

In the attics and basements, we didn't find anything, and thereby proved to the crowd that there were no machine-guns in the Astoria. I appointed second lieutenant Orel to be the commandant of the Astoria (he was later killed), and after giving several speeches to the crowd, I returned to the Duma. As I was approaching the Duma, I saw military cadets heading toward it.

At the Duma, in the Military Commission, I met an officer of the General Staff, Prince Tumanov, who had set up the Commission's headquarters. Two more officers of the General Staff were working with him—Tugan-Baranovskii and Iakubovich. In my subsequent work, I dealt with these three young and very energetic officers more than with anyone else. On the 28th, various military units from the immediate environs of Petrograd started to arrive. In the beginning, their intentions in coming to Petrograd were unknown, but soon it became clear that they were coming to support the Temporary Committee. I received instructions to meet the arriving troops. This kept me very busy. In addition to greeting them, I had to feed them and find accommodation. But there was nothing to feed them with, and nowhere to quarter them. We had to put them in cheap hotels near the train stations. The problem of food was especially acute. The mood of the arriving troops was panicky; they were expecting traps everywhere. They did not know where to go, and I had to take care of them. I was sending all arrivals to the Baltic Railway Station under the command of Captain Kossovich,[14] whom I had put in charge.

The following example of this panicky mood made an especially bad impression on me: I was talking to one of the arriving units, who came with the intention of defending the revolution against all sorts of perils. Just then, a gunshot was heard nearby that was answered by several others. As a result of this small, accidental shooting, all the units immediately ran away, leaving their artillery behind. What would have happened if an actual armored train had arrived and the revolutionary troops had had to engage it in battle?

Some units were not yet committed. A battery of the Artillery Guard, after long arguments with me, pretended that it was going to the Baltic Railway Station, but actually went to Beliaev in the Admiralty. But they soon left there and went to Kossovich, who arrested their commander. One of the arriving infantry regiments exhibited similar behavior. On another occasion, the Cossacks interrupted me repeatedly with hostile comments; some of their lower ranks directly harassed us, but soldiers took them away. I had to make trips particularly often to the Baltic and Tsarskoe Selo Railway Stations to meet and greet arriving troops. On the night of the 1st [March],

I was again called to the Baltic Station for this purpose. While there, I was informed that the treasury was being robbed. It was necessary to send soldiers in automobiles to defend it. Therefore, I drove to the Technological Institute to pick up trucks. There, Svatikov[15] told me in confidence that things were not going well in the Izmailovskii Regiment. Two armed companies of this regiment were taken by their officers to the Manège, and they disarmed the rest. The regimental officer-in-charge ordered the officers to lock their personal weapons in the armory.

The officers were inviting disarmed soldiers into the Manège to talk, but the soldiers hesitated, uncertain what to do. I advised them not to go, but instead to invite the officers to their barracks for discussion. Later, it turned out that, in fact, the two companies of the Izmailovskii Regiment went to the Admiralty and placed themselves under Khabalov's command. During that time, the Duma deputies were popular, and crowds in the streets would immediately start listening when they realized that a deputy was speaking. That is why, everywhere that there was ransacking, shooting, or where a police station was burning, the crowd would immediately listen to me and disperse. This is how I cleared Zagorodnyi Avenue when the crowds were awaiting the arrival of the famous armored train.

My most significant and vivid memories during the first days of the revolution come from the tense and emotional night when the final text of the declaration was worked out and the Provisional Government was formed.[16] The situation was overwhelming. Kerenskii had just received permission from the Soviet—but not the authority—to join the government. The mood brightened. Suddenly, the door flew open and a very pale but excited Skobelev walked into the room.

"So?…" Miliukov asked him. Skobelev quietly walked up and kissed him. It was the same unforgettable and uplifting mood during the night, when Guchkov and Shul'gin were sent to Pskov. (Guchkov showed up in the Duma on the 27th; Rodzianko wrote his second telegram to the tsar together with Guchkov.)[17]

About March the 2nd, quite accidentally, we succeeded in seizing the papers of Aleksandra Fedorovna.[18] In the street, a technology student arrested a suspicious couple—both of them carrying a suitcase—a gentleman in civilian clothes and a young lady. The student sent them to the Duma, to me, and I turned them over to an officer for questioning. Soon, the officer reported that the gentleman turned out to be a courier for the tsarina, and the young lady was his acquaintance. On the orders of the empress, they were on their way to the sovereign in Pskov. In one of the suitcases there were envelopes addressed to the sovereign, but the courier had not dared to open them. I immediately informed Rodzianko. He ordered that the suitcases be sent to him, and we turned the gentleman over to Papadzhanov's investigative commission.[19] The documents unquestionably pointed to a certain duplicity in the intentions of the empress. The young lady was soon released. She explained that the gentleman had visited her place in the afternoon, and that from there they left for Pskov. The Duma deputy Vershinin[20] could tell you more details about this interesting episode.

I specialized in maintaining liaison with the troops, and in dealing with the consequences of Order Number One. For two days, I was acting city police chief, and was therefore on call in the city police building [gradonachal'stvo], where every 10–15 minutes telephone reports came in with information about lootings, the burning of houses, and so on. All these reports were remarkably inaccurate. Eighty percent turned out to be false. There were very few soldiers at the disposal of the city police office, and there was no one to send when help was asked for. I had to give up this duty. Apparently, these false reports were generated either as pranks or as the work of remnants of the old authorities trying to scare us with impending anarchy. The same was happening at the State Duma. It was contacted through the Military Commission—where reports that were similarly unfavorable to the revolution were consistently coming in—that a train had come with a punitive expeditionary force; that the troops had already disembarked and were moving toward the Duma; that there was already a battle raging on Zagorodnyi Avenue; and so on. The city thrived on fantastic rumors.

There was unrest in the barracks. The officers were very nervous, and their nervousness played a big role in disorders and developing events. Soldiers insisted on their newly received civic freedoms; whereas officers, nervous and not yet fully acclimated to the revolution, viewed this insistence as rebellion. Afraid of being slaughtered for some little thing, they were constantly telephoning the Duma and calling deputies for help. At that time, the deputies had enormous influence, and with their authority, immediately tamed the most aggressive soldiers. The deputies were able to calm the sharpest conflicts between soldiers and officers without much difficulty. But this picture soon began to change dramatically: as our soldiers came under the influence of radical parties, our hold over them was quickly evaporating. In the barracks, the reason for that was becoming clear. I happened to visit the 4th Company of the Pavlovskii Regiment, where the effects of propaganda were becoming quite obvious.

While there, I was continuously followed around by a gentleman who objected to my speeches and demanded proof that I was a Duma deputy, etc. The Moskovskii Regiment very quickly escaped the influence of the Duma. It was open to all, with lithographed police leaflets of a reactionary nature and other similar literature. Already during March the 2nd and 3rd quickly penetrating, extreme maximalist propaganda was gaining ground in Oranienbaum Machine-Gun Regiment, in the 180th Reserve, and in the Finland Regiment stationed on Vasil'evskii Island.

After the agreement between the Provisional Government and the Soviet of Workers' Deputies had been reached, the barracks were visited by one representative from the Soviet and one from the Duma. Captain V[r]zhosek[21] did us a great favor. There was a lot of work to do. Everywhere we went, we had to conduct discussions for three to four hours, and it always turned out to be very constructive, even in such regiments as the Finland Regiment, which very quickly slid toward the Left. By the way, their officer corps was very poor and spoiled many things. The wave spread further, into the suburbs and different provinces (Novgorod) as well as to the northern front. We even had to send delegates there. As for myself, I did not have time to travel outside Petersburg, and went only to Porokhovye[22] and to Tsarskoe Selo.

From among the Duma deputies, the following can say interesting things about their impressions from visiting the front: Stepanov, Taskin, Lebedev (Don Region), Demidov Igor',[23] Karaulov (this one is a very effusive person, with mood swings).

The absence of the officer corps, who were hiding, was very dangerous. The relationships with soldiers were becoming very tense. The mood and atmosphere in the barracks intensified. This gave a push to the creation of the Propaganda Commission [*agitatsionnaia komissiia*], which from the very first moment had to work a lot and intensively. The Commission quickly grew and expanded, and its character gradually changed because of its activities. Newspapers and literature were needed for all those who visited us. Newspapers of all political shades were donated to us. But we had to create the literature. We got into the business of publishing. About 7,000,000 pieces of literature have been sent to the front and to the provinces, establishing ties with the country. The report about our publishing activity was printed in *Izvestiia Vremennogo Komiteta Gosudarstvennoi Dumy*.[24] Rodzianko, Shul'gin, Nekrasov,

Vershinin (Secretary), Kerenskii, and Chkheidze visited the provinces on behalf of our commission.

Besides myself, others were attached to the Temporary Committee, including Guchkov (from February 27) and G. E. L'vov, the Muscovite (from March 1). The following were also attached to the Committee, and stayed continuously in the Duma: Volkov, Vinogradov, and Lashkevich (from Kharkov),[25] through whom the Committee received all its reports. In addition to Duma deputies, a number of officials of the Duma Chancellery worked with the Committee: Iakov Vasil'evich Glinka[26] (who knows many interesting things about the revolution), Batov, and others. Ivan Ivanovich Pushchin[27]—who was the city's commandant during March the 3rd and 4th—was a specialist on Petersburg's "moods." Pepeliaev is a specialist on Kronstadt. Mansyrev,[28] and especially Bublikov,[29] have interesting information about the revolution. The last was receiving all telegrams which tracked the movement of trains. He made it impossible for troops to arrive to suppress the revolution. He was our "rescue committee."

My recollections about the arrest of ministers. Shcheglovitov was brought to the Duma on the 27th. Everyone in the [Tauride] Palace immediately ran to stare at him, but I did not go, and saw him only when he was taken to the Ministerial Pavilion. He was pale, but walked with dignity. Maklakov[30] was brought in, head bandaged, with some people who had been beaten. Beliaev was pitiful. Sukhomlinov was not brought to the room of the investigative commission (next to Rodzianko's office), but into Bobrinskii's office.[31] He looked awful. His eyes were filled with horror; he did not quite grasp what was happening around him. He was put in a chair, and at that very moment, Papadzhanov flew into the room and jumped on him, hysterically screaming, "epaulets, epaulets!" Several soldiers and others from the public ran in, following him. Papadzhanov cut the epaulets off of Sukhomlinov's coat and immediately went back out to the troops. "You see, the epaulets," he shouted. It turned out that soldiers in Catherine Hall, once they learned that Sukhomlinov had been brought in, were on the way to skewer him on their bayonets. They were stopped only after they had been promised that his epaulets would be cut off. Sukhomlinov himself cut the epaulets off of his overcoat, after asking permission to do so. He also took off his Cross of St. George and put it in his pocket. I did not see what happened next, but I was told that Sukhomlinov was taken from Bobrinskii's office to the Ministerial Pavilion with Kerenskii (who told the soldiers that they could get to Sukhomlinov only over his dead body) in front and the guards walking behind.

Kerenskii and Papadzhanov questioned the ministers who were brought in, whereas Volkov was in charge of sending them to the Peter and Paul Fortress.

NOTES

1   Vasilii Aleksandrovich Stepanov (1872–1920) was a mining engineer and a prominent Kadet deputy in the last Duma from Perm province. During the February Days he was the Duma Committee's commissar for liaison with the troops of the Petrograd, Tsarskoe Selo, and Kronstadt garrisons; on March 13 he was appointed commissar to the ministry of trade and industry and assistant to the minister. He died on his way to France from the Crimea while on a mission for General Wrangel, on August 29, 1920.

2   Aleksandr Nikolaevich Eksten (1873–1917) was a colonel in the Russian imperial army, and since January 1917 served as commander of the Pavlovskii Guards Regiment's reserve battalion. He was murdered by a group of armed demonstrators as he stepped out of the 4th Company barracks into Koniushennyi Square around 7:00 in the evening on February 26, minutes after promising his soldiers that their patrolling of the streets would be halted. Earlier that day, soldiers from the 4th Company of the Pavlovskii Regiment fired on a police force near the City Duma on Nevskii Avenue, killing one policemen and wounding another in an attempt to prevent further shooting at the demonstrators by their comrades from the Pavlovskii training detachment. This incident was the first act of open revolt by a military unit and a prelude to the larger events, which came less than 24 hours later. Both sides of the rapidly worsening conflict took notice of the event; some saw it as grave and alarming, others as hopeful and encouraging. For the most reliable scholarly account of the Pavlovskii revolt, see V. Iu. Cherniaev, "Vosstanie Pavlovskogo polka 26 fevralia 1917 g.," *Rabochii klass Rossii, ego soiuzniki i politicheskie protivniki v 1917 godu*, (Leningrad: Nauka, 1989), 152–77.

3   This important conversation between the last (since November 20, 1916) tsarist minister of foreign affairs, Nikolai Nikolaevich Pokrovskii (1865–1930) and Vasilii Alekseevich Maklakov (1869–1957)—in Shul'gin's words, "the smartest and most moderate of the [Duma] Kadets"— took place at about 10:30 on the morning of February 27. Maklakov telephoned the minister to inquire about the government's failure to fulfill its promise made the previous day. According to Maklakov, he and several of his moderate and conservative Duma colleagues (N.V. Savich, I. I. Dmitriukov, P. N. Balashev) met with the liberal ministers Pokrovskii and A.A. Rittikh, at the ministers' invitation, to find a mutually agreeable solution to the current political crisis and avert a full-scale revolution. The deputies proposed the Duma be suspended for a very short cooling-off period. This was to be announced concurrently with the collective resignation of the cabinet and the naming of a new premier "who can enjoy the confidence of the country." Maklakov specifically mentioned the name of General Alekseev. Both sides appeared to agree to the terms. Thus, when he was woken up the next morning (February 27) to speak with N.V. Nekrasov, Maklakov was unsurprised to hear of the tsarist prorogation decree, but was surprised that the rest of the plan had not been followed—the cabinet had not resigned and the new premier had not been named. Bewildered, Maklakov went to the Duma and telephoned Pokrovskii at his residence. The minister had just woken up and knew nothing about the soldiers' revolt. He told Maklakov that at least one part of their agreement (the prorogation) had been fulfilled while the rest would be addressed on March 1, after the tsar's anticipated return to Tsarskoe Selo. Outraged, Maklakov ended the conversation. See N. N. Pokrovskii, *Vospominaniia* [1922], no pagination, S. E. Kryzhanovskii Collection, box 3, Bakhmeteff Archive, Columbia University;

Maklakov, "Review of [Bernard] Pares' book [*The Fall of the Russian Monarchy: A Study of the Evidence*]," Coll. Maklakov, box 16-8, p. 14, HIA; Maklakov, "Kanun revoliutsii," *Novyi zhurnal* 14 (1946): 303.

4 This conversation indeed took place around 12:00 noon on the 27th. War minister Beliaev telephoned the Duma and proposed to Rodzianko that in the interest of the nation the Duma and the government should act together to restore order. Rodzianko was indignant at the proposition and demonstratively refused any cooperation with the government after it had prorogued the Duma.

5 Gerasimov refers to several consecutive (but separate, if overlapping) meetings of the Council of Elders (approximately from 11:00 to 12:00), as part of the private meeting of the Duma deputies (from approximately 2:30 to 4:00), and with the Duma Presidium (from approximately 4:30 to 5:00 on the same afternoon).

6 The Arsenal stood across from the Circuit Court on Liteinyi Avenue, adjacent to the Main Artillery Administration building. The insurgents captured the Arsenal and seized close to 40,000 rifles, 30,000 revolvers, and countless ammunition.

7 The reference is to I. Lukash's brochure *Preobrazhentsy* (Petrograd: Izdanie "Osvobozhdennaia Rossiia," no. 4, 1917), 10, published in Petrograd in April of 1917. Ivan Sozontovich Lukash (1892–1940) was a prolific Petrograd writer, poet, and journalist. He later emigrated and lived in Latvia, Estonia, and France. The officer in question was "a very young ensign" Nikolai Petrovich Pertik, who joined the initial group of 700 insurgents from the Volynskii and Preobrazhenskii Regiments and led them to the barracks of the Moskovskii Regiment, located on the Vyborg Side. As the rebels approached and prepared to storm the barracks, the loyal troops inside opened machine-gun and rifle fire, forcing the attackers to retreat. Pertik was not killed during the skirmish. He left the scene but resurfaced among the insurgents later that day.

8 The reference is to the private meeting of the Duma deputies that had actually started one and a half to two hours earlier, close to 2:30 in the afternoon. The first part of the meeting ended just before 4:00. After a short break, the deputies reconvened for less than an hour to elect the Temporary Committee of the Duma.

9 Gerasimov's admission of his authorship of the minutes (also known as protocol) of the private meeting is of paramount importance. Considered until now anonymous, they represent the single most important source, used by generations of historians, documenting the creation of the first Duma-based revolutionary authority. It appears that sometime in May or in the early summer of 1917, Gerasimov provided his transcript to Ia. V. Glinka who, at Rodzianko's request, was compiling the official chronicle of the Duma Committee. V. M. Vershinin, who served as the Duma Committee's secretary at the time, took a draft of Glinka's document, including the minutes, with him when he emigrated and subsequently published a shorter version of the minutes, anonymously and without any attribution, in a Russian newspaper in Prague ("Iz zametok o pervykh dniakh revoliutsii," *Volia Rossii*, March 15, 1921, 4). For additional information on the complicated history of this document, see S. Lyandres, "Protokol'naia zapis' 'chastnogo' soveshchaniia chlenov Gosudarstvennoi dumy 27 fevralia 1917 g. kak istochnik po istorii parlamentarizma v Rossii," in V. I. Startsev, ed., *Istoriia parlamentarizma v Rossii (k 90-letiiu I Gosudarstvennoi dimy). Sbornik nauchnykh statei* (St. Petersburg, 1996), II: 28, 30, 106–7; Lyandres, "On the Problem of 'Indecisiveness' among the Duma Leaders during the February Revolution: The Imperial Decree of Prorogation and Decision to Convene the Private Meeting of February 27, 1917," *The Soviet and Post-Soviet Review* 24, 1–2 (1997): 123; A. B. Nikolaev, *Revoliutsiia i vlast: IV Gosudarstvennaia duma, 27 fevralia–3 marta 1917 goda* (St. Petersburg: RGPU, 2005)," 73–84.

10 Vladimir Ivanovich Charnolusskii (1865–1941) was a well-known Popular Socialist and educator. He was among the first to bring a group of insurgent soldiers to the Tauride Palace on the morning of February 27 and on his arrival joined with the Kerenskii group (the future MC)

to organize insurgent soldiers. He continued to work with the MC throughout the February Days. Under the Provisional Government, he was one of the founders and leaders of the State Committee for Education; he later worked in the People's Commissariat of Enlightenment and various Soviet educational institutions.

11 Georgii Stepanovich Khrustalev-Nosar' (real name: Petr Alekseevich Khrustalev) (1877–1918) was a lawyer by training and a veteran labor and political activist. In October 1905 he was elected chairman of the first St. Petersburg Soviet and subsequently joined the Social Democrats. He was arrested at the end of 1905, tried, and exiled to Siberia, but in 1907 was able to escape to Europe. An ardent patriot, he returned to Russia after the outbreak of the First World War but was again arrested and imprisoned. He was released by the insurgents only on February 27, 1917, together with K. A. Gvozdev and other members of the workers' group of the WIC. Following his release from the Kresty prison and accompanied by a group of insurgent soldiers, Khrustalev came to the Duma between 3 and 4 in the afternoon on February 27 and proceeded to organize the Petrograd Soviet. His leading role in creating argu-ably the most important revolutionary institution was later deliberately minimized by his political rivals, mostly from the Petrograd Socialist establishment. His last appearance in the Soviet was recorded on March 3. Later that year he resurfaced in his native Pereiaslav (not far from Kiev) as a vocal critic of his former socialist colleagues, especially the Bolsheviks. He supported Hetman P. P. Skoropadskii and for a short while organized his own tiny auton-omous "Khrustalev republic" in 1918. Following the Bolshevik takeover, he was arrested and shot as a counterrevolutionary and profiteer.

12 Aleksandr Fedorovich Orel (1879–1917) was a first lieutenant in the Chechen Cavalry Regiment. He was discharged from the military for health reasons in March 1908 but was recalled to service in January 1916 and assigned as staff officer to his old regiment. On the morning of February 28, 1917, he came to the Duma to offer his services as "officer-citizen." He received a detachment of revolutionary troops (sailors and military cadets) with an assign-ment to capture Hotel Astoria, which was used by the military authorities to quarter officers on leave, their families, and the Allied military personnel. He was killed near the hotel around 2:00 that afternoon either by the officers who defended the hotel against the looters or by the drunken mob that broke into its famous wine cellars. Shortly after the incident, the insurgents captured the Astoria and at 2:45, Engel'gardt appointed Colonel V. A. Iurkevich as the hotel's new commandant.

13 Reportedly, the same general fired on the insurgents' representatives from one of the windows as they approached the Astoria and demanded that the Russian officers living in the hotel sur-render. According to some reports, the general's body was thrown into the Moika River. Stinton Jones, *Russia in Revolution, Being the Experiences of an Englishman in Petrograd during the Upheaval* (London, 1917), 164.

14 Kossovich (sometimes referred to as Kosovich) was apparently a lieutenant colonel in the so-called Special Brigade. He came to the MC on February 28 and before noon was assigned to Gerasimov and his Kadet colleague Stepanov to meet the troops arriving in Petrograd from the direction of Oranienbaum. On March 1, he was appointed commander of the troops in the districts surrounding the Baltic and Warsaw Railway Stations.

15 Sergei Grigor'evich Svatikov (1880–1942) was a well-known Socialist activist (at one time a Social Democrat) and an expert on the history of the Russian revolutionary movement. During February 27–8, 1917, he was the commissar of the Duma Committee and the Petrograd Soviet for the Technological Institute and the surrounding area, where many military schools and regimental barracks, including Izmailovskii, were located. On March 1, he was appointed deputy to the first public city police and administration chief (Iurevich).

16 Gerasimov refers to the night of March 1–2, when the basic agreement on the formation of the Provisional Government was reached between representatives of the Duma Committee

(principally Miliukov) and the Soviet Executive Committee (represented by Sokolov, Steklov, Sukhanov, and Chkheidze). Then on the morning of March 2, the negotiations broke off but were soon reconvened to finalize the text of the Provisional Government's declaration by early afternoon. It was published the next day. Kerenskii secured the Soviet's permission to join the cabinet retroactively, after he had already committed himself to the justice portfolio. For the circumstances of Kerenskii's dramatic appeal to his Socialist colleagues on the afternoon of March 2, see the interview with M. I. Skobelev in this volume.

17 Rodzianko wrote his so-called second telegram to the tsar between 11:00 and 12:00 noon on February 27 (the first telegram had been sent the previous evening but had received no reply) and sent it to General Headquarters at 12:40 p.m. Guchkov helped Rodzianko to compose the telegram, in which the Duma President reported about the soldiers' revolt, deplored the prorogation decree, and asked that the Duma be reconvened and a new cabinet named that could be trusted by the population as a whole (*Krasnyi arkhiv* 21, 2 (1927): 6–7; *Fevral'skaia revoliutsiia. 1917. Sbornik dokumentov i materialov* (Moscow: RGGU, 1996), 110–11).

18 That is, the spouse of Nicholas II and the last Empress of Russia.

19 The reference is probably to the so-called Higher Investigative Commission (HIC), organized in the early evening of February 27 in room 34 of the Tauride Palace by a group of intelligentsia volunteers led by A. F. Kerenskii, in order to receive and register the detained high-ranking officials of the old regime who were being brought into the Duma by the insurgents. Later that day, the Duma Committee appointed the Kadet deputy Mikhail Ivanovich Papadzhanov (1869–1930) as the HIC's first chairman (February 27–March 3). The detainees were kept in rooms 35, 35a, and 36. However, the most notorious and highest-ranking officials were transferred to the so-called Ministerial Pavilion, the spacious chambers meant to accommodate ministers and other state officials during their appearances before the Duma. The Pavilion was not used by the Duma deputies or staff, and was considered outside of the Duma's jurisdiction. The HIC was dissolved on March 30, its records were incorporated, and the remaining detainees were transferred to the Provisional Government's Extraordinary Investigative Commission under the Social Democratic lawyer N. K. Murav'ev. During its short existence, the HIC processed some 600 detainees.

20 Vasilii Mikhailovich Vershinin (1874–1946) was a leading Labor Group deputy to the last Duma from Tomsk province. During the first days of the February Days he was effectively in charge of keeping the Duma Committee records and distributing assignments. On March 7, he was appointed commissar of the Duma Committee to accompany the former tsar on his way from General Headquarters to Tsarskoe Selo. Vershinin emigrated after October 1917, and lived in Berlin and Prague.

21 This may have been Sergei Karlovich Vrzhosek (1867–1957), a graduate of the Military-Juridical Academy in Petersburg and a prominent defense lawyer. He was also a well-known Petersburg Social Democrat and later a member of the Labor Group. During the First World War he was mobilized with an officer's rank. On February 27, 1917 he came to the Tauride Palace and joined the MC. He subsequently helped organize and then chaired the executive committee of the Petrograd Soviet of Officers' Deputies.

22 Porokhovye District, located approximately 3 km (2 miles) outside the city limits northeast of Bol'shaia Okhta District, was the home of two large Okhta gunpowder plants (*Okhtenskie porokhovye zavody*). Both factories were taken over by their workers on February 28, 1917, who also organized and controlled the local soviet.

23 Sergei Afanas'evich Taskin (1876–1952) was Kadet Duma deputy from the Baikal region. During the February Revolution he performed various tasks assigned to him by the Duma Committee and its MC. Iurii Mikhailovich Lebedev (1874–?) was a Kadet deputy to the last Duma from the Don Region. On March 2, 1917 he was commandeered by the Duma Committee to Luga to ensure the resumption of regular railroad operation; on April 21 he was

sent as the Duma Committee commissar to the 6th Army on the Romanian front. Igor' Platonovich Demidov (1873–1946) was another Kadet deputy to the fourth Duma from Tambov province. In the fall of 1914, he organized one of the first frontline sanitary detachments that operated on the southwestern front; during the February Days he performed many different tasks assigned to him by the Duma Committee, including visits to Tsarskoe Selo and to units of the Petrograd garrison and the Kronstadt naval base, primarily to restore the authority of the officer corps. On March 15, 1917, he was appointed commissar of the Duma Committee and of the Provisional Government to the southwestern front, which he toured until April 21.

24 This report was published in the first issue of the official publication of the Duma Committee, *Izvestiia Vremennogo Komiteta Gosudarstvennoi dumy* (*IVKGD*), on April 27, 1917 (p. 3). Only 13 issues of *IVKGD* were published, all between April 27 and August 28, 1917.

25 Nikolai Konstantinovich Volkov (1875–1950) was a Kadet deputy to the fourth Duma from Baikal Region. On February 28, 1917 he was sent by the Duma Committee as commissar to the ministry of agriculture and then, together with M. I. Skobelev, to the Peter and Paul Fortress. He served as assistant minister of agriculture under A. I. Shingarev in the first Provisional Government. He later emigrated and lived in Paris. Vladimir Aleksandrovich Vinogradov (1874–after 1923) was a Kadet deputy to the fourth Duma from Astrakhan' province. On February 28, 1917, he was sent as commissar by the Duma Committee to the ministry of finance, and after March 3 served as assistant minister of transport (under Nekrasov). Valerian Valeriianovich Lashkevich (1876–after 1920) was yet another Kadet deputy to the fourth Duma from Khar'kov province; during the February Days he participated in the work of the MC. At the end of March he was sent by the Duma Committee and the Provisional Government as commissar to the Donetsk Coal Mining Basin.

26 Iakov Vasil'evich Glinka (1870–1950) was a longtime aide and confidant of the Duma President Rodzianko and a senior staffer in the Duma Chancellery throughout its existence (1906–17). On March 2, 1917 Rodzianko appointed him manager of affairs of the Duma Committee Chancellery. On Rodzianko's recommendation, he was also appointed senator by the Provisional Government on April 29, 1917. In March 1917, Rodzianko asked Glinka to compile a detailed chronicle known as the "Protocol of Events," documenting the activities of the Duma Committee from its inception on February 27 through March 4, 1917 (an incomplete version of the Protocol was published in *Fevral'skaia revoliutsiia 1917 goda: sbornik dokumentov i materialov* (Moscow: RGGU, 1996), 109–45). His work on the Protocol, which is considered one of the most valuable sources on the Duma Committee, was well known to his Duma colleagues at the time. Glinka also kept an informative diary about his service in the Duma and later wrote memoirs on his participation in the February Revolution. Both documents were unknown until Petersburg historian B. M. Witenberg discovered and published them, just recently (Ia. V. Glinka, *Odinnadtsat' let v Gosudarstvennoi dume, 1906–1917: dnevnik i vospominaniia* [Moscow: NLO, 2001]).

27 Ivan Ivanovich Batov (1875–) was a senior staffer (since 1911) in the Duma Chancellery; on March 3, 1917 he became senior staffer of the Duma Committee chancellery; on June 14 he was appointed assistant man-ager of affairs (de facto manager of affairs) of the Duma Committee. Lavrentii Ivanovich Pushchin (1874–1929) was a Progressive Nationalist deputy to the fourth Duma from Orlov province and a member of the Progressive Bloc's Bureau (since November 1915). During the February Days he was deputy commandant and (since March 4) commandant of the Tauride Palace and the surrounding district; during March 7–18 he was temporary commissar of Petrograd and of the Tauride Palace.

28 Prince Serafim Petrovich Mansyrev (1866–1928) was a Kadet and then a Progressist (since August 1915) deputy to the fourth Duma from Riga. He came to the Duma on the first day

of the February Days, participated in the private meeting of the deputies, and helped establish Duma-based revolutionary authority. On March 1 he was appointed commissar of the Duma Committee to the units of the Petrograd garrison; on March 19 he was sent by the Duma Committee to the western front, and on 6 April to the Romanian front. After the Bolshevik takeover, he lived in Latvia and Estonia.

29 Aleksandr Aleksandrovich Bublikov (1875–1941) was a prominent railway engineer and a Progressist deputy to the fourth Duma from Perm Province. From 1914 to 1917, he was deputy chairman of the Central WIC; from February 28 to March 2, 1917, he was the Duma Committee's commissar to the ministry of transportation.

30 Nikolai Alekseevich Maklakov (1871–1918) was a notoriously conservative minister of internal affairs from February 1913 to July 1915, and a younger brother of the prominent Kadet Duma deputy Vasilii Maklakov.

31 Count Vladimir Alekseevich Bobrinskii (1867–1927) was a leading Progressive Nationalist deputy to the last Duma from Tula province and a member of the Bureau of the Progressive Bloc. He also served as assistant Duma President (beginning on November 5, 1916) but resigned this position shortly before the February Days for medical reasons and left Petrograd. He returned only after March 20, 1917, but because the Duma had been prorogued and his replacement was not chosen, Gerasimov continued to refer to room no. 4 (next to the Duma President's) as Bobrinskii's office.

6

Mikhail Vladimirovich Rodzianko

MIKHAIL VLADIMIROVICH RODZIANKO (1859–1924) was a wealthy land-owner from the southern Ekaterinoslav province, one of the founders of the moderately conservative Octobrist party, and the President of the last two imperial Dumas. First elected to the (third) Duma in 1907, he became President of the lower chamber in March 1911 and continued to serve in this role during the fourth Duma from 1912 to 1917. By the time the Provisional Government dissolved both chambers of the national legislative assembly on October 6, 1917, Rodzianko had become the Duma's longest-serving and arguably most influential leader.

Castigated and at times mocked by former colleagues and rivals for his explosive temperament, empty rhetoric, and supposedly limited vision, Rodzianko in fact proved to be a very able politician. It was Rodzianko who steered the battered Duma ship for six long years, having been reelected annually to his post by large majorities of deputies, and for the most part he successfully navigated the lower chamber through the stormiest of times and amidst the vicissitudes of court, government, oppositionist, and later revolutionary politics. Hardly a committed monarchist—despite his relentless post-1917 efforts to prove the opposite[a]—his main political motivation was to advance the standing and expand the powers of the legislative institution over which he presided. During 1915–17, he greatly increased his national visibility by helping organize such important wartime organizations as the Special Council on Defense and the Duma Progressive Bloc. He also closely cooperated with the leaders of the Zemstvo and Towns Unions and the national nobility organizations. Moreover, by late 1915 he positioned himself as the chief liaison between the country's opposition and the "obstinate monarch," from whom

[a] See "Dopros M. V. Rodzianko, September 4, 1917," *Padenie tsarskogo rezhima. Stenograficheskie otchety doprosov i pokazanii, dannykh v 1917 g. Chrezvychainoi Sledstvennoi Komissii Vremennogo Pravitel'stva*, ed. P. E. Shchegolev, VII (Moscow and Leningrad: Gosizdat, 1927): 116–75; M. V. Rodzianko, *Gosudarstvennaia Duma i fevral'skaia 1917 g. revoliutsiia* (Rostov na Donu, 1919); Rodzianko, "Iz vospominanii," *Byloe* 21 (1923); "Krushenie imperii (Zapiski predsedatelia Russkoi Gosudarstvennoi Dumy)," *Arkhiv russkoi revoliutsii*, 27 (Berlin, 1926); A. B. Nikolaev, "M.V. Rodzianko," *Gosudarstvennaia Duma i fevral'skaia 1917 g. revoliutsiia* (Rostov na Donu, 1919), 525–6.

he had constantly sought to wring political concessions which would allow for greater public participation in the administration of the country. His last-minute negotiations with representatives of the old regime for a peaceful transition of government authority to the Duma, on February 25–7, 1917, unmistakably point to where his political priorities had been and real loyalties lay.

During the February Revolution, he chaired the Duma Committee in whose name he assumed temporary government authority, conducted negotiations with military leaders, demanded (and received) Nicholas's abdication, convinced Grand Duke Mikhail Aleksandrovich to renounce the throne, and sanctioned the formation of the Provisional Government. That his vision for establishing a more permanent Duma-based authority failed to materialize should not be viewed as solely Rodzianko's political failure. It was an epochal failure of the forces of political moderation as they succumbed to the overwhelming pressures of the war and were swept away by a hurricane of popular rebellion that in the end produced no winners, only losers.

In the months following the February Revolution, Rodzianko tried without much success to reconvene the Duma, prorogued by tsarist degree since February 27, but had to be content with chairing private meetings of its members and presiding over the increasingly superfluous Duma Committee. After the Bolshevik takeover, he went to the Don region, participated in the White movement, and again tried to reconvene the Duma (which he hoped would boost the legitimacy of the White cause), all to no avail. He left Russia in 1920 and settled in Serbia, disillusioned, ostracized, and with no financial means. Rodzianko spent the rest of his days answering his critics and defending his record as the Duma President and the tsar's loyal servant.

One of the most striking aspects of his May 16, 1917 interview, though only the first of two planned sessions ever took place, is that it was recorded at a time when participation in the revolution was still considered an asset and *before* Rodzianko discovered the need to defend himself against accusations that he betrayed his sovereign and supported the February uprising. Less guarded, he thus acknowledged his preference for removing Nicholas II by means of a palace coup, an admission never repeated in subsequent testimonies.

The interview below is reproduced on the basis of a master copy, originally compiled by Viktor Pavlov and subsequently copied by Rusudana Polievktova-Nikoladze, and compared against three draft transcripts written by Tamara Nikoladze, Rusudana Polievktova-Nikoladze, and M. A. Polievktov.

★ ★ ★ ★ ★ ★

The President of IV State Duma, Mikhail Vladimirovich Rodzianko. May 16, 1917

The Duma had long been apprehensive that a revolution would take place during the war, and not without reason. Everything that happened just confirmed this premonition. I lived through the Revolution of 1905; I understood what revolution is all about. Given the tsar's obstinacy, I could not envision the salvation of Russia without a coup. For me personally, revolution seemed to be a great impediment. I do not believe the Leninists— the German money undoubtedly plays a role.[1]

Our work focused on criticizing the government with the purpose of establishing a responsible ministry. This thread ran all through our activity. We considered a revolution dangerous not because we were apprehensive about revolution itself, but because we knew the danger posed by the process of structural change during a war, when blood is being shed. I myself am an adherent of democracy, not some kind of Black Hundred reactionary.[2]

A political coup was the only way out. For a palace coup to be successful, one has to have firm and courageous people, and not the kind of slush which the tsarist family represents.[3] With the murder of Rasputin,[4] we saw what can be achieved through a palace coup, but because of spinelessness, it did not succeed. This is my personal view. Others had different points of view, and different plans. They thought that a palace coup was possible, and the only reason it did not succeed was because of wishy-washiness. They did not take into account that a coup can be successful only when it has real force behind it. Troops should have been behind it, but were not. They should have started by organizing a military force that would have supported a coup. The Petrograd Garrison was unfit for this purpose. This is not a regular army unit. These were primitive peasants. They were politically illiterate, and were only interested in land. In my political work, I used the army as leverage to extract a responsible ministry at any cost, which would have had the temporary effect of bromine. But from among the front commanders, I could only rely on one. Others did not understand that their support was essential for the sake of the country. All officers and corps-level commanders understood this, but the commanders at the highest level did not—therefore, I did not succeed.

Events were moving very quickly. Russian industry was working very hard and patriotically, producing artillery shells and munitions which would have been sufficient for four months of intense combat. The ruinous state of food and coal transport was stopping everything. Since I had my own sources of information, I was well informed. I knew everything that was happening among the popular masses. I therefore knew that if a movement was to break out, it would not be inconsequential. When the disturbances in the streets began, I understood that they were not the result of hunger— nobody was dying from hunger, and there were no perceptible shortages of food. In general, I was not inclined to exaggerate things in order to intimidate. I did not see colossal disruptions in food consumption. When people were saying that there were food riots, I did not believe it. My colleagues and I helped organize small food cooperatives in all state enterprises. I knew that what was going on was not hunger, and that the shortage of food was only a pretext.

Since February 7, Prince Golitsyn,[5] the Chairman of the Council of Ministers, had two prepared and signed copies of the decree suspending the Duma. He was even showing it to acquaintances. This was a very unwise decision on the part of the emperor. I always thought that Golitsyn was an idiot, but please do not write that down, write "a limited person." I had known him for a long time. He is even my distant relative, but I was very surprised when he was appointed to such a post.[6] The tsarist decree existed in two variants: complete dissolution, or prorogation. Golitsyn threatened me with the dissolution of the Duma if we did not stop criticizing the government: "The Duma is stirring the country up."

My response was: "The war is a people's war, the Duma is the people's Duma. It cannot stop its interest in the war. By dissolving the Duma, you would damage the war effort and insult the troops. It is not the Duma which is stirring the country up." Indeed, we were following the mood of the country, and consciously so. We were holding off the spread of the waves from the Left, and attempting to localize the revolutionary wave inside the Duma—by doing this, we were restraining revolution, otherwise it would have happened long before. The Duma was a ram which was used cautiously. We succeeded in certain things. After all, the Duma was taken seriously. No one expected such vigor from the fourth Duma. But I must tell you that from the beginning of the war, even Rightist elements (Purishkevich[7]) turned out to be true citizens. There was no element of the Black Hundreds in the mood of the Duma, except for Markov II.[8] A hunchback can only be cured by the grave.

The prorogation decree was issued as the result of Golitsyn's lack of prudence. The tsar should not have given the decree to Golitsyn when he left for General Headquarters. When the first signs of the movement became apparent, I went to Golitsyn and declared: "What are you doing?! I'm going to arrest you." This was on the 24th or the 25th [February], after I visited the factories which were on strike. When I heard that the disturbances had begun, I drove to the factory districts, and realized that the situation was serious. I went to pick up Rittikh[9] (about 9:00 in the morning); near Troitskii Bridge, I saw disturbances on the embankment. After collecting Rittikh,

I went to the war minister [Beliaev] and Golitsyn. I said to them: "What is the necessity of concentrating everything in your hands? Delegate the problem of food to the city. Revolution has begun."

Golitsyn objected, "What can we do?"

I said, "You and your entire government should go to General Headquarters."

"How can we, when the sovereign is there?"

I replied, "The direct wire is in your hands."[10]

I am convinced that, had a responsible ministry been granted on the 25th and Aleksandra Fedorovna sent to Livadia,[11] the movement would have been stopped and revolution could have been avoided. The popular masses—and everyone agrees with this—were not inclined to excesses. This was the life-saver. Everything could have succeeded if vigorous, legal, and responsible measures had been quickly introduced. Prince Golitsyn, given his stupidity, did not listen. He arranged for a meeting to deal with the food question, and on the night of the 26th (at 10:00),[12] sent the prorogation decree.

I consider Rittikh to be one of the most decent people. He was sincere in his passion for Russia. I have known him since the time of the third State Duma, when he was Chairman of the Land Committee. He is a sincere, honest, and good man, but he was underappreciated.

When I received the decree, I realized that everything was lost, and sent out my first telegram to the tsar.[13] General Beliaev did not want to accept the telegram. He refused to send it because he objected to the following phrases: "State authority is paralyzed" and "on the head of the sovereign." The situation was so serious that I could not change a single word, so I ventured out into the midst of the stormy sea to go to the post office myself. Pokhvisnev[14] sent the telegram via direct wire. The second telegram,[15] which was more blunt, went out the next day. The tsar did not listen, even then.

After everything happened, I was asked (both in the Duma and by the crowds), "Tell us, did the tsar reply to the telegrams?" My situation was a difficult one—the tsar was still the reigning monarch. At the same time, no one is as sensitive as children and crowds. I always talk to the crowds as if I am talking to children. You cannot be insincere with them. And so I replied, "No."

Then people shouted, "Rodzianko, free us from the Romanovs!" The crowd consisted of townspeople—those who are now called the petty bourgeoisie—civil servants, and ladies who were bringing me flowers. At that time, I had to deliver numerous speeches. These days, it seems that I will no longer be greeted with flowers.

On the 26th everything became clear to me. As the President of the Duma, the country's focal point, I was well informed on all events and clearly realized all the positives and negatives. I had a complete picture before my eyes. I had a good idea that a profound revolution would occur, and chaos would follow. This is why I decided against assuming power. I could not abandon the Duma. It could become useful again. We do not know what will happen now. The Provisional Government and the coalition cabinet are in terrible shape, especially the socialist ministers. They took unilateral responsibilities upon themselves, and are now facing the collapse of industry. But anyway, they are well-intentioned people.

On the 26th, before the prorogation, Grand Duke Mikhail Aleksandrovich called me from Gatchina and expressed a desire to see me. Obviously, I could not leave Petrograd. I replied, "With pleasure, because you are the only person who can save the situation, and you only have until tonight." Revolution is a dangerous business. We tried, somehow, to hold on until the spring, until the spring offensive—to crush the Germans. After that, we could revolutionize as much as we wanted, and get all the freedoms. From the perspective of the Russian state, I am correct. Liberty would not have escaped us in any case, because it was impossible to continue living like we were. Revolution was inevitable. I told the grand duke, "Come while it is still possible." We decided to meet in the Mariinskii Palace. I declared that I would not speak with him alone, but only in the presence of witnesses. The meeting took place. We told him everything: "You must get in touch with your brother via direct wire, and tell him that he is falling into the abyss—unless, tomorrow, Aleksandra Fedorovna is expelled to Livadia, and he allows an announcement in the Duma that a responsible government is to be promulgated."

Golitsyn, who was present at this meeting (on the 26th between 5 and 7:30), did not utter a word about prorogation even though the decree had already been typeset. I received a printed copy at 11:00. Mikhail Aleksandrovich might have been changed by his wife's[16] influence, but I consider him one of the noblest, most honest, and incorruptible people in the world. He is just an unusually shy person (the only one in the current Romanov family); he inherited this trait from Alexander III.[17] He has a uniquely pure soul. He is smart and absolutely clear-headed, and the typical

Romanov haughtiness is completely absent in him. He immediately grasped the situation, and at once declared his consent to all of our demands—that if disorders continued the next day, he would agree to assume the regency at the request of the Duma (how devious of Golitsyn, who was there!).

The grand duke said, "I consent. I will either perish or be killed, but I will help you." Nekrasov, Dmitriukov,[18] and Savich[19] were present. Golitsyn was there as well, and kept silent the whole time. When everything had been said, the grand duke went to the direct wire at the war ministry and spoke with the tsar. The answer...well, you can see for yourself what kind of answer it was—indecisive. However, it was clear nonetheless that the tsar took everything to heart, because he immediately asked for a train and left General Headquarters in the direction of Petrograd. But on the 27th, after we took over the leadership of the movement, we did not allow him to proceed, and stopped him in Bologoe.[20]

The tsar should simply have appointed Mikhail as regent, and trusted him to settle everything with the Duma or give him dictatorial powers, at the least. Had there not been the stupid decree of prorogation! It was unthinkable for me to open the Duma on the 27th, because the army's attitude was still unknown. To assemble the Duma in order to read out the decree of prorogation would have resulted in the proclamation of a Constituent Assembly. I did not have the right to assemble the Duma after the prorogation decree.

The correlation of forces was unclear. We knew that the troops did not shoot at the people, but that was not enough, and we did not know which side they would take. I could not risk the Duma. If I were to do so, the Duma would have been swept away. It would not have remained a reserve force which could assemble at a moment of need, and do what was required—as it had done. The State Duma, even though it was the June 3rd Duma, is the only lawful representative body. I am sure that the revolutionary element would have swept everything away, perhaps with the benevolent participation of the government, for which "the rebellious bourgeoisie" was less threatening than the social democrats and other radical elements. Such was the situation on the morning of the 27th. I could not risk the Duma, the country, or the army. The revolution was not organized.

The journal of the Duma[21] was very meticulously put together. It can be obtained at the office. Glinka—an official in the [Duma] Chancellery.

Recorded by T. V. Krupskaia, T. N. Nikoladze, V. I. Pavlov, and R. N. Polievktova, from the words of M. V. Rodzianko on May 16, 1917. A compilation of the four transcripts, as well as the master version, was completed by V. I. Pavlov. The interview should have continued. Rodzianko set a meeting with us for the morning of May 19. However, when we got together, he excused himself, saying: "I have an urgent meeting right now; things are not going well with the socialist ministers. Konovalov[22] is about to arrive for consultation." In the evening, the papers reported on Konovalov's resignation. We agreed to meet again on Tuesday the 23rd. But on that day, M. V. Rodzianko once again could not receive us, because he had to go somewhere. M. Polievktov.

NOTES

1 Rodzianko's comment reflects a widespread contemporary belief in a German hand behind Russia's military and political ills that predates the accusations of German-Bolshevik conspiracy put forward by the Provisional Government in July 1917. During the war years, Rodzianko readily adopted the notion that "Rasputin and his clique" acted on orders from Berlin (see, for example, his deposition in *Padenie tsarskogo rezhima*, VII: 128–9), whereas Lenin's controversial return to Russia in April 1917, traveling in a "sealed train" across German territory, gave him grounds to suspect collusion between the two sides. However, it is quite unlikely that, at the time of this interview, Rodzianko was privy to any specific information. The first documentary evidence concerning financial ties between German agents in Scandinavia and some of Lenin's close associates in Russia and abroad did not emerge until June 1917 and were not publicized until early July. Although the Provisional Government failed to prove the German-Bolshevik connection in the so-called July case, documents of the German Foreign Ministry captured by the Allies after the end of the Second World War showed that by December 1917, the total amount spent by Germany for propaganda in Russia reached the staggering number of 30 million marks. How much of that amount had actually reached the Bolshevik coffers and by which specific channels remains obscure. For the most recent estimates and analysis of the charges, see S. S. Popova, *Mezhdu dvumia perevorotami. Dokumental'nye svidetel'stva o sobytiiakh leta 1917 goda v Petrograde (po frantsuzskim i rossiiskim arkhivnym istochnikam)* (Moscow: Ladomir, 2010); S. M. Lyandres, "Novye dokumenty o finansovykh subsidiiakh bol'shevikam v 1917 godu," *Otechestvennaia istoriia* 2 (1993): 128–43; Lyandres, *The Bolsheviks' "German Gold" Revisited: An Inquiry into the 1917 Accusations* (Pittsburg: The Carl Beck Series in Russian and E. European Studies, 1995); David S. Foglesong, "Foreign Intervention," in Edward Acton et al., eds., *Critical Companion to the Russian Revolution, 1914–1921* (Bloomington and Indianapolis: Indiana University Press, 1997), 107–8, 113–14.

2 Here "anti-revolutionary, right-wing." The Black Hundreds, or *chernosotentsy*, were extremist right-wing, nationalistic, and anti-Semitic paramilitary groups formed during and after the 1905 Revolution.

3 For Rodzianko, who in all his subsequent testimonies claimed to have been the sovereign's faithful servant and a committed monarchist, to describe the imperial family as "slush" was both astonishing and unprecedented. Not only does this betray his deep frustration with some of the tsar's close relatives (including Nicholas's brother-in-law Aleksandr Mikhailovich and uncle Pavel Aleksandrovich), whom Rodzianko repeatedly urged to persuade the emperor to introduce constitutional changes, it also suggests his willingness to support a palace coup. Yet Rodzianko's strongest indignation was probably reserved for Grand Duke Mikhail Aleksandrovich for refus-

ing, without his reigning brother's explicit consent, to become a temporary dictator and rule over the country in agreement with the Duma, as was insisted on by the ambitious Duma President on February 27, 1917.

4 Grigorii Efimovich Rasputin (Novykh) (1869–1916), whose influence over Aleksandra Fedorovna and the tsar was believed to have made him a threat to the empire and the ruling dynasty, was murdered on the night of December 16–17, 1916 by a group of conspirators led by Prince Feliks Feliksovich Iusupov, Grand Duke Dmitrii Pavlovich, and the right-wing Duma politician V. M. Purishkevich.

5 Prince Nikolai Dmitrievich Golitsyn (1850–1925) was an appointed member of the State Council and the last tsarist prime minister (December 27, 1916–February 27, 1917). He was arrested on February 28 and brought to the Ministerial Pavilion; on March 4, he was transferred to the Peter and Paul Fortress but was released after nine days. He remained in Russia after October 1917 and worked as a shoemaker in Moscow and Rybinsk until his arrest and execution by the Soviet secret police on July 2, 1925.

6 Golitsyn and Rodzianko were related by way of the Duma President's marriage to the prime minister's distant relative Anna Nikolaevna (née Golitsyna) and via Rodzianko's second cousin, who happened to be the prime minister's wife.

7 Vladimir Mitrofanovich Purishkevich (1870–1920) was a notorious right-wing nationalist deputy to the second and third (from Bessarabia province), and fourth (from Kursk province) Dumas, and one of the founders and leaders of the reactionary Union of the Russian People and Union of Archangel Michael. However, from 1915 to 1917 he basically supported the Progressive Bloc's criticism of the government's conduct of the war. In 1916, he played a leading role in the conspiracy to assassinate Rasputin, whom he blamed for the regime's rapidly declining prestige and for discrediting the monarchy in the eyes of the general population. Remarkably, he was not arrested during the February Days and was among the very few known figures on the Right who did not disappear from the political scene in 1917.

8 Nikolai Evgen'evich Markov (1866–1945) was another Rightist deputy to the last two Dumas from Kursk province. During the war years, he remained a vocal opponent of the Progressive Bloc in the Duma, supported the government's policies for the most part, and tried to unite the most reactionary pro-monarchy organizations into an anti-Progressive Bloc.

9 Aleksandr Aleksandrovich Rittikh (1868–1930) was a very able and reform-minded tsarist bureaucrat and a specialist on land and peasant questions. He served as the last tsarist minister of agriculture (starting on November 16, 1916), and was chairman of the Special Council on Food Supply.

10 Rodzianko's rendition of this episode in his September 4, 1917 deposition to the Provisional Government Extraordinary Investigative Commission appears to have been much less forthcoming. See *Padenie tsarskogo rezhima*, VII: 158–9.

11 Livadiia Palace was the Black Sea summer retreat of Nicholas II and his family, located just 2 miles (3 km) west of Yalta, in the Crimea.

12 In all likelihood, Rodzianko received the prorogation decree sometime between 11:00 and midnight on February 26.

13 This so-called first telegram from Rodzianko to the tsar was sent from Petrograd on February 26 at 21:52 and received at General Headquarters at 22:40. For the English translation of the telegram, see *RPG*, I: 40. Rodzianko sent copies of this telegram to the commanders at the front and in the navy as well as to General Alekseev.

14 Vladimir Borisovich Pokhvisnev (1859–1927) was director of the main administration of posts and telegraph in the ministry of internal affairs from October 1913 to February 28, 1917. He later lived in Yugoslavia.

15 See n. 17 to the Gerasimov interview.

16 The reference is to the Countess Nataliia Sergeevna Brasova (1880–1952) (née Sheremet'evskaia; Mamontova from her first marriage,Vulfert from her second), who from 1912 was morganatic spouse of Grand Duke Mikhail Aleksandrovich. By the end of 1918, after having failed to secure her husband's release from exile in Perm', Brasova left Soviet Russia with their son Georgii Mikhailovich (1910–31). She later lived in France.

17 Aleksander Aleksandrovich Romanov (1845–94) was Alexander II's son and father of Nicholas II. He ruled Russia as Alexander III from March 1, 1881 until his death.

18 Ivan Ivanovich Dmitriukov (1871–after August 1918) was an Octobrist deputy to the fourth Duma from Kaluga province, and the Duma's elected Secretary (November 20, 1912–October 6, 1917). On February 27, he became member of the Duma Committee and participated in the negotiations with Grand Duke Mikhail Aleksandrovich for the transfer of state authority to the Duma. Rodzianko confused the date of these negotiations, which took place on the evening of the 27th (not the 26th). For additional descriptions of these important, if unsuccessful, negotiations see the N.V. Nekrasov interview in this volume and N.V. Savich's recollections (N.V. Savich, *Vospominaniia* (St. Petersburg: Logos, 1993), 200–2).

19 Nikanor Vasil'evich Savich (1869–1942) was a leading Octobrist deputy to the last two Dumas from Khar'kov province, a member of the Council of Elders, and Rodzianko's trusted adviser and ally. At Rodzianko's request, Savich was one of the four Duma deputies who negotiated with ministers Pokrovskii and Rittikh on February 26 (see the Gerasimov interview, Chapter 5) and was also invited by Rodzianko to join the members of the Duma Presidium (Dmitriukov, Nekrasov, and himself) to negotiate with Grand Duke Mikhail Aleksandrovich on February 27, 1917. During the February Days, he served as commissar of the Duma Committee to the ministry of the navy.

20 Bologoe, a railroad station on the Petrograd–Moscow line, was located approximately halfway between the two cities. During March 1, while trying to get through to Tsarskoe Selo, the tsar's train passed twice through Bologoe, then turned west to Dno—a railroad station on the Petrograd–Vitebsk line, located 135 miles (218 km) south of Tsarskoe Selo and 70 miles (113 km) east of Pskov—before finally arriving at Pskov at eight o'clock on the evening of March 1.

21 That is, the journal of the Duma Committee or "Protocol of Events," compiled by Ia. V. Glinka. See nn. 9 and 26 to the Gerasimov interview.

22 Aleksandr Ivanovich Konovalov (1875–1949) was a leading Progressist deputy to the fourth Duma from Kostroma province. From 1915 to 1917, he was deputy chairman of the CWIC and head of its Moscow branch. On February 27, 1917 he became a member of the Duma Committee and from March 2 to May 18, 1917 served as minister of trade and industry in the first Provisional Government.

7

Lev Stepanovich
Tugan-Baranovskii

L EV STEPANOVICH TUGAN-BARANOVSKII (1880–1955) was a colonel of the
General Staff in the Russian imperial army. At the time of his interview he was
acting chief of the War Minister's Chancellery under Kerenskii and chairman of the
ministry's executive commission. In June he was appointed Kerenskii's special assistant "for the duration of the war" and together with his friends and peers Colonels
G. N. Tumanov and G. A. Iakubovich belonged to the troika of Kerenskii's most
trusted military aides during his tenure in the Provisional Government.[a]

Tugan-Baranovskii was a son of the career artillery officer Major General Stepan
Ivanovich Tugan-Baranovskii, whose family came from the hereditary nobility of
the Grodno province and had Tatar roots (hence the "Tugan" part of his surname).
Although Tugan-Baranovskii senior practiced Islam, he did not impose it on his
son, who was duly baptized and registered as Russian Orthodox. Lev Stepanovich
studied in the prestigious First Moscow Cadet Corps and the Mikhailovskii Artillery
School in St. Petersburg. After a brief stint in the Far East during the 1904–5 war,
he entered the General Staff Academy. Following graduation—between 1908 and
1913—he served in various infantry and grenadier units. In March 1913 he was
assigned to be a staff officer to the Mobilization Department in the Main Administration of the General Staff. In 1916 he was promoted to the rank of colonel and
appointed chief of the department's 4th subdivision.[b]

On the morning of February 28, 1917 he received a telephone call from his old
acquaintance Colonel Engel'gardt, the newly appointed chairman of the Military

---

[a] Kerenskii's brother-in-law, Lieutenant Colonel Vladimir L'vovich Baranovskii (1882–1931),
was not part of this *troika* and served as Kerenskii's personal adjutant.

[b] *Spisok General'nogo shtaba. Ispravlen na 1 iiunia 1914 g.* (Petrograd, 1914); *Spisok General'nogo
shtaba. Ispravlen na 1 ianvaria 1916 g.* (Petrograd, 1916); *Spisok General'nogo shtaba. Ispravlen na 3 ianvaria 1917 g.* (Petrograd, 1917); RGVIA, f. 409, op. 1, p/s [Service Record] 149-008 (1917), ll. 1–12.
See also A. B. Nikolaev, *Revoliutsiia i vlast': IV Gosudarstvennaia duma, 27 fevralia–3 marta 1917 goda*
(St. Petersburg: RGPU, 2005), 599.

Commission (MC), who invited Tugan-Baranovskii to join the MC as his deputy. From March 1 until his transfer to the War Ministry two months later, Tugan-Baranovskii was one of the most senior and influential officers on the MC and devoted his inordinate energies, experience, and fine-tuned political instincts to the monumental task of democratizing the old army.

Tugan-Baranovskii's two-part interview with the Polievktov Commission represents his only known testimony; it is also one of the longest and most informative accounts recorded by the Commission. The interview covers the last years of his service in the General Staff, his tenure on the Duma Military Commission during and after the February Revolution, conditions in the army before and during the revolution, and the efforts by the first Provisional Government to reform the imperial officer corps and internal organization of the army more generally. Tugan-Baranovskii's account of the political maneuverings leading to Kerenskii's appointment as war minister is particularly revealing and unprecedented. The portrait of Tugan-Baranovskii that emerges from the interview is that of a very intelligent, politically Left-leaning, and able, if overly ambitious, military officer in the prime of his life and career, who had no misconceptions about the old system and clearly saw his own relatively limited prospects of advancement within it. At the same time, one cannot help but notice that his early fascination with the new revolutionary order and some of its leaders was motivated at least in part by opportunistic considerations. That his aspiration for a more appropriate recognition of his talents proved ephemeral precisely because he was a prime beneficiary of the old system was not something he was apparently able (or willing) to accept during the early revolutionary euphoria.

In any event, he stayed with Kerenskii until the demise of the Provisional Government. Not long thereafter, in January 1918, he was discharged from military service, officially for health reasons.[c] As far as can be established, he was not among those former officers who joined the anti-Bolshevik forces during the civil war; nor is there any information about his service in the Red Army. His military service record ends with a note dated September 2, 1918. We next find Tugan-Baranovskii in France. During the 1920s and 1930s he was involved in the work of a local chapter of the Union of the Graduates of Russian Cadet Corps in Emigration, but it appears that he otherwise kept a low profile. He spent his last days in an émigré sanatorium near Trieste.

Tugan-Baranovskii's interview is reproduced here on the basis of the three draft transcripts. The first and the longest—on twenty-three and a half legal-sized leaves—is written by Margarita Feliksovna Ropp; each leaf has a wide left margin containing numerous stylistic edits by Polievktov in pencil and black ink, suggesting perhaps that he approached the text on more than one occasion. The second transcript contains only the record of the interview session that took place on May 20, and is written in shorthand by Tamara Nikoladze. The final transcript, in

[c] RGVIA, f. 409, op. 1, p/s [Service Record] 149-008 (1917), ll. 13–16.

M. A. Polievktov's hand, contains only the text of the first interview, recorded on May 17.

★ ★ ★ ★ ★ ★

An account by Colonel Tugan-Baranovskii, head of the War Minister's Chancellery. [Recorded in the War Ministry on] May 17 and 20, 1917

The declaration of war raised the regime's prestige. But it failed to utilize the surge in popular enthusiasm, systematically killing it instead. This was the cause of the revolution. I served on the commission of inquiry which investigated Sukhomlinov, the former war minister.[1] Everyone knew that Sukhomlinov was guilty, and yet he was discharged with honors. Was this thoughtlessness, or was it a crime? There was a rumor in the war ministry about a letter of honorable discharge Sukhomlinov received. The letter, which could have been apocryphal, recently surfaced in our newspapers. The next step which drew the revolution nearer was the appointment of Beliaev, the head of the General Staff (who had a bad reputation), to the position of war minister. Beliaev's behavior was provocative and indecent. The following phrase was typical for him: "I wonder why the condition of the army in the field preoccupies you so much." To be exempted from conscription, one would have to have good connections, especially with ladies-in-waiting. For them, Beliaev would lay down flat. He would often say, "One needs to know for whom one should do favors." A very pernicious man, he corrupted the ministry. One of Beliaev's last outrageous acts was his reply to the requests to send 500 noncommissioned officers, prisoners of war, to the coal mines. They numbered in the thousands, but they were not sent to work. Beliaev's reply was a bald-faced lie: "We have no prisoners." These facts explain why, already on February 28, all of the officers of the General Staff had sided with the people and the Duma.

There was no question that the revolution was unplanned, yet everyone was openly siding with the opposition. State Duma deputy Engel'gardt visited. It was clear that we could not go on like that anymore; something was in the making. There was talk of a military plot. Some units were supposed to capture the tsar's train at Volkhov Station, overthrow the tsar without regicide, and declare Mikhail regent.[2] In my opinion, such a plot was a joke—an attempt with inadequate means. There were many discontented officers in the regiments. Unfortunately, the soldiers were oblivious. The officers were constrained by their oath (this is the reason for the carnage between soldiers and officers), even though they were quite critical. If the efforts to involve a few regiments had been successful, then a larger part of them would have resisted. There would have been more blood shed than there was. The plot was unsuccessful because it had been worked out by a theoretician, Prince Viazemskii (who was killed during the revolution).[3] The plot was more childish than that of the Decembrists. The 1st Guard Cavalry Division was supposed to participate. There was no revolutionary propaganda because the extreme Left thought the timing was wrong. The masses were not revolutionized by proclamations, but by Rasputin, Beliaev, Sukhomlinov, and Protopopov.

I first met with Shtiurmer regarding the supply of horses. Before going to him, I was expecting questions related to the business at hand, and prepared myself in earnest. But Shtiurmer only spoke about my family connections; he asked about my relatives. The second meeting concerned conscription. It was the same thing—conversations about family. It was becoming clear to me that the man had no interest in what was really going on in the country.

Beliaev exhibited the same attitude: holding back, shelving things. Regiments in the field did not have their own reserve units, whereas a moral connection between the army in the field and its units in the rear is very important and desirable. Sukhomlinov destroyed this link. I decided to take the matter into my own hands; but for reasons of personal vanity Beliaev delayed the matter despite General Headquarters' approval. While on a visit from the front, Dmitrii Gurko attended a private dinner at Polivanov's.[4] The host gave him my memorandum. This was the method I usually used when I wanted to get something through. General Adlerberg,[5] a stupid man, who usually did what he was asked during the tsar's audiences, gave my memorandum to the sovereign. The sovereign made a notation that this should be implemented. There were no results, however. Not until Gurko came again (in about twenty days), did I learn about the tsar's reaction. It was clear that secret documents had been intercepted somewhere. I wrote a report to Beliaev, who made this notation: "I have your memorandum." All this prepared the ground for revolution, and therefore when the first shooting started between soldiers and precinct policemen, on February 27, everyone happily assumed it would lead to something.

I spent the night of February 26–7 with the Izmailovskii [Life Guards] Regiment, where two officers were being seen off to the front. Towards midnight, the regiment's commander, Danil'chenko,[6] arrived. He returned from Khabalov, who had summoned him to prepare a plan of action for Petrograd on the next day. Danil'chenko gave a speech in which he conveyed the decision taken at Khabalov's: "Save no bullets, use live ammunition. Don't use blanks or fire into the air." He expressed hope that the Izmailovskii Regiment would fulfill the duty of their oath. The speech was received without enthusiasm. What is more, it was delivered in the presence of orderlies. Danil'chenko did not mince words. He spoke of an incident between an officer of the Finland Regiment named Iost and a worker. The latter appealed to the soldiers not to kill their brothers and sisters. Iost allowed him to talk himself out, and then killed him. For my part, I recall turning to my neighbor at the table and expressing condemnation of Iost.[7] Danil'chenko was a limited man, uneducated, and a careerist. Earlier, he had served as secretary to Konstantin Konstantinovich,[8] and was dreaming of becoming aide-de-camp. He managed to obtain funds to restore Troitskii Cathedral,[9] contrived to be introduced to the sovereign, and was probably thinking that by suppressing the uprising he would receive the position of aide-de-camp (this had happened in 1905). However, Danil'chenko's calls for executions did not resonate, even with career officers.

Around 4:00 in the morning, we were walking home; there were long "tails" at the bakeries. The Izmailovskii soldiers who were on guard were peacefully chatting with the people standing in the queues. On the morning of the 27th, a doorman told me: "The Volynskii soldiers are at war with the Preobrazhenskii soldiers." I went out onto the street. In the area of Kirochnaia-Preobrazhenskaia-Znamenskaia-Basseinaia streets, there was sporadic shooting. Nobody laid hands on me. Toward 12:00 noon, Iakubovich and I, with two staffers, went by automobile to the General Staff. There I heard rumors about shootings, about an attack on the [Main] Artillery Administration, and about the murder of officers.[10] Toward 3:00, it became known that some units of the Preobrazhenskii Regiment had joined the insurgents. Other Preobrazhenskii units were kept standing for 2–3 hours on Palace Square, doing nothing, at 11 degrees below zero. At the General Staff, some wondered whether they were trying to turn them into revolutionaries by freezing them. Toward 5:00, Prince Tumanov, Iakubovich, and I, after removing our sabers, decided to walk home. At that moment, a gendarme (who had been sent by the chief of the General Staff, Zankevich[11]) came in and reported that Zankevich demanded my presence at the building of the city police chief, where he was at the time. We already knew that the Duma had not dispersed. I assumed that a meeting of the General Staff was taking place at the city police chief's, and that they wanted to send me to the Duma as an envoy of truce. On my way to the city police chief's, I heard the music of the Pavlovskii and Preobrazhenskii Regiments' marches from the direction of Millionnaia Street. It should be pointed out that when regiments come across each other, they customarily play the march of the other regiment.

At the city police chief's, I witnessed a frightful scene. Everyone was scared and agitated. Khabalov, Colonel Pavlenkov,[12] and some gendarme officers were there. Nobody could tell me why I had been summoned. Pavlenkov guessed that I had been appointed chief of the General Staff. Then Zankevich came in and reported that Beliaev had appointed him commander of the government forces, and asked me to be his chief of staff. I was surprised by this, because I knew Zankevich as a person of different convictions (he was thought to be on the far Left). His offer dropped like a bombshell. I refused, and advised him to refuse: "We serve the motherland, not Beliaev."

He objected: "I am a soldier. What can I do?" For my part, I said that an assignment from Shuvaev[13]—who was decent, if not very smart—could have been obeyed. But not from Beliaev, whom I was ready to shoot myself. Zankevich asked me to wait, and to contact Vsevolozhskii[14] regarding bullets. I refused.

In the meantime, they started counting the number of loyal troops: Izmailovskii, riflemen, several cavalry squadrons from Tsarskoe Selo. They were also waiting for artillery units from Strel'na.[15] All in all, they counted 19–20 companies, several dozen squadrons, and 12 artillery pieces, with shells. There was a feeling that the majority of the troops were still on the government's side, and that they needed to hold out until the morning, when troops from the front were expected to arrive (which units they had in mind, I do not know). Precinct policemen ran in with the news that Pavlovskii soldiers with machine-guns were moving from Millionnaia Street to take over the city police chief's building. The most terrible panic ensued. People were hiding in closets. Someone gave an order to prepare for a siege. The decision was made to relocate from the city police chief's (*gradonachal'stvo*) to the Admiralty. General Adlerberg came in from Palace Square, where he had seen Pavlovskii soldiers entering the Winter Palace, playing "God Save the Tsar."

The news that there were loyal regiments had a calming effect. I recalled my own encounter with the same regiments. Zankevich left to talk to the

Pavlovskii Regiment. Despite the news, the rest relocated to the Admiralty. Taking advantage of this moment, and not wanting to take part in the dirty business of shooting women (*baby*) and children I returned to the General Staff. Regiments were refusing to shoot. The wife of one Pavlovskii soldier was killed on the eve, and the next day, Pavlovskii soldiers rebelled.

At 6:00, I got ready to walk home. There was not a soul on Nevskii, but there was shooting. I could not get to Prince Tumanov's via Millionnaia either. I returned to the Staff. The second attempt to get home, along Morskaia [Street], also failed. There was intense shooting, and I did not want to get killed by a stray bullet. I stayed in the Staff until 2–3:00 at night, then spent the night at a relative's nearby.

On the morning of February 28, at 7:00, I was already back at the Staff. There were reports that Moskovskii and Borodinskii Regiments of the 17th (19th?) [*sic!*] Division, Sevskii Regiment of the 9th Division, and the 2nd Cavalry Division, along with artillery and machine-guns, were all coming in from the front. The mood was desperate. I worried about my family, because refusing Zankevich the night before might have brought trouble. There was no illegal literature at home, only a caricature of Nicholas II from 1905. I wanted to call home and tell them to burn it. I didn't know anything about the fate of the Duma. For me, as a career military officer, it was clear that two regiments with machine-guns would have been sufficient to bring Petrograd back into submission.

Somebody reported that the remaining members of the former military authorities were to be found in the office of the chief of the General Staff. Indeed, Pavlenkov and Zankevich were there. Some said that Beliaev was also at the Staff. Only five companies were still loyal, but reinforcements were expected to arrive from the front. Pavlenkov greeted me with a phrase laden with meaning: "Many people are going to pay the price for this." [Here follows, on the left margin, a notation in Polievktov's handwriting: *I copied the text up to here. From here, and until the words "the beginning of Rusia's* [Rusudana Polievktova-Nikoladze] *notes," on page 14, I am asking you to rewrite it, with all my corrections. After that phrase, change the narrative to the first person. There is no need to put the text in quotation marks; only Tugan-Baranovskii's specific turns of phrase, exactly as recorded by Margo* [Margarita Ropp].—M.P.]

After relocating to the Admiralty on the 27th, Beliaev, Zankevich, and Khabalov took some units with them. Others, they sent out to patrol. But those who were sent out did not return, and joined the insurgents. The Preobrazhenskii soldiers left for supper, and did not return. An order was given for the Automobile School to bring ammunition to the Admiralty from a railway station. They picked it up, but delivered it to the Duma instead. On the night from the 27th to the 28th, the Council of Ministers was supposed to hold a meeting in the Winter Palace. Those who were in the Admiralty moved to the Winter Palace too. But soon they were all "smoked out" of there and returned to the Admiralty. At 8:00 in the morning on the 28th, an envoy of truce was sent to the Admiralty to announce that, if they did not surrender within the hour, the building would be shelled. After that, everyone went to the General Staff. They were leaving one by one, and making their way to the Staff. Khabalov was the last to leave. He shaved so it would be more difficult to recognize him. But he was caught and taken to the Duma.

The arrival of these men at the Staff caused resentment, especially Beliaev's, who was abhorred by the entire General Staff. He was there until 4:00, expressing strong anxiety when an armed automobile was shooting at the crowd on Palace Square. Before leaving, he flipped his epaulets over so that they would look like a common soldier's. He walked in procession, with his adjutant in front and another bringing up the rear. This trio went to the House of the War Ministry at Moika 67. Later, Madame Kamenskaia[16] told me how Beliaev came and begged her to hide him. But not empathizing with him or wanting to undermine her husband, she refused. Then, Beliaev went to an official named Petrov who lived in the same building. But she (Madame Kamenskaia) also "smoked him out" from there.

Guchkov came to the Staff for negotiations.[17] At about 5:00, Engel'gardt summoned me to the Duma. I could not get there on foot because there was shooting all over and armed automobiles were driving around searching for policemen. I tried to get a ride in a truck, but was unsuccessful. An ambulance finally took me to the Duma on the morning of March 1.[18] Everything there was a horrible mess. I had to work on the issue of liaison between the Duma and the troops. The work was quite difficult because orders were not followed (however, I did succeed in disposing of alcohol). Iurevich asked me to help him with the duties of the city police and administrative chief. I refused and instead sent him officers of the General Staff Academy who had come to the Duma.

In the Military Commission there were troops, petitioners, and railroad business, "noise, hubbub, and shouting." The troops were coming into the Catherine Hall with music. Speeches were delivered to them from the second floor railing. They were hard to hear, but everyone still shouted

"Hurrah!" The situation was becoming clear: the crowd (workers, soldiers, and intelligentsia) was hostile toward the house of the Romanovs; there were shouts of "Down with the Holsteins!" Clearly, preserving the Romanovs was impossible. The government's intention to keep Mikhail and Alexei was unacceptable.

On March 2, there was a difficult situation in the Duma. Placards with the inscription "Down with the Romanovs!" popped up. A crisis was brewing; slaughter was becoming a real possibility. I had to speak with delegations that were coming in and asking whether it would be the Romanovs or a republic. I had to answer them with general phrases, because nobody knew for certain. It was becoming intolerable. Privatdozent Pletnev[19] and I turned to Savich. I said that any push for the Romanovs should be abandoned. Then I spoke to Skobelev, asking him to influence the government so that it would get off a monarchical platform. I brought the same issue up with minister Miliukov (before his speech), and I pointed out that the idea of continuing with the monarchy had been invented by the Kadets. I argued that it should be dropped. Soldiers were asking whether there would be a president. "And you are telling them that there will be?" Miliukov asked angrily, "You shouldn't!"

Prince Tumanov, Iakubovich, and I spoke with Shingarev in the same spirit. Shingarev expressed uncertainty about whether he would serve as minister of agriculture under control from the Soviet of Workers' and Soldiers' Deputies. I argued for the importance and advantages of such control (more support from the Left for the minister's measures, given the difficult situation with food in Russia), after which Shingarev conceded.

In my conversation with Manuilov[20] before the meeting of the council of ministers, I asked him to introduce the following: (1) rejection of the monarchy; (2) strengthening the left wing of the cabinet (we spoke about a coalition; Kerenskii alone was not enough. Skobelev was proposed as minister of labor; Gor'kii[21] for the arts); (3) to convince Shingarev of the desirability of control from the Soviet of Workers' and Soldiers' Deputies. Manuilov did nothing. The war minister, Guchkov, disappeared somewhere, and left General Potapov in his place. Rumors circulated that he and Shul'gin had gone to look for the tsar. Nobody knew for sure why Guchkov had disappeared, and in the meantime I needed him badly.

The question of the relationship between officers and soldiers (Order Number One) was getting very serious. Officers were being arrested and brought to the Duma. General Kutaisov[22] was involved in this.

Chkheidze and Kerenskii were giving speeches. They were able to build a bridge between officers and soldiers (Chkheidze was carried out on shoulders). At the same time, a hostile attitude toward Miliukov was beginning to be felt—especially striking was his speech. It was beautiful, but because of its faulty thesis,[23] it turned the crowd against him. It became clear that, if Miliukov did not concede, scandals would erupt and this smart, energetic man would be lost.

During the night from March 2 to 3, the crisis ripened (here, Prince Tumanov played a role). As a result, after Nicholas's abdication in favor of Mikhail, Kerenskii refused to serve in the cabinet. Around 8–9:00, Rodzianko spoke on the direct wire; the crisis was about to be favorably resolved. Everything nearly fell apart. On the 3rd, at 11:00, Nekrasov replied to my question about Guchkov's whereabouts with: "There is no point in concealing it: Guchkov submitted his resignation." On his return from the Warsaw Railway Station, Guchkov gave a speech near the Technological Institute, for which he was arrested by the crowd. The Military Commission got him released, but because of the arrest, Guchkov decided to resign.[24] Thus, we were left without a war minister. Prince Tumanov, Iakubovich, and I suggested to Duma deputy Engel'gardt, a very energetic man, that he become the war minister (at first he refused, but then agreed in principle). We spoke with ministers and members of the Duma. Engel'gardt received congratulations. General Filat'ev needed the war minister's signature to release 32 million [rubles] to the army. Engel'gardt signed the order "for" the war minister. General Alekseev asked that the war minister come to the direct wire. Engel'gardt went, but Alekseev informed him that he had already spoken with Guchkov. The Synod's L'vov discovered that Guchkov had been talked into staying. Beginning on March 4, Guchkov was in the war ministry. That evening, in the House of the War Minister, Guchkov received the generals. Guchkov did not say much, but gave a few necessary orders. Prince Tumanov, Iakubovich, and I wanted to clarify our roles, but the generals turned their noses up at us.

With the creation of the Polivanov Commission,[25] the question of the continued existence of the Military Commission was up in the air. Some even wanted to transfer it over to the war ministry. It would have lost any significance as a result. Guchkov supported this move, but pressure was brought to bear on him via Pal'chinskii, who was the only one who had influence over him.

The Commission stayed in the Tauride Palace. It dealt with a broad variety of issues. Delegates from the front, who came to deal with the Soviet of Soldiers' and Workers' Deputies, ended up going to the Military Commission. The Commission was considered a revolutionary organ, and thus might be helpful. Telegrams were received all at once at ten different addresses: the Military Commission, the Soviet of Soldiers' Deputies, the war ministry, the ministry of transport, and others. As long as I worked with Guchkov, I was able to introduce many measures. When help from the war ministry was needed (to remove commanders, or concerning living conditions in the military), people would turn to Prince Tumanov, Iakubovich, and myself. When we left the Polivanov Commission, we developed contacts with Manikovskii,[26] and through him arranged the matters of the Military Commission.

In the beginning, the relationship between the Military Commission and the Soviet of Soldiers' and Workers' Deputies was shaky, because the Soviet thought that the Military Commission wanted to grab power over military matters. But soon they understood that this was not the case and that the Military Commission was a kind of conciliatory chamber between the Soviet of Soldiers' and Workers' Deputies and the War Ministry or the Provisional Government, and that therefore it was needed. The relationship improved, and the Soviet of Soldiers' and Workers' Deputies began to send many documents over to the Military Commission. When the question of its dissolution came up, the Soviet of Solders' and Workers' Deputies voted to keep the Commission.

The Work of the Military Commission to Support the Army in the Field
Before the revolution, troops from Oranienbaum and Strel'na—78 machine-gun companies and detachments (about 900 machine-guns), as well as an artillery brigade—were ready to be sent to the front. But because of the breakdown of the transportation system, they did not leave Oranienbaum and Strel'na before the revolution broke out. They came to the Duma during the initial days (March 2–3) leaving all of their machine-guns strewn along the way. The machine-guns have yet to be located, despite many efforts to find them. The artillery pieces had come from France and England.

The Military Commission attempted to raise the question of sending troops to the front, but the Soviet objected, referring to point 7 of the government's declaration,[27] which stated that the troops of the Petrograd garrison would remain in the city. Then the three of us (Prince Tumanov, Iakubovich, and I) started a campaign against that provision. We soon found support in the Soviet of Soldiers' Deputies. Soldiers themselves began to support us. The first to leave for the front was the guard infantry, followed by machine-gunners. The best situation was, and still is, with the artillerymen. I agreed to their departure, and all I needed to do was get the sanction of the Soviet of Workers' and Soldiers' Deputies. In general, during the revolution the artillerymen showed themselves to be more sophisticated. They did not lose their common sense, and even showed an interest in technology. *This exhibited itself sometimes in a rather curious form. When other troops were marching with placards, the artillerymen*[28] also carried, together with placards reading "Land and Freedom!" others which read "Give Us Caterpillar Tractors!" (Trucks which can go over plowed-up fields and across ditches are the dream of any technician.) They were stationed in Tsarskoe Selo.

After about a month and a half of struggle over reinforcements, they started to be deployed, even though many of the soldiers did not want to go. At that time, the work of the Polivanov Commission started, and we, Prince Tumanov, Iakubovich and I, also worked there. We were invited by Guchkov, via Polovtsov.[29] There were many people in that commission who, like Guchkov, had not deeply felt the whirlwind of the revolution. They clung to the old norms, did not understand how extraordinary the times were, and always resisted initiatives required by the moment. For example, the questions of saluting, salary, and so on. On March 4–5, we introduced the question of soldiers' salaries. But it was defeated, and was put through regular channels instead. We therefore had to deal with it in April–May. Under pressure, we had to approve a salary of 15 rubles, without distinguishing between war- and peacetime. (Initially, 7 rubles was proposed.) The question of saluting was another such issue. Today, this has come back as Kerenskii's grand gesture. Guchkov thought that these changes caused disorganization in the army, but, in fact, the arguments about them were what actually contributed to disorganization. Dissatisfaction with Guchkov grew. He—and this is true—fired numerous commanders, but did not introduce anything new, even though reforms were necessary.

All undertakings which emanated from the Polivanov Commission were passed on by Guchkov to General Filat'ev, who delayed them. Two of my projects were killed in this way: one was about the creation of a liaison office under the war ministry; the other concerned the High Command. I knew Filat'ev from my time at the Academy. He never offered to shake hands with academy cadets, and he did not return salutes on the street. He acted like a brute, treating them like dogs. Some of Guchkov's other officials were also unfit. For example, Kondzerovskii was decent, but was not well liked in the army.[30] Guchkov removed him from General Headquarters and, following the example of the old government, appointed him to the minister's council. In the war ministry, everything stayed the same; there were no new trends. The ministry was nervous; everyone had lost heart. We (Tumanov, Iakubovich, and I) had an ally in Pal'chinskii. He viewed us as the young blood that Guchkov could count on for support. Once, we dined with Guchkov and had a very long, friendly conversation with him. But in practice, he was not interested in what we thought, and in general we saw that he would not change anything. Polovtsov had also served under Guchkov, but he too decided to get away from him. During the initial days of my appointment, I traveled to General Headquarters with Guchkov.[31] Through Polovtsov, Guchkov offered to decorate staff officers from the Polivanov Commission. He said that he valued our talent, but he thought that this talent was wasted. We refused his offer. Instead, we asked to take a picture with him, for the record. When we met to do that, we sensed that, in fact, this was a subtle way of suggesting that we leave. We simply did not fit in. Afterwards, we returned to our old posts in the General Staff. We lobbied for the needs of the Duma Military Commission through Manikovskii. Polovtsov left at the same time we did; he went back to the Savage Division [*Dikaia diviziia*].[32]

In the [war] ministry, everything continued as usual. No new trends or spirit of innovation was felt. The opposition to Guchkov was coalescing and growing. This caused apprehension in military circles and in the ministry. There was a feeling that Guchkov and the ministry were on a collision course, and that soon he would no longer be there. At first, everyone expected that he would be forced to go, either because of his health or because of ever-intensifying events.

I kept up a good relationship with the Soviet of Workers' and Soldiers' Deputies. The Provisional Government needed support and an organization which would represent public opinion. The State Duma no longer exists (its active members are traveling on assignments). The mouthpiece of public opinion is the Soviet of Workers' and Soldiers' Deputies, even though it is true that it was created by usurpation. It is in the interest of the Provisional Government to strengthen the Soviet.

I spent April 20–1 in Moscow, where things were calm.[33] When I returned to Petrograd, Pal'chinskii invited me to come to the Polivanov Commission in the evening, but I was tired from traveling and did not go. Later, I deeply regretted this decision. It turned out that Tumanov, Iakubovich, Polovtsov, Engel'gardt, and Pal'chinskii went to see Kerenskii that night to talk about the war ministry and the High Command. Earlier, on April 10–12, Pal'chinskii told me that he had spoken with Kerenskii, who said that he wanted to establish contact with young officers of the General Staff, those who had not lost their will and independence because of their time at the Military Academy. Pal'chinskii thought that Tumanov, Iakubovich, and I were the best candidates. Indeed, when Beliaev was the head of the Military Academy,[34] he used to call us the "Revolutionary Department" instead of the "Mobilization Department." So that it would not look like a conspiracy, Polovtsov told Guchkov about the late-night meeting. They all came back euphoric from that meeting. But I was devastated that I had paid so heavily for my laziness.

I first met Kerenskii on March 1. Earlier, during peacetime, he had struck me as an extremely nervous, unbalanced person. In short, I did not approve of him. However, after my very first encounter with him in the Duma on March 1, I realized that he was the only person who could really get things done. I came over to his side at once. The majority in the General Staff and the war ministry, as well as various generals and the like, including Guchkov, had no sympathy for Kerenskii, and disliked him intensely.

Although he was expected to resign, Guchkov still surprised everyone by leaving when he did. With regard to the Provisional Government, his departure was indecent. On a Saturday,[35] at 9:00 in the evening, Guchkov announced to the council of ministers that he had made a decision, without telling them what it was. The government had previously agreed that members could not resign from the Provisional Government on their own. On Sunday morning, Guchkov sent L'vov a letter of resignation. Without waiting for an answer, he at once went to the Congress of Delegates from the Front, where he announced that he was no longer a minister.[36] The Congress accepted this news with absolute calm and indifference. However, the military officers, conscious of their duty, were indignant. Everyone found his departure inappropriate, coming at the most difficult of moments. Without giving advance notice, he left like a house servant. This undermined any trust in him, but did not provoke any regret whatsoever. On the other hand, his departure was actually very timely: while some went into a panic about the state of affairs, we saw this as an opportunity to install a person quite different from Guchkov to head the ministry. Concurrently, the Miliukov crisis ripened.

The war ministry was left without a minister, and was completely unprepared for that eventuality. It was necessary to find his successor quickly. On
Monday night, the three of us went to ask Kerenskii if he was interested in
the post. We decided amongst ourselves that there was no suitable career
military man who would adequately understand the situation, and that a
minister should be chosen from among the civilians. From that group, we
considered Kerenskii and Pal'chinskii to be the two most fitting candidates
because of their energy and zeal. Petr Ioakimovich [Pal'chinskii] was in
favor of Kerenskii. Some thought that Kerenskii was the last card that should
be played—if that card was beaten, the outcome would be unclear. At first,
we asked Pal'chinskii. He agreed (this is the reason why some newspapers
reported that he was a candidate for the minister's post). Only after that did
we drive over to see Kerenskii. When we asked him his opinion on taking
the vacant post of war minister, Kerenskii replied, "This question has been
floated, but I am still vacillating." When we told him that our only other
candidate was Pal'chinskii, he said that, in his opinion, Pal'chinskii would
not be accepted because he was little known in the army. Furthermore, the
cabinet would not support him since he had given a favorable report on
Guchkov (even though Pal'chinskii was in opposition to Guchkov), and
that was a negative. We stayed at Kerenskii's until 10:00. He proposed
Nekrasov, but we opposed that idea. Kerenskii then promised us to put
Pal'chinskii's candidacy forward and left for the council of ministers. From
there, we (Tumanov, Iakubovich, and I) went back to Pal'chinskii's and
stayed and talked with him until 2:00 in the morning.

On Tuesday [May 2], Parshin and the three of us went to Kerenskii, who had
called us in to tell us that the Soviet had decided the issue: he himself would
become the war minister. He also told us that he would be unable to perform
his duties if he were undermined from both the Left and the Right. Kerenskii
said that he was being undermined from the Right by the Kadets. Miliukov
wanted to resign, but if he were to remain in the cabinet, he would take the
ministry of popular enlightenment. Kerenskii continued that Manuilov would
take the ministry of agriculture, and Shingarev (who had turned out to be an
unsuccessful minister of agriculture), would resign. Miliukov's departure would
cause a rupture. All the Kadet ministers might go with him. The situation
would be particularly worrisome if Nekrasov left, as he was not only a candidate
for war minister, but was also much-needed for the Provisional Government. In
addition, if Nekrasov left, Tereshchenko would go with him. Again, this was
highly undesirable. Those two could not be lost. In view of all this, Kerenskii

suggested that we get in touch with the Kadets, calm them down, raise the question of a coalition ministry, and work with them to put it in place.

At once, the three of us drove to the Executive Committee of the Soviet, where its bureau (Tsereteli, Privatdozent and economist Bogdanov, Sokolovskii) was in session.[37] We gave a report, painted a picture of disintegration at the front, and emphasized the necessity of Soviet support; we said that Kerenskii was the last card, pointing out that he would be undermined by the Kadets. After spending an hour with the bureau, we left. At about 7–8:00, the entire Executive Committee gathered and introduced a resolution on the necessity to form a coalition ministry.[38] Only a few days before, an overwhelming majority (22–23, with 2 abstentions) had voted against this idea.[39]

From the Executive Committee, the three of us drove to the Kadet Club.[40] We told the bureau of the Executive Committee that we would start by talking unthreateningly with the Kadets, but if they continued to disagree, we would threaten to incite the officers and troops against them because they were hampering our efforts while the fatherland was perishing. At the Club, we spoke with Vinaver.[41] He objected, but would say neither nay not yea. He said that, by their refusal, the Kadets were seeking to sober people up. We left the Club unsatisfied, even though we managed to impress on them the imperative that Nekrasov not resign as a result of Miliukov's departure. We spent the entire night from Wednesday to Thursday[42] at Kerenskii's. He gave all of us assignments, and during that night, we discussed various technical changes, the appointment of new commanders, and the like.

The troops worship Kerenskii as if he were a deity, and this is completely understandable. I share that admiration, and bow before him. He is a man of amazing energy who has an extraordinary intelligence and an ability to quickly grasp situations. He is a committed revolutionary, but not a blind fanatic. If not for him, no one would be able to cope with the situation. There is an unbelievable smear campaign directed at him from different directions, especially the Left, who are both jealous of him and afraid of a future Bonaparte. He receives masses of anonymous letters in which he is called a dictator, a Bonaparte, and is threatened with assassination.

Pal'chinskii is a mining engineer, and is the Director of Lys'venskie Mining Enterprises (Urals).[43] Politically, he is a committed Socialist Revolutionary. In 1905, he was the President of the Chita Republic,[44] and was almost executed. From Siberia, he escaped abroad. He is so energetic that, as an émigré, he was sent on trips by some ministry, and later his reports from those trips were published. He wrote a classical study of Mediterranean seaports and received a travel assignment to Sweden on commercial-industrial matters from the French government. In the fall of 1916, he established the Committee of Military Technical Assistance; he still administers its operations admirably.[45] There was a request to the General Staff to assess this committee. I was asked to provide an opinion. I supported the committee, and as a result, 3 million rubles were allocated to it.

Pal'chinskii thinks like a statesman. He never loses his presence of mind. On March 2, we received reports in the Duma that, at 8–9:00 in the evening, an echelon had arrived at the Baltic Railway Station, and that a battle was raging. Everyone got scared and lost their heads. The extreme Left—those who had come with red flags—took to their heels. Pal'chinskii did not panic, and sent Balabin[46] to bring the Izmailovskii Regiment. Balabin, with the Petrograd and Izmailovskii Regiments, went straight to the Baltic Railway Station in armed cars. Afterwards, several witnesses to the battle (officers, workers) came to the Duma both on foot and by automobile. Someone called the commandant of the railway station. It turned out that Filatov[47] had come from Oranienbaum with machine-gunners. As they were getting off the trains, shots were fired into the air. That was it. At around 10:00, they arrived at the Duma. A slew of similar reports were constantly coming into the Duma, and in such cases Pal'chinskii never lost his presence of mind.

Order Number One

This order was of a purely revolutionary nature. Sokolov and someone else (I do not know who) are being named as the authors. Engel'gardt was an indirect participant. This order is a revolutionary creation. At a time when, in the Soviet and in the Duma, the situation was unknown and there was a fear that the army would turn against the revolution, efforts were made to revolutionize the army and cause its collapse. These efforts achieved their goals quite well. In my view, the order can logically be explained as a revolutionary act. But there is still something that is unclear to me: Engel'gardt knew two to three hours in advance that the Soviet was working on the order. He wanted to preempt them by issuing his own order. But it was not well received in the government. Guchkov decisively rejected it. Some soldiers in the Soviet of Worker's Deputies, upon learning about Engel'gardt's intentions, offered to issue a joint order with him. But once Engel'gardt told them that the government was against it, they said: "In that case, we will write it ourselves." Seen in this way, the order cannot be considered a revolutionary act, but rather a military order. (It was a big mistake, which caused disorganization.) Orders number 2 and 3, which were written with the purpose of correcting, and in part retracting, had no impact. It was too late.

We had to carry out a series of reforms in the army. We presented them as continuations of Order Number One so they would be more acceptable, softening and smoothing over the effects of that order. These days, however, the real trouble in the army is not Order Number One, but the formula: "Without annexations and indemnities." Soldiers do not understand this, and think that both money and land should be taken from the Germans. They shout: "Down with annexations and indemnities!" and use it as an excuse not to man the trenches. Sometimes, the lack of bayonets and the unfitness of division commanders are given as reasons for not going to the front. Even if those demands have been met, they still will not go to the trenches. For example, in Pskov soldiers have argued, "We are not traitors; we are from the Perm' area. We would not let Germans into our province. But Riga is not ours." What kind of conversation is possible about annexations and indemnities when dealing at this level?

"Lentils"

You have probably heard about the famous "lentils" of our revolution, which revolutionized the army and now threatens the Provisional Government. There was an interruption in the supply of foodstuffs from Siberia. The southern provinces, which are closer to the front, are rich in lentils. It was calculated that lentil beans are a superbly nutritious food because they contains calories, protein, and the like. They began feeding the front with them. The soldiers came to hate lentils; they threw them away and starved. (It is said that they are only fit for mice. Lentils and herring started disorders in the army.) What occurred in the rear because of the shortage of flour and bread was accomplished at the front by lentils. Soldiers say that the stomach can demoralize any regiment. During the revolution, a wave of protest against lentils arose instantly. It is possible to say that "the stomach made the revolution." Sometimes, when there was a demand that an officer be removed and he asked why, the answer was, "You are good, but you fed us lentils." Now, an order has been given to abolish the use of lentils; we are replacing them everywhere in order to save Kerenskii and the government.

Grekov[48] knows about the summoning of Regiment 180 to the Duma. The regiment came after it learned about Chkheidze's radio-telegram to capture the tsar,[49] who was rumored to be heading for England. (*Roder was in charge of the radio-telegraph.*)[50] Kotsebu, the Commandant of the Aleksandrovskii Palace at Tsarskoe Selo,[51] described how Maslovskii turned up at Tsarskoe Selo (with machine-guns) to verify that the tsar was actually there.[52]

Kornilov's rise was accidental. He was a general of the General Staff, and he was in opposition. He had escaped from enemy captivity. The thinking was that he would be suitable, but it soon turned out that he was quite inflexible. On April 21, he gave an order for troops to take to the streets, but under pressure from the government, he told them to go back to the barracks.[53]

I will tell you an interesting fact which is still an absolute secret. Yesterday, May 19, during the night, I was called to the Soviet of Soldiers' and Workers' Deputies. There, the Commission on Defense, which consists almost entirely of soldiers, discussed both the question of an offensive (the Bolsheviks were against it) and how to minimize desertion. At 11:00, a delegation from the 2nd Baltic Marine Equipage (a commander, an adjutant, and two sailors) arrived in order to make a very important announcement: an (uneducated) sailor had escaped from Kronstadt and was inquiring, on behalf of the 6th Company, whether they would be readmitted to the Corps, in light of the resolution that had been decided the Wednesday before in Kronstadt. The plan was to take *Liberty* (formerly *Aleksander*)[54] and sail to Petrograd, anchoring it near Nikolaevskii Bridge at about 5:00 on May 20, in order to arrest Guchkov and force the Petrograd garrison to join with the Kronstadters under the threat of shelling the city (the Kronstadt Soviet apparently supported them). Helsingfors was against Kronstadt's plan to capture Petrograd, threatening to send *Gangut*[55] and one more ship to crush the Kronstadters, and sink their old galosh *Liberty*. After that, however, the news came in that Helsingfors had also decided, "Down with the Provisional Government, Guchkov, Kerenskii, and the like!"

We started searching for the members of the Executive Committee. Chkheidze was unavailable. We were unable to reach him by telephone. I found Gots,[56] and he said that he thought all this was rubbish. Personally, I also thought these were rumors, but if something like that were to happen, I would not be surprised; we still do not have a very reliable force. The Soviet of Soldiers' and Workers' Deputies also does not represent a substantial force. They are only trusted insofar as (*postol'ku poskol'ku*). They do not think or act like statesmen; the minority (which speaks against Kerenskii) does not subordinate itself to the majority.

Prince Tumanov can tell you very many interesting things about the revolution. He was the officer on duty in the Duma during the most interesting night, from March 2 to 3.

Krasnov, Captain of the General Staff, went with his aide to arrest the tsarina. He offers a detailed account of his trip, including such details as the fact that she wore a pink peignoir. He also has a diagram of the inside of the room, including its furniture, even marking the place where her needlework was. You must talk to him this spring; he has cancer, and he may not be around in the fall.[57]

[Here follows Polievktov's comments: *After our session with Tugan-Baranovskii at the war ministry, we encountered Tumanov on the stairs, and he set a meeting with us for 10:00 in the evening on Sunday the 21st, assuming Kerenskii, who had returned from the front for two days, did not need him on that date. Tumanov wanted Kerenskii to give us an hour too, because he thought that it was very important to interview Kerenskii right away: "Since you are leaving for the entire summer, it is necessary that you catch us and force us to tell everything we know right now. God knows if we will be alive in the fall." Kerenskii did not release him on the 21st. His interview did not take place in the spring, and on 25 October, he was killed.*]

NOTES

1 General V. A. Sukhomlinov was appointed minister of war in 1909 and removed in June 1915 following the poor performance of Russia's armed forces and the March 1915 conviction of his protégé, colonel of the gendarmes S. N. Miasoedov (along with his associates), on spying charges. In July 1915, the Supreme Investigative Commission under General N. P. Petrov was instituted to look into the circumstances of acute shortages of ammunition and other military supplies at the front during Sukhomlinov's tenure as minister. In March 1916, Sukhomlinov was discharged from military service, arrested on charges of gross misconduct and treason, and confined to the Peter and Paul Fortress. But by October 1916, he was released and placed under house arrest, thus confirming the allegations that Nicholas II wished to suspend the case against his former minister. He was again arrested on March 1, 1917, and brought to trial over the summer on the same charges. He was found guilty of lesser charges (inadequate preparations for the war) and sentenced to life at hard labor, was amnestied by the Bolshevik government in May 1918, and emigrated to Finland and from there to Germany.

2 For a discussion of prerevolutionary conspiracies to depose Nicholas II, see chapter 13.

3 Prince Dmitrii Leonidovich Viazemskii (1884–1917) was a graduate of St. Petersburg University's law faculty, an officer in the Life Guards Cavalry Regiment, and an elected member (*glasnyi*) of the Petrograd City Duma. In August 1914 he organized and commanded the 17th Frontline Detachment of the Red Cross (financed by the Petrograd Equestrian Society); in the winter of

1915 he was severely wounded and sent home to Petrograd to recuperate. He returned to the front in the summer of 1916. During late 1916–early 1917 he was one of the five leaders of the Guchkov conspiracy, in charge of recruiting officers from the guard units. He returned to Petrograd shortly before the outbreak of the February Revolution. He joined Guchkov on the first day of the uprising and participated in the work of the MC. On the night of March 1, while touring the revolutionary city in an automobile in the company of Guchkov and General Potapov, Viazemskii was mortally wounded by a stray bullet. He died of his wounds on the morning of March 2.

4 Dmitrii Iosifovich Gurko (Romeiko-Gurko) (1872–1945) was major general in the Russian army. From August 1915 to April 1917, he was chief of staff of the 14th Army Corps. His brother, Vasilii Iosifovich Gurko (1864–1937), was Nicholas II's chief of staff from November 11, 1916 to February 17, 1917. It is probably no coincidence that Dmitrii's visit to the capital was treated as a special occasion at a time when his brother was in a position to speak to the emperor directly and on a daily basis.

5 Aleksandr Aleksandrovich Adlerberg (1849–1931) was general of the infantry; from August 1915 on, he served as general under the direct command of Nicholas II at General Headquarters, and in 1916, he also became inspector general of the reserves. He retired from service in April 1917.

6 Petr Vasil'evich Danil'chenko (1873–1953) was a colonel in the Russian imperial army and spent most of his military career in the Izmailovskii Regiment; from July 13, 1915 to February 25, 1917, he served as commander of the Regiment's reserve battalion. On 25 February he was appointed commander of the 7th Revel Infantry Regiment on the Romanian front but was not able to assume the new post until March 14. On the evening of February 27, General Khabalov appointed Danil'chenko temporary commander of the loyal (pro-government) forces defending the Winter Palace. He was decommissioned on September 24, 1917. His memoirs on February 27, 1917 provide a useful corrective to Tugan-Baranovskii's dismissive tone and partisan description of these same events. See P. Danil'chenko, "K istorii gosudarstva Rossiiskogo. Rokovaia noch' v Zimnem dvortse. 27 fevralia 1917 g.," *Voennaia byl'* 126 (January 1974): 3–9.

7 This incident—when second lieutenant Iost (probably Aleksandr Georgievich Iost or Josts, b. 1881), the commander of a company of the Finland Regiment's reserve battalion, killed a worker on February 25—was described in the Bolshevik *Pravda* on April 11, 1917. According to *Pravda*, a group of strikers from nearby factories gathered in front of Petrograd Pipe Factory on Vasil'evskii Island, not far from the barracks of the Finland Regiment's reserve battalion, and tried to break into the factory in order to force the workers barricaded inside to join the strike. When Iost's company arrived at the scene, one of the striking workers began harassing the officer and shouting obscenities. Iost pulled his gun and reportedly shot the worker without warning. See "Vystuplenie leib-gvardii Finliandskogo polka," *Pravda*, April 11, 1917, as cited in Tsuyoshi Hasegawa, *The February Revolution, Petrograd, 1917* (Seattle and London: University of Washington Press, 1981), 250.

8 Grand Duke Konstantin Konstantinovich (1858–1915) was a grandson of Nicholas I, general adjutant and general of the infantry, and an accomplished pianist, actor, and poet. During the decade 1900–10, he was the commander of Russia's military schools and academies and, from 1899, the Academy of Sciences' president. Danil'chenko's official service record does not indicate that he had served as the grand duke's secretary (RGVIA, f. 409, op. 1, p/s 52–661 [1917]).

9 Or the Trinity Izmailovskii Cathedral, which was the official church of the Izmailovskii Life Guards Regiment, designed by V. P. Stasov and built between 1828 and 1835. The Cathedral is located on Izmailovskii Avenue, not far from the Technological Institute and the former site of the regimental barracks.

10 See the interview with Tereshchenko in this volume (Chapter 12).

11 Mikhail Ippolitovich Zankevich (1872–1945) was a career army officer at the rank of major general; he served as General Quartermaster and acting Chief (from August 1916) of the General Staff. On the afternoon of February 27, he replaced Colonel V. I. Pavlenkov as temporary commander of the military units guarding Petrograd (*voiskovaia okhrana Petrograda*) but did not undertake energetic measures against the insurgents. He was widely suspected of having secretly collaborated with the Duma leaders, especially Guchkov.

12 Vladimir Ivanovich Pavlenkov (1865–after January 1920) was a colonel in the Russian army; from 1906 he served in the Preobrazhenskii Regiment and from 1916 was deputy commander of the Regiment's reserve battalion in Petrograd. On the eve of the February Revolution he served as acting commander of the reserve guards battalions stationed in Petrograd and the units guarding the capital (temporarily replacing lieutenant general A. N. Chebykin, who was on medical leave). However, on February 27 he failed to report for duty, having suffered from angina, and was replaced by Major General Zankevich.

13 Dmitrii Savel'evich Shuvaev (1854–1937) was a career army officer, general of the infantry (1912) and chief of the quartermaster department of the Russian army (since 1909). He preceded Beliaev as minister of war, serving from March 15, 1916 to January 3, 1917. He was thought to have belonged to a more reform-minded liberal wing of the tsarist cabinet. Guchkov appointed him to an advisory military council on March 10, 1917.

14 Sergei Sergeevich Vsevolozhskii (1869–1930) was lieutenant general (1916) in the Russian imperial army and chief of the department of military communications of the General Staff (August 1914–June 1917).

15 Strel'na, a suburb of Petrograd, is located 12 miles (19 km) southwest of the city on the southern shore of the Gulf of Finland on the direct line Oranienbaum–Peterhof–Strel'na–Petrograd (to the Baltic Railway Station). On the morning of February 28, soldiers from Strel'na, including the Second Machine-Gun Regiment, as well as soldiers from the Oranienbaum and Peterhof garrisons, reached Petrograd and joined the insurgents.

16 This may have been Countess Tat'iana Aleksandrovna Kamenskaia, the wife of Major General Mikhail Pavlovich Kamenskii (1874–after 1923), who served as a department chief in the General Staff during Beliaev's tenure as chief of the General Staff. The Kamenskiis resided at no. 3 Kavalergardskii Avenue.

17 Guchkov came to the General Staff to negotiate with General Zankevich on February 27 (not the 28th), not long before 5:00 in the afternoon. They apparently agreed that Zankevich would not pursue active operations against the insurgents and used the absence of reliable troops as an excuse to his commanders.

18 Actually, Tugan-Baranovskii came to the Duma and began working in the Military Commission on the morning of February 28.

19 The reference is to the military jurist, Colonel Vladimir Dmitrievich Pletnev (1878–1954), who was a graduate of the Military-Juridical Academy and later taught criminal law at Petrograd University as well as several higher military schools. He was also a gifted writer and editor of the short-lived illustrated journal *Petersburg Courier*. During the February Revolution, he was active in organizing insurgent troops under command of the Duma but apparently was not formally associated with the MC. An ardent patriot and anti-monarchist, in mid-March 1917 he was one of the organizers of the concerted pro-war propaganda effort among the troops of the Petrograd garrison, and was founder and editor of the weekly paper *Svoboda v bor'be* (*Freedom in Struggle*). He also advocated deferring the introduction of the eight-hour workday until after the war and ending the dual power system by concentrating all power with the Provisional Government, for which he was smeared in the Socialist press and vilified by the leadership of the Petrograd Soviet. In late March or early April, he and his colleagues among the pro-war non-factional Socialists began to focus on General Kornilov as a potential

temporary military dictator. In early April, he joined forces with B. V. Savinkov, V. S. Zavoiko, and E. P. Semenov to organize the patriotic officers' Union of the Motherland and Peoples' Army, and later wrote the first popular biography of General Kornilov (*Pervyi narodnyi glavnokomanduiushchii general-leitenant L. G. Kornilov* [Petrograd:"Novoe vremia," 1917], 48 pp.). This organization had extensive ties with moderate non-Socialist groups and politicians, including A. I. Guchkov, P. B. Struve, and V. A. Maklakov, and was considered a precursor to the more motley collection of military, political, and public figures that coalesced around General Kornilov during the summer. See E. Semenov, "Nachalo kornilovskogo dvizheniia," *Russkaia nedelia* (Paris), June 28, 1925, 20–1; Alexander Rabinowitch, *The Bolsheviks Come to Power. The Revolution of 1917 in Petrograd* (New York: W. W. Norton & Co., 1976), 98; GARF, f. 1780, op. 1, d. 28.

20   Aleksandr Apollonovich Manuilov (1861–1929) was a prominent Kadet of the liberal-populist bent, professor of political economy and former rector of Moscow University. He served as minister of education in the first two Provisional Governments (March–July 1917).

21   Maksim Gor'kii (Maxim Gorky) was the nom de plume of the "proletarian writer" Aleksei Maksimovich Peshkov (1868–1936), who was a radical in his youth and maintained close personal and professional relationships with leading socialist writers and publicists before and during the revolution.

22   This may have been Colonel Konstantin Pavlovich Kutaisov (1876–1918), an aide-de-camp and commander of the 3rd battery of the Life Guards Cavalry Artillery. He was one of the two sons of the General of the Infantry Pavel Ippolitovich Kutaisov (1837–1911).

23   The reference is to Miliukov's famous speech in the Catherine Hall of the Tauride Palace, on the afternoon of March 2, in which he announced the formation of the Provisional Government and, when asked, briefly spoke about the necessity of preserving the monarchical form of government under the regency of Grand Duke Mikhail Aleksandrovich.

24   In actuality, Guchkov was not arrested upon his return from Pskov. When he and Shul'gin arrived at the Warsaw Railway Station, they were met by insurgent soldiers and railway workers. Guchkov was asked to attend a meeting of the workers during which one of the speakers called for his arrest. But another participant intervened on his behalf. Guchkov was allowed to deliver a brief speech and right after that, he and Shul'gin were rushed in a car provided by the Military Commission to Millionnaia Street where the historic meeting between their Duma and Provisional Government colleagues and Grand Duke Mikhail Aleksandrovich had already begun. Guchkov indeed submitted his resignation on March 3, yet the reason for it was not his alleged arrest. It was his and Miliukov's failure to convince the grand duke to accept the throne. Miliukov too submitted his resignation that day, but by the evening both he and Guchkov had been persuaded to change their minds and remain in the cabinet.

25   The so-called Polivanov Commission was created by the Provisional Government's first minister of war, Guchkov, on March 6, 1917 "for the purpose of revising [military] statutes and regulations in precise conformity with the new legal norms." *RPG*, II: 854. In practice, this meant that the Commission was to prepare wide-ranging democratizing reforms of the armed forces. The Commission was chaired by the former tsarist war minister General A. A. Polivanov. The Octobrist deputy N. V. Savich supervised the Commission's naval division. Also included were many ranking members of the MC, among them Pal'chinskii, colonels Engel'gardt, Tugan-Baranovskii, Iakubovich, and Tumanov, and Generals P. I. Aver'ianov, N. S. Anosov, and A. S. Potapov. The Commission developed a set of statues and procedures that recognized but also regulated the soldiers' committees created by Order Number One, and recommended major personnel changes within the officers' corps. On the whole, however, the Commission failed to introduce sweeping reforms, and did little to contain the growing anarchy or restore the fighting capacity of Russia's armed forces.

26 Aleksei Alekseevich Manikovskii (1865–1920) was a general of the artillery and chief of the Main Artillery Administration (since May 1915). Before the February Revolution, his name was often mentioned by various opposition circles as a likely temporary dictator and head of a public ministry in the event of a successful palace coup. On February 27, 1917, he was in fact offered such a role by the Duma leaders, which he apparently declined (see the Tereshchenko interview). On March 6, 1917, he was appointed assistant minister of war in charge of supplies, and from April 30 also served as manager of affairs of the war ministry. From 1918 to 1920 he served in the Red Army as chief of the Main Artillery Administration.

27 The reference is to point 7 of the so-called "8-point declaration of the Provisional Government," dated March 3, 1917, that was to serve as the program of action for the government before the convocation of the Constituent Assembly. The program was negotiated by the representatives of the Provisional Government and the Petrograd Soviet and promulgated, *inter alia*: immediate political amnesty; political and civic liberties; social, religious, and ethnic equality. It also called for preparations for the convocation of a Constituent Assembly. Point 7, insisted upon by the Petrograd Soviet, guaranteed that military units that had participated in the revolution would not be disarmed or sent to the front.

28 The italicized text, in Rusudana Nikoladze-Polievktova's hand, was written in the left margin.

29 Petr Aleksandrovich Polovtsov (Polovtsev) (1874–1964) was a graduate of the St. Petersburg Mining Institute and colonel of the General Staff. By the time of the February Revolution, he was chief of staff of the Caucasian Natives Cavalry Division (better known as the Savage Division: see n. 32 below). He was on a visit to Petrograd during the February Days. On March 1, 1917, he joined the MC and became its chief liaison officer with the General Staff. His participation in the work of the MC can in part be explained by his long-standing friendship with P. I. Pal'chinskii, who had been his classmate at the Mining Institute. After 3 March, Polovtsov was assigned to the war ministry and on 22 May he replaced General Kornilov as commander of the Petrograd Military District (until 12 July).

30 Petr Konstantinovich Kondzerovskii (1869–1929) was a lieutenant general of the Russian imperial army and the general in charge of new assignments of high-ranking officers at the General Staff (1908–14) and at General Headquarters (1914–17). Both of these positions, by their very nature especially when held for such a long time, earned him many enemies as well as friends. On April 2, 1917, Guchkov relieved Kondzerovskii of his duties at General Headquarters and appointed him to the war minister's advisory military council.

31 According to his service record, Tugan-Baranovskii visited General Headquarters on March 15–16, 1917 (RGVIA, f. 409, op. 1, p/s 149-008 [1917]).

32 The Savage Division (*Kavkazskaia tuzemnaia konnaia diviziia*) was comprised primarily of mountain tribesmen from the northern Caucasus who were legendary for their ferocity in combat (hence its name). It was attached to the Third Corps at the southwestern front, which at the end of August 1917 constituted the main force, under General A. M. Krymov, that marched on Petrograd.

33 That is, in contrast to Petrograd, where for two days on April 20 and 21 thousands of armed workers and soldiers calling for the removal of "bourgeois ministers" confronted the supporters of the Provisional Government. The immediate cause of the April Crisis was the so-called "Miliukov's note to the Allies" of April 18, in which the foreign minister reaffirmed Russia's strong commitment to the war aims of the tsarist government. The most immediate political outcome of this first major crisis of the post-revolutionary period was the resignation of Guchkov (30 April) and Miliukov (2 May) and the formation of the first coalition cabinet.

34 Tugan-Baranovskii was probably referring to Beliaev's tenure as acting chief of the General Staff (1914–16), when he and his two friends, Tumanov and Iakubovich, had served in the Mobilization Department.

35 That is, on April 29, 1917.

36 Guchkov addressed the opening session of the First Congress of Delegates from the Front on
    April 29, 1917 and, according to the published text of his speech, did not mention his impend-
    ing resignation, (*Rech'*, April 30, 1917, 4, and *Vestnik Vremennogo Pravitel'stva*, April 30, 1917, 2).
    In his memoirs, Guchkov also stated that he did not announce his resignation but warned the
    front delegates of the coming disintegration and humiliating defeat of the armed forces at the
    front. He also recalled that Kerenskii joined him at the Congress, which is confirmed by the
    newspaper reports, and that they both left together and rode in the same car. During the ride,
    Kerenskii tried to persuade Guchkov to stay in the office and even offered his own candidacy
    as deputy minister. S. Lyandres and A. V. Smolin, eds., *Aleksandr Ivanovich Guchkov rasskazy-
    vaet...Vospominaniia predsedatelia Gosudarstvennoi dumy i voennogo ministra Vremennogo pravitel'stva*
    (Moscow: "Voprosy istorii," 1993). 109. The Congress of Front Delegates lasted until 4 May,
    but there is no indication that Guchkov addressed it again, that is, after 29 April.

37 Irakli Georgievich Tsereteli (1881–1959) was a leading Georgian and Russian Social Democrat
    (Menshevik), deputy to the Second Duma, and advocate of socialist collaboration with the
    liberal opposition. He spent a decade in prison and exile (since 1907), returned to Petrograd
    on March 19, 1917, and quickly emerged as the leader of the influential revolutionary defensist
    bloc in the Petrograd Soviet. He was the strongest supporter of the coalition among the lead-
    ership of the EC and himself served in two coalition cabinets between May 5 and July 24, 1917.
    Boris Osipovich Bogdanov (1884–1960) was another leading Menshevik; he served as secre-
    tary of the Labor (Workers) Group of the CWIC until his arrest on January 27, 1917. He was
    released from prison by the insurgents on February 27 and took part in organizing the
    Petrograd Soviet. Like Tsereteli, he belonged to the revolutionary defensist bloc and supported
    the coalition. Eduard Ksaver'evich Sokolovskii (V. Shatrov) was a Petrograd Menshevik-
    Internationalist, and a member of the Soviet EC from the evening of February 27. On March
    1, he was sent to represent the EC on the MC.

38 The reference is to a meeting of the EC that began in the evening of May 1 and lasted well
    into the early morning hours on May 2. The final vote was 44 in favor of coalition, 19 against,
    with 2 abstentions. Of the three Menshevik leaders mentioned by Tugan-Baranovskii, only the
    Internationalist Sokolovskii voted against the coalition. See *Petrogradskii Sovet rabochikh i soldat-
    skikh deputatov v 1917 g. Protokoly, stenogrammy sektsii, zasedanii Ispolnitel'nogo komiteta i fraktsii.*
    Vol. II: *1 aprelia–5 maia 1917 g.* (St. Petersburg: Biblioteka Zvezdy, 1995), II: 477, 484–6.

39 This vote took place on April 28, with 22 voting against the coalition and 8 abstaining. See
    Ziva Galili, *The Menshevik Leaders in the Russian Revolution: Social Realities and Political Strategies*
    (Princeton: Princeton University Press, 1989), 176–7.

40 In 1917, the Kadet party headquarters, including the newly created Party Club, was located on
    the French Embankment (no. 8), between Palace Embankment and Liteinyi Bridge. I am
    indebted to Professor A. B. Nikolaev for providing this information.

41 Maksim (Maks-Gil') Moiseevich Vinaver (1863–1926) was a founding member of the Kadet
    party and a member of the Central Committee (CC) from 1905 to 1921. During the Provisional
    Government period, he assumed the role of the CC liaison with the government and as such
    exerted enormous influence over the Kadet participation in the coalition, and on Miliukov.

42 That is, from the third to the fourth day of May.

43 Lys'venskie Mining Enterprises were among the oldest (since 1785) and largest metallurgical
    works in Russia, located in the town of Lys'va near Perm' in the Urals.

44 The reference is to the short-lived revolutionary dictatorship by the Chita Soviet of Workers',
    Soldiers', and Cossacks' Deputies that ruled over that Eastern Siberian city from December
    1905 to January 22, 1906.

45 On Pal'chinskii's extraordinarily wide-ranging interests, technical and organizational talents,
    and spheres of economic, technical, and political activities, see his biographies by Loren

Graham, *The Ghost of the Executed Engineer: Technology and the Fall of the Soviet Union* (Cambridge, MA: Harvard University Press, 1993) and especially I. A. Garaevskaia, Petr Pal'chinskii. *Biografiia inzhenera na fone voin i revoliutsii* (Moscow: Rossiia molodaia, 1996).

46 Filipp Ivanovich Balabin (1881–1938) was a colonel of the General Staff, and general quartermaster of the Petrograd Military District headquarters (1916–17). He was rumored to have maintained close ties with Guchkov and his co-plotters. During the February Revolution, he participated in the work of the MC and was sent to different units of the Petrograd garrison, including, on March 1, the reserve battalion of the Chasseurs Regiment. During May 25 –July 13, 1917, he was acting chief of staff of the Petrograd Military District. He remained in Soviet Russia after October 1917.

47 Nikolai Mikhailovich Filatov (1862–1935) was lieutenant general in the Russian imperial army and a department chief in the Artillery Committee of the Main Artillery Administration. He was the principle designer of a three-wheeled armored car (*broneavtomobil' Filatova*) built in the works of the officers' school in Oranienbaum in 1916. On March 1, 1917, he and all the officers of the First and Second Machine-Gun Regiments stationed in Oranienbaum received orders from the MC to come to the Tauride Palace.

48 Konstantin Fedorovich Grekov (1890–1947) was a first lieutenant in the 7th Finland Riflemen Regiment, to which he was assigned after his injury in June 1916. In December of that year, he was sent to his native Petrograd to recuperate from his injury. He joined the MC shortly after the outbreak of the military uprising. On February 28, 1917 he was appointed commandant of the Nikolaevskii Railway Station and played an important role in blocking the movement of imperial trains toward Tsarskoe Selo. On March 5 he was appointed officer for special tasks under the chairman of the MC, and from July 10 to August 12 he served as commandant of the Tauride Palace.

49 The reference is to the telegram sent by Chkheidze (and signed by him and M. I. Skobelev) on the morning of March 9 on behalf of the Soviet EC to the railroad workers and stationmasters along the route of the former tsar's train from General Headquarters to Tsarskoe Selo, requesting his arrest. However, by the time the telegram reached its destinations, the former tsar had already arrived at Tsarskoe Selo (shortly before 12:00 noon on March 9) and was reunited with his family. To prevent the Provisional Government from allowing Nicholas "to escape to England," the EC increased pressure on their "bourgeois" colleagues and mobilized military units in the capital. Later that evening Chkheidze reported to his Soviet colleagues that the Provisional Government agreed not to allow the former tsar and his family to leave Tsarskoe Selo without the explicit agreement of the EC. See S. Mel'gunov, *Sud'ba Nikolaia II posle otrecheniia* (Paris: La Renaissance, 1951), 22–47; *Petrogradskii soviet*, I: 218–19. Chkheidze's telegram is reproduced in "Fevral'skaia revoliutsiia 1917 goda...," *Krasnyi arkhiv* 1, 21 (1927): 67.

50 The italicized text, in M. A. Polievktov's hand, was inserted here. Roder was a captain in the Finland Radiotelegraph Company. On March 2, he was appointed chief of the MC's radio-telegraph department and operated the telegraph, which had been obtained earlier that day by Pal'chinskii. On March 28, Roder was appointed chief of the radio-telegraph department of the Petrograd military district's headquarters. RGIA, f. 1278, op. 10, d. 58, l. 146, 202.

51 Cavalry Staff Captain (*shtab-rotmistr*) Pavel Pavlovich Kotsebu (1884–1966) was an officer of the Second Life Guards Lancers Regiment. After the February Revolution, he was appointed commandant of the Aleksandrovskii Palace (the main residence of Nicholas and his family) in Tsarskoe Selo. His tenure did not last long and on March 21, under pressure from the Soviet leaders, he was dismissed from his post. On the face of it, the Soviet leaders objected to his humane treatment of the former tsar and his family, now under house arrest in Aleksandrovskii Palace, and Kotsebu's alleged failure to censor their correspondence with the outside world. However, a more convincing reason for his removal appears to have been his resistance to S. D.

Maslovskii's demand to arrest the former tsar and confine him in the Peter and Paul Fortress (see the next note).

52 Sergei Dmitrievich Mstislavskii [real name Maslovskii] (1876–1943) was a librarian of the Academy of the General Staff at the rank of lieutenant colonel, a well-known Socialist Revolutionary (Left SR after the 1917 split) and a prolific writer. He was part of the core group (with Kerenskii, Pal'chinskii, and Filippovskii) that organized the MC on the afternoon of February 27, 1917. On March 9, he was dispatched to Tsarskoe Selo as commissar of the Soviet EC with an ambiguous order "to gain control over the situation," which, as it became clear during his visit, meant to arrest Nicholas and take him to the Peter and Paul Fortress. His mission failed, however, because of the resistance of the soldiers and officers guarding the Aleksandrovskii Palace, who were determined to prevent the former tsar's arrest and transfer to a different custody. According to Kotsebu—as told by his close acquaintance, the prominent defense lawyer N. P. Karabchevskii—when Maslovskii showed up at the Palace, Kotsebu conveyed to him the mood of the garrison. Unable to enforce his will, Maslovskii demanded to see the former tsar to verify that he indeed was in Tsarskoe Selo and had not escaped. In the end, it was agreed that he only be allowed to see Nicholas in a hallway, from a distance. Frustrated and "visibly shaken," he returned to Petrograd empty handed. The next day he requested to be relieved of his duties as commissar for Tsarskoe Selo. See *Petrogradskii sovet*, I: 224; Mel'gunov, *Sud'ba Nikolaia II posle otrecheniia*, 42–5; N. P. Karabchevskii, *Chto glaza moi videli*, vol. II: *Revoliutsiia i Rossiia* (Berlin: izdanie Ol'gi Iakovlevoi, 1921), 144–6; P. N. Apraksin, "9-go marta 1917 goda v Tsarskosel'skom dvortse (po dnevniku)," *Novoe vremia*, March 17, 1922, 2–3. For Maslovskii's much different interpretation of this episode, see his famous account of the Russian Revolution: Sergei Mstislavskii, *Five Days Which Transformed Russia* (Bloomington: Indiana University Press, 1988), 82–107.

53 Tugan-Baranovskii may have referred here to one of two separate but related developments. On April 20, General Lavr Georgievich Kornilov (1870–1918), the commander of the Petrograd military district at the time, proposed to the cabinet his plan to disperse armed demonstrations against the government that were taking place in the city center with reliable troops at his disposal, and urged the ministers to act without delay. However, his request was met with strong opposition from Kerenskii and Prince L'vov, and was denied. On April 21, Kornilov issued an order for two batteries of light artillery from the Mikhailovskii Artillery School to deploy on the Palace Square as a warning to the armed demonstrators. The order went into effect but was soon rescinded, after intervention by the Soviet EC's representatives, M. I. Skobelev and A. R. Gots, who insisted on the Soviet's exclusive right to approve any such order by civilian or military authorities.

54 The reference is to the battleship *Emperor Alexander II*, which on May 9, 1917 was renamed *Zaria svobody* (Dawn of Liberty). Built in 1893, the battleship had been used as a training artillery unit (hence "old galosh") since 1906, and in 1918 it was decommissioned altogether. The crew included 638 sailors and officers.

55 *Gangut* was a much newer, more advanced and powerful battleship; it was built in 1914 and had a crew of 1,094 men. In 1925 it was renamed *October Revolution*, and was decommissioned only in 1956.

56 Abram Rafailovich Gots (1882–1940) was a well-known SR (longtime member of the CC), and the leader of the SR faction in the EC of the Petrograd Soviet. He spent eight years in hard labor (released in 1915) and then lived in administrative exile in Irkutsk, where he belonged to the group of Siberian Zimmerwaldists led by Irakli Tsereteli. He returned to Petrograd in March 1917. In April, he was elected to the EC and belonged to the Tsereteli-led revolutionary defensist bloc. During the April Crisis, he supported a coalition on the condition that Social Democrats also join the cabinet.

57 Staff Captain Nikolai Nikolaevich Krasnov, who died in the fall of 1917, began his military career in His Majesty's Life Guards Cossack Cavalry Regiment, where he served with F. I. Balabin. During the February Revolution, he joined the MC and worked in the communications department, then under colonel Balabin. From 2 to 10 March he served as an orderly officer under the new commander of the Petrograd Military District General Kornilov, whom he also accompanied to Tsarskoe Selo, on March 8, to arrest the tsarina. Krasnov's account of this mission was recorded by M. A. Polievktov on June 5, 1917.

8

Nikolai Vissarionovich Nekrasov

NIKOLAI VISSARIONOVICH NEKRASOV (1879–1940) was a prominent Left Kadet and deputy to the third and fourth Dumas, from Tomsk province. Born in St. Petersburg to the family of a parish priest, Nekrasov was the oldest of six children and had to earn everything through hard work and perseverance. A gifted and diligent student, he graduated in 1897 with a gold medal from a classical gymnasium and later excelled as a student in the prestigious St. Petersburg Institute of Railway Engineers. Following graduation, he was invited to join the faculty of the recently established Tomsk Technological Institute, and in 1903 was sent to Germany and Switzerland as part of his preparations for a professorial position. In 1906 he defended his dissertation on the theoretical foundations of bridge construction and was promoted to professor in the department of statistics and the construction of railway bridges. Nekrasov's active involvement in politics dates back to the beginning of his European tour where, mostly in Switzerland, he established contacts with Russian political exiles from the (socialist) revolutionary and liberal circles. Upon his return to Tomsk he joined a local branch of the Union of Liberation, and at the end of the turbulent year of 1905 became a member of the recently founded Kadet party. By the time of his election to the (third) Duma in 1907, Nekrasov had just turned 28 but was already a well-established professional and a rising star in the left wing of the Kadet party (one of his preferred paths to the "people's freedom" was through abolishing the private ownership of land).

In the Duma he distinguished himself as a gifted orator and efficient legislator, especially on questions related to the area of his technical expertise and the introduction of institutions of local self-government in Siberia. He also showed himself to be a talented organizer for the party. He began serving as the Kadet Duma faction secretary in May 1909 and was co-opted to the party's Central Committee in the fall. Surrounded by many lawyers and apparently sensing the need to perform on par with his party colleagues and in the Duma, Nekrasov taught himself law, and in 1910 successfully passed the bar examination. During the war years, Nekrasov served on the Special Council on Defense and was an influential member of the

Progressive Bloc's leadership in the Duma. In November 1916 he became one of the Duma President's two elected deputies which assured him membership in the select group of the Duma Presidium and access to the highest echelons of the Duma leadership.

Alongside his official roles, however, he also appears to have developed an appetite (or perhaps he had an inherent tendency) for conspiratorial activity. He was one of the revivers of Russian political Masonry in the post-1905 period, which emphasized above-party-lines Center-Left cooperation aimed at changing the existing political and social order. Here too Nekrasov played an important and increasingly leading role—from the "venerable Master" of one of the Duma lodges in 1909 to the general secretary of the nationwide Masonic network, the Grand Orient of the Peoples of Russia, during 1910–16. This penchant for behind-the-scenes conspiratorial activity, "leading from the background," would manifest itself ever more strongly in the fall of 1916, when he and the future foreign minister Tereshchenko joined the so-called Guchkov plot to remove Nicholas II. Nekrasov's active involvement in the plot reveals a great deal about his mode of thinking on how to achieve regime change and his political *modus operandi* more generally. It also helps explain his otherwise baffling insistence, throughout the first day of the February Revolution, on the establishment of a temporary military dictatorship under the leadership of a popular general and a council of public figures, despite the absence of viable candidates and widespread popular revolt.

Although Nekrasov chose not to dwell on this topic in his interview with the Polievktov Commission, he nevertheless provided many previously unknown details about some of his other activities during the February Days, including his participation in the two historic negotiations with Grand Duke Mikhail Aleksandrovich: on the evening of February 27 for the transition of authority to the Duma, and on March 3 when the grand duke was persuaded to renounce the throne. Nekrasov was one of the architects of the Temporary Duma Committee which, as a member of the Duma Presidium, he joined from the outset. Together with Kerenskii and Engel'gardt, he was among the most active and influential organizers of revolutionary forces in the Duma. He is especially credited with leading the efforts to manipulate the movement of the imperial train while on its way from General Headquarters to Petrograd. Nicholas II was deliberately misled about the conditions on the railroads, prevented from returning to the capital, and was instead diverted to Pskov where—trapped and confronted by his generals—he abdicated.

While on the Duma Committee, Nekrasov joined forces with Kerenskii and Miliukov to oppose Rodzianko's strategy of expanding the Duma's authority, and at the same time successfully blocked Miliukov's efforts to preserve the monarchy under Grand Duke Mikhail Aleksandrovich. He would continue to undermine his long-time party rival and *bête noire* in the first cabinet, contributing in no small measure to Miliukov's eventual departure from the Provisional Government and consolidating the leading role for the Kerenskii-led triumvirate of Tereshchenko and himself. He served as minister of transportation in the first two cabinets

(March–July) and then as minister of finance and assistant premier (July–August). He played a decisive role during the Kornilov–Kerenskii confrontation at the end of August, supporting the latter and declaring the former a traitor. A declaration to that effect was expeditiously transmitted across the country via the railway telegraphic network under the transportation ministry. However, his alliance with Kerenskii soon came to an end when Kerenskii discovered that his longtime political collaborator had secretly sided with those who argued for the premier's resignation in the aftermath of the Kornilov debacle. In early September, Nekrasov was dismissed from the cabinet and sent into "honorary exile" in Helsingfors as the last Russian governor general of Finland. This marked the end of his extraordinary decade-long political career.

Following the Bolshevik takeover, he disengaged from politics but remained in Soviet Russia and spent the rest of his life under the watchful eye of the secret police. His motives for staying cannot be established with certainty. However, the traditional (and romanticized) view that he chose not to emigrate in order to "work for Russia" even under Lenin and Stalin does not easily fit with Nekrasov's very ambitious, self-serving, and manipulative personality. In any event, his subsequent fate was anything but enviable. For the first several years he was constantly on the move, living under the assumed name of Golgofskii (a curious and telling choice, given the name's etymology—*golgofa* or Calvary) and working in various Soviet cooperative and financial institutions in Moscow, Omsk, again in Moscow, and Kazan'. In the spring of 1921 his true identity was exposed. He was arrested in Kazan' and sent to Moscow's notorious Butyrki prison. But he somehow succeeded in convincing highly placed *chekisty* that he had become a loyal Soviet citizen and was soon released on Dzerzhinskii's orders. For the next nine years he appears to have been left alone, started a new family, and worked in the Central Union of Cooperatives and Consumers. From time to time he was even allowed to teach statistics and finances in several Moscow institutions of higher education.

But then in November 1930, with preparations for the so-called Menshevik trial underway, his troubles began in earnest. Although never a Menshevik, he was arrested, forced to confess to crimes against the Soviet State that he had not committed (sabotaging supplies of consumer goods), and in 1931 he was sentenced to ten years in the labor camps. He spent two years in the infamous Solovki camps, working on the construction of the White Sea Canal, where he quickly demonstrated the extraordinary organizational skills that helped earn him an early release in 1933. Yet he stayed on the Canal and continued to work as a construction manager until 1937. His final arrest came in June of 1939. This time he was sent to the Moscow Lefortovo prison. Accused of taking part in the attempted assassination of Lenin in 1918, anti-Soviet activity (as a member of an underground terrorist organization), and sabotage, he was subjected to months of interrogations and in the end "agreed" to all charges. He was sentenced to death on April 14, 1940 and executed three weeks later.

Nekrasov never wrote memoirs. This is hardly surprising considering the trying circumstances of his post-revolutionary life. He was, however, "persuaded" to share his recollections with "historians" in black leather jackets and the blue cap-bands of the Lenin and Stalin secret police during his arrests in 1921, 1931, and 1939. On two of these three occasions he very briefly touched upon on his role in the February Revolution.[a] But those comments pale in comparison with his May 25, 1917 interview, which not only represents the earliest and most complete account of his activities during the February Days, but remains his only testimony provided of his own free will.

The interview is reproduced here on the basis of a master copy compiled by Rusudana Polievktova-Nikoladze, with stylistic edits written between the lines in Tamara Nikoladze's hand.

★ ★ ★ ★ ★ ★

The Minister of Transportation Nikolai Vissarionovich Nekrasov. May 25, [19]17

The morning of February 27 began with a phone call from State Duma Deputy Vostrotin,[1] who informed me that in the street in front of his apartment (he lives at the corner of Paradnaia [Street] and Grecheskii [Lane])[2] there were soldiers with red flags causing a disturbance. I, in turn, telephoned Rodzianko, who was already aware of all that. "The State Duma has been dissolved," he said, "I just received the *ukase*."[3]

"When does it go into effect?" I asked.

"Yesterday. What is there to do?" He replied.

"Mikhail Vladimirovich, we should gather in the Duma," I said.

"Call in whomever you can find, and then go there yourself." I picked up the phone and explained to the operator girl that I needed to be connected urgently to as many Duma deputies as possible. She very quickly connected me with more than fifteen people. I summoned them all to the Duma, and soon went there myself. Shortly thereafter, Rodzianko also arrived. On my way, I heard shooting all around me: on Kirochnaia, Tavricheskaia, and Paradnaia.

In the Duma, it was known that soldiers had rebelled and were moving in the direction of the Tauride Palace, but none were yet in sight. As it turned out later, they were pressing the *Preobrazhentsy* [Preobrazhenskii soldiers] to join them, but not all did. Around 11–12:00, the first armed insurgent soldiers arrived at the Duma. Kerenskii went out to greet them with a

---

[a] "Iz sledstvennykh del N. V. Nekrasova 1921, 1931 i 1939 godov," *Voprosy istorii* 11–12 (1998): 19–20, 38.

speech. At that time, we received a report that the Soviet of Workers' Deputies would soon be formed. Also, a number of outsiders showed up who had no Duma affiliation, but some of us knew that these people were connected to each other. By the way, I remember how one prominent public figure[4] approached Rodzianko and categorically declared, "Proclaim yourselves a provisional government, topple the Romanovs, and chase out all Rightists, including the Octobrists." He had completely forgotten that Rodzianko himself was an Octobrist. Rodzianko was at a loss.

Soon, the first meeting of the Duma began. I was running around the whole time taking care of all sorts of matters. There was already revolutionary chaos in the Tauride Palace. At that time, the first shootings took place in the Duma. One of the officers of the Duma guard was wounded by soldiers. Rodzianko categorically forbade Osten-Sacken[5] to mount any resistance. Crowds of people, soldiers, and automobiles began to arrive. The Duma was overtaken by revolution.

In the morning, Mikhail Aleksandrovich telephoned Rodzianko from Gatchina[6] asking for a meeting. He knew what was happening, and was very worried. Rodzianko set the meeting for 5–6:00 in the evening at the Mariinskii Palace.

In the turmoil of the first part of the day, the Temporary Committee of the Duma was formed. At its first meeting, it was decided that the Presidium of the Temporary Committee (Rodzianko, Nekrasov, Rzhevskii,[7] Dmitriukov) and Savich would go to negotiate with Mikhail Aleksandrovich. We took two cars. As we were leaving, we were stopped by soldiers, who asked us questions: who are you, where are you going, and why? Once we told them, they became our revolutionary cortège, and accompanied by revolutionary shouting we drove, escorted by the rebellious soldiers. We drove by the circuit court building, which was on fire, and along the embankment. We stopped before approaching Troitskii Bridge. The revolutionary zone ended there, so the soldiers jumped off. We entered the government zone. We did not see pro-government troops before we reached the building of the city police chief. There were detachments of infantry with machine-guns near the building, as well as Cossacks. We did not see any more troops. There was shooting all around us. From time to time, we could hear the characteristic rat-a-tat-tat of machine-guns. But there were no obvious signs of revolution.

Mikhail Aleksandrovich was already waiting at the Mariinskii Palace. We went to the office of the state secretary. We stated that the situation was very serious, and that this required urgent measures. We asked him to assume regency and to appoint temporarily (before the tsar's arrival from General Headquarters) a provisional government of public figures to administer the country, headed by a popular general devoted to a constitution. Mikhail quickly and readily agreed, but declared that he first needed to talk with General Headquarters via direct wire—that he would do so at once and act as soon as he got an answer. The council of ministers was in session, and he went to talk to the ministers (before his conversation with the tsar) to ask Beliaev to connect him with the tsar.

The ministers categorically objected, which was mainly because of Beliaev's influence. He claimed that the government was on solid ground, and that the broad measures he was undertaking would pacify the situation; this was his line. Right then, we also learned that Protopopov was no longer a minister. The government, in an effort to save itself, had thrown him overboard. The former chief military procurator Makarenko,[8] who was there with us, and with whom we chatted, was appointed minister of internal affairs. His mood was far from victorious. I told him what I knew—that soldiers were refusing to fire, and so on. Makarenko threw his hands up in despair: "And nobody is going to fire, and no one holds out any hope for that."

There was a strange moment while we were with the council of ministers. Even Nikolai Nikolaevich Pokrovskii, who is a person of the highest degree of decency, argued in favor of suppressing the uprising without mercy. He and some other ministers were determined to emerge victorious; other ministers exhibited open hostility toward us Duma deputies. They knew about Shcheglovitov's arrest. Kryzhanovskii[9] made it clear that he suspected the arrest was made on Rodzianko's orders. The hostility toward us was quite pronounced. We attempted to come up with conditions which would be acceptable to Mikhail. The ministers denied us access to direct wire, and the conversation (between Mikhail and the tsar) did not take place. The matter was closed. Mikhail Aleksandrovich did not consider himself free to act without the consent of the council of ministers.

At 9–10:00 in the evening, we drove back via Voznesenskii [Avenue], Sadovaia [Street], Sennaia [Square], Fontanka [Embankment], Stremiannaia [Street], Povarskoi [Lane] (where we dropped Savich off),[10] Nevskii, and Znamenskaia—we drove through a revolutionary city. There were no longer any zones. It was all one continuous revolutionary wave—revolution had taken everything over. Armed automobiles repeatedly stopped us and asked us for a pass. At times, they appeared to be satisfied, but at other times, Rodzianko's name met with disapproval. For several blocks, we rode under a peculiar guard. An old man, around 50 years old, jumped onto our running board. Once he learned who was in the car, he began declaring everywhere: "Here comes the deputy of the State Duma, Nekrasov, member of the Party of People's Freedom.[11] Hooray!" We made it through a large section of the city on the strength of the name "Nekrasov." Everywhere, police stations were burning. The picture was quite clear. We drove Dmitriukov[12] and Savich home, [then] proceeded in one car. The whole time, Rodzianko spoke about the blindness of the old regime, which did not see where it was headed. After bidding farewell to Dmitriukov and Savich, we went back to the Duma.

The Duma was completely under revolutionary dominance. An incredible amount of things of all sorts was brought in: flowers, silver bullion, and so on. In the hallway, there was a piece of explosive on the floor, and near it just a small sign, "No Smoking." Masses of people were somehow fed there for several days. It was a decisive moment, and the question arose: What do we do now? The entire Temporary Committee of the Duma was pleading with Rodzianko to head up the movement, but he continued to refuse. At long last, the news came over the telephone that the Preobrazhenskii Regiment had sided with the Temporary Committee of the Duma. I burst in with this news, and everyone shouted, "Mikhail Vladimirovich, you must agree!"[13] He got up, waved his hand, and said: "All right." From that moment until the end of the revolutionary days, Rodzianko behaved admirably, firmly, without wavering—in a word, this was a man at his very best. With this, the first period ended.

An armored car was sent to arrest the council of ministers. There was only one mishap: no one knew the ministers by sight, and so they slipped away. When soldiers burst into the Mariinskii Palace, the council of ministers was in session. Everyone was terribly frightened. Nobody knew what was happening. One of the ministers subsequently told me that he does not remember how, but he found himself under a table. When everything calmed down, he came out from under the table. When Pokrovskii—and following him, Protopopov—were leaving the palace, they ran into soldiers coming in with bayonets ready and shouting, "Where is Protopopov?" Pokrovskii did not know what to say, so he said, "He is over there somewhere." The soldiers ran past them, and Pokrovskii and Protopopov were able to escape.[14] From that moment, the government no longer existed. But we did not figure that out for more than 24 hours. Then began the continuous, round-the-clock sitting, appeals, meetings, and so on.

The Moment of Abdication of Nicholas and Mikhail: The Last Night

On March 2, Guchkov and Shul'gin left for Pskov to get Nicholas's abdication. We stayed behind in anticipation. The situation was desperate. The waiting was long and torturous. Finally, during the night we received a report that they were on their way back, and that a coded telegram had been sent in Rodzianko's name to the Main Staff. Only Rodzianko could receive the telegram, and he had to go and pick it up personally. He and [Prince] L'vov left to use the direct wire. We waited for them.[15] At that time, we received, from Bublikov in the Ministry of Transportation, the first report that the abdication had taken place. There were two copies of the abdication manifesto—one was left with Ruzskii,[16] the other was taken by Guchkov. Ruzskii transmitted it in a coded telegram to the chief coordinator of troop movement for the Warsaw District, who started to decipher it. We were told only that some kind of coded telegram had been received, and that the chief coordinator was deciphering it. This caused a terrible uproar. At that time, we were living under fear of possible suppression by Ivanov,[17] and therefore sent someone to arrest the chief coordinator. Later, everything was cleared up. Bublikov received the text of the abdication. The abdication was not in favor of the son, as we expected, but in favor of Mikhail. The question of what to do arose. Many differed, but the majority (with the exception of P. N. Miliukov) thought that Mikhail's abdication should also be demanded. Right then, I composed the text of an abdication in favor of the people, which would be in force until the Constituent Assembly. It was used as the basis for the final abdication. We still did not know the whereabouts of Guchkov and Shul'gin and of Rodzianko and L'vov. The latter pair, unable to reach Ruzskii on direct wire—it was broken—came back to the Duma at 7–8:00.[18]

Mikhail invited Duma deputies to come for talks. At 4 in the morning, we informed him that he would be visited by Duma deputies at 6–7:00 in the morning.[19] Apparently he was awake when we called him, and already knew about the abdication.[20]

We were waiting for Rodzianko and L'vov. When they arrived, a stormy meeting took place. Miliukov decisively defended his position, and was even prepared to resign. We persuaded Miliukov not to resign by allowing him to defend his point of view before Mikhail Aleksandrovich. Members of the

Provisional Government and of the Temporary Duma Committee gathered
to see Mikhail Aleksandrovich. Guchkov and Shul'gin arrived later. They
had been delayed by a brief arrest in the locomotive shop at the Warsaw
Railway Station, after they tried to advocate in favor of Mikhail
Aleksandrovich's candidacy and nearly lost their copy of the text of the tsar's
abdication. They came late.

The very scene of the Mikhail's abdication was unforgettable: the splen-
did noble's apartment on Millionnaia [Street], Hussars standing guard, ele-
gant furniture in the living room and boudoirs. Into this setting poured in
an unspeakably strange company of people—dirty and unwashed, with
creased faces, eyes red and bloodshot from sleepless nights, uncombed hair,
and wrinkled collars. These were representatives of the Provisional
Government and the Temporary Committee of the Duma—the only organs
of power in the country. On the other side was a person who could be
considered emperor. Mikhail Aleksandrovich was very calm, reserved, and
proper. After initial greetings, Rodzianko described the purpose of our visit.
In the presence of Mikhail Aleksandrovich, the question of whether or not he
should be emperor was discussed and decided. Guchkov, Shul'gin, and Miliukov
spoke for the necessity of accepting the title. Everyone else was against it,
including Rodzianko and L'vov. After Rodzianko spoke, I read my text of
abdication[21] and discussion ensued. All those involved were exceptional debat-
ers who knew how to defend their points of view. The tension reached its
maximum. All etiquette was completely forgotten. Mikhail was sitting, and
near him people were speaking loudly, getting up, and leaving the room. Some
listened; others whispered in corners. The anxiety was unbelievable.

The main line of argument for accepting regency was built on the
premise that it was essential to take this step, even though they (Guchkov,
Miliukov, Shul'gin) did not deny its potential risks. Russia and the army
would be against the promulgation of a republic. He must accept the throne
to save Russia.

We were arguing the opposite: that the dynasty was completely compro-
mised, and therefore regency would likely provoke a civil war. Petrograd
might be soaked in blood, and the army and the country would find themselves in open civil war in the face of the external enemy. We thought to
leave the question of regency up to the Constituent Assembly. The debate
continued for about two hours. Mikhail Aleksandrovich expressed the desire
to consult with Rodzianko and L'vov, and then be left alone in order to
make a final decision. As Kerenskii was exiting the room, he overheard

Guchkov talking on the telephone, and concluded that Guchkov was trying to somehow influence things in his desired direction.[22] Kerenskii came back to the room quite agitated, and turned to Mikhail Aleksandrovich with a passionate appeal: not to talk to anyone on the phone while he was left alone, except for his wife. Mikhail calmed him down, saying: "My wife is in Gatchina, and I do not want to talk to anyone else. I would like to be left alone with my conscience." After that, we left the room and began waiting.

The waiting was tense. Mikhail Aleksandrovich conversed with Rodzianko and L'vov. Rodzianko, when he left the room, remarked: "He cannot reign, and he knows it." And indeed, judging by his behavior, it was clear that Mikhail was only looking for a moral excuse to refuse. When he was left to himself, the atmosphere reached the apex of intensity. One of the ministers was so worried that he came to me and said, "Nikolai Vissarionovich, give me a revolver, I cannot go on like this." He could not wait until the end, and left. About five minutes later, Mikhail Aleksandrovich emerged and with calm, measured voice—which simultaneously betrayed a certain anxiety— said that he had decided to abdicate. I remember the general tone. I was a passionate supporter of abdication, but when the moment came, I felt all the weight of this decision fall on my shoulders.

Everyone left. Price L'vov stayed at Mikhail Aleksandrovich's, and some-one else was called in (Nabokov and someone else) for the final editing of the abdication (Boris Nolde and perhaps also Lazarevskii), the document was changed, and many legal nuances were inserted.[23] Mikhail himself did not do much editing. He replaced the word "We" with "I," "demand" with "ask"; and he inserted, "And so help me God." Nicholas wrote his own abdication in advance, but only a few phrases were put into the copy which was delivered by Guchkov.

On the night of March 1, we were hunting for [General] Ivanov. Bublikov was sitting in the ministry of transportation, and on our orders, directing the movement of trains and echelons via telegraph. In the Duma, we were in charge of the telephone [lines] and were informing everyone what the movements were, and what was happening with trains. At 2–3:00 in the morning [of February 28], I received a report from Bublikov that imperial trains, marked with the letters "A" and "B,"[24] had left General Headquarters and were moving toward Bologoe. What should we do? The Temporary Committee of the Duma decided to allow the trains to move, but to keep us informed on everything. About this time, General Tatishchev's train left Tsarskoe Selo in the direction of Gatchina and Tosno[25] to meet the imperial trains, but we did not know if the imperial family were with Tatishchev (we did not know that the children were sick).[26] From Tosno, the general wanted to proceed to Liuban', but could not. The imperial trains reached Malaia Vishera, but stopped because movement on the next segment had not been cleared. Tatishchev was sitting in Tosno.

Every 10–15 minutes, Bublikov was asking us what to do next. He kept us informed on the movement of the imperial trains. We received a report that they had turned back toward Bologoe, and we allowed them to proceed. In the meantime, Tatishchev had reached Liuban', but was not allowed to go any further. Once he learned that the imperial trains had turned back to Bologoe, he returned to Tsarskoe Selo. We then received a report that the imperial trains arrived at Bologoe and were asking for permission to go in the direction of Dno. We allowed them to proceed, thinking that we would let them leave Bologoe but detain them halfway to Dno. That order was given, but somehow arrived too late. Bublikov asked Grinchuk-Lukashevich,[27] who is the current director of Aleksandrovskaia Railroad,[28] to stop at nothing—even to go as far as sending freight trains into the path of the imperial trains. By that time, all of Dno's station agents had been detained by the police, so that order was not received either. The tsar was able to reach Dno. Then the question again arose whether we should let him continue on to Tsarskoe Selo. We gave the order that he could go in the direction of Petrograd as long as he did not go back to General Headquarters. He could not travel south, but his way to the north was still open. It was a surprise to everyone that he went to Pskov. He was allowed to travel there because it was safe for us—we were sure of the mood in Pskov. He got stuck there, and abdicated. Such is the history of our pursuit on the railroads. He was afraid to go to Piter;[29] he went to Pskov and abdicated there.

NOTES

1 Stepan (Stefan) Vasil'evich Vostrotin (1864–1943) was a leading Kadet deputy to the third and fourth Dumas from Enisei province. During the war years, he was active in the CWIC, the Zemgor, and the Special Council on Food Supply. During the February Revolution, he participated in the work of the joint Soviet–Duma Commission for Food Supply (from February 28); on March 1, 1917, he was appointed Duma Committee commissar to the Special Conference on Food Supply; he also served as an assistant minister of agriculture under A. I. Shingarev (March–May 1917).

2 Vostrotin resided at no. 12 Grecheskii Lane.

3 That is, the prorogation decree, dated February 25, 1917, but received by Rodzianko after 11:00 at night on February 26.

4 The reference is to Popular Socialist Vladimir Ivanovich Charnolusskii.

5 Vladimir Fedorovich von Osten-Sacken (1860–1920) was a career army officer, major general (1910), and chief of the security guards of the Tauride Palace (1906–17).

6 Grand Duke Mikhail Aleksandrovich and his wife Countess N. S. Brasova lived in Gatchina, a town and railway station 28 miles (45 km) south of Petrograd, which was also the favorite residence of his father, Alexander III.

7 Vladimir Alekseevich Rzhevskii (1865–after July 1917) was the leader of the liberal Progressists' faction in the fourth Duma. Starting in June 1913, he also served as senior deputy to the Duma Secretary (I. I. Dmitriukov) and thus was a member of the Duma Presidium. From 1915 to 1917, he represented his faction on the Bureau of the Progressive Bloc; he took part in the private meeting of the Duma members on February 27, 1917 and was elected to the Duma Committee. He was also supposed to join his Duma Presidium colleagues in the negotiations with the grand duke on the evening of February 27, but ended up not going to the Mariinskii Palace.

8 Aleksandr Sergeevich Makarenko (1861–1932) was a prominent military jurist at the rank of lieutenant general, and the last chief military procurator under the old regime (1911–17). He replaced A. D. Protopopov as minister of internal affairs during the night of February 26–7, 1917. He was decommissioned on March 15, 1917.

9 Sergei Efimovich Kryzhanovskii (1862–1935) was the last state secretary of Imperial Russia (1911–17). A radical in his youth, he later became a conservative and loyal defender of the old regime, and proved himself a very able jurist and administrator. He served as assistant minister of internal affairs (1906–11) under P. A. Stolypin, and was the principal architect of the electoral law of June 3, 1907. He was arrested during the February Revolution, but was soon released. After 1920 he lived in France.

10 Savich resided at 12 Povarskoi Lane.

11 That is, the Constitutional Democratic or Kadet party.

12 Dmitriukov resided at 40 Sergievskaia Street, also within walking distance of the Tauride Palace.

13 The honor of receiving a telephone call from the Preobrazhenskii Regiment on the night of February 27 and then delivering "the extraordinary important news" to the wavering Rodzianko was also claimed by the Octobrist deputy S. I. Shidlovskii, while the non-factional Social Democrat N. N. Sukhanov remembered talking on the telephone with someone from the Preobrazhenskii Regiment but failing to inform his "bourgeois" colleagues, who waited anxiously for Rodzianko's decision in the adjacent room. S. I. Shidlovskii, *Vospominaniia* (Berlin, 1923), 2: 67–8; Nik.[olai] Sukhanov, *Zapiski o revoliutsii*, 7 parts (Berlin, Petersburg, Moscow: Izdatel'stvo Z. I. Grzhebina, 1922–3), I, 1–2: 97.

14 A. D. Protopopov came to the Tauride Palace on his own around 11:00 at night on February 28 and turned himself in. Pokrovskii was never arrested and, in fact, continued to perform his duties as minister of foreign affairs (presumably with the Duma leaders' tacit consent) for another 24–36 hours.

15 Rodzianko and L'vov went to the Main Staff to receive the telegram and then to the war ministry to use the Hughes apparatus, the only place in the capital with a direct connection to General Headquarters at the time, to talk to General Alekseev. They apparently left the Duma no later than 3:00 in the morning on March 3, but Rodzianko's conversation with General Headquarters (with L'vov standing by his side) did not start until 6:00 and lasted until 6:45. During the three or so hours that separated their departure from the Tauride Palace and the Rodzianko–Alekseev conversation, the two leaders decided to take a quick nap in quiet places where they could not be reached. L'vov went to the home of his long-time associate D. M. Shchepkin at 42 Furshtatskaia Street, and Rodzianko to that of his old

friend and fellow former cavalry guard, V. M. Vonliarliarskii at 16 Manezhnyi Lane, only a few blocks from Rodzianko's own residence on Furshtatskaia. The pair returned to the Duma only after Rodzianko's conversation with General Ruzskii, which ended at 8:45, that is, after the meeting between Grand Duke Mikhail Aleksandrovich and the representatives of the Duma and Provisional Government had already been set up. See N. V. Savich, *Vospominaniia* (St. Petersburg: Logos, 1993), 219, 221; V. M. Vonliarliarskii, *Moi vospominaniia, 1852–1939 gg.* (Berlin: Russischer National-Verlag und Versandbuchhandlung, 1939), 114, 197–225; "Fevral'skaia revoliutsiia 1917 goda (Dokumenty stavki)," *Krasnyi arkhiv* 22, 3 (1927): 26–9; RGIA, f. 1278, op. 10, d. 9, l. 19.

16 Nikolai Vladimirovich Ruzskii (1854–1918) was general adjutant and general of the infantry. At the time of the February Revolution, he was commander in chief of the armies of the northern front (August 1, 1916–April 25, 1917).

17 Nekrasov probably exaggerated the threat or confused the dates. The Ivanov expedition had already been halted on the night of March 1–2. See n. 46 to the Engel'gardt interview.

18 It is quite possible that Rodzianko kept Nekrasov in the dark about his conversation with General Ruzskii, during which the Duma President pretended that a Duma-based authority was about to be formed while knowing full well that Nekrasov and his allies in the Provisional Government had drastically different plans (see the transcript of Rodzianko–Ruzskii conversation in "Fevral'skaia revoliutsiia 1917 goda (Dokumenty stavki)," 26–9). In any case, Rodzianko and L'vov could not have returned to the Duma "at 7–8:00," for Rodzianko's conversation with the commander of the northern front only ended at 8:45. See n. 15 above.

19 Nekrasov is off by about two hours. Kerenskii telephoned the grand duke around 6:00 in the morning to inform him of the abdication and to set up a meeting with the members of the Provisional Government and the Duma Committee. It was agreed that they would come to Princess O. P. Putiatina's apartment on Millionnaia Street (no. 12), where the grand duke had been staying since the night of February 27–8. Considering the timing of Rodzianko and L'vov's return to the Duma, the delegation could only have arrived at Putiatina's after 9:00. Guchkov and Shul'gin joined their colleagues a half hour to an hour after the meeting had begun.

20 See the Kerenskii interview in this volume (Chapter 11).

21 See n. 23 below.

22 Guchkov later recalled that Kerenskii thought that he and his allies were somehow conspiring to preserve the monarchy. According to Guchkov, he telephoned his wife to inform her about his safe return from Pskov, which he had not done earlier because he was delayed at the Warsaw Station and then rushed to Millionnaia. See S. Lyandres and A. V. Smolin, eds., *Aleksandr Ivanovich Guchkov rasskazyvaet ... Vospominaniia predsedatelia Gosudarstvennoi dumy i voennogo ministra Vremennogo pravitel'stva* (Moscow: "Voprosy istorii," 1993), 109–10.

23 According to Nol'de, Nekrasov's draft of the manifesto had to be almost completely rewritten because it mentioned nothing about the position of the Provisional Government or the concept of a Constituent Assembly (B. E. Nol'de, *Dalekoe i blizkoe: istoricheskie ocherki* (Paris: "Sovremennye zapiski," 1930), 144. See also George Katkov's insightful discussion, in *Russia, 1917: The February Revolution* (New York: Harper & Row, 1967), 409–14. Vladimir Dmitrievich Nabokov (1869–1922) was a leading Kadet jurist specializing in criminal law. At the time of the February Revolution, he was a senior clerk (drafted as a noncommissioned officer) at the General Staff; on 3 March, he was called to Millionnaia to edit Nekrasov's draft of the grand duke's abdication manifesto. Boris Emmanuilovich Nol'de (1876–1948) was another leading Kadet jurist, known for his expertise in international law. At the time of the February Revolution, he served in the ministry of foreign affairs, and on March 3 was summoned to assist Nabokov and Shul'gin. Nikolai Ivanovich

Lazarevskii (1868–1921) was a well-known specialist in constitutional law, *privatdozent* of Petrograd University and professor at the Higher Women's Courses. In contrast to Nekrasov's contention, the available sources do not corroborate Lazarevskii's direct participation in editing the manifesto, even though he would have been the only expert in constitutional (state) law among those involved in the process.

24 One train was carrying the tsar; the other – his entourage.

25 Tosno, a railroad hub on the Petrograd–Moscow (Nikolaevskaia) line, located 34 miles (54 km) southeast of Petrograd.

26 Count Il'ia Leonidovich Tatishchev (1859–1918) was adjutant general in the imperial suite, and lieutenant general in the Life Guards Hussar Regiment. Beginning in 1914, he served directly under Nicholas II's command. In August 1917, he followed the imperial family into exile in Tobol'sk, and was executed by the Bolsheviks on July 10, 1918. All five of Nicholas's and Aleksandra's children (Aleksei and four daughters) were sick with measles from February 23, and stayed with their mother at Tsarskoe Selo.

27 Liutsian Avrelievich Grinchuk-Lukashevich (1879–after 1939) was a graduate of the St. Petersburg Institute of Railway Engineers. At the time of the February Revolution, he was chief of operations and telegraph (in charge of coordination of passenger and cargo transfers, technical services, and supervising stationmasters) of the Moscow–Vindava–Rybinsk Railway. In March 1917, he was appointed by the Provisional Government as chief (*nachal'nik*) of Aleksandrovskaia Railroad in Moscow. Nekrasov is referring to the famous telegram sent by Grinchuk-Lukashevich on February 28, 1917 to the chief of Dno station (I. I. Zubrilin) ordering that the imperial train be prevented from reaching the headquarters of the northern front in Pskov at all costs.

28 Aleksandrovskaia, or the Moscow–Brest Railroad, was one of the oldest and longest (684 miles/1,100 km) privately constructed railroads in Imperial Russia, connecting Moscow with Smolensk, Mogilev, Minsk, and Grodno provinces.

29 That is, Petrograd (St. Petersburg).

9

Nikolai Semenovich
Chkheidze

Nikolai (Nikoloz) Semenovich Chkheidze (1864–1926) was a leading Georgian Social Democrat (Menshevik) of his day, deputy to the third and fourth Dumas from Tiflis province, and the chairman of the Petrograd Soviet during February 27–September 9, 1917. Chkheidze came from a petty noble family in the Kutaisi (Imereti) province in western Georgia. He graduated from a local gymnasium, then briefly attended Odessa's Novorossiiskii University, and in 1889 transferred to Kharkov's Veterinary Institute, from which he was quickly expelled for taking part in student protests. He then lived in Austria for two or three years, studied in a mining academy, and also expanded his political "training" in the local Social Democratic circles and among political exiles from the Russian Empire. In 1892 he returned to his homeland and by year's end founded the first Georgian Social Democratic organization, called Mesame-Dasi, or the Third Group. For the next fourteen years he lived in Batumi, capital of the Adjara region, on the Black Sea, where he worked in the municipal administration and was a leader of the regional Social Democratic organization. By 1907 his political activity became so conspicuous that he was ordered to leave Batumi, but was allowed to settle in Tiflis (Tbilisi). Later that year he was elected to the Tiflis city Duma and from there began his swift rise in national politics.

In October 1907, he was elected to represent Tiflis province in the (third) State Duma, joining the ranks of the unified Social Democratic faction, which at that time included both the Mensheviks and Bolsheviks. He quickly established himself as an active parliamentarian, speaking on or co-sponsoring bills aimed at improving the socio-economic conditions of the lower classes, and as a stern and fearless critic of government policies and officials. During 1908–12 he was banned from the Duma for an unprecedented twenty-three sessions for his fiery speeches and obstruction of cabinet ministers who came to address the national legislature. But his voters at home must have approved of his radical behavior, and in 1912 he was easily reelected to the next Duma. Although already a leading member of the Social Democratic faction before its November 1913 split, Chkheidze's influence in the Duma and his national visibility increased dramatically thereafter. Not only did he become the chairman and unquestionable leader of the now separate Menshevik faction, a position that assured him a seat on the important Council of Elders, but he also emerged as the most senior "official" (that is, not in foreign or Siberian exile) Social Democrat in the country. His attacks on the government became ever more vocal, his opposition more unflinching. In November 1914 he joined the Bolshevik deputies to vote down the government request to authorize war credits and on several occasions (in 1914, 1916, and especially in February 1917) openly called for a regime change.

Yet neither his seemingly uncompromising opposition and confrontational (at times bordering on scandalous) behavior in the Duma, nor his dogmatic mistrust of "bourgeois" politicians prevented him from understanding the need for broad interparty cooperation among Left-leaning politicians and public figures. In 1909 he answered the Left Kadet deputy V. A. Stepanov's invitation to join the so-called Duma lodge under the "mastership" of the "venerable" N. V. Nekrasov. Two years later, he himself established a political Masonic lodge in Kutaisi and during 1912–16 belonged to the ruling Supreme Council of the Grand Orient of the Peoples of Russia, a position which brought him into close contact with his future colleagues and allies in the Petrograd Soviet and the Provisional Government, including Kerenskii, Nekrasov, A. I. Konovalov, N. D. Sokolov, N. N. Sukhanov, and M. I. Skobelev. There is little doubt that these informal ties, while not necessarily superseding party allegiances or affecting ideological preferences, helped develop a cohesive strategy and assured closer cooperation between diverse liberal and revolutionary elements, inside and outside of the Duma, during the February Revolution.[a]

But as the events of 1917 would demonstrate, Chkheidze's political and ideological flexibility had its boundaries. His presumed ability to see beyond narrow party or class interests before the revolution did not translate into action once he was catapulted to power during the February Days. His outright refusal to accept the labor portfolio in the first "bourgeois" cabinet of the Provisional Government is one of the better-known examples of his ideological rigidity. His class-based jargon, his habitually confrontational tone—as demonstrated in his countless statements and speeches as the Soviet Executive Committee chairman—was unnecessarily politicized and polarizing. Even in his interview with the Polievktov Commission, to which he reluctantly agreed after inordinate persuasion, he remained single-mindedly focused on interpreting almost every episode he agreed

---

[a] See Chkheidze's interview with B. I. Nikolaevskii, August 24–6, 1925. B. I. Nikolaevskii, *Russkie masony i revoliutsiia* (Moscow: Terra, 1990), 82–7. For a more complete version of this interview, see B. I. Nicolaevskii Collection, Box 525-3, notebook 1: 116–17, HIA; On the significance of Masonic ties, see Hasegawa's comments in *Critical Companion to the Russian Revolution, 1914–1921*, ed. Edward Action et al. (Bloomington and Indianapolis: Indiana University Press, 1997), 59; Rex A. Wade, *The Russian Revolution, 1917*, 2nd edn (Cambridge: Cambridge University Press, 2005), 19; and Barbara T. Norton, "Political Masonry," in Harold Shukman, ed., *The Blackwell Encyclopedia of the Russian Revolution*, 2nd edn, rev. and updated (Oxford, UK, and Cambridge, MA: Blackwell, 1994), 92–3.

to discuss in terms of the "dual power" relationship between the Petrograd Soviet and the Provisional Government, which to his mind meant that the government's authority was counterbalanced by and dependent on the Executive Committee's conditional support.

Despite his deep familiarity with the politics of the February Days, in which of course he played a leading role, he offered his interviewers exceedingly frugal answers and rarely, if ever, strayed from answering the exact questions posed to him. His interview contrasts sharply with the more expansive and less doctrinaire testimonies of his close political friends Skobelev and Kerenskii. The reason for this reticence is not entirely clear. Some of it can probably be attributed to his reserved and cautious personality, toughened by years of conspiratorial work. Another and more immediate reason might have been depression caused by the terrible personal tragedy that struck his family just two months prior to the interview. On March 26 his 15-year-old son accidentally killed himself while playing with a loaded revolver.[b]

In any event, here we encounter a diligent and skillful party functionary, not without political talent or a loyal following, and someone who knew how to hold his nose and toe the party line. Initially against the Socialists' participation in the Provisional Government, he supported it, albeit conditionally, once it was formed. During most of his tenure on the Soviet Executive Committee, he belonged to the inner circle of the revolutionary defensists' faction, led by his old and admittedly more politically gifted friend and ally Irakli Tsereteli. Though not after power per se, Chkheidze did cling to his leadership position for six agonizing months, and resigned only after the moderate Socialists lost their majority on the Executive Committee. But on the whole, he proved to be more of a doctrinarian than a strategic thinker or problem solver, a general who was more concerned with winning a battle than with losing a war.

During the Bolshevik seizure of power in October, he was in Georgia and thus avoided arrest and possible prosecution. In February 1918 he was asked to preside over the so-called Transcaucasian Seim, which under his leadership declared the separation of the Caucasus from Soviet Russia. In May 1918 he was elected chairman of the Constituent Assembly of the newly proclaimed Democratic Republic of Georgia, and later was one of the authors of the Republic's first constitution. In March 1921, after the Bolsheviks took control of the country, he left Georgia and settled in France. He never adjusted to his new life. Uprooted and disillusioned, he committed suicide on June 13, 1926. His last testament to his Menshevik party

---

[b] *Izvestiia*, March 28, 1917, 1; *Petrogradskii sovet rabochikh i soldatskikh deputatov v 1917 g. Protokoly, stenogrammy sektsii, zasedanii Ispolnitel'nogo komiteta i fraktsii*, vol. I: *27 fevralia–31 marta 1917 g.* (Leningrad: Nauka, 1991), I: 598, 611. Chkheidze's only other two known testimonies, which are not about his participation in the February Revolution, corroborate this impression. See his August 24–6, 1925 interview with Nikolaevskii, and his deposition to the Murav'ev Commission in *Padenie tsarskogo rezhima, Stenograficheskie otchety doprosov i pokazanii, dannykh v 1917 godu v Chrezvychainoi sledstvennoi komissii Vremennogo pravitel'stva*, ed. P. E. Shchegolev (Moscow and Leningrad: Gosizdat, 1923–7), III: 485–506.

comrades read: "Keep up with the movement and lead [it]" (*Sledite za dvizheniem i rukovodite*).[c]

Chkheidze did not write memoirs. His speeches in the State Duma were collected by an admirer and published in Petrograd in 1917 and in Tiflis in 1919.[d] His May 27, 1917 interview represents his only known testimony on the February Revolution and provides important, albeit brief, glimpses into the mindset of a revolutionary leader, the establishment of the Soviet authority, and the workings of "dual power" during March–April 1917.

The text is reproduced on the basis of three draft transcripts: two of them in Tamara Nikoladze's hand and the third, slightly shorter, transcript compiled by Margarita Feliksovna Ropp.

★ ★ ★ ★ ★ ★

Nikolai Semenovich Chkheidze, Deputy of the State Duma, Chairman of the Soviet of Workers' and Soldiers' Deputies. May 27, 1917

Nikolai Semenovich Chkheidze set the interview for 1:00 in the afternoon, in the Duma. Upon our arrival to the Duma, we discovered that Chkheidze was at Skobelev's residence,[1] where the two of them were meeting with Tsereteli. Chkheidze told us on the telephone that he would receive us at 3:00. At 3:00, we found him having [second] breakfast in the Duma building, sitting at a table piled with papers and talking to people who were continuously coming to him with questions and papers to sign. Chkheidze looked tired, with a mournful, exhausted look in his eyes. To our request to share with us his recollections pertaining to the first days of the revolution and the birth of the Soviet of Soldiers' and Workers' Deputies, he said that it would be very difficult for him to reconstruct the events of those days from memory. When he was working around the clock, events and days ran together. Now, however, he is so overwhelmed with work that he is afraid that he will be unable to talk about the events with clarity and exactitude. Therefore, he asked us to write up our questions; he would then provide written answers. Even though Chkheidze at first refused to give us his account on the spot or to share his detailed memories, we were able to lure him into talking by asking some questions. One such question was about the idea

---

[c] *Politicheskie deiateli Rossii 1917 g. Biograficheskii slovar'* (Moscow: BRE, 1993), 356.

[d] *Rechi Nikolaia Semenovicha Chkheidze*, published by A. D. Arabidze, part 1 (Petrograd: Gosudarstvennoe izdatel'stvo 1917), 87 pp.; N. S. Chkheidze, *Parlamentskie rechi* (Tiflis, 1919), 120 pp.

*of sending the tsar abroad. Chkheidze told us that he had learned from L'vov that
there was an inclination to send the former tsar abroad, to England. Whether this
question had already been decided was difficult to say. But the Provisional Government
saw that the Soviet would resort to extreme measures.*

I [Chkheidze] formed the impression that they thought it was prudent to
isolate the tsar. Otherwise, he might be surrounded by people who, because
of memories and associations, could hatch all sorts of plans. (This discussion
had taken place in the Mariinskii Palace.) I think this concern was the main
reason for the idea of sending him abroad. They themselves did not formulate this, however, and we did not ask for such a formula, because for us the
issue had been decided, and their concern did not play a substantive role.
For us, it was clear that the tsar should not be allowed to leave the country—there was money abroad, and with money, much can be done.

Here, the much-discussed dual power [*dvoevlastie*] surfaced, the character
of which should be explained. We received a report that the tsar was on his
way to Tsarskoe Selo. The Soviet, without waiting for the government to
reply (whether the tsar would be in Tsarskoe Selo), called on troops, took
over all railway stations, sent out telegrams along railway lines, and so on.[2]
This example shows the nature of *dvoevlastie* unambiguously. Before the
government could implement its intended measures, we undertook our
own measures. In actuality, this was the rightly talked-about *dvoevlastie*. I will
point out the crux of our attitude toward the Provisional Government: it
was trusted *postol'ku poskol'ku* [insofar as]. Now, it is vested with the plenitude of power and trust, but we still demand that they be accountable to
us.[3] It is well known that an agreement was concluded between the government and the Soviet. But in the process of implementing its conditions, we
did not exclude the possibility that the government would go one way, and
we would go the other without waiting for the government.

Here is one more example: we had an agreement with the Provisional
Government that we would not send the troops of the Petrograd Garrison
out of Petrograd. The government agreed, but then questions arose about
sending marching companies and special units to the front. Even though we
had an agreement, the government could implement some measures each
time—but not without asking the Soviet—it was impossible to send troops
out without asking us. The situation is different now. Kerenskii can exercise
power without asking us,[4] but afterwards he has to report to us why, for
what purpose, and which units were deployed.

My answer to the question of whether there were any cases when the Soviet overruled a decision of the Provisional Government is "Yes."

On April 20, Kornilov issued an order to send troops to defend the Mariinskii Palace. I learned about it over the telephone, and I forbade the carrying out of this order. For our part, we issued an order that the troops stay inside.[5] Although there was an agreement, a skirmish might occur at any minute.

The arrest of the former tsar also shows the character of *dvoevlastie*. The Soviet could still come into conflict with the Provisional Government, even though here we had an agreement with them. The Soviet took its own steps, not waiting for the government. As well as showing confidence in the actions of the government, the Soviet has the right to criticize it and express distrust.

You are asking if there was a delegation from Moscow, which demanded that the tsar not be allowed to go abroad? No, there was not. I do not remember any practical measures, there was no such delegation.

This is what I can say about the events of April 20–1. We were awaiting, and at long last received, Miliukov's diplomatic note along with his explanations for it. The note made an enormous impression, and our attitude toward it, as could be expected, was negative. Anxiety was strong, but I did not expect that there would be a need to introduce a state of siege. At the meeting of the Soviet on the 21st, we were told about the bloodshed.[6] That forced us to introduce a state of siege. An order was given to keep the troops in the barracks, but they were still taking to the streets in the name of the Soviet. On the 21st, all street demonstrations were forbidden. This is a good example of how Soviet orders were followed: some from the Petrograd Side turned to us with the question of whether a funeral procession could be mistaken for a demonstration. There were other such incidents. The effect of the order forbidding demonstrations apparently had a strong effect.

On April 21, as comrade Voitinskii[7] and I were driving across the Field of Mars,[8] we met columns of factory workers, mostly women, carrying flags and posters: "Down with the Provisional Government!" I stopped and spoke to them, explaining the significance of Miliukov's policy, and of the diplomatic note. I told them that the demonstration should go back and await the Soviet's decision. But they did not agree, and kept on. On Nevskii I met another demonstration. It was moving toward the Naval Corps, where a meeting of the Soviet was supposed to be going on.[9] I wanted to talk to these demonstrators as well, but since they were moving too fast, I was unable to do so. Perhaps they did not recognize me, even though I think they did. Maybe these were Bolsheviks. I sensed that from conversations. Orders had not yet been given that workers should not take part in demonstrations that day, but in my speeches I tried to persuade them to disperse, since they had already demonstrated. But they did not heed me.

QUESTION: How was the Temporary Committee formed, and how was the Provisional Government selected from within it?

ANSWER: People who stood to the Right of L'vov (Procurator of the Holy Synod) could evidently not enter the Provisional Government.

QUESTION: Why, was this a precondition?

ANSWER: No, it happened on its own.

QUESTION: Did they decide for themselves not to join, or did you refuse to accept them?

ANSWER: I don't know. We didn't discuss it. They just fell away on their own. The situation showed that, under the circumstances, the parties to the Right of Vl[adimir]. L'vov could not join.

QUESTION: When did discussions regarding the cabinet begin?

ANSWER: It was at night. I do not remember the date.[10] The list of members of the Provisional Government was being put together. Prince L'vov was suggested as a candidate. Miliukov was taking notes. Steklov and I repre-sented the Soviet. N. [D.] Sokolov was coming and going, but at the time when the list was composed, I don't recall him being there. We didn't propose anyone ourselves. The list was composed by them. It was clear that we, the Social Democrats, were not going to join. Kadets and Progressists were being put forward. Prince L'vov was named. We didn't object to anyone. Maklakov was mentioned for minister of justice,[11] I think, but I don't remember exactly. That post remained uncertain for a long time. Kerenskii was asked to join the cabinet, but we didn't propose him. We were not consulted about him. Kerenskii came to the Soviet and declared that he was a minister—so he acted on his own initiative.

The question of joining the government was not on the Soviet's agenda that day.[12] We were discussing other things. Kerenskii asked to speak ahead of those who were scheduled. The meeting took place in room number 13 (of the Tauride Palace). He climbed onto a table and delivered a speech: "Do you believe in me, comrades?" Applause followed. In other words, the impression was created that he was approved. This was the second or third meeting of the Soviet. I don't remember Kerenskii being at those meetings at all. That was his first time. The presidium of the Soviet was only recently elected; I had been elected during my absence. I don't think that Order Number One was ever presented to a general meeting of the Soviet. Kerenskii was not there, and I doubt he was there when the election for chairman was held.

When the list of ministers was composed, there were no objections from us; nor were there questions concerning Guchkov and Konovalov. In general, we didn't see any need to reject candidates. Miliukov offered me the post of minister of labor. I categorically refused. [His] reply was not serious. For me, personally, it was quite clear that we were not going to participate in power. I don't know whether Miliukov was serious about his offer.

[QUESTION:] Was the cabinet formed before the declaration was worked out?

[ANSWER:] The declaration came first. We proposed our "nine points" to them.[13] They did not have their own. No one proposed Rodzianko for anything.

On February 27, at 12 noon, a private meeting of the State Duma took place in the semicircular hall. It did not give the impression of being a session, but rather of a broad exchange of opinion [*vpechatlenie bol'shogo "oprosa"*].

NOTES

1 M. I. Skobelev, whose close ties with Chkheidze date back to the early 1900s when both men worked together in the Social Democratic organizations in the Caucuses and then served together in the Duma (1912–17). Skobelev resided on Tverskaia Street (no. 13), right around the corner from the Tauride Palace.

2 See n. 49 in the Tugan-Baranovskii interview (Chapter 7). For further details on the measures undertaken by the Soviet EC, see *RPG*, I: 179–90. Chkheidze's telegram of March 9 requesting to detain the former tsar is reproduced in *Krasnyi arkhiv* 2, 21 (1927): 67.

3 Chkheidze refers here to the coalition cabinet formed on May 5, 1917 that included his comrades-in-arms, the Socialists Kerenskii, Skobelev, P. N. Pereverzev, V. M. Chernov, A. V. Peshekhonov, and I. G. Tsereteli. Legally speaking, however, the Provisional Government had been vested with plenitude of power from the very beginning, when Grand Duke Mikhail Aleksandrovich abdicated in its favor on March 3.

4 This probably refers to Kerenskii's joint membership on the Soviet EC and as minister of war in the Provisional Government.

5 For the circumstances of the Kornilov order and how it was rescinded, see n. 53 to the Tugan-Baranovskii interview. The EC order to refrain from demonstrating in the streets and await instructions from the Petrograd Soviet was issued in Chkheidze's name on April 21, and sent by way of radio telegram at 4:00 that afternoon to all soviets and army and navy committees. See G. N. Golikov, Iu. S. Tokarev, "Aprel'skii krizis 1917 g.," *Istoricheskie zapiski* 57 (1956): 47; *Petrogradskii Soviet*, II: 297–300, 317; *RPG*, II: 1240–1.

6 There were two meetings on 21 April: in the morning, the EC met to discuss the situation concerning the Miliukov note to the Allies, as well as the demonstrations and clashes it provoked; that evening, around 7:20, the general session of the Soviet commenced in the Hall of the Naval Cadet Corps. For details on both meetings, see *Petrogradskii Sovet*, II: 288–316; "Aprel'skii krizis 1917 g.," 47.

7 Vladimir Savel'evich Voitinskii (1885–1960) was a prominent Russian Social Democrat (Bolshevik from 1905 to March 1917). Shortly after his return from Siberian exile to Petrograd on March 20, 1917, he became a member of the EC. On April 23, at the height of the April Crisis, he was elected to the Bureau of the Soviet EC. He had already left the Bolshevik party by then, and joined the Mensheviks over disagreements with Lenin's divisive politics and defeatist position. Voitinskii became close personally with Tsereteli during the years of exile in Irkutsk, and from the spring through the autumn of 1917, identified himself with Tsereteli's brand of revolutionary defensism. Voitinskii supported the coalition, and on May 1 joined a commission of the EC that negotiated the conditions of the Socialists' participation in the coalition cabinet.

8 Or Marsovo pole, a large park and parade ground named after Mars, the Roman god of war. It was situated in the center of the city, between the barracks of the Pavlovskii Regiment (to the west) and Moika River (to the south).

9 The reference is to the meeting of the Petrograd Soviet that took place in the Naval Cadet Corps, located on the Neva's Nikolaevskaia Embankment between the 11th and 12th Lines of Vasil'evskii Island. The reason for holding a session at a location other than the Tauride Palace was that the rapidly expanding ranks of the Petrograd Soviet could no longer be accommodated in the Duma's main (White) assembly hall. According to the meeting's minutes, Chkheidze opened the session at 7:20 in the evening and reported on the EC's measures to prevent street clashes and demonstrations. He then left the session to attend a cabinet meeting, scheduled for 9:00. See *Petrogradskii Sovet*, 2: 304, 306; "Aprel'skii krizis 1917 g.," 47.

10 The first known negotiations between representatives of the Soviet EC and the Duma Committee began during the night of February 28–March 1, and continued, with interruption, throughout the day on March 1 and until the early afternoon of March 2, when agreement was finally reached and the composition of the new cabinet announced to the revolutionary crowds inside the Tauride Palace. Miliukov was the principal negotiator on behalf of the Duma Committee, while the Soviet EC was represented, with varying frequency of participation, by Sukhanov, Chkheidze, Sokolov, and Steklov. Chkheidze probably refers here to the night of March 1 (early morning, more accurately) when the first round of negotiations lasted until about 4:00 in the morning. According to Sukhanov, Chkheidze was present during these negotiations, but was very tired (he was still suffering from a severe cold). He then disappeared for the rest of the morning. (Nik.[olai] Sukhanov, *Zapiski o revoliutsii*, 7 parts (Berlin, Petersburg, Moscow: Izdatel'stvo Z. I. Grzhebina, 1922–3) I, 1–2: 154). This might explain Chkheidze's foggy recollection of the timing of the episode.

11 V. A. Maklakov had been considered the leading candidate for the justice portfolio ever since the first lists of future public cabinets began circulating in 1915. He was mentioned in four of the six most circulated lists between August 1915 and February 25, 1917. Kerenskii's name did not appear once. On February 28, it was Maklakov who, in anticipation of his post, was appointed commissar for the ministry of justice by the Duma Committee. Yet his candidacy

was sacrificed in favor of Kerenskii by Miliukov during his negotiations with the representatives of the Soviet EC because Kerenskii was seen as a link with the Petrograd Soviet and thus as guarantor of the cabinet's stability. For more on the circumstances of this last-minute change, see the interviews with Skobelev and Kerenskii in this volume.

12 The meeting in question took place on March 2. Kerenskii's dramatic appeal to his Petrograd Soviet colleagues to approve his participation in the "bourgeois" cabinet took place during that meeting (on March 2), and was variously reported in the Petrograd press over the course of the next few days. See *Petrogradskii Sovet*, I: 61–78.

13 The reference is to the "program" (also known as the declaration) prepared by the EC and presented to the Duma Committee, namely, to Miliukov, on March 1, as the basis for negotiations and a condition for supporting the government. Although the final product came to be known as the 8-point program of the Provisional Government, the so-called "ninth point" (originally "third point"), which concerned the form of the future government, was dropped at the insistence of Miliukov. The Socialist leaders wanted to leave that question to a resolution by the future Constituent Assembly, whereas Miliukov was adamant in his defense of preserving the monarchical form of government and rejected the Soviet demand upfront (Sukhanov, *Zapiski o revoliutsii*, I, 1–2: 149–50, 175). The final text of the 8-point declaration of the Provisional Government was published on March 3, 1917 and included a watered-down version of the original point 3, now under point 4, promising immediate preparations for the convocation of the four-tailed Constituent Assembly "which will determine the form of government and the constitution of the country." (*RPG*, I: 135–6).

10

Matvei Ivanovich Skobelev

MATVEI IVANOVICH SKOBELEV (1885–1938) was a Menshevik deputy in the fourth Duma, assistant chairman of the Petrograd Soviet Executive Committee during February 27–early September 1917, and minister of labor in the coalition cabinet of the Provisional Government from May to August 1917.

His "love affair" with revolution began at an early age. He grew up in Baku where his father, a sectarian Molokan, owned mill factories and was a rich real estate magnate. While still in his teens he and his brothers inherited a large mill factory but instead of looking after the family business, Skobelev turned his energies and talents to "the service of the people." By the time of the 1905 revolution he was already a locally recognized Social Democratic activist and a seasoned labor organizer. In 1906 he left Baku in the wake of the post-revolutionary crackdown and from 1907 to 1912 lived in Vienna, studying (though he did not graduate) in the Polytechnic but paying considerably more attention to revolutionary politics and to forging ties among Russian political exiles. One of his closest acquaintances was Lev Trotskii, who had just begun publishing his Viennese *Pravda*, the precursor to the famous Bolshevik paper, and was looking for contributors and devoted followers. Skobelev happened to be one such suitable candidate. According to an early biographer, Trotskii considered Skobelev to be his favorite disciple at the time and would soon offer him a position as the paper's secretary.[a] Their association continued through the second half of 1912 when Skobelev, with Trotskii's blessing, returned to Baku in time for elections to the fourth Duma. In October 1912, thanks to his old labor connections and family resources, he was elected to the national legislature to represent the Russian population of the Caucasus.

In the Duma he served as secretary of the united (and later the Menshevik) Social Democratic faction, and was active on a number of commissions and committees while continuing to spread the Social Democratic gospel among oil industry workers when visiting back home. His principal mentor was now his Duma faction leader and a fellow Caucasian, N. S. Chkheidze. It was Chkheidze who

---

[a] Isaac Deutscher, *The Prophet Armed, Trotsky: 1879–1921* (New York and London: Oxford University Press, 1954), 192.

introduced this provincial yet motivated novice to the conspiratorial world of St. Petersburg revolutionary circles, including Masonic lodges, where he met many of his future collaborators in the Petrograd Soviet and the Provisional Government, from N. D. Sokolov and N. N. Sukhanov to Kerenskii, Nekrasov, and Konovalov.

By all counts, Skobelev's contribution to the success of the February Revolution was enormous. He was among the chief organizers of the insurgent forces and the founders of the Petrograd Soviet. His many roles and responsibilities during and in the aftermath of the February Days—some self-assumed, others requested by his revolutionary colleagues—are recounted in his long and extraordinarily informative interview with such lucidity, conviction, and detail that no additional elaboration is required here. Suffice it to say that in this interview he was unusually forthcoming, not hesitating to contradict his colleagues in the Socialist camp or to challenge conventional wisdoms. Consider, for example, his bold statement that it would be premature to speak about "dual power" during the first days of the uprising, before the Provisional Government was formed and began to function. Or take his extraordinary revelation concerning the correlation between the timing of elections to the Petrograd Soviet and the announcement of its formation on February 27, hours *before* the voting had been completed and the results counted ("revolutionary tricks"). His disclosure of the true motives that guided one of the principal organizers of anti-government demonstrations during the April Crisis (F. F. Linde) should serve as a useful corrective to the traditional interpretation of this pivotal event, and represents yet another welcome example of Skobelev's willingness to ignore the unspoken taboos of the excessively secretive culture of his revolutionary milieu.

Hardly an original thinker or strategist, Skobelev proved himself a capable, energetic, and pragmatic organizer ideally suited to occupy important, if secondary roles. According to the great Menshevik archivist and historian B. I. Nikolaevskii—who had plenty of opportunities to observe him at close range during Skobelev's years in the Duma and in the Petrograd Soviet and, admittedly, did not have much good to say about his personal qualities—Skobelev harbored far-reaching political ambitions for himself but also knew how, at least for the time being, to be content with lesser roles.[b] Skobelev realized that the path of advancement lay in associations with strong and authoritative leaders, hence his early gravitation toward Lev Trotskii and Chkheidze, and especially his close association with Irakli Tsereteli and his revolutionary defensist majority in the Petrograd Soviet. Skobelev's subsequent behavior, his increasing tendency to change sides, may well prove Nikolaevskii right. But we should remember that it was Skobelev's desire to please his then political guru that ensured his consent for an interview with the Polievktov

[b] B. I. Nikolaevskii to I. G. Tsereteli, November 8, 1928, Letter no. 180; Nicolaevskii Collection, Box 505, folder 1, HIA. This letter was kindly brought to my attention by Professor A. P. Nenarokov.

Commission, whose principal members were "Kaki" Tsereteli's two favored cousins, Rusudana Nikoladze-Polievktova and her sister Tamara.

In a sense, Skobelev was an ideal interviewee. In contrast to the reluctant Chkheidze or cautiously suspicious Nekrasov, he did not hesitate to go beyond the interviewers' questions and offer his opinions or dwell at length on his revolutionary experiences and accomplishments. Fully engaged and talkative, he was eager to tell his side of recent history even if that entailed repeated interviewing sessions in the middle of the night, in between cabinet meetings, and at the cost of postponing a myriad of other and more pressing responsibilities. This was a man in the prime of his life, fully aware of his contribution to history. His political career was on the rise and although he was hoping to play an even bigger role one day, this was his time to enjoy every bit of the sudden limelight. No amount of attention, it seems, could be considered excessive to this young and energetic revolutionary. No task was too big for him to undertake. Whether in politics or his personal life, this was the time to take full advantage of his newly gained status and fame and to use it to its fullest.[c]

And so he did, and from his perspective he was probably right. Soon enough his luck would run out. In early September the Menshevik–SR leadership lost their majority on the Soviet EC and collectively resigned. During the same week Skobelev also gave up his labor portfolio and left the Provisional Government. Then, two months later, he resigned from the Menshevik Central Committee in disagreement over the party's negotiations with the Bolsheviks, which he saw as damaging to the workers' cause and harmful to the revolution. This marked the end of his association with the Menshevik party.

Initially, he strongly objected to the Bolshevik seizure of power and even attempted to organize a military expedition to recapture Petrograd. Yet he later changed his mind and remained there in the former capital until the end of 1918. In 1919–20 he lived in Baku and was reportedly involved in unseemly financial operations and war profiteering. He also tried to reinvent himself politically. One of his better known adventures was to persuade the independent Menshevik Georgian government to launch joint military operations with the Red Army against the White armies of General A. I. Denikin. It went nowhere. Following the Communist takeover, he moved to Paris, but soon established contact with the Soviet diplomatic mission and from 1921 to 1925 served as Soviet trade representative in France. In 1922, in yet another twist of his colorful life, he joined the Bolshevik party over the objections of both Lenin and, notably, his former mentor Trotskii.[d] He returned to the USSR in 1925 and until his arrest in 1938 served in

[c] During this time, he also divorced his first wife (with whom he had three children) and married M. S. Davydova, an attractive opera singer and social butterfly.

[d] I. S. Rozental', "Skobelev Matvei Ivanovich," *Gosudarstvennaia Duma Rossiiskoi imperii, 1906–1917. Entsiklopediia*, ed. V. V. Shelokhaev et al. (Moscow: ROSSPEN, 2008), 562.

various trade, state planning, and propaganda institutions.[e] He was executed in Moscow on July 29, 1938.

His interview is reproduced on the basis of a master version compiled by Rusudana Nikoladze-Polievktova, with minor stylistic corrections also in her hand; and a draft transcript written in shorthand by another interviewer (either T. V. Krupskaia or V. I. Pavlov) who also recorded a draft transcript of the Tereshchenko interview.

★ ★ ★ ★ ★ ★

Matvei Ivanovich Skobelev, Minister of Labor and Deputy Chairman of the Petrograd Soviet of Soldiers' and Workers' Deputies, a former deputy of the IV Duma from the Russian Population of the Caucasus

This account was given in three sessions, impromptu. Part I: May 29 (7–9:30 in the evening), before the meeting of the Provisional Government. Part II: On the same night (2:30–4:00 in the morning in the presence of Tsereteli), after the meeting of the Provisional Government. Part III: The next night (3–5 in the morning), on May 31, after the meeting of the Provisional Government and after greeting Kropotkin at the Finland Railway Station.[1]

PART I

Before the February session of the State Duma, a discussion began in workers' circles concerning the question of a possible demonstration on the day that the Duma was going to open [February 14, 1917]. Some proposed marching to the Kazan' Cathedral,[2] others to the Duma. On the initiative of the Social Democrats and the Labor Group [*trudoviki*], an inter-party committee was organized that included public figures.[3] Its purpose was to maintain contacts and monitor the popular mood, as well as to prepare and to have everything necessary in case street clashes developed. The underground party organizations were very skeptical

---

[e] In March 1927, on the occasion of the tenth anniversary of the February "bourgeois" revolution, he published brief memoirs in the Soviet press, which were heavily edited, filled with customary hindsight, and, most important, reflected Skobelev's own radically changed circumstances ("Gibel' tsarizma. Vospominaniia M. I. Skobeleva," *Ogonek*, 11 (207), March 13, 1927; "25 fevralia–3 marta: (Vospominaniia b[yvshego] chlena Sotsial-demokraticheskoi fraktsii Gosudarstvennoi dumy M. Skobeleva)," *Vecherniaia Moskva*, March 11, 1927.

about all this, arguing that the necessary mood did not exist, and that there should be a march not to the Duma, but to the Kazan' Cathedral—in order to avoid supporting the Duma—and so on. On the 14th, the demonstration did not take place. The Duma opened. The mood lapsed. And not until February 20–2, when "tails"[4] began to swell—that is, when they branched into more than one row—did the first signs of street activity become apparent.[5] On the 23rd, the first street gatherings appeared. The common city-dwellers began to group together in the city center more frequently. Similar gatherings began to appear in workers' neighborhoods. On the 24th, such gatherings became more orderly, and red flags appeared over demonstrations that assumed a clearly political character. The Cossacks fraternized with the crowd. On the 25th, the Cossacks were replaced with military units, who looked more like police in some places. Karaulov questioned whether these "Cossacks" were in fact disguised police officials.

On the 25th, the atmosphere started getting more intense, worrisome, and formidable in comparison with February 23 and 24, when it had been idyllic, with some comic elements. On the 24th, unverified reports appeared that a police official, or a police agent, had been murdered. On the 25th, there were already reliable reports on the murder of a police agent[f] on Znamenskii Square. During those days, there was an atmosphere of disarray and a lack of direction among underground mass workers' organizations. There was no agitation. Individual workers (about twenty people) and mostly old underground party operatives showed up to visit members of both Socialist factions[6] in their homes and in the Duma. All were asking: "What is to be done?"

So, around the 20th, I and other members of the Social Democratic and Labor group (both factions in the Duma) decided, at our own risk, to form the Soviet of Workers' Deputies, and advised the workers to make "Organize the Soviet!" the slogan of the day. The [revolutionary] parties opposed this on the grounds that parliamentary circles did not have such a right. Our efforts met with opposition from their side, but on the 22nd–23rd, we put that slogan forward anyway. During this time, the mood in the Duma reflected that in the street: idyllic smiles on the 23rd–24th; and on the 25th everyone was already anxious. The working class was lagging behind the street. But on the 25th, we were informed that elections to the Soviet of Workers' Deputies had taken place at some factories. Around 6:00 in the evening on the 25th, I was called to the City Duma and was informed about shootings on Nevskii. I

---

[f] This may have been police captain (*rotmistr*) M.E. Krylov, who was the chief of a nearby police station.

immediately drove there, but the shooting had stopped and the wounded had been taken away—some to their homes, others to pharmacies and Merchants' Row [Gostinnyi Dvor, the main department store].

In the City Duma, I saw 2 bodies and 6–7 wounded—in all, 8–10 victims. On the sidewalk in front of the Duma thermometer, there was a big pool of blood, one *sazhen*[7] in diameter. Khaustov and Dziubinskii,[8] who witnessed what happened, told me the following: around 5:00 in the afternoon, on Znamenskii Square, after the gathering was over, an attempt was made to organize a demonstration without flags because all along Nevskii there were patrols. But all of a sudden, the patrols disappeared somewhere, so the demonstrators were able to reach Anichkov Palace[9] unimpeded, and then unfurled their red flags. Once again, no one stopped them and they moved further, until they saw mounted soldiers crossing Nevskii at the corner of Catherine Canal. The crowd got confused, hid their flags several times, and pausing along the way, made their final stop near Merchants' Row. An officer ordered that the horses' tails should be turned toward the crowd. The soldiers dismounted. The crowd, with some hesitation, started to move again. The cavalry followed it, and when the crowd came to the City Duma, across from Mikhailovskii Street, all of a sudden a volley rang out—without any warning, and most likely shot into the air. Judging by the wounds, it was clear that they were not shooting point-blank, and were hitting those who were lying down. Apparently, all such wounds came from above. Khaustov glued himself to the wall, and saw everything in detail. The first rifle volley was delivered from the hip. The second was done the same way, but an officer on the right flank, striking the barrels downwards with his saber, made the bullets fly point-blank into the left flank of the crowd. Indeed, the killed and wounded that had been shot point-blank all turned out to have been among the demonstrators on the left flank.

There was a need to evacuate the wounded from the City Duma. The crowd was agitated. As we crossed Nevskii, all of a sudden a line of soldiers with their rifles at half-ready crossed Mikhailovskii Street. I suddenly sensed something serious in the air—the smell of blood. We went through the line with no problem. Whether they recognized us as Duma deputies or let us through by accident I do not know, but right after we passed, the mounted patrols dispersed the entire crowd. Dziubinskii and I, along with several other deputies, five to six in all, proceeded. On Mikhailovskii Street, Kerenskii drove up to us; on the corner we were joined by a group of several journalists.

On the 26th, everyone came to the State Duma early; the atmosphere was quite uneasy. Disturbing news was coming in on the telephone from Nevskii. Members of the City Duma (Shnitnikov[10] and others with whom we, and I personally, were communicating on the phone) were reporting that from the windows of the City Duma, they saw that on the corner of Nevskii and Sadovaia Street, two lines of soldiers were in the prone position. One line had their rifles turned toward Znamenskii Square, the other (a training unit of the Pavlovskii Regiment) was facing the Admiralty, toward Aleksandrovskii Garden, and clearing the whole of Nevskii by shooting at selected people as well as every silhouette. Around 12:00 [noon] the reports came in that masses of wounded women and children had started to be brought to the City Duma. After that, General Khabalov showed up with his staff. He had organized this massacre, and began personally to direct the gunfire on Nevskii. Later, it became clear that this had been done by the training unit of the Pavlovskii Regiment.[11]

There was confusion in the State Duma. Everyone was asking each other, "What is to be done?" I remember how we—a group of deputies (Konovalov, myself, and others)—gathered near a desk in the Catherine Hall, wondering how we should react to what was happening. I was saying that we, as deputies of the Duma, needed to find honest officers and convince them that they should put an end to the shooting of women and children, which brought shame on Russian officers and soldiers. "We must," I specifically proposed, "at this very moment, send officers to the units of the Pavlovskii Regiment that are shooting at women and children." Someone from among the moderate members of the Duma was communicating with some ministers . . . This is how that day went.

Massacres moved from Nevskii onto the side streets, then the Rozhdestvenskie streets, Peski, along Sadovaia and onto the Field of Mars. On the same day, we were told that Pavlovskii soldiers—upon learning that their training unit was shooting at the people—poured out, unarmed, onto the Field of Mars, and told the trainees to stop shooting. They refused. Then, the regular Pavlovskii soldiers seized their arms and moved toward Nevskii along the Moika River. N. D. Sokolov witnessed what happened afterwards. On Nevskii, they were met by precinct policemen, with whom they exchanged fire. After that, the Pavlovskii soldiers returned to their barracks, and went out onto the Field of Mars and demanded to see their commander, with whom they began to talk things over. At that moment, a civilian came out of the crowd and inflicted several wounds on the commander with cold steel; the precinct policemen, using hatchets, came to his aid.[12] The next day, the news came in that Pavlovskii soldiers had herded workers onto the Field of Mars.

In the evening, I was wandering along Suvorovskii Avenue, near Nikolaevskii [Military] Academy. Under the influence of everything I had seen earlier, I cursed at some precinct policemen: "Your brothers are executing your wives and children. Why are you shooting?"

"Just wait," they replied, "tomorrow we'll show them." And, at that moment, for the first time I realized that something might happen as soon as tomorrow.

That night, I placed a telephone by my bed—and not for nothing. On the 27th, at 8:00 in the morning, I was awakened by a telephone call from Iordanskii,[13] who lives on Furazhnyi Lane, across from the Preobrazhenskii Regiment.[14] He reported that the Preobrazhenskii soldiers had unlocked the armory and were taking rifles. At that point, our conversation ended. I quickly dressed and telephoned Kerenskii. His wife[15] answered and said that, because the Duma had been dissolved, he was already at the Tauride Palace. As soon as I finished talking to her, the telephone rang again. It was Iordanskii again, reporting that a different stage of events had begun. The armed Preobrazhenskii soldiers had gone to the corner of Suvorovskii Avenue and the 9th Preobrazhenskii Street, and were stopping all cars, ordering the passengers to get out, taking their seats, and driving off to capture Nevskii.

I ran to the Duma, where I found many deputies. At about 10–11:00, we went to Rodzianko's office and insisted that he convene the Council of Elders, but Rodzianko, who was working on his second telegram to the tsar,[16] asked to be left alone: "Please do not disturb me." We went without him to one of the committee rooms, the 11th, and commenced a private meeting under the chairmanship of Nekrasov, as deputy of the Duma President. I sat in for Chkheidze, who was absent. At first, Kerenskii and I spoke (followed by others), arguing that the Duma should not disperse, and that it would have to assume power. At that very moment, I was called to the telephone. Bonch-Bruevich[17] was calling. He reported that mutinous soldiers were moving to capture Nevskii, and that a group of public figures without party affiliations was in the process of being organized and was moving in the same direction in order to lead the uprising, capture railway stations, and so on. They proposed that the State Duma not disperse—that it declare itself a national assembly and await the arrival of troops so that when the troops came, they would see peoples' representatives in place.

I came back to the meeting, requested to speak, and reported everything I had heard, adding at the end that it would be imprudent for the whole Duma to declare itself a national assembly, but that it was necessary to assume power in order to stay in responsible positions and fulfill the mission imposed on us by the moment. To this, Miliukov replied, "If the Duma were to assume power now, it would be a farce. Regarding the attitude of the Duma to the developing events, for my part I can say that I am not yet certain how far the movement will go. But on the positive side, party leaders are heading it up, which means that it will be organized. Whether I myself would join the movement depends on which party would lead it, and which tasks and slogans would be put forward by the movement. Specifically, what would its attitude be towards the war?"

I replied to Miliukov (and Kerenskii also objected to him in the same vein), that the group of public figures were not parties, and that the group feels a responsibility for the moment (according to Bonch-Bruevich's report). At that time, we were told that soldiers had arrived, and we ourselves saw, from the windows, mutinous soldiers approaching the Duma in several automobiles. Pointing to them, I told Miliukov that every word should be weighed carefully at such a moment. For example, his word "farce," or his declaration that the movement was being headed by "parties." "Grey coats and tall hats [*papakhi*] with rifles are not Social Democrats, Socialist Revolutionaries, Kadets, or Octobrists—they are the whole nation, and when the nation rises up, its attitude cannot be held back by slogans. Therefore, we must become national leaders and the center of the awakened nation." At that moment (this was between 11 and shortly after 12:00 noon), Nekrasov burst in and reported that the [Main] Artillery Administration on Liteinyi had been taken over by troops.

Reacting to that, Shingarev nervously exclaimed, "Only Germans could have done this!"

I immediately asked to speak: "I could understand that, in the Duma, you used to say from the podium that the strike movement and the disturbances during the war were in the interests of the Germans, but to use these words in reference to the mutinous army, that I cannot allow. I demand that you take back your words." I do not recall for certain whether he took back his words (I think he did). Nekrasov came in again and reported that General Manikovskii had apparently been killed in the Artillery Administration. This report was depressing. Manikovskii was well respected. But then, Nekrasov once again ran into the room and clarified that Manikovskii was still alive and that Kerenskii said that Manikovskii had apparently escaped just in time by leaving his office and going downstairs, through the backyard of the building.[18]

Miliukov, Shingarev, Shidlovskii,[19] and Shul'gin were leaning, as always, in the direction of adopting a wait-and-see position because it was not yet clear to them whether there was just a mutinous regiment or something else. At that time, Rodzianko flew into room 11, where we were meeting. "Who is meeting in here?" he asked. "This is a private meeting. Who had the right to start it?" Nekrasov explained that this was a private meeting, but that we were demanding that a real meeting be convened and insisting on the opening of the Council of Elders. So we moved to Rodzianko's office and began the meeting of the Council of Elders. Our private meeting was interrupted by Rodzianko between 11 and 1:00. Between the private meeting and the meeting of the Council of Elders, news and rumors began to come in that Kresty Prison[20] had been opened, political prisoners had been released, and that they, together with troops, were moving towards the Duma. We started to get worried, and clustered in the hall and near the entrance.

I don't remember everything exactly, but I do know that we were in Rodzianko's office before the troops arrived (I do not recall whether it was during the private meeting or the Council of Elders), and it was there that Colonel Bertgoldt, deputy security chief of the Tauride Palace, rushed in: "I have information that mutinous troops are moving toward the Duma," he declared.[21] "What should be done with the security guards?" Rodzianko categorically and firmly replied that there should be no resistance, none whatsoever, no provocative shooting, and absolutely no use of arms against the crowds by the guards. "Yes sir, but I report to the commandant of Petrograd and I have to communicate with him."

Chkheidze and I (he was not feeling well and only showed up toward the end of the private meeting in room 11) put on fur coats and went outside toward the main exit from the Duma, but saw that the gate in the fence was locked. I ran back to Rodzianko's office and, without taking my coat off, demanded that the gate be opened. Otherwise, I said, we would open them on our own authority. Rodzianko calmed me down and ordered Bertgoldt to open the gate.

Chkheidze, Kerenskii, and I went out to the crowd, which was still rather small, and gave speeches. The circuit court was in flames; the preliminary detention chamber [*predvarilka*] was open. Chkheidze spoke first, then Kerenskii, then I spoke. Our speeches were short: "We hear your cry to be the masters of your own fate, but you need to exercise self-restraint. You must be calm and organize yourselves." We went back into the building. The crowd swelled and poured into the garden, toward the portico. The crowd was mixed: workers with rifles, and soldiers. We went back out to them. One of the workers, who had been released from Kresty and had obtained a rifle from the soldiers, turned out to be an old acquaintance of mine; we kissed. This time, when we went out to the crowd, we told the soldiers that they should stop wandering around as a mob, and that they needed to organize and form up. "Where are your officers?" we asked them.

The crowd replied, "They are gone; they hid. They don't want to be with us." Then Kerenskii proposed that they select the most experienced from among themselves, place them in command, and put the soldiers into formation.

The worker from Kresty came to us inside the Duma and demanded, "Comrades, Social Democrats and Laborites, come out!" Chkheidze, Kerenskii, and I stepped forward. There were only three of us. The worker told the crowd, "Here, Comrades, these are our representatives in the Duma. Only they can be trusted and obeyed. We should only listen to them."

Kerenskii began to mount a guard. He took two to three squads and went to the old guard, which all came over to the side of the people and joined us. Nevertheless, there was one wounded second lieutenant brought out of the guardroom. All of the guards were replaced by six soldiers. After that, the meeting of the Council of Elders began; it was fairly general, just talk.

A delegation arrived and was greeted by the Laborite [*trudovik*] Ianushkevich, Savvateev,[22] and me. It turned out that these were medical workers and military cadets, who had been sent from a gathering of several thousand on the Vyborg Side, to find out from the Duma what they should do.[23] "We don't want instructions from two factions," they said. "We were sent here to receive guidance from the State Duma as a whole." Rodzianko, who went out to greet them, told them that the Duma was busy imposing order, and that the people should not commit excesses, but maintain complete calm.

At the time when we were mounting the guard in the semicircular hall— I do not recall exactly when it was—the private meeting commenced. Rodzianko insisted that this meeting would not be held in the regular hall, but in the semicircular hall, under his chairmanship.[24] Chkheidze, Kerenskii, and I were not present at the start because we were busy in the street, delivering speeches from the fence. I gave two to three speeches from there. Soldiers entered the Tauride Palace. Our comrades placed them by the telephones and the telegraph. A Bolshevik refused to allow a young lady from the post office through to Rodzianko with a telegram (from either Ruzskii or Brusilov).[25] She was let through on my orders. Because of all this, Chkheidze, Kerenskii, and I were late for the private meeting. I went in before they did, after the meeting was already in full swing. When I ran in, the discussion was centered on the concrete question of transferring command of the Petrograd troops to Manikovskii. As I walked in, Nekrasov and Rodzianko turned to me: "What would be the attitude of your Left factions toward this?"

I replied: "I can't comment on it because we have not discussed it, and it's not important. It makes no difference to us whether it will be A or B. The first words from the insurgent troops were: 'Where is the new authority? Where is the new government?' Therefore, it is important right now to provide a clear answer to these questions from the street, and to say that the Duma has taken matters into its own hands so that when we go back out to the street, we can be specific in answering the crowd's questions of where the new authority and government are." Upon saying this, I ran back out. None of them went out to the people. They carried out elections to the Temporary Committee of the Duma, which was meeting in Rodzianko's office. I was not there; Chkheidze and Kerenskii were. This took place at about 5:00.

At about 3:00, when the private meeting began, comrades who had been released from prisons showed up in the Duma. At about 4:00, in room 13, there were: Gvozdev, Bogdanov, Frankorusskii,[26] myself, and two or three more—in all, six to seven people. Because most factories had already elected delegates, we took the risk of declaring ourselves the Temporary Executive Committee of the Soviet of Workers' and Soldiers' Deputies, and I at once (at about 5:00) announced this to the crowd in the street. I did not know where Chkheidze was; I saw him in passing at the private meeting. I went out to the street—there were very few people; I continued to the corner of Shpalernaia and Tavricheskaia Streets and saw many more people there. I asked two workers to lift me onto their shoulders, and from there announced the formation of the Soviet of Workers' and Soldiers' Deputies. This provoked indescribable enthusiasm because the crowd, following its instinct for self-preservation, was hungry for new authority and a center around which it could coalesce. I told them, "Now that you took a new position, you can no longer see-saw—you have to organize!" (The crowd was mixed.)

The following formula had been worked out for elections to the Soviet: one delegate from each 1,000 workers and one soldier from each company (that is, from only 280 men). This happened because we did not expect so many troops—we thought that there would only be a few mutinous units. As a consequence, we had a disfigured Soviet. Everything that was printed in *Izvestiia petrogradskikh zhurnalistov* on February 27—about the formation of the Soviet, the invitation to come to the Soviet, and the appeal to the citizens to feed the soldiers[27]—all of that came from us (a revolutionary trick). It was at the time of the elections that I first saw the faces of Steklov and Sokolov.

Kerenskii, apparently on his own initiative, started organizing the Military Commission. Here too, the Duma Temporary Committee was lagging behind. Kerenskii, Filippovskii (the old SR from the artillery plant of the naval ministry, who was the first to show up),[28] myself, and Pal'chinskii (who came later) formed the kernel, the would-be foundation, of the Military Commission. No one was elected, everyone came on his own. Those who were not lazy came to join us. The Commission settled in room 42, and formed a sort of headquarters to which all revolutionary soldiers came for instructions.

At around 8:30 [in the evening], in the hallway, somebody told me that Chkheidze, Kerenskii, and I had been elected to the Presidium of the Soviet of Workers' and Soldiers' Deputies: Chkheidze as chairman, and Kerenskii and myself as deputy chairmen. I went by room 13; Chkheidze was not there. I ran to look for him, but could not find him anywhere. I glanced again into room 13, and he was already sitting there. I came in and sat next to him. Soon Kerenskii ran in. He expressed his thanks for the trust in him, but immediately apologized that he had to leave at once to go to the Military Commission because he was fully occupied with military affairs. Having said that, he ran right away to the Military Commission. I asked the Soviet to free Kerenskii from his responsibilities and entrust him to direct all his energy and work to the Military Commission in the Soviet's name. Everyone agreed, and Kerenskii received a sort of mandate as a result. I did not spend much time in the Soviet, and soon joined him at the Military Commission.

I spent most of that evening there, with Kerenskii. Around midnight, everyone left. Only a few Duma deputies, some military doctors, and some recently arrived officers remained. After midnight, things got anxious. Chkheidze was ill, and went home to sleep. We, on the other hand, spent the entire night in the Duma, in the Military Commission.

After the Military Commission had already been formed, the Temporary Committee proposed to invite Colonel Engel'gardt there and put him in charge. No one objected: neither in the Commission, nor in the Soviet. He was accepted without conflict. I spent the night running between the Military Commission, the Temporary Committee, and Rodzianko's office, where Miliukov and I "slept" on his fur coat on the same corner bench, with our heads meeting at the corner. Rodzianko's telephone was being used the whole time. All of us: Nekrasov, Grodzitskii, Efremov,[29] Miliukov, Konovalov, Shul'gin, and I were trying all night long to establish which of the city quarters were under our control, and which were still under the government's. I remember how Nekrasov replied to a report over the heavily crackling telephone about looting: "This quarter is under our control."

Units were formed from among the insurgents. While in Rodzianko's office, we figured out where the government was hiding and what should be done with it. The first report stated that the government was in the Department of Police. This was unconfirmed (the information came from Nekrasov's personal acquaintances). The second report suggested that the government was in the building of the city police chief. Reconnaissance reported that it had been there, but had moved on to the Admiralty. We developed a plan of siege. During the day, dynamite and gunpowder had been brought into the Duma. Forgetting about that, we smoked cigarettes right next to it, stepping over mines, crates of dynamite, and so on. Despite all that, nothing blew up. Only toward the morning did we think of placing two soldiers near each entrance to room number 1, where all these things were piled, to remove cigarettes from smokers' mouths. At about 3:00 in the morning, it became clear that the government was in the Admiralty. Reconnaissance was sent there, and reported back that it would be impossible to capture the building without cavalry because there were artillery units from Pavlovsk everywhere, loaded with buckshot. It would be impossible to fight them without artillery.

We decided to occupy the St. Peter and Paul Fortress, so that we could shell the Admiralty from there. Colonel Myshlaevskii (son of the general)[30] was at the Guards Economic Society[31] (Nekrasov spoke with him on the phone). He reported valuable information. During the day, a rumor circulated that the St. Peter and Paul Fortress was held by a Keksgol'mskii unit,[32] but that turned out to be untrue. It became clear that the old garrison was still there, and that General Nikitin was not resisting the Duma. Even so, he considered it his soldier's duty to preserve what was inside and defend everything in order to turn it over to the new authority intact. Shul'gin happened to know Nikitin. Myshlaevskii found out that Nikitin wanted an official delegation of deputies to come to him from the Duma. They decided to send Shul'gin, and gave him two trucks. This was about 4:00 in the morning [on February 28]. It was still very dark. But because of rumors of artillery fire, Shul'gin's expedition was delayed until 7:00 in the morning. At that time, we had tea in room number 4, in the Deputy President's office. Shul'gin grabbed a cloth napkin off a writing desk to use as a white flag of truce, and left. He came back at 9–10:00 with the report that Nikitin was observing complete neutrality, perhaps with a slight leaning to the side of the Duma. This meant that the St. Peter and Paul Fortress could not be used as the position from which to shell the Admiralty. At about 12 noon, Nikitin telephoned and reported that a crowd of soldiers had gathered near the fortress, and wanted to burst in. They did not believe that there were no political prisoners inside. Nikitin asked us to send Duma deputies to pacify the workers. The Temporary Committee decided to send Volkov and myself as its official representatives. We equipped ourselves as if we were going on a "military" expedition, taking one truck for machine-guns, which we failed to procure, and one car. Then, an artillery officer offered to gather cavalry in the street for us. No such force was available to the Duma. He thought to gather Cossacks, place himself at their command, and escort us. But we could not wait for the Cossacks, so we took two soldiers, got into the car, and embarked on our journey.

Not counting the speeches which I had given near the Duma, this was my first trip into the city since the beginning of the revolution. I was astonished by the picture on the streets. This was something completely unexpected for me, a disgusting picture of nonstop automobile cruising by show-offs from among the soldiers, accompanied by young women. Our car died twice on the road, and as we drove over Troitskii Bridge, it stopped completely. At that moment, shooting erupted. Some said it was coming from the St. Peter and Paul Fortress. I brought my Browning pistol along, but did not shoot. In order to move on, we stopped one of the cars passing by, told the military show-offs and their young women to get out, and sped off toward the fortress. There, we saw a huge crowd in front of the gate. I climbed onto the roof of the car, explained to the workers what was happening, and asked whether they trusted us. They said that they did. We went inside, accompanied by a deputy commandant, and searched all of the chambers. They indeed turned out to be absolutely empty: on the morning of the 28th, nineteen Pavlovskii soldiers were released, along with several officers who had been kept there for criminal offenses. The new fortress commandant—a young Georgian (with a very short surname that I cannot remember now),[33] wearing a *papakha* [tall hat] and a long Circassian coat, surrounded by militiamen and soldiers—asked me for help. He did not have any identity papers with him, and wanted me to vouch for him. I did. The deputy commandant was an old general of German descent. There's something funny about a Georgian and a German together . . .

Going home (to Tverskaia 13) that day from the Duma, I saw that nearby (Tverskaia 15), the Gendarme Administration was in flames. I began to argue to the crowd that they should not torch everything just like that, on the spur of the moment. "Only the archive is burning," they replied.

[PART] II

On the 27th, at the first evening meeting of the Soviet of Workers' and Soldiers' Deputies, four secretaries were elected: Gvozdev, Sokolov, Pankov, and Grinevich. The Executive Committee, numbering fifteen people, was also elected.[34] The principle of representation for political parties was set. Each party organization was to send one representative to the Soviet and three to the Executive Committee (two from the central committees of the parties and one from their Petrograd organizations). The soldiers' executive committee was formed much later.

I did not participate in the first stage of negotiations about the Provisional Government. They began towards the evening on the 28th. I do not recall where I was that evening. I had been taking part in negotiations since March 1. On March 1, we received a report from Warsaw Railway Station that a special tsarist train had been prepared for Rodzianko to travel to Pskov. Local railway workers were asking us whether they should release it. We received reports that the tsar was in Pskov, and we also knew that the question of abdication was in the air. We thought that the moment was very important, but that negotiations behind the Soviet's back were unacceptable. We therefore took measures so that nothing could be done without the Soviet of Workers' and Soldiers' Deputies. Yours truly was appointed commissar of all railroads of the Petrograd hub, and I even had the opportunity to serve in that capacity on the 28th. I gave instructions over the telephone to the workers at the Warsaw Station that they should not release the train.

We were very concerned and asked Nikolai Semenovich Chkheidze, who was a member of the Temporary Committee, to find out which train this was, with what purpose, where and by whom it was being sent, and why any of this was done without notifying the Soviet's Executive Committee. This was a struggle for power. The episode took place at 11:00 in the morning. Before Chkheidze could even get off his seat to fulfill this assignment, an unusually agitated Kerenskii ran into room 13 and said to us in a loud voice: "Was it you who ordered that the train not be released? This is a very important matter for us, and in our mutual interests."

I replied, "Aleksandr Fedorovich, I speak to you of behalf of the Executive Committee, and as a commissar, and I ask you to maintain a formal tone. We consider it unacceptable that steps be taken without the Executive Committee. The train was cancelled on our orders."

"You are obstructing our common cause," Kerenskii replied in the same raised tone of voice, trying to explain himself. I had to remind him to use a formal tone. He fell down in a dead faint. After that the episode was over, and it became clear that Rodzianko was going to travel in order to get the abdication. We said that, in that case, we would send the train, but that we could not trust Rodzianko to go alone. We objected to him. Rodzianko did not go, and instead Guchkov and Shul'gin traveled in this train (either right away, or a few hours later).[35] I cannot say exactly how their candidatures came up, or how they replaced Rodzianko.

On March 1, for the first time, we grappled with each other. Our Soviet and the Temporary Committee for the first time struggled for power, and for the first time we taught them to see us as a real force to be reckoned with.

The Soviet gathered in room 13. The meeting was set to begin at 1:00, but we delayed it for a couple of hours by arriving late because the train issue had not yet been resolved. There was therefore a need to call for a break, because there was nothing to report at the meeting. We could not talk about this matter because of its conspiratorial nature, but it was impossible for us to conceal from the meeting that something was going on. I was asked to go to the meeting and get them to take a break. I went and succeeded by proposing a break in the following way: "The Executive Committee needs to resolve a very important and responsible matter, which cannot be delayed. Therefore, we declare a two-hour break." That did not go very smoothly. The atmosphere was very tense. The mood of the meeting was aggressive toward the Executive Committee. I asked them to accept my proposal unanimously, but critics raised objections. They did not object to the matter itself, but (since they were aggressive to the Executive Committee) they declared that the Executive Committee was doing something without disclosing everything to the Soviet.

Generally speaking, though, the mood was favorable. I saw that our proposal could get enough votes. But at that time, a group of soldiers—about two hundred—who seemed to be the newly elected representatives from the companies, barged in from room 12. Before that, there had been about two hundred workers and fifteen soldiers. The soldiers had been as unobtrusive as the workers now became. I created much confusion because I failed to see that I could no longer control the meeting. Still, I did not allow the newcomers to settle in before I put the question to a vote, and a break was voted for by the majority of voices. That caused the soldiers to become so outraged that I had to cancel the vote and put the question to a vote again. I was unable to make the meeting take a break. I had to continue, but it was very difficult to conduct the meeting because the mass of soldiers turned out to be unruly. Finally, I somehow managed to cope with the meeting. At that time, Nikolai Dmitrievich Sokolov showed up, and I transferred the duty to him and left to fulfill my responsibilities as commissar of the railroads. I situated myself by the telephone and contacted railway personnel. I asked them to notify me if there were any changes.[36]

After that, I returned to the Soviet, where the soldiers were talking, each about their own companies. They asked what they should do because, pursuant to Rodzianko's order,[37] the officers who had gone into hiding were returning to their regiments. They were imposing order. They wanted to disarm the soldiers and restore the old ways. The soldiers declared that they needed instructions from the Soviet. At that moment, I turned my chairmanship over to Sokolov, left the meeting, and joined the negotiations about the Provisional Government. All the theses, from A to Z, which were later accepted by the Provisional Government and became part of its program, were worked out by us in the Executive Committee. We outlined nine points, and presented them to the Temporary Committee.[38] We declared that the program was the important thing—not personalities—but that we reserved the right to reject their candidates. We left the text of our program with them, but when we returned to the Soviet at about 6–7:00 in the evening, we were shown Order Number One, typed and in multiple copies. It turned out that in the heat of the moment a commission of soldiers had been elected under Sokolov's chairmanship. Without leaving the meeting, the commission had written the order right there, with Sokolov editing. An ad hoc assembly of soldiers voted on the spot to confirm and accept it, because the atmosphere was very heated, influenced by what the soldiers were saying about the officers. Nobody was talking about dual power yet, because there was no Provisional Government and the new authority had only just sprung up. So it is really a misunderstanding to speak of dual power on March 1. [Here, Tsereteli inserted the following comment into Skobelev's account: "But this means that dual power was coming into being."]

[Skobelev:] At that time, the [new] authority was just taking root. We conducted negotiations with the Temporary Committee in room 45. The Executive Committee authorized a few comrades for this task: Chkheidze, Steklov, and myself. But at first, I was busy, and joined the negotiations only toward the end. We quickly agreed on a program, but we could not immediately agree on the specific people. Soon, during the night, we came to agreement on that as well. We had some disagreements on the program, but they were not extensive. I remember what Shul'gin said on the question of the Constituent Assembly: "If two weeks ago someone had told me about a constituent assembly, I would not have believed it, and would have said that this is folly. But now, there is nothing that I can say against it." People such as L'vov,[39] Shul'gin, and Godnev[40] quickly agreed with everything. It was very interesting to observe the changes in their psychology because of the coup; the previously unimaginable was now a reality. Shul'gin, L'vov, and Godnev were much more agreeable than the skilled politician Miliukov, who was considerably more stubborn. In the evening, a list of ministers coalesced. Only the ministry of justice remained an open question. It was offered to Maklakov, but he turned it down in favor of Kerenskii. In the evening, when it became clear that the candidacy was still open, the Temporary Committee demanded two official candidates from the Executive Committee: Kerenskii and Chkheidze. The latter was nominated for the ministry of labor. I think the same was proposed [again] on the 1st, but I cannot remember exactly.

On the morning of the 2nd, or perhaps even during the night, Steklov and I went to the Temporary Committee to finalize the list, and made an attempt to reject Guchkov. But they made it clear to us that the combination would be impossible without Guchkov, that none of them would agree to join the cabinet without him, and that there was no better candidate for war minister. The ministry of justice was intended for Maklakov, but the post was still open for Kerenskii. The ministry of labor was for Chkheidze. On the 2nd, we convened the Executive Committee in room 12, and discussed the question of joining the Provisional Government. It was voted down, 9–6. It was decided not to take part in a coalition government. In the morning, Konovalov and others insisted that Kerenskii join the ministry. In a private conversation, Konovalov told me that he would not join the Provisional Government without Kerenskii. Nekrasov told me the same. He too refused to enter without Kerenskii. It was clear that the whole arrangement could collapse. After the decision not to join the ministry, we convened the Soviet.[41] The question of the minister of justice was still open.

At about 12 or 1:00, Chkheidze opened the meeting, sitting on a table under a small opening windowpane [fortochka]. We protected him (I called him, jokingly, "the future minister of labor") from the cold by covering him with a soldier's coat. Iurii Mikhailovich Steklov gave a thorough, impeccable, brilliant report defending our tactics and program, without saying a word about our negotiations, for which we had not gotten sanction from the Soviet. The Soviet had not been informed about our negotiations. On the 2nd, we opened the meeting and stated up front that the Duma Committee had accepted the program which we proposed. On the question of the ministry, we suggested the formula that we should support their actions as long as they follow our program [postol'ku poskol'ku]. The floor was opened for discussion. We were quite apprehensive of the way the audience would react to this, but from the very first speeches, it became clear that the position of the Executive Committee would be approved by the Soviet. At that time, no one could last in the chairmanship for more than half an hour, so Chkheidze handed it over to me. All of a sudden Kerenskii showed up, and I received a note that he wanted to make an unscheduled announcement. I gave him the podium.

He climbed onto a desk and delivered the speech which was later reproduced in Izvestiia, justifying his joining the Provisional Government.[42] He delivered it with great pathos, in his first attempt to use the language of power: "Will you listen to me? Do you trust me? Do you believe me?" and so on. To all these direct questions, he received unambiguous, definitive, positive answers. The meeting very passionately accepted him with unequivocal enthusiasm. "Comrades, all of the detainees—the officials of the old regime—were in my hands. I was given five minutes to think it over and decide whether I should pass them off to Maklakov or take the post of minister of justice myself. I made the decision, but if you do not agree, I will leave the post of deputy chairman of the Soviet. But if you let me, I will become the minister of justice." This provoked a new storm of enthusiasm and applause. His questions were not put to a vote. The meeting gave him answers by their reactions, and lifting him up, carried him to the Temporary Committee. After that, we continued the discussion of Steklov's report, but in a few minutes—a couple—Kerenskii came back and declared that the British Military Attaché,[43] with whom he had just spoken, had asked him (in his capacity as minister of justice) to give the Soviet greetings from English democracy. This was Kerenskii's first appearance as minister. Thus ended the blessing of Kerenskii by the Soviet.

The discussions soon ended. Our tactic was accepted and approved, I think unanimously. We decided to inform the Temporary Committee through Chkheidze, Steklov, and Sokolov. Thus this creation—the Provisional Government—was born. After that, we (Sokolov, Steklov, and myself) went to the Provisional Government. When we informed them about our decision, Miliukov and someone else (Shul'gin, as I recall) sighed, "Thank God! Russia is saved!" Steklov and I entered first, and Miliukov kissed us. There was one point which was missing from our negotiations, and it was not included in the declaration of the Provisional Government. This was the demand for a republic, which they did not accept, and (mainly Miliukov) let us understand that they thought regency was possible. We then changed our position, demanding that the Provisional Government not undertake any steps that would predetermine the future form of government before the Constituent Assembly. On this question, we yielded, in the sense that we did not insist and left it an open question. However, Miliukov immediately used this, and developed the question of regency in his speech.[44] This provoked a stormy reaction from everyone who had welcomed his speech before he raised the question of regency. He was almost toppled from the desk on which he was standing.

On the 2nd, a rumor about Nicholas's abdication was spread in the city.[45] Toward the evening, groups gathered carrying slogans: "Down with the Regent!" "Long Live the Democratic Republic!" In the evening, clusters of people were showing up near the Duma, calling us to come outside, and asking us the question whether it would be a republic or a regency. On the

3rd, the entire city was on its feet. Everyone was in the streets. Here and there street demonstrations and gatherings sprung up with the slogans: "Down with Regency!" "Long Live the Provisional Government!" "Long Live the Democratic Republic!" We have Miliukov to thank for raising the question of regency right away.

From some members of the Provisional Government—Nekrasov, Kerenskii, and Konovalov—I heard the following about the negotiations between the Provisional Government and Mikhail Aleksandrovich on the same question of regency.[46] The final resolution of the question of regency came when, on the 2nd,[47] the manifesto of Nicholas's abdication was brought in and the Provisional Government went to Mikhail Aleksandrovich on the morning of the 3rd. (I heard this from Nekrasov.) The Provisional Government found itself in an uneasy situation before the grand duke because its members argued amongst themselves in his presence. Participation in these negotiations was a heavy responsibility. Mikhail Aleksandrovich did not know what to say. Miliukov was most decisively trying to convince him to accept the throne. Miliukov insisted. Shingarev supported him, but was not particularly insistent. Miliukov aggressively criticized rejection. In contrast, Rodzianko, Shul'gin, and Godnev were very cautious and did not impose anything on the grand duke, letting him decide on his own. Kerenskii did not apply any pressure either. He did not stubbornly defend the opposite point of view, thinking that it was a question for the grand duke's conscience. I don't know what Guchkov was saying. After listening to all of them, Mikhail Aleksandrovich expressed the desire to talk to Rodzianko and Shul'gin in private.[48] Some objected to this, but others, particularly Kerenskii, declared that they had nothing against it. After the private conference, Mikhail Aleksandrovich came out and declared to everyone: "I do not feel that I have the strength to assume such a heavy burden, and I do not see unanimity in your ranks. On the contrary, since I see disunity among you, I refuse the regency until a decision by the Constituent Assembly." A manifesto of abdication was edited there. Who edited it I do not know, but Aleksandr Fedorovich Kerenskii told me that he had taken part in it.

On the eve, the talk was about the establishment of the Provisional Government. This was on the evening of the 1st, when we still wondered how things would turn out. Kerenskii told me tête-à-tête that, during discussions on the formation of the Provisional Government, he and those on the Left in the Temporary Committee (Nekrasov and Konovalov) had declared that they considered Rodzianko unacceptable as premier, and they would not tolerate his candidacy. As the worst-case scenario, they would agree on Prince L'vov. They decided not to cause a stir on the question of regency. They did not speak decisively against it because they thought that if a regency were to be introduced it would be possible to influence the regent through his wife,[49] who was connected to certain Moscow radical circles. Not even Kerenskii thought it was necessary to put up a fight and cause a breakup over this question; events were developing too fast, and it was impossible to grasp the meaning of them all. Before our very eyes, a coup was taking place in the psyche of many. The night from the 27th to the 28th, when Miliukov and I slept on the same fur coat in Rodzianko's office, was a turning point for Miliukov. When it became known that the St. Peter and Paul Fortress was maintaining neutrality, and when we raised the question of what would happen next, Miliukov said: "It is absolutely clear to me that everything is over for that scoundrel Nicholas."

On the 27th, during the day, the Temporary Committee was insisting that Rodzianko assume power, but he hesitated to do so for several hours. Miliukov declared that without Rodzianko the creation of the Temporary Committee would be impossible. Only when Rodzianko started receiving phone calls with requests for instructions, and when delegates of troops arrived, did he overcome the crisis. He outgrew his responsibilities before the tsar, and declared: "The inevitable has occurred. I take power into my hands," and placed himself at the head of the Temporary Committee. I cannot say how we felt about the question of regency during that night. I do not recall what I myself thought about regency . . . I don't think I thought about it at all. We did not reject regency. This was a time when we were everywhere at once. As far as I recall, the state of mind at the Executive Committee on the night of the 1st was as follows: events were developing so incredibly that we could not have a clear view of the further successes of the revolution. We were running around during these three days, carried by events. Therefore, we didn't think it was worth putting up a real fight over the question of regency, or causing a rupture. We couldn't see the whole extent of the revolution ourselves, and didn't know whether we were in control of Petrograd. The membership and the program of the Provisional Government finally calmed us down. The question of regency became confrontational only on the evening of the 2nd, when we came out, furious, after Miliukov's speech. Then, we openly spoke against regency and in favor of a republic. Before that, our position was somewhat indecisive.

On the morning of the 3rd, a telephone report came in from the Warsaw Railway Station. We were told that another train (Guchkov and Shul'gin had already slipped away from us) was ready to leave for Pskov. I dashed to the station, because I still retained the duties of a commissar. There I was told that Guchkov had returned from Pskov, gathered workers at the station and spoke before them, trying to agitate in favor of regency. They arrested him for that, but soon, after an explanation, let him go.[50] It turned out that there was no new train. The station chief reported that the train that was about to depart for Pskov was only a passenger train. I asked if there was a Duma deputy on board, and was told that, indeed, there was one in a first-class compartment. This turned out to be Krivtsov.[51] I ran to the train, entered the compartment, took Krivtsov into the office of the assistant station chief, and interrogated him about his purpose in going to Pskov. He replied that he and his wife were going to visit his son. To that, I told him: "Colleague, I consider it inappropriate for you to travel. It would be better if you didn't." He got off, and I drove him and his wife to their residence, asking him to pledge his word that he would not go to Pskov over the next two days. As for Guchkov, I am not quite sure whether he was arrested or not.

The Provisional Government appointed Rodichev minister for Finland without consulting with the Executive Committee.[52] On the evening of the 1st, the Provisional Government turned to the Executive Committee with information about a sailors' uprising in Sveaborg. There was abuse and lynching of officers, and the Provisional Government was asking someone from the Executive Committee to go to Sveaborg, leaving at about 10:00 in the evening.[53] The Executive Committee decided that I should go. I refused, saying that I did not feel I had the strength to cope with this task, but my comrades insisted, and were convincing. I agreed, but on the condition that I would not be judged for this step. The Executive Committee demanded written consent from the Provisional Government to arrest any officers who I deemed necessary. I spoke with Kerenskii, and he and L'vov agreed verbally to my request. I wanted written consent, but I did not get it. I was trying to catch L'vov to get it from him, but missed him and just wasted time. After that, I went home (it was the first night since the beginning of the revolution that I went home). At 2 in the morning, I received a telephone call that a train had been prepared, and that Rodichev was already on board, waiting for me. I called L'vov again, but he was asleep. I was told not to wake him up, and thus was unable to secure the document from him. I decided to leave anyway.

In Sveaborg, we were met by an unexpected scene. A writ from the Provisional Government was unnecessary. On the contrary, we had sufficient authority to rescue the Provisional Government ourselves. At the railway station, we were met by an honor guard and Admiral Maksimov,[54] who rushed to me, not to the minister for Finland. We were introduced to the guard, and from there proceeded to a square, where the garrison was standing in formation. We gave speeches, and saw that we were in control of the garrison. Admiral Maksimov took a telegram from his pocket, in which Guchkov appointed him commander of the [Baltic] fleet. (About two hours earlier, Nepenin had been murdered, and Maksimov had reported to Guchkov that command of the fleet had passed on to him because he had been elected by the crews.[55] Guchkov had sanctioned these elections, and confirmed him.) After the speeches, we went to the local executive committee, where we were told about what had happened. From there, we proceeded to a gathering of officers and a parade.

The sailors were in a state of great confusion and alarm, not knowing what was going on. It turned out that they had received no reports or leaflets from Petrograd. We told them about everything. Once they learned that the coup was already an accomplished fact, and that calm had been restored in Petrograd, they solemnly lifted us up and carried us around. After that we went to the ships in order to resolve the painful question of the arrested officers. We spoke carefully about it. Our goal and tactics were to sanction the uprising, but then to refashion things into a normal condition. We asked them to take the red signal lights down from the mutinous ships. This was the first time we applied a brake to the revolution. This was difficult, but the question of taking down the lights received unanimous support in the [Sveaborg] Soviet. We sent a radio transmission to every ship. From a window, we watched the red lights taken down, one after another—but they remained on a couple of ships. These were *Andrei Pervozvannyi* and *Pavel* (Bolsheviks).[56] We received a radio response from them that they would not take the lights down until their demands were met. Their demands were: a democratic republic, "war until victory," and along with that, a whole bunch of naval housekeeping items of a petty military nature. We insisted that the [local Soviet] committee subordinate them. After putting on airs for an hour and a half, they finally took the lights down. The next morning, Rodichev and I visited the ships and attended a number of large gatherings at which we delivered speeches. Although our speeches differed quite a bit on the question of the war, we both delivered them in a proper manner. On one of the ships, I demanded that all the officers be brought out from the punishment cells, and insisted that they be entrusted to us in the Executive Committee. It worked. Even before we could reach the next ship, they were released.

[PART] III

[*While parts I and II represented his narrative account of the first days of the revolution, the third evening was structured around Skobelev's answers to questions posed to him by members of the Society for the Study of the Revolution.*]

We received (I do not remember the date) information from I do not know whom, that the tsar, who was at General Headquarters, had gotten permission from the Provisional Government to travel in a special train through Petersburg to Murman,[57] so that he could leave from there for England. Alarmed, we at once called an urgent meeting of the Executive Committee. It was decided to take every measure to keep him from doing so, even to arrest him in the name of the Executive Committee. We prepared military units. Some of them were called in to take over all of the railway stations. A radio-telegram was composed immediately. We presented the situation as if our measures had been undertaken with the knowledge of the Provisional Government. Therefore, the text of the radio-telegram went like this: "According to information we have received, the former tsar is trying to escape to England. We consider it to be the duty of a revolutionary, or of anyone who is able, to detain him. To all executive committees; to all soviets of soldiers' and workers' deputies; to all railway committees, railway employees, and other citizens."[58]

The radio-telegram was sent out immediately. It created a big stir in Finland. At the same time, we sent a contact commission to the Provisional Government to clarify the matter. At that time, we received information that the train was traveling along the Tsarskoe Selo Railway Line, and that it was approaching Tsarskoe Selo—but then the flow of information was interrupted.

In the Provisional Government, we learned that the tsar was at his palace in Tsarskoe Selo. From General Headquarters, however, he had indeed petitioned the Provisional Government to travel to Murman via Tsarskoe Selo and Petrograd, and the government had given him permission. Miliukov told us about this. Then we said that this should not be, and that we would not allow it. It was clear that Guchkov and Miliukov were maintaining a position of quiet non-resistance. In return, they promised to keep him in

Tsarskoe Selo, not allowing him to leave, and to take no steps without our consent. This was the last revolutionary step in the activity of the Soviet as a rebuff of the Provisional Government. (On the eve of our negotiations with the Provisional Government, Chkheidze made a presentation to the Soviet.) At that time, we were also told that England was offering its services to take the former tsar into "safekeeping." The British ambassador, under pressure from Guchkov and Miliukov, conducted negotiations in this regard.[59] We pressured the Provisional Government to stop these negotiations. The whole time, Chkheidze and I insisted on the tsar's arrest. Because they were apparently conducting negotiations behind the Soviet's back, they gave us evasive answers.

They received the act of abdication, then let the tsar go. He immediately proceeded to General Headquarters.[60] The contact commission was formed much later. During the entire first period of the revolution, the situation was such that the Temporary Committee, acting under pressure from us, was liquidating autocracy. We ourselves did not undertake any aggressive steps or decisive measures, fearing that we might go too far and do too much. We were pushing them (the Temporary Committee) to take these actions.

Now the question emerged where to put the tsar in order to prevent his escape. Our circle came up with the idea of putting him in the St. Peter and Paul Fortress. Aleksandr Fedorovich Kerenskii opposed this, insisting that this would be unsuitable: the tsar could not be kept there without creating an aura of martyrdom around him, thereby preparing the ground for counterrevolution. He thought that it would be better to keep the tsar on the outskirts of the city. We agreed, and decided on Tsarskoe Selo. Because we received information that the tsar was under insufficiently reliable guard, we undertook one more step. We, the Executive Committee, sent officer Maslovskii with a company of soldiers to verify, on behalf of the Executive Committee, whether the tsar was being held under sufficiently strict conditions. Maslovskii went to Tsarskoe Selo, but received a chilly reception. Even so, he managed to get into the palace to observe, and personally saw the tsar.[61] Afterwards, a delegation from the Finland Regiment of the Tsarskoe Selo garrison came and declared that the Finland Regiment was very unhappy about his visit.

During the first days of the Provisional Government, we pushed them on the question of the tsar. The contact commission presented several proposals, "seven points," of our demands regarding the tsar.[62] The most important of them were as follows. Point I: Confiscation of all of the property of all grand dukes. Point II: To place all members of the imperial family, including the tsar, under arrest until they renounced all of their property rights in writing, both inside Russia and abroad. Point III: To strip them of their Russian citizenship, and only then to raise the question of whether they should be permitted to travel abroad. None of this was carried out, however. Some members of the Provisional Government were saying that they found it impossible to place all members of the imperial family under arrest because some of them had previously fought against the tsarist regime, and were still in responsible positions. Information about the extent of their property holdings was given to an appropriate special commission. Later, this question lost its relevance. Now, the question of property is slowly being dissected. But it is not easy to determine which parts are personal property and which parts belong to the state treasury.

The idea of a contact commission came up in connection with the question of the tsar, especially in connection with frequent conflicts between the Soviet and the Provisional Government in the last third of March.[63] We were coming up against each other constantly because we were ill-informed about each other's actions. Our worries were often the fruits of our own misinformation. Most importantly, we and others took steps without coordinating our actions. We presented our seven points after the commission had already been created. In the beginning, it included Chkheidze, Steklov, Sukhanov, Filippovskii, and myself. Later Tsereteli, who had recently returned from Siberia, joined us. Still later, Chernov,[64] who came back from abroad, was added. We would set our meetings with the Provisional Government over the telephone. When they needed us, they would call; when we needed them, we would call. At present, with the creation of the coalition cabinet, this commission is dissolved.

Khrustalev showed up at the first meeting of the Soviet, and was elected to one of the commissions, either the finance or the food commission.[65] He did not show any initiative in the creation of the Soviet, and in a few days (two days, it seems), he disappeared from Petersburg. Our Soviet has nothing in common with the first Khrustalev Soviet. That Soviet dissolved, and its life ended with a trial. We only inherited the idea of the Soviet. We adopted it, fully formed. Trotskii and Khrustalev had not reestablished old party ties when they were abroad. Khrustalev had conducted himself in such a way that he was completely isolated from the entire émigré colony. Some comrades in Siberia had preserved their ties.

Crisis of Power

The first days after the establishment of the Provisional Government, even during the first days of the revolution, the Executive Committee suggested to the Temporary Committee that they issue an appeal asking the peasants to bring bread.[66] I participated in this effort. The food commission of the Temporary Committee of the Duma was established during the first days [*sic!*]. Another food commission was established by the Executive Committee and later they were combined under the leadership of Shingarev and Groman.[67] There, an appeal was worked out as a common text from both the Duma and the Soviet. But we were not satisfied because of its military tone, with their language about the war. We decided to put together our own separate appeal to the peasants. When our text was ready, we gave it to Chkheidze to sign. He refused, without giving us a reason or an explanation. It was evident, however, that he had done so because he did not want to lend his support to the war. At one night meeting, since Nikolai Semenovich was not present and because of the alarming rumors about the impending danger of hunger, we issued an appeal without his knowledge or signature. This appeal to deliver food and bread was the first instance in which we had to clarify our attitude toward the war.

On March 1, one worker and I decided to raise the question of the need to appeal to the democracies of all other countries so that they would not think badly of us, and so that they would understand that we did not have aggressive intentions. For the first time, we understood the difficulty in which Russia found herself: the duality of the Russian revolution lies in the fact that defending revolution and liberty can also be understood as a strengthening of Russia's power. That is why the first appeal to the population to support the army prompted our sense of the need to formulate these thoughts, to express our position on the war, and to issue an appeal to the peoples of all countries.

When I returned from Sveaborg,[68] this question of an appeal to other peoples had to be dealt with in a concrete way. We started to work on it. The writing was assigned to Nikolai Nikolaevich Sukhanov. The first version of the text was much more decisive and antiwar than the one we finally introduced, and which was published in the newspapers. I, the ardent internationalist, softened the text. This happened under the influence of everything I saw in Sveaborg, where even in the revolutionary resolutions of the Bolshevik crews, there was one overriding theme: the radical destruction of

everything inside, and a very energetic defense of the country from outside—sometimes even of conducting the war to a "victorious end."[69]

This is how it was. The idea of an appeal was born on March 2. A week
later, upon my return from Sveaborg, the text of the appeal was already
prepared. On March 7 I found myself in the Executive Committee, where
Sukhanov's text was discussed.[70] An atmosphere of internationalism pre-
vailed at the meeting. Not without profound soul-searching did I dare to
be the first to speak, against everyone, by proposing to soften the tone of
the appeal. This surprised everyone: Chkheidze, Steklov, Sukhanov, and
even myself. Even I was quite shocked by what I had to say. This was
external pressure, the influence of external circumstances (Sveaborg), on
our position. That was the influence of the general situation and of the
nation. I insisted that we had to take the revolution into account, as well
as the mood of the country. I ran home and brought back a stack of resolutions by sailors, which I then showed to my comrades. I succeeded in
conveying my point. Under the influence of those resolutions, my corrections were introduced, and the following was inserted: "The Russian
Revolution will not allow itself to be crushed by the bayonets of foreign
aggression."

Sukhanov's first text underwent changes. Only the first introductory
paragraph—"Ardent greetings!"—remained intact. There were many subsequent changes and additions. The formula "without annexations and
indemnities" was already part of his text. After that, the question of war and
peace was raised when we appealed to the people of the whole world. The
delegations from the front went first to the Provisional Government and
from there came to us. We felt that, concerning questions of foreign policy,
we had no common language with the Provisional Government. Especially
striking were the issues raised by the delegates from the front who visited
the government. In the beginning they regarded us with suspicion, because
from the start of the war through to the revolution, we had a definite position in the Duma on the question of war. Because of the growing influence
of the Soviet on the army, we felt that we, members of the Social Democratic
faction of the fourth Duma, were not trusted on war matters. The delegates
thought that we wanted peace with the Germans. They told us, "We want
to fight, but what about you?" The majority of them were asking us directly,
"How do you see the war? What is your attitude toward peace?" We referred
them to our written appeal, which had to be clarified, so we read it to them
ourselves and commented on it, explaining such phrases as "peace without

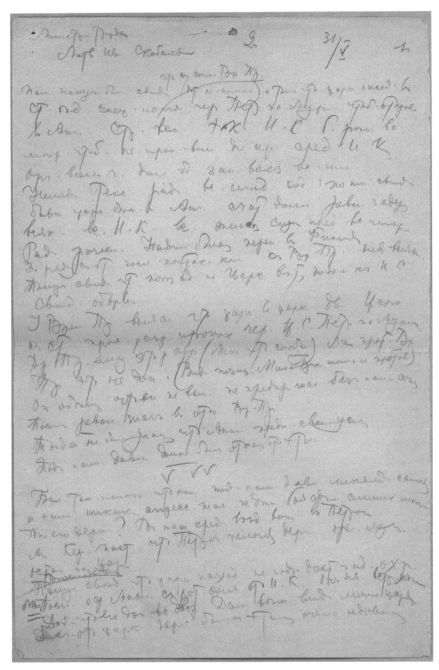

Figure 1 Two folios from the original transcript of the interview with M. I. Skobelev, May 31, 1917. Skobelev's head is sketched by one of his (evidently) bored interviewers.

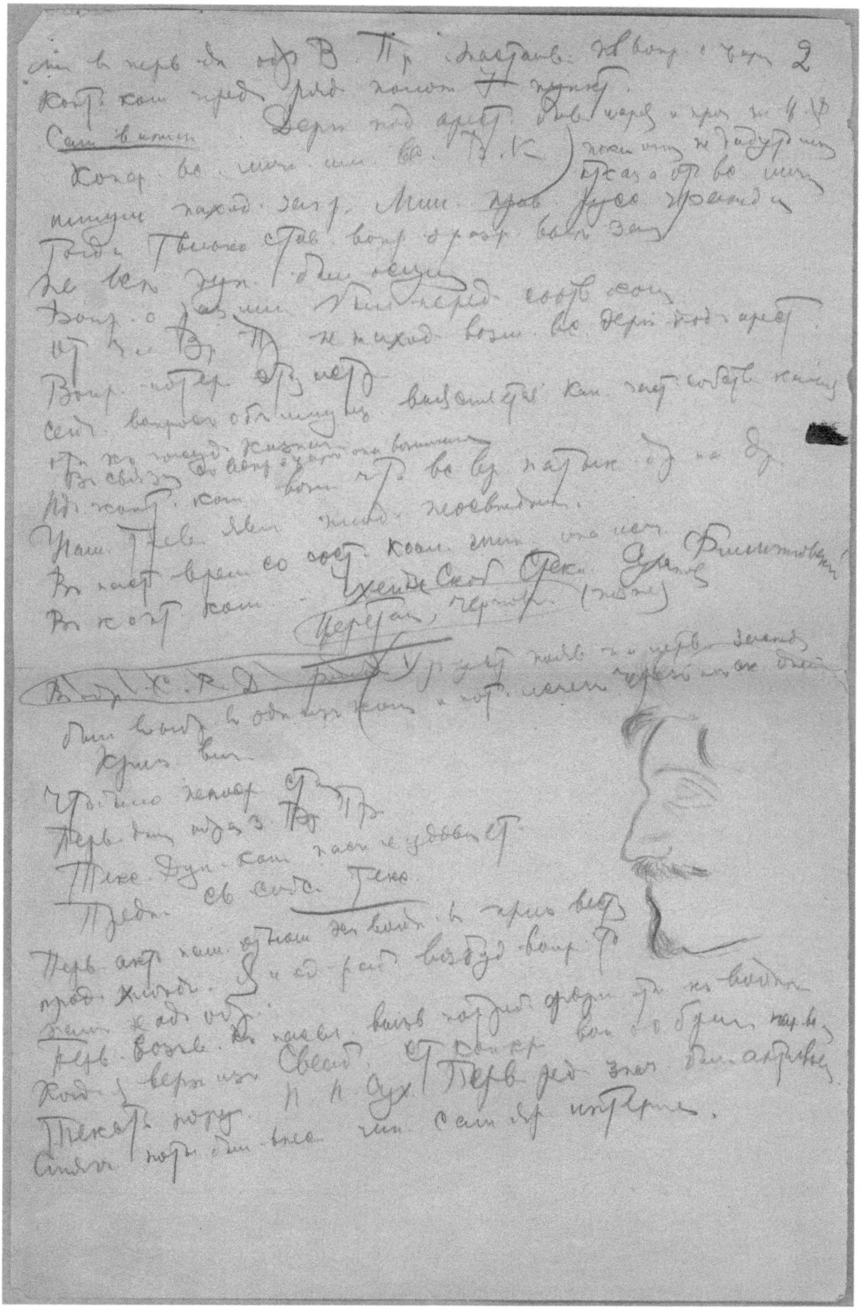

annexations and indemnities." The word "peace" troubled them. We had to explain it.

Because of all of this, we started addressing the troops, which were continuously coming to the Duma during that time. We gave a huge number of speeches. We had to speak so often that one day I counted fifteen speeches. Sometimes we listened to each other and lifted our hands in dismay. Before each other's eyes, we drifted from the sphere of abstract internationalism into defensism [*oboronchestvo*], transformed from abstract internationalists into ardent defensists. All of us leaned more and more in this direction. Nikolai Semenovich Chkheidze increasingly keeled over. We delivered our speeches from atop a table. Once, upon finishing my speech, after I got off the table a gentleman approached me and shook my hand, "We, the Muscovites, send you special greetings," he said, "because you put the issue so plainly, quite definitely, and clearly." The Danish press, quoting one of my speeches, ascribed this phrase to me: "The Russian Revolution will speak with German Social Democracy using bayonets!!!"

We, who the army suspected of wanting to conclude peace with Germany, began to show a pro-war bent. We felt that the attitude of the government created a dangerous situation for us, placing responsibility for the army on our heads. Pressure from the army was already being felt. We decided to pressure the Provisional Government, and began pushing, demanding that they express themselves on the matter and insisting that a new position was needed on the war. The result was a declaration to citizens, but it was very difficult to extract it from them, and cost us a lot of effort. The Minister of Foreign Affairs[71] put up special resistance. He declared that a new position would threaten a break with the Allies. As a last resort, he would have been willing to tell the country that we were against conquests; but it would be impossible to say this to the Allies, especially in a diplomatic act. At the same time, he did not deny that conditions in the country might become such that he would risk conveying this to Allied governments.

During our work on the text of the declaration, intense skirmishes were taking place between Kerenskii and Miliukov. Several times, Kerenskii threatened to resign from the government. That marked the beginning of a struggle between Miliukov and the government—initially with a part of it, then with the whole Provisional Government. Finally, and with difficulty, the text was agreed upon. We achieved that, and on March 27, the declaration was finalized.[72]

1. Mikhail Polievktov with wife, young son, and other family members *ca.* 1922

2. Polievktov holding a cigarette, 1930s

3. Rusudana Polievktova-Nikoladze surrounded by her books and family archive, 1970s

4. Boris Aleksandrovich Engel'gardt,
St. Petersburg, 1913

5. Petr Vasil'evich Gerasimov,
St. Petersburg, 1913

6. Mikhail Vladimirovich Rodzianko, President of the fourth Duma, St. Petersburg, 1913

7. Nikolai Vissarionovich Nekrasov, Petrograd, May 5, 1917

8. Nikolai Semenovich Chkheidze,
Petrograd, 1917

9. Matvei Ivanovich Skobelev,
Petrograd, May 1917

10. Aleksandr Fedorovich Kerenskii, Petrograd, ca 1917

11. Mikhail Ivanovich Tereshchenko, Petrograd, 1917

12. Duma Committee, Petrograd, March 1917, Rodzianko's Office, Tauride Palace. Seated (*left to right*): V. N. L'vov, V. A. Rzhevskii, S. I. Shidlovskii, M. V. Rodzianko. Standing (*left to right*): V. V. Shul'gin, I. I. Dmitriukov, B. A. Engel'gardt, A. F. Kerenskii, M. A. Karaulov

13. "Grandiose Funerals of the Revolution's Casualties", Petrograd, March 23, 1917. Standing, front row (*left to right*): V. A. Iurevich, I. I. Dmitriukov, M. S. Adzhemov, M. V. Rodzianko, A. I. Guchkov, A. I. Konovalov

This took place after the exiled deputies of the Second Duma had returned. I was not there to greet them when, on the morning of March 19, they arrived from Siberia. Chkheidze reported that he had seen them on the Petrograd Side, and was surprised by the first thing Tsereteli told him to do: "Take us to the Soviet, we want to present our point of view there." Chkheidze was a bit alarmed by that, but soon calmed down because it turned out that the arrivals shared our views and our tactics. Tsereteli's position, his point of view, ended up being the same as ours. He developed it the next day, when he joined the Soviet. Together with him, besides Mensheviks, were former Bolsheviks Anisimov and Vinogradov,[73] who identified themselves as non-party Social Democrats and shared Tsereteli's viewpoint. Thus, these second Duma deputies at once, and enthusiastically, joined our work.

The situation was very different with the émigrés. We had to digest each dose of them painfully and with great difficulty. Of course, Plekhanov was an exception. Chkheidze met him at the Finland Station, and in his speech of greeting, he said that we all had hope that we could find a common language and work together.[74] Chkheidze's short speeches to Plekhanov and Lenin were quite telling. At the same railway station, in the rooms reserved for special passengers, Chkheidze said very clever things to Lenin which immediately provoked Lenin to reply. Chkheidze told him about the duties of a revolutionary, about the defense of revolution from foreign threats, and offered to march in close ranks. In reply, Lenin immediately hit him with: "Civil War!" and "Power to the Soviets of Workers', Soldiers', and Farm Laborers' Deputies!"[75] They are no longer using these.

The next dose came with the arrival of Martov, Aksel'rod, and Martynov.[76] This was very interesting. Aksel'rod was tactful, and preferred not to speak out before he made himself familiar with the situation. But at the Menshevik Conference,[77] Martov and Martynov spoke out sharply and aggressively against us, against war, and against coalition government. On the very same day, we (Tsereteli and I) were elected honorary chairmen of the Conference. Unexpectedly, the Conference turned out to be entirely on our side, and attacked their teachers, Martov and Martynov. Aksel'rod was more cautious. He agreed with us on almost everything. Martov stood further from us, in some opposition; Martynov stood even further away.

The declaration of the Provisional Government which we secured on the 28th [March] greatly improved our situation in the country, and especially our position on the war.[78] At the All-Russian Conference of [Local]

Soviets, on the 30th, a resolution was passed that developed and defined our first proclamation and our position more precisely, especially because of these insertions: "strengthening military power" and "the army should be capable of conducting active operations."[79] These were made on the initiative and under the influence of delegates from the front, especially Romov[80] and Diubua.[81] The entire congress of the front, at Minsk,[82] confirmed our position.

Now we come to April 20–1, when we succeeded in working out the declaration for internal consumption (as they say), but we could not get it made public. We later forgot about it because the question lost its edge. Around the 20th, we learned that the Provisional Government was working on a diplomatic note to the Allies. We immediately went to the government to find out if this was true. They said that it was indeed so, and told us about the tenets upon which the note had been developed. We quickly agreed, by and large, on all general points; then we left. Later, all of a sudden, we received the final text of the note. At first, Prince L'vov told us about it over the telephone, on the 17th or 18th, that the note had already been developed and written, but that we could not see it before it was handed over to the foreign ambassadors. Supposedly, this part of the etiquette in international affairs, but I do not know to what extent that was accurate. After the note was presented to the ambassadors, it was delivered to us on the 19th at about 5–6 in the evening. At last, we began reading it in the Executive Committee. We received it in a spirit of victory. Tsereteli was reading it as he walked down the corridor, in order to present it victoriously to the Bolsheviks. But as he was reading it, the victorious feeling trickled away with every line. We sank lower and lower, and at the end, we were utterly despondent. The mood was terrible. A permanent session of the Soviet began, and it lasted all night—until 4:00 in the morning. The whole Soviet argued about what was positive and negative in the note, and whether it should be seen as a step forward or backward.

The next day, the note was published. We again gathered in the morning to decide what we should do. We came to the realization that we were not satisfied with the note. At that time, we received a telephone call from the Provisional Government, and were told that there were troops on Mariinskii Square, and that regiments were approaching the Mariinskii Palace, demanding Miliukov's arrest. Others were already demanding the arrest of all of the ministers. My role as *Mädchen für Alles*[83] was immediately remembered in the Executive Committee, and I was asked to drive to the square at once and make the regiments go back. I drove there and found a separate group of leaders in addition to the troops, standing near the entrance to the palace and trying to get in. It turned out that regiments were taking to the streets on the initiative of a soldier named Linde.[84] He was a former member of the Executive Committee of the Soviet of Soldiers' and Workers' Deputies, but was unhappy that he had not been reelected. He considered the new elections invalid, and continued to see himself as a member of the Executive Committee. Representing himself as such, he had called troops into the streets. Gots was with me. I had to use a commanding tone, and described the situation to the troops. The units realized that they had been misled. I suggested that they go back—that they should not put themselves in such a stupid situation. Linde, along with other leaders, was insisting that the troops demonstrate in the streets before returning to their barracks. I did not insist on an itinerary, and allowed this, having made sure that they left Mariinskii Square at once.

By the way, the Provisional Government was not in the Mariinskii Palace. At that time, General Kornilov arrived. He was very confused, asking what had happened. We calmed him down. I explained everything to him. The regiments were sent back to their barracks. We spoke to the troops, explaining to them that all of us were concerned and that we welcomed their support, but for the sake of the cause, it would be better if they dispersed. This was received with relative calm and little controversy. They obeyed fairly quickly. Once this was done, we returned to the Executive Committee. More and more new rumors and information were arriving there suggesting that the note was causing confusion and indignation everywhere among the troops, that there were disturbances in the barracks, and that the street movement had begun.

On the 21st, we received information that Kornilov had ordered certain military units to deploy on Palace Square. Together with this, we had information that some regiments were agitating for all soldiers to take to the streets. Chkheidze was not present. I proposed that all military units stay off the streets. Nikolai Semenovich showed up, and was asked to contact Kornilov by telephone and inform him of our decision. Kornilov replied that he had already ordered the troops to deploy, and therefore could not rescind his order. We categorically objected, and Chkheidze conveyed this to him. Again, things were at "the point of the sword." We adopted a resolution to undertake the most decisive measures to prevent that order from being carried out. It was decided to issue a proclamation from the Executive

Committee, and to post it in the streets. Its basic points were agreed upon right away. Kornilov asked us to send him someone from the Executive Committee, for negotiations. This was assigned to Dobranitskii,[85] Bogdanov, and myself. We drove there and spoke with Kornilov, from one side to the other, in official language. I told him, "Recognizing the responsibility for the moment, the Executive Committee has decided this and that, this and that, this and that, and suggests that you rescind your order."

Kornilov replied, "Is your goal really to preserve order and calm on the streets?"

Then I said, "You and I have totally different worldviews. I won't even consider your question if it is addressed to me personally. The position of the Executive Committee remains unchanged. It stands on a well-defined political platform—supporting the Provisional Government as long as it follows our program [postol'ku poskol'ku]. We, the representatives of the Executive Committee, hereby inform you of its decision." After that Kornilov, while we were still standing there, telephoned his adjutant and rescinded his order.

Leaving Kornilov, we drove to Mariinskii Square. A pro-Kadet mass meeting was taking place there. People were giving speeches on the square. Bogdanov was pulled off the platform because he gave an inappropriately long speech in defense of Lenin. Dobranitskii was taken for a Leninist, and arrested. He asked the crowd to bring him to me, so that I could testify that he was not a Leninist. I did so without delay, and he was released. We ran into a huge, pro-Bolshevik demonstration on the corner of Moika and Nevskii. I climbed onto the bed of a truck and tried to give a speech, but they did not listen because the Leninists and anti-Leninists got into a scuffle. Later, they listened to me. I proposed that they stop beating each other up.

An extraordinary session of the Soviet of Workers' and Soldiers' Deputies was scheduled to take place on the evening of the 21st [April], at the Naval [Cadet] Corps. On the same day, we went to the historic, emergency meeting of the Executive Committee with the Provisional Government and the Temporary Committee at the Mariinskii Palace. There we agreed on a new, additional diplomatic note. The Soviet gathered at the Naval Corps, and we informed them that a joint session of the Executive Committee, the Provisional Government, and the Duma Committee was necessary. The Soviet approved. We were in session. (We were also in session the next night. This new note was deemed acceptable. The Executive Committee proposed its resolution to the Soviet.) At that time, unexpectedly,

Dan,[86] Voitinskii, and Steklov came in and told us that they had run into a scuffle, with bloody victims. This invigorated the mood of the meeting, and interrupted it. Dan declared that in his opinion the Soviet should take steps to prevent such skirmishes by putting an end to mass meetings in the streets. I took the podium and suggested that we write a concrete proclamation forbidding all demonstrations and street protests for two days. Even though my speech was risky and I was afraid that my tone was too firm, my proposition was unanimously accepted.

We were confident that this incident had been resolved, that this conflict was over, and most importantly, that the question of power had been resolved. Upon resolving all this, we calmed down and got busy with the question of the international conference. As it turned out, however, this conflict was far from over at that point. The Provisional Government was unhappy about our actions concerning the troops, as well as our proclamation, which they regarded as beyond the scope of our responsibilities and an interference with their authority. We provided our explanation for what happened; they gave us theirs. No one thought that this was the beginning or the eve of a coalition ministry.

Mollified by the fact that the conflict had apparently been resolved, we focused on the conference. We received a telegram about the Stockholm Conference of Left Socialists,[87] along with an invitation to send delegates. The aims and goals were mentioned, but were vague. The date of the convocation was very near. We assumed that this was going to be the second Zimmerwald conference;[88] we decided to take part, and in accordance with my usual role of *Mädchen für Alles*, I was assigned to go. This was on a Friday, and on Saturday we informed the meeting of the Soviet. The Bolsheviks were against participating, but the majority of the Soviet supported us.[89] On Sunday, I obtained a passport; on the way, I nearly ran over a bicyclist. On Monday morning, May 1, Comrade Erlikh[90] and I departed for Stockholm. Before evening on that same day, while sitting in the train car in Rikhomiaki,[91] we were handed a telegram asking us to return: "The conference postponed. Need to return." Before taking the return train, we visited a nearby regiment. In the evening, we left to go back. On Tuesday morning, we were in Petersburg. I went to the Executive Committee, but none of the leaders were there. I found all of them in a private room of the First Association's restaurant.[92] They greeted me with a round of applause, as if I were a naval minister. Like Chatskii, I went directly from a ship to the dance.[93]

Tsereteli could describe all of the negotiations and perturbations leading up to the formation of the coalition ministry much better than I can. He was the center of it all, and headed up the efforts on our side.

Was Kornilov following a specific policy? He would not have been against that, he would not have minded being more decisive, but each time he ran into a lack of authority. There was one period when the troops were flocking to the Duma, the period of the Pletnev organization, when Colonel Pletnev was agitating among the troops.[94] Kornilov could have played a role then, but he was smart enough to know that there was no authority. He knew how to assess the situation, since he had stumbled onto that problem every time. But generally speaking, it was hard to figure him out.

About the army? During the first days of the revolution, the army was suspicious of us because of our attitudes toward war and peace. Now the situation is such that pacifism is developing so fast in the army that we are giving it subcutaneous injections. Many think that we were the ones who corrupted the army's psychological condition; that this resulted from our mistakes. They attribute the current condition to the effects of Order Number One, "peace without annexations and contributions," and so on.

Personally, I cannot agree. I see things differently, and I think that what is happening in the army is an objective and unavoidable development. Everyone thinks that a revolution invigorates the army, that it acts as a cold shower for the troops. But I would say that this is not a cold shower, but a warm, relaxing, and calming bath. When a tired person with strained and tense nerves takes a warm bath before bed, he gets up in the morning calm but weak. This is the condition of the army. Two years of strained nerves created a need to rest. This need became a push toward revolution. But revolution served for the army as a warm bath before bed. The army emerged limp from this bath, and was even weaker the next day. Now, the army is getting better and we have not lost hope that it could be capable of advancing, that we could mount an offensive. We have hope as well as objective information that the army could advance. I speak not as a member of the cabinet, but simply as an objective observer. There are now striking facts and incidents of complete demoralization which provoke sharp condemnations from the soldiers themselves; decisive reprisals are coming from within the army itself. For example, when four regiments recently refused to go into battle, the army itself disowned them. This reflects its recovery. Blisters are being localized and burst. The organism of the army is getting healthier. It is being cured. Kerenskii and I think that the army is being cured. We are both confident about this. There will not be much decisive force, but it will be capable of launching an offensive. The first stage in the weakening of the army's pulse is already over. Now, the pulse is strengthening, and is beating rapidly.

Order Number One was not exactly smart or appropriate. N. D. Sokolov and a few soldiers—two, I think—put it together in a hurry, without asking anyone, not even the Executive Committee (as if it had been amputated). Steklov had nothing to do with it. All in all, of course, it is true to a degree that mass meetings and revolution corrupted the army. Once it took the bath, it ceased to be capable of launching an offensive. It was not used to taking part in politics; it had no experience with political life. Then all of a sudden, it started debating things because it had nothing else to do. Rodichev put it best when we went to Helsingfors: "Is the army really the place for debates [*raz've armiia mozhet vechevat'*]?" From an active army, it turned into a kind of public forum, a place for referendums. The difference between the Allied armies and ours is that the English and French armies are reading about politics which are being made at home. Our army is making politics, and it reads nothing at all. As a member of the Provisional Government, I would like to have a mechanical army that isn't talking, but doing.

Intimate Details from Prince L'vov's Office
During the first stage of the Provisional Government, Konovalov was on the left wing, politically speaking. In terms of economic issues, however, he has moved to the right.

Yes, the telegram: "Catch and Execute Revolutionaries," which was reported on in the meeting of officers on 6 March, was indeed sent by General Alekseev. This was not a communiqué from the first three days of the revolution that had been delayed en route. It had been sent after the Provisional Government had been recognized, but at that time Alekseev did not understand our revolution. He mistook the formation of the new government for a simple change in cabinets. Therefore, when agitators were sent to the army from Petersburg, he gave the order, "Catch and Execute."[95] From his perspective, he was right. Radko-Dmitriev did the same thing, but quickly realized his error.[96]

Skobelev's account was recorded by:
Part I: Marg[arita] Fel[iksovna] Ropp, Tat'iana Vsevolodovna Krupskaia, Tamara Nikolaevna Nikoladze, and R. Polievktova.

Part II: T. V. Krupskaia, T. Nikoladze, R. Polievktova, and Viktor Ivanovich Pavlov.

Part III: The same people who recorded Part II, plus: Zoia Fedorovna Pokrovskaia. Compilation of transcripts and final presentation by R. Polievktova.

NOTES

1 Prince Petr Alekseevich Kropotkin (1842–1921), the revered revolutionary and theoretician of anarcho-communism, returned to Russia on May 30, 1917 after thirty-one years of exile in Western Europe. He was greeted at the Finland Railway Station by A. F. Kerenskii, N. V. Chaikovskii, Skobelev, and other Socialist dignitaries.

2 Also known as the Cathedral of Our Lady of Kazan, built between 1801 and 1811 and dedicated to one of Russia's most venerated icons. The Cathedral is located on Nevskii Avenue, just a short block away from Merchants' Row and the City Duma.

3 The reference is probably to an informal committee of the representatives of different Socialist groups (Kerenskii, Sokolov, and Skobelev among them) that during the first days of the February uprising organized the so-called information meetings of the Socialist intelligentsia to discuss the developing situation and coordinate activities. The participants of these meetings ranged from the Bolsheviks (led by A. G. Shliapnikov and P. A. Zalutskii) on the Left to the Popular Socialists, the moderate Social Democrats and the Socialist Revolutionaries (A. V. Peshekhonov, Skobelev, Chkheidze, Kerenskii, and Zenzinov) on the Right. They met on February 24, 25, and 26 in the homes of N. D. Sokolov, Maksim Gor'kii, and Kerenskii, respectively. The moderate SR Zenzinov later described these meetings as "the general staff of the revolution," a claim disputed by subsequent historians, who nevertheless acknowledged the importance of these informal gatherings in creating the loose coalition of Socialist leaders that came together to form the Petrograd Soviet on February 27. See Tsyuoshi Hasegawa, *The February Revolution, Petrograd, 1917* (Seattle and London: University of Washington Press, 1981), 324–5; B. I. Nikolaevskii, *Russkie masony i revoliutsiia* (Moscow: Terra, 1990), 89; *RPG*, I: 32–3; Nik.[olai] Sukhanov, *Zapiski o revoliutsii*, 7 parts (Berlin, Petersburg and Moscow: Izdatel'stvo Z. I. Grzhebina, 1922–3; repr. 1991), I, 1–2: 57–60; V. Charnoluskii, "Desiat' let nazad. Vospominaniia o pervykh momentakh Fevral'skoi revoliutsii," *Izvestiia VTsIK*, March 12, 1927, 6. Skobelev is correct in pointing out that representatives of the radical underground groups advocated a much more cautious approach than their moderate colleagues. See also the interview with Kerenskii (Chapter 11).

4 "Tails," in this context, means queues for bread.

5 For a useful brief chronology of the February Days in English, see Hasegawa, *The February Revolution*, Appendix I, and *RPG*, III: 1821–2. For a more detailed but still a very compact summary, see Rex A. Wade, *The Russian Revolution, 1917*, 2nd edn (Cambridge: Cambridge University Press, 2005), 29–39.

6 That is, the Social Democratic faction, headed by Chkheidze and the Kerenskii Labor Group.

7 Approx. 6½ feet (or slightly over 2 meters).

8 Valentin Ivanovich Khaustov (1884–after 1917) was a Social Democrat (Menshevik) deputy to the fourth Duma from Ufa province. Vladimir Ivanovich Dziubinskii (1860–1927) was a leading Labor Group deputy to the third and fourth Dumas from Tobol'sk province. On February 25, 1917, he visited the city center and witnessed the clashes between demonstrators and the soldiers from the Volynskii and Lithuanian Regiments, then travelled to Nikolaevskii Railway Station where similar clashes were occurring between demonstrators and police.

9 *Anichkov dvorets*, so named after the nearby Anichkov Bridge across the Fontanka River, is located at the intersection of Nevskii Avenue and the Fontanka. Originally built for the Empress Elizabeth in 1754, by the time of the February Revolution the palace was occasionally used by Nicholas II's mother, the Empress Maria Fedorovna, as her Petrograd residence.

10 Nikolai Nikolaevich Shnitnikov (1861–?) was a well-known Petrograd sworn attorney and deputy to the City Duma. In October 1905, he was one of the founders of the Kadet party, and in 1905–6 one of the leaders of the legendary Union of Unions. In later years, he drifted toward the Popular Socialists (he was good friends with Charnolusskii). During the First World War, he was active in the Zemgor and the City Duma; in June 1917, he was elected to the central committee of the unified Labor Popular Socialist Party.

11 See the interview with P. V. Gerasimov (Chapter 5).

12 *Sic.* This is the text as written.

13 Nikolai Ivanovich Iordanskii (1876–1928) was a publicist, a prominent Social Democrat (a follower of G. V. Plekhanov), and a member of the first St. Petersburg Soviet of 1905. From 1909 to 1917, he edited the popular left-leaning journal "Contemporary World" (*Sovremennyi mir*) and through his literary and publishing work maintained extensive ties with various Socialist, neo-populist, and liberal circles (for example, he collaborated closely with the Bolshevik V. D. Bonch-Bruevich and employed V. M. Molotov as the journal's secretary). After the February Revolution he served as commissar of the Provisional Government to the south-western front. In 1917, he lived on Furazhnyi Lane (no. 4), two blocks from the Duma and the Tauride Garden.

14 This refers to the so-called Tauride barracks (*Tavricheskie kazarmy*) of the Preobrazhenskii Regiment's reserve battalion, located just south of the Duma and the Tauride Garden, between Kirochnaia, Preobrazhenskaia, and Paradnaia Streets.

15 The reference is to Ol'ga L'vovna Kerenskaia (1886–1975), née Baranovskaia.

16 See the interview with Gerasimov. For the English translation of this telegram, see *RPG*, I: 42.

17 Vladimir Dmitrievich Bonch-Bruevich (1873–1955) was an Old Bolshevik and Lenin's trusted ally since the split of the Russian Social Democratic Party in 1903. He was also a well-known publicist and publisher of literature on Russian religious sects. On February 27, 1917, he organized (apparently on his own initiative) a seizure of the printing house of a low-brow popular daily, and the next day began publishing there *Izvestiia*, the Petrograd Soviet's newspaper. He later served as the executive secretary of the Lenin Council of People's Commissars (1918–20).

18 Skobelev's description of the reports on the seizure of the Main Artillery Administration and the rumors concerning General Manikovskii's fate suggests a very close cooperation between himself, Tereshchenko, Nekrasov, and Kerenskii during the first crucial hours and days of the February Revolution. See also the interview with Tereshchenko (Chapter 12).

19 Sergei Iliodorovich Shidlovskii (1861–1922) was a leading Octobrist deputy to the third and fourth Dumas from Voronezh province. After the split of his party in January 1914, he became the leader of the left Octobrists faction in the fourth Duma; from September 1915 to February 27, 1917, he served as chairman of the Bureau of the Progressive Bloc. On February 27, 1917, he became a member of the Duma Committee, but reportedly refused to join the Provisional Government. Beginning in March, he served as commissar to the Academy of the Arts.

20 Kresty (literary, "crosses") is a colloquial name of the Petrograd solitary confinement prison, reflecting the building's cross-like shape, through which generations of Russian and Soviet political prisoners have passed. Kresty is located on the Vyborg Side (on Arsenal'naia Embankment behind the Finland Railway Station and across the Neva River from the Tauride Palace). Built in the late 1880s, at the time of the February Revolution Kresty housed both criminal and political prisoners (ca. 2,400 inmates) all of whom had reportedly been released between 12:00 and 2:00 in the afternoon on February 27, 1917.

21 The timing of Bertgoldt's announcement is usually given as around 2:00 in the afternoon. See
    Fevral'skaia revoliutsiia 1917 goda. Sbornik dokumentov i materialov (Moscow: RGGU, 1996), 112.
    See also *Velikie dni rossiiskoi revoliutsii 1917 g. Fevral': 27 i 28-go. Mart: 1, 2, 3 i 4-go* (Petrograd:
    Biuro rossiiskoi pressy, 1917), 3. Grigorii Pavlovich Bertgoldt (1877–after 1917) was a colonel
    in the gendarmes, and served as deputy security chief (1907–17) and as acting commandant of
    the Tauride Palace (from November 1914).

22 Nikolai Osipovich Ianushkevich (1886–after March 1918) was a leading Labor Group deputy
    to the fourth Duma from Kovna province; during the February Revolution he served as a
    commissar of the Duma Committee, and in early March as the Provisional Government's
    commissar to the northern front. Aristarkh Petrovich Savvateev (1869–after 1917) was a Kadet
    deputy to the fourth Duma from the Don Cossacks' Region (in 1914 he joined the
    Independents faction); during the February Revolution he served as the Duma Committee
    commissar to the ministry of war.

23 The reference is to the representatives of the cadets and faculty of the Military Medical
    Academy and of the military units deployed on the Vyborg Side, who came to the Duma
    around 1:00 in the afternoon. See *Fevral'skaia Revoliutsiia 1917 g.*, 112; A. B. Nikolaev, *Revoliutsiia
    i vlast': IV Gosudarstvennaia duma, 27 fevralia–3 marta 1917 goda* (St. Petersburg: RGPU, 2005),
    168–9, 176.

24 This must have been between 2:00 and 2:30 in the afternoon. For Rodzianko's reasons to hold
    the private meeting in the semicircular hall, see Semion Lyandres, "On the Problem of
    'Indecisiveness' among the Duma Leaders during the February Revolution: The Imperial
    Decree of Prorogation and Decision to Convene the Private Meeting of February 27, 1917,"
    The Soviet and Post-Soviet Review 24, 1–2 (1997): 115–27.

25 The reference is to the telegrams sent on February 27 by generals Ruzskii and Brusilov in
    reply to Rodzianko's so-called first telegram to the tsar, his chief of staff, and the commanders
    of all fronts, which was sent from Petrograd at night on February 26 (see n. 13 to the Rodzianko
    interview, Chapter 6). Ruzskii and Brusilov were the only generals who replied to Rodzianko.
    They confirmed the receipt of his telegram and promised to fulfill their duty "before the Tsar
    and the Motherland," that is, to support Rodzianko's appeal to Nicholas II to grant major
    political concessions. See *Fevral'skaia Revoliutsiia 1917 g.*, 111; *Krasnyi arkhiv* 21, 2 (1927): 7; *Kak
    sovershilas' Velikaia russkaia revoliutsiia. Podrobnoe opisanie istoricheskikh sobytii za period vremeni s
    23 fevralia po 4 marta 1917 goda* (Petrograd: Narodopravnaia Rossiia, 1917), 8. Aleksei Alekseevich
    Brusilov (1853–1926) was general of the cavalry and commander in chief of the southwestern
    front (March 1916–May 1917).

26 A. Frankorusskii (real name B. N. Leont'ev) was a prominent Petrograd Socialist and activist in
    the workers' consumer cooperatives. Later that night (February 27) he was one of the organ-
    izers of the temporary food supply committee created to feed insurgent soldiers who strayed
    from their units and barracks.

27 This appeal (*vozzvanie*) to the population from the Temporary EC of the Petrograd Soviet
    appeared under Chkheidze's name in issue no. 1 of *Izvestiia Komiteta Petrogradskikh zhurnalistov*
    (*IKPZh*), February 27, 1917, p. 1. *IKPZh* was a publication of the relatively non-partisan
    Committee of Petrograd Journalists, which was established on the morning of February 27, on
    the basis of the Committee of Duma journalists, in order to print only news (*izvestiia*) and
    information pertaining to the revolutionary events. *IKPZh* was produced in the printing
    house used by the conservative Petrograd newspaper *Novoe vremia*, and should not be confused
    with the better known *Izvestiia* of the Petrograd Soviet, which began its publication a day later.
    Only ten issues of the *IKPZh* ever appeared—no. 1, February 27 to nos. 9–10, March 5, 1917.

28 Vasilii Nikolaevich Filippovskii (1882–1940) was the second lieutenant-engineer in the navy
    and a longtime member of the Socialist Revolutionary party. He served as commandant of the
    Tauride Palace from the evening of February 27 until the morning of February 28. After the

February Revolution, he played an active role in the Petrograd Soviet and was a member of the EC and the so-called Contact Commission. He was an ardent revolutionary defensist and an advocate of cooperation with the Provisional Government.

29 Mitrofan Iosifovich Grodzitskii (1861–after 1917) was a Progressist deputy to the third and fourth Dumas from Orenburg province; during the February Revolution he served as the Duma Committee commissar to the state controller's office. Ivan Ivanovich Efremov (1866–1945) was a leading Progressist deputy to the third and fourth Dumas from the Don Cossacks' Region, and chairman of the Progressists' faction in the fourth Duma (until October 1916 when he left the faction). He was also one of the founders and leaders of the Progressive Bloc. On February 27, 1917, he urged his colleagues to defy the prorogation decree and continue to hold regular Duma sessions. During the February Revolution, he served as commissar to the ministry of internal affairs and was frequently dispatched by the Duma Committee to greet the troops arriving in Petrograd from nearby garrisons.

30 The reference is to colonel Vsevolod Aleksandrovich Myshlaevskii (1889–1951), the son of the infantry general A. Z. Myshlaevskii (1856–1920). He began serving in the 3rd Life Guards Riflemen Regiment in 1908 but in May 1916, after suffering serious shell-shock, was sent to the Regiment's reserve battalion. By the time of the February Revolution, he was undergoing treatment for his injury in Petrograd under the auspices of the Aleksandrovskii Committee for the Wounded. During the night from February 28 to March 1, 1917 he was indeed contacted by the MC about the feasibility of shelling the Admiralty from the Peter and Paul Fortress. GARF, f. 3348, op. 1, d. 131, l. 2.

31 That is, the Economic Society of the Officers of the Guards Corps (*Ekonomicheskoe obshchestvo ofitserov Gvardeiskogo korpusa*), a corporate joint-stock company founded in St. Petersburg in 1891 to serve the consumer needs of the officers of the Guards units stationed in the capital. By the time of the February Revolution, the Society's large new building stood on Bol'shaia Koniushennaia Street (nos. 21–3), off Nevskii Avenue in the direction of Koniushennaia Square and the Moika.

32 The reference is probably to a small unit (about forty men) of the Life Guards Keksholm Infantry Regiment's reserve battalion, which during February 28 was assigned to guard the Senate building. See GARF, f. 3348, op. 1, d. 128, l. 40.

33 This may have been *pod'esaul* (cavalry lieutenant) of the Savage Division's Tatar Cavalry Regiment Andrei Aleksandrovich Bers, who was appointed by the MC on the afternoon of February 28 as the fortress's temporary commandant. On the morning of March 1, he was named deputy to the fortress's permanent commander, the artillery staff captain F. E. Kravtsov.

34 Skobelev probably refers to the first meeting of the Soviet of Workers' Deputies, which started at 9:00 at night on February 27 and elected the first permanent EC (as opposed to the Temporary EC formed that afternoon). In addition to the four secretaries (Gvozdev, Sokolov, K. S. Grinevich-Shekhter, and the Menshevik and cooperatives' activist G. G. Pankov), the members of the first EC were: Chkheidze, Skobelev, Kerenskii, Steklov, Sukhanov, N. Iu. Kapelinskii (non-factional SD), B. O. Bogdanov, P. A. Krasikov (non-factional SD), the SR V. A. Aleksandrovich (real name P. A. Dmitrievskii), and the Bolsheviks A. G. Shliapnikov and P. A. Zalutskii.

35 Guchkov and Shul'gin left Petrograd around three o'clock in the morning on March 2 and arrived at Pskov at nine o'clock in the evening. Although significant, the opposition of the EC to Rodzianko's trip was not the main reason for sending Guchkov and Shul'gin in his stead. It appears that Miliukov and his allies on the Duma Committee were concerned that a meeting between Rodzianko and Nicholas II would result not only in the tsar's abdication but also in the transferring of authority to a Duma-based government—a far cry from Miliukov's own vision of an all-powerful Provisional Government independent of the "reactionary" fourth Duma.

36 The available records of this important meeting do not start until the point when Sokolov replaced Skobelev as its chairman. See *Petrogradskii Sovet rabochikh i soldatskikh deputatov v 1917 g. Dokumenty i materialy. Vol. I: 27 fevralia–31 marta 1917 g.* (Leningrad: Nauka, 1991), I: 47–56, esp. 55.

37 See n. 35 to the Engel'gardt interview (Chapter 3).

38 See n. 13 to the Chkheidze interview (Chapter 9).

39 That is, V. N. L'vov, member of the Duma Committee and the future Procurator of the Holy Synod.

40 Ivan Vasil'evich Godnev (1854–1919) was a medical doctor, a zemstvo activist, and a moderate Octobrist deputy to the third and fourth Dumas from Kazan' province; on February 27, 1917 he was elected to the Duma Committee. From February 28 to March 2, he served as the Duma Committee commissar to the Senate and from March 2 to June 24 as state controller in the Provisional Government.

41 There is no record of this meeting of the EC. For the most complete protocol of the Soviet meeting on March 2, including Steklov's report on the negotiations with the Duma Committee and the EC decision against joining the cabinet, see *Petrogradskii Sovet*, I: 61–75.

42 See *Izvestiia* [of the Petrograd Soviet], March 3, 1917, p. 2. Kerenskii's speech was mentioned (but not reproduced) in the protocol of the Soviet session on March 2. *Petrogradskii Sovet*, I: 66. See also Hasegawa's rendition of this meeting in English, in his *The February Revolution*, 539–41.

43 Major General Alfred W. F. Knox (1870–1964) was a career military officer in the British Army and later a conservative politician. He served as the British Military Attaché in Russia from 1911 to 1918.

44 That is, in his famous announcement on the formation of the Provisional Government to the revolutionary crowds in the Catherine Hall of Tauride Palace on the afternoon of March 2. For the most complete and accurate text of Miliukov's speech, see *IKPZh*, nos. 6–7, March 2–3, 1917, 1. For an analysis of the speech and the crowds' reaction to it, see George Katkov, *Russia 1917: The February Revolution* (New York: Harper & Row 1967), 375–7, and Hasegawa, *The February Revolution*, 530–4.

45 This must have been March 3, as the abdication only took place on the night of March 2.

46 Skobelev's retelling of the circumstances of the March 3 meeting between Grand Duke Mikhail Aleksandrovich and the representatives of the Provisional Government and the Duma Committee, which is based on the information that had been provided to him by several of the participants, is not always dependable.

47 That is, with the abdication of Nicholas II on the night of March 2. However, the text of the manifesto and the news that Nicholas had unexpectedly abdicated in favor of his brother (not his son under the regency of Grand Duke Mikhail Aleksandrovich) reached the Tauride Palace only in the early hours of March 3.

48 Before announcing his decision, the grand duke consulted in private with Rodzianko and Prince L'vov (not with Shul'gin). For more reliable first-hand accounts of what happened during that fateful meeting, see the interviews with Kerenskii and Nekrasov (Chapters 11 and 8).

49 That is, Countess N. S. Brasova.

50 See note 24 to the Tugan-Baranovskii interview (Chapter 7).

51 This may have been Iakov Vasil'evich Krivtsov (1854–after 1917), a Rightist deputy to the third and fourth Dumas from Kursk province. By the time of the February Revolution, his two sons were serving at the front.

52 On March 1, Rodichev was appointed by the Duma Committee as Commissar for office of the state secretary for the Grand Principality of Finland (his appointment as minister came three days later, on March 4). The Duma Committee rarely, if ever, consulted their Socialist colleagues before appointing commissars.

53 Skobelev was sent by the EC in the late evening of March 3 to the Sveaborg Fortress—a major naval and army base of the Baltic Fleet, situated on a group of islands at the entrance to the harbor of Helsingfors (Helsinki)—after reports of disorder among the ship crews in Helsingfors and Sveaborg. He was accompanied by three other members of the EC, the Duma commissar Rodichev, a soldier of the Automobile division named Iu. A. Kudriavtsev, and two sailors. The delegation arrived at Helsingfors at 4:00 in the afternoon of March 4, and later that evening visited the Sveaborg Fortress. Upon their return, Kudriavtsev and Skobelev presented a detailed report to the Soldiers' section of the Soviet on March 6. See *Petrogradskii Sovet*, I: 159–61, 170.

54 Andrei Semenovich Maksimov (1866–1951) was a vice-admiral and the commander of the mine defense in the Baltic Sea (1915–17). On March 4, 1917, after the murder of vice-admiral A. I. Nepenin, he became the commander of the Baltic Fleet and remained in this post until June 2, 1917. According to some contemporary accounts, Maksimov appears to have been collaborating with the mutinous sailors, and had gotten himself "elected" commander of the fleet even before Nepenin's murder (see Fedor Mikhailovich Rodichev, *Vospominaniia i ocherki o russkom liberalizme*, ed. Kermit E. McKenzie [Oriental Research Partners, Newtonville, MA, 1983], 229).

55 Adrian (Andrian) Ivanovich Nepenin (1871–1917) was a vice-admiral and the last prerevolutionary commander of the Baltic Fleet (since August 1916). He spent most of his naval career in the Baltic Fleet and was the founder and first commander of the communications service, which included intelligence and counterintelligence operations. In the early afternoon of March 4, 1917, he was shot and killed in Sveaborg by mutinous sailors for his refusal to be relieved of his duties without an order from the Provisional Government. See D.A. Bazhanov, "Ubiistvo komanduiushchego Baltiiskim flotom vitse-admirala A. I. Nepenina 4 marta 1917 g.," *Revoliutsiia 1917 goda v Rossii. Novye podkhody i vzgliady. Sbornik nauchnykh statei* (St. Petersburg: RGPU, 2010), 30–9.

56 The reference is to the two battleships *Andrei Pervozvannyi* (Andrew the First Called) and *Imperator Pavel I* (Emperor Pavel I, renamed *Respublika* or Republic after April 16, 1917) that were in service in the Baltic Fleet during 1912–23 and 1911–24 respectively. Each battleship had a crew of 957 sailors and officers. The sailors of both ships, but especially those on *Pavel*, were considered the most radical in the fleet and included a disproportionally large number of Bolsheviks or Bolshevik sympathizers. On March 3, after killing several of their officers and locking up the rest, the sailors from *Pavel* led the mutiny of the other ships' crews stationed in Helsingfors harbor. The red signal lights were mounted on a mast and lit when a ship called for urgent help or attention; it was usually followed by a telegraph or radio transmission containing additional information on the nature of the alarm and requesting action. In this case, the lighting of the red lights on other ships signaled solidarity with the rebellious crews of *Andrei Pervozvannyi* and *Pavel*.

57 Permission for the former tsar to travel to Tsarskoe Selo to join his family and then to continue on to Romanov-on-Murman (renamed Murmansk in April 1917) was granted by the Provisional Government and transmitted in a telegram to General Alekseev in General Headquarters at midday on March 6, 1917. See *RPG*, I: 178. Romanov-on-Murman, sometimes referred to as Romanov or Murman, was the main railway center on the eastern shore of the Kol'skii Peninsula, with access to the largest seaport in the Barentsov Sea that did not freeze in winter.

58 See n. 49 to the Tugan-Baranovskii interview (Chapter 7). Skobelev's remembering the exact wording of the March 9 telegram to detain the former tsar might be explained by the fact that it was sent out in his and Chkheidze's names.

59 The British ambassador to Russia from 1910 to 1918 was Sir George Buchanan (1854–1924). The request to grant the imperial family asylum in England came from the newly appointed

foreign minister P. N. Miliukov on March 6, who informed Buchanan of Nicholas's request for safe passage to Murman and from there, presumably, to England. On March 8, the Foreign Office replied to Buchanan's request but instead of issuing an invitation to the former tsar, asked the ambassador to inquire about the possibility of the Romanovs receiving asylum in Denmark or Switzerland. Buchanan conveyed this to Miliukov, who insisted that Nicholas should go to England. The British government agreed, but in return asked the Provisional Government to bear the cost of transporting the former imperial family to England. On March 9 the matter was discussed by the EC. The Soviet leadership insisted that Nicholas not be allowed to go anywhere, let alone abroad, without the prior consent of the EC. Then, however, larger events interceded. Both governments succumbed to internal political pressures and in the middle of June, London informed Petrograd that the transfer of the former monarch and his family within the boundaries of the British Empire was no longer feasible. Nicholas and his family remained in Tsarskoe Selo under house arrest until August 14. They were then transferred to Tobol'sk, and eleven months later murdered by the Bolsheviks near Ekaterinburg. The question of blame for preventing the imperial family from leaving the country has been the subject of many judicial, historical, and literary investigations. For the most judicious and still valid treatment of this question, see S. P. Mel'gunov, *Sud'ba Nikolaia II posle otrecheniia. Istoriko-kriticheskie ocherki* (Paris: La Renaissance, 1951). See also *Rossiiskii arkhiv,* vol.VIII, *N. A. Sokolov. Predvaritel'noe sledstvie, 1919–1922 gg.,* ed. L. A. Lykov (Moscow: Trite, 1998). For the most up-to-date discussion in English, see Mark D. Steinberg and Vladimir M. Khrustalev, *The Fall of the Romanovs. Political Dreams and Personal Struggles in a Time of Revolution,* Russian documents, trans. Elizabeth Tucker (New Haven: Yale University Press, 1995), 117–21.

60 After signing the abdication manifesto, the former tsar left Pskov at 1:00 in the morning on March 3 and arrived in Mogilev nineteen hours later.

61 For the circumstances of Maslovskii's visit to Tsarskoe Selo, see n. 52 to the Tugan-Baranovskii interview (Chapter 7).

62 The "seven points" proposal referred to here cannot be located among the available records of the Petrograd Soviet, but a similar (in spirit and some of the details) resolution was voted on at the March 3 session of the EC. It called for arrests or tight surveillance of the grand dukes Mikhail and Nikolai Nikolaevich, and asked the MC to carry out "gradual" arrests of "the women of the House of Romanov . . . depending on the role each played in the activities of the old regime." Chkheidze and Skobelev were instructed to inform the Provisional Government of this decision. See Steinberg and Khrustalev, *The Fall of the Romanovs,* 10; *Petrogradskii Sovet,* I: 81–2.

63 The so-called Contact Commission, which met from March 8 to May 5, 1917, was created by the Soviet EC to maintain liaison with the Provisional Government and "to exercise uninterrupted control over the implementation of the demands by the revolutionary people . . ." According to Ziva Galili, the contact or liaison commission originated with Sukhanov's proposal (March 4) to reconsider the dual power policy of the Petrograd Soviet by establishing "institutional channels through which the soviet's pressure on, and *kontrol'* of, the Provisional Government might be implemented in a planned and consistent manner." (Ziva Galili, *The Menshevik Leaders in the Russian Revolution: Social Realities and Political Strategies* [Princeton: Princeton University Press, 1989], 144–5). Galili also notes that "of the commission's members, Sukhanov and Steklov were advocates of pressure, and Skobelev and Filippovskii of cooperation. The fifth member, Chkheidze, appeared to be in a state of depression and was not very active in the commission's work." (Ibid., 145n).

64 Viktor Mikhailovich Chernov (1873–1952) was one of the founders and the leading theoretician of the Socialist Revolutionary party. He returned to Petrograd from European emigration on April 8 and was co-opted into the EC the next day. He served as minister of agriculture in the coalition cabinets between May 5 and August 26, 1917.

65 Khrustalev was apparently elected to the so-called mandate commission, which was organized by the EC just before its first official session on February 28. Yet it remains uncertain whether he actually took part in the commission's work, for he and Gvozdev were removed from the members' list on the same day under the pressure from representatives of the workers' underground organizations (*Petrogradskii Sovet*, I: 28, 45 *n.* 5; n. 11 to the Gerasimov interview, Chapter 5). Khrustalev's last appearance in the general session of the Soviet took place on March 3. Warmly greeted by the audience and asked to speak, he proposed to broaden the current representation in the Soviet by holding elections among the general city population. In his view, elected representatives of these relatively moderate and numerous groups would have guaranteed the complete and final defeat of the old regime (*Petrogradskii Sovet*, I: 87–9, 97–8). There is little doubt that such a "heretical" proposal was meant to undermine the established minority rule based only on representatives of workers and soldiers. His proposal was not even brought to the floor for discussion. Khrustalev was subsequently denounced and ostracized. Any connections between his 1905 Soviet and its 1917 namesake were purposefully minimized. Skobelev's comments about Khrustalev should probably be viewed in this context.

66 This joint appeal from the Duma Committee and the Petrograd Soviet to "citizens, to feed the insurgent soldiers as best you [they] can" was published in the first issue of *IKPZh* on February 27, 1917 (*RPG*, I: 71).

67 The reference is to various food supply initiatives organized by the Petrograd Soviet on the evening of February 27 and closely coordinated with the Duma Committee. This resulted in the creation of the joint Food Supply Commission during the late evening–early night hours of February 27–8. The commission had 9 members: 6 from the Soviet and 3 from the Duma. Vladimir Gustavovich Groman (1874–1932), the veteran Menshevik economist and statistician, was chairman of the joint Soviet/Duma Food Supply Committee, while Shingarev was the leading member on the Duma side.

68 Skobelev returned to Petrograd late at night on March 5.

69 Skobelev's surprise at what he witnessed at the Sveaborg naval base can, in part, be explained by the fact that he and other Socialist leaders in Petrograd were accustomed to interacting with wounded, sick, or newly conscripted soldiers from reserve units, whose radicalization was often predicated on their reluctance to return to the front lines, especially considering the high casualty rate sustained during the first two and a half years of the war. In contrast, the naval crews of the Baltic Fleet suffered relatively minor losses but were subjected to much stricter discipline and harsher service conditions. According to Evan Mawdsley, the Baltic fleet sailors were also "demoralized by inactivity," and they "tended to come from a working-class background" and thus were generally better educated than their predominantly peasant coevals in the army. (Evan Mawdsley, "Soldiers and Sailors," in Edward Acton et al., eds., *Critical Companion to the Russian Revolution, 1914–1921* (Bloomington and Indianapolis: Indiana University Press, 1997), 585–6.) Thus, the Sveaborg sailors apparently had no trouble keeping their political views separate from their pro-war patriotic feelings.

70 The available records of the Petrograd Soviet from March 7, 1917 do not contain this discussion. Sukhanov's rendition of the discussion of the draft manifesto to "the peoples of the whole world," which was written by M. Gor'kii and then, on March 6, transformed into a political document by Sukhanov, is presented in his *Zapiski o revoliutsii* (vol. I, 1–2: 232–41, 265–8). Sukhanov also reproduced the final text of the manifesto on p. 268. He first discussed the document with Chkheidze late at night on March 6 and also probably at the meeting of the EC on the 7th before it became the main item of business during the Petrograd Soviet's general session on March 14. See *Petrogradskii Sovet*, I: 302–23. The final text (identical to the one reproduced by Sukhanov) was published in *Izvestiia* [of the Petrograd Soviet], March 15, 1917, 1; *Pravda*, March 15, 1917, 1; *Den'*, March 15, 1917, 3; *Rech'*, March 15, 1917, 5; and other Petrograd newspapers.

71 The reference is to Pavel Nikolaevich Miliukov, who served as foreign minister from March 2 to May 2, 1917.

72 After pressuring the Provisional Government to revise Russia's war aims in accordance with the new democratic order—especially in the wake of Miliukov's March 23 interview to the press in which he confirmed that Constantinople and the Straits should remain part of the war aims—the Soviet leadership authorized separate negotiations with the cabinet and asked Kerenskii to play a go-between role. The Soviet wanted the government to issue a new declaration that would emphasize the defense of the country as the main goal and to renegotiate a new agreement with the Allies concerning war gains. The status of these negotiations with the cabinet was discussed at the meeting of the EC on March 27, 1917. (*Petrogradskii Sovet*, I: 599–604).

73 Vasilii Anisimovich Anisimov (1879–1939) was a teacher and a Social Democratic deputy to the second Duma from Saratov province. He returned to Petrograd in mid-March 1917 after spending nearly ten years in prison and exile. During his time in Siberia he maintained correspondence with Lenin and other Bolsheviks. Soon after his return to Petrograd, he was co-opted to the Soviet EC. Aleksandr Konstantinovich Vinogradov (1869–1938) was a medical doctor and a Social Democratic deputy to the Second Duma from Akmolin Province. He too returned to Petrograd in mid-March 1917 but apparently withdrew from politics soon thereafter.

74 Georgii Valentinovich Plekhanov (1956–1918) was "the father of Russian Marxism." He returned to Russia on March 31, 1917 after thirty-seven years of exile and was greeted at the Finland Station by Chkheidze, Tsereteli, and Skobelev, among others.

75 V. I. Lenin (Ul'ianov) returned to Petrograd on April 3, 1917. The next day he revealed to his dumbfounded party loyalists a set of policies that contrasted sharply with the relatively moderate line pursued by Petrograd Bolshevik leaders in the Soviet since February 27. Lenin's directives, which came to be known as the April Theses (published in *Pravda* on April 7), consisted of ten well-formulated and forcefully expressed points. The two slogans mentioned by Skobelev were perhaps the most radical and better known part of the April Theses, reflecting the content of the first and fifth theses.

76 Iulii Osipovich Martov [real name Tsederbaum] (1873–1923) was the founder and principal ideologue of the Menshevik party. He lived in emigration from 1906. During the war years he was the main spokesmen for the internationalist wing of the party, and after the February Revolution he also became one of the leading critics of the Mensheviks' participation in a coalition government. Pavel Borisovich Aksel'rod (1850–1928) was one of the founders of Russian Social Democracy (with G. V. Plekhanov and V. I. Zasulich); he sided with the Mensheviks after the 1903 split and was one of the party's leading theoreticians. He lived in emigration between 1881 and 1917. Aleksandr Samoilovich Martynov [real name Pikker] (1865–1935) was a veteran Menshevik theoretician; he lived in emigration starting in 1900. Like Martov and Aksel'rod, Martynov was a leading voice in the internationalist wing of the party and strongly opposed the Menshevik participation in the Provisional Government. All three Menshevik leaders returned to Russia on May 9, 1917.

77 The (first) All-Russian Menshevik Conference met in Petrograd from May 7 to 12, 1917 to discuss, principally, two most pressing issues: the party's participation in the coalition and its standpoint vis-à-vis the war. Skobelev and Tsereteli spoke on the first day and defended their decision to join the coalition. On May 8, the conference voted in support of Tsereteli's stance. The next day was dominated by discussion on the question of war. Tsereteli, Skobelev, and others defended the "defensist" position and spoke forcefully against the internationalists (or decidedly anti-war wing) as represented by the just returned "émigrés" Martov, Martynov, and Aksel'rod. The conference again supported Tsereteli's "defensist" position. For an insightful discussion of the May Conference and its implications for the Menshevik party in 1917, see

Galili, *The Menshevik Leaders*, 189–203. The stenographic reports and resolutions of the Conference are included in *Men'sheviki v 1917 godu*. Vol. I: *Ot ianvaria do iiul'skikh dnei*, ed. A. P. Nenarokov et al. (Moscow: Progress-Akademiia, 1994), 270–463.

78 At the March 28 meeting of the EC with its Bureau, Tsereteli reported that the Provisional Government agreed to publish a revised declaration on the question of the war in accordance with the March 14 declaration of the Petrograd Soviet, which stipulated that in foreign affairs democratic Russia would pursue a policy consistent with its domestic policies based on law and freedom, not on violence toward people of other countries. The Soviet leadership also resolved to continue to apply pressure on the Provisional Government until it issued an appeal to the Allies spelling out Russia's new war aims. *Petrogradskii Sovet*, I: 615, 622–3. As the subsequent events would demonstrate, the Provisional Government did not succumb to pressure from the EC. Instead, in his April 18 "Note" to the Allies Miliukov reiterated Russia's old war aims, thereby provoking what came to be known as the April Crisis that led to the formation of the coalition government.

79 The (first) All-Russian Conference of Local Soviets took place in Petrograd from March 29 to April 3, 1917. It was called by the Petrograd Soviet and included 432 representatives of local soviets, 37 from the Petrograd Soviet, and 46 delegates representing army units from both the front and the rear. Chkheidze chaired the opening session. Skobelev, Tsereteli, B. O. Bogdanov, and A. R. Gots were among the members of the conference's presidium. Tsereteli urged the delegates to adopt, without a discussion, a resolution that would send an appeal to "world democracy" to defend Russia, as her defeat would bring the defeat of democracy in Russia. The majority voted in favor of the resolution, with 40 against and 30 abstaining. See *Petrogradskii Sovet*, I: 638. The Conference adopted several resolutions, the most important of which were on the question of war (it included the phrases cited by Skobelev) and on the attitude toward the Provisional Government (conditional support). The conference also elected an organizational bureau to prepare, in coordination with the Soviet EC, the convocation of the First All-Russian Congress of Soviets. See *Vserossiiskoe soveshchanie Sovetov rabochikh i soldatskikh deputatov. Stenograficheskii otchet* (Moscow and Leningrad: Gosizdat, 1929), 291–306.

80 This may have been M. D. Romm, a soldier-member of the soldiers' section of the Petrograd Soviet, who was nominated by the EC at its meeting on March 28 to represent the army on the presidium of the Conference of Local Soviets together with Skobelev, Steklov, and Tsereteli. See *Petrogradskii Sovet*, I: 613; *Politicheskie deiateli Rossii 1917 g.*, 372.

81 Anatolii Eduardovich Diubua (1881–1958) was a sworn attorney by training, a union organizer, and a prominent Social Democratic operative (Bolshevik until 1906). During the war he served as a non-commissioned officer in Petrograd; after the February Revolution he was elected to the Petrograd Soviet, supported Tsereteli's line of revolutionary defensism, and spent time as commissar to the 12th army (Northern front). He served as a deputy minister of labor in the first coalition cabinet (under Skobelev).

82 The reference is to the first Congress of the Western Front in Minsk, April 7–17, organized by the officers' soviet and the workers' and soldiers' soviet of Minsk. It was attended by more than 1,200 delegates and guests, including Tsereteli, Chkheidze, and Skobelev for the Petrograd Soviet EC and Rodzianko, Rodichev, and Maklakov for the Duma. The policies put forward by the Tsereteli-led defensist bloc received overwhelming support by the majority of delegates. More broadly, the congress also endorsed the front committees and the soviets as main defenders and guarantors of democratic freedoms and social justice (i.e. the transfer of all the land to those who work on it).

83 Or a maid-of-all-work.

84 Fedor Fedorovich Linde (1881–1917) was a non-party (reportedly an SR sympathizer) Petrograd revolutionary activist, some time mathematician, and an adventurist. By the time of

the February Revolution, he was serving as a noncommissioned soldier in the reserve battalion of the Life Guards Finland Regiment. He was a member of the Soviet EC from February
28 to early April 1917, and became one of the main organizers of the April 20–1 demonstrations against the Provisional Government. On May 13, he was appointed by the Petrograd
Soviet as deputy commissar to the Special Army on the southwestern front, and on August 25
was lynched by the soldiers of the army's 443rd regiment. He later became the prototype for
Commissar Gintse in Boris Pasternak's novel *Doctor Zhivago.*

85 Mechislav Mikhailovich Dobranitskii (1882–1937) was an attorney by training and a veteran
Social Democrat (Menshevik from 1903 to 1920). By the time of the February Revolution, he
was serving as a noncommissioned wartime clerk in Petrograd. From February 28 to May 10,
1917, he was a member of the Military Commission, and after March 1 served on it as a representative of the Petrograd Soviet. In the spring and summer months of 1917, he was also a
member of the Soviet EC.

86 Fedor Il'ich Dan [real name Gurvich] (1871–1947) was a medical doctor by training, Martov's
brother-in-law, a veteran Social Democrat, and a leading Menshevik figure in Petrograd before
his arrest at the start of the First World War and exile to Irkutsk. He returned to Petrograd in
March 1917 and joined the EC, where he became a key political force and organizer behind
Tsereteli's defensist faction. After the Bolshevik takeover, he joined Martov's internationalist
faction and led the left wing of the Menshevik party and its Foreign Delegation in
emigration.

87 The reference is to the proposed Stockholm Peace Conference that never took place. In April
1917, a Dutch-Scandinavian organizing committee led by Camille Huysmans, the Secretary of
the Second International, sent out invitations to all socialist parties and organizations. However,
by early May the idea was abandoned because of opposition from the British, French, Belgian,
and Russian governments and dissention among socialists. This conference should not be
confused with the Stockholm (third) Peace Conference of the anti-war Zimmerwald movement that was held in September 1917.

88 The reference is to the Zimmerwald Conference of European socialists, which was organized
by the Swiss Social Democrat Robert Grimm and held in Zimmerwald, Switzerland,
September 5–8, 1915. After considerable debate and an open split between the internationalist
(revolutionary) wing, led by Lenin, and the centrist-leaning majority led by Grimm, the conference issued a famous anti-war manifesto calling for the mobilization of the international
proletariat to fight against the imperialist war.

89 The EC first discussed the possibility of participating in the Stockholm Conference on Sunday,
April 23, after hearing a report on its goals and prospective participants from the prominent
Danish Social Democrat Frederick Borgbjerg, who was sent by the Dutch-Scandinavian
Committee to Russia to gain support for the proposed conference and the participation of the
Soviet. The question of participation was again brought up during the meetings of April 24–6.
At the general session of the Soviet on April 26, Skobelev proposed a resolution calling for the
convocation of the international peace conference (and by implication, for the Soviet's partici-
pation in it), which was supported by all those present except for the Bolsheviks, who chose
to abstain. See *Petrogradskii Sovet rabochikh i soldatskikh deputatov v 1917 g. Protokoly, stenogrammy
sektsii, zasedanii Ispolnitel'nogo komiteta i fraktsii.* Vol. II: *1 aprelia—5 maia 1917 g.* (St. Petersburg:
Biblioteka Zvezdy, 1995), II: 351–401; *RPG*, II: 1169–72.

90 Genrikh (Gersh-Volf) Moiseevich Erlikh (1882–1942) was a leading Bundist who also worked
closely with the Mensheviks (from 1907); from 1914 to 1917, he lived in Petrograd and contributed to various Bundist and Menshevik publications. He joined the Petrograd Soviet EC
on February 28, supported the defensist bloc and Socialist participation in a coalition (from
May on), and continued to occupy leadership positions in the Soviet and the All-Russian
Central EC until October 1917.

91 The reference is probably to the southern Finnish railway station Riihimäki, located on a direct line to Petrograd, 43 miles (69 km) north of Helsingfors.

92 That is, the famous Petrograd Restaurant of the First St. Petersburg Society of Waiters (later renamed Metropol), located on the corner of Sadovaia Street and Krylov Lane, just a block off Nevskii Avenue.

93 Chatskii was the central character in A. S. Griboedov's comedy *Woe from Wit*. The phrase "from a ship to the dance" is a variation on A. S. Pushkin's phrase from his novel in verse *Evgenii Onegin*. The connotation here is of a sudden change of circumstances.

94 This must have been around the middle of March 1917, before Pletnev was banned from the Tauride Palace in the second half of the month at the insistence of the Soviet's leaders. On Pletnev's activities, see n. 19 to the Tugan-Baranovskii interview.

95 The reference is probably to the telegram sent by general Alekseev to Prince L'vov on the morning of March 4, summarizing reports that he had received from two army commanders on the northern front about an invasion by "a large group of delegates of a workers' party" who were opening up prisons, disarming guards, police, officers and other military personnel, and burning garrisons' headquarters and police stations. The general asked the newly appointed premier to undertake all measures possible to prevent sending any such delegations to the front. Alekseev also informed his front commanders that "should any such gangs (*shaiki*) show up, they should be seized and court marshaled on the spot." ("Fevral'skaia revoliutsiia 1917 goda . . .," *Krasnyi arkhiv* 3, 22 (1927): 49). The text of the telegram must have been leaked to the Soviet leaders and the press. On March 8, the telegram was published in *Izvestiia*, and on March 10 it also became the topic of an informal discussion among the EC leaders. However, according to Sukhanov, his and his colleagues' reaction to the "retrograde general" seemed to have been more of a condescending amusement than anger, and did not result in calls for Alekseev's head. See Sukhanov, *Zapiski o revoliutsii*, I, 1–2: 238–9.

96 Radko Dmitrievich Radko-Dmitriev [Radko Rusko Dmitriev] (1859–1918) was a Bulgarian general and *chargé d'affaires* in St. Petersburg. With the outbreak of the First World War, he became a Russian citizen and enlisted in the imperial army with the rank of lieutenant general. From March 1916 to July 1917 he was the commander of the 12th army in the northern front. On March 5, 1917, Radko-Dmitriev informed his front commander, general Ruzskii, about a number of recent cases where lower ranks refused to salute their officers, citing Order Number One, which abolished this age-old military practice. The general ordered the perpetrators punished and at the same time appealed to Ruzskii "to convey to those who write such orders" that their actions only deepen the rift between the officers and the rank-and-file. *Revoliutsionnoe dvizhenie v russkoi armii, 27 fevralia–24 oktiabria 1917 goda*. Sb. dokumentov, ed. L. S. Gaponenko (Moscow: Nauka, 1968), 25–6. Radko-Dmitriev's order was also published in *Izvestiia* on March 10, 1917, and was repeatedly referred to by the Petrograd Soviet leaders together with Alekseev's "counterrevolutionary" telegram of March 4. See, for example, Steklov's remarks to the delegates of the first All-Russian Conference of Soviets of Workers' and Soldiers' Deputies on 30 March. *Vserossiiskoe soveshchanie sovetov rabochikh i soldatskikh deputatov. Stenograficheskii otchet* (Moscow and Leningrad: Gosizdat, 1927), 116, 330.

I I

Aleksandr Fedorovich
Kerenskii

Among the personages interviewed by the Polievktov Commission, Aleksandr Fedorovich Kerenskii (1881–1970) stands out as the best known yet most controversial figure. No other leading personality of the February Revolution was admired by so many when he came to power in March 1917 yet became so universally loathed by the time his government was toppled by the Bolsheviks in October. None of his revolutionary colleagues has been more scorned and ridiculed; none has been blamed more squarely for the failure of Russia's first experiment at democracy.

Yet Kerenskii would not only outlive *all* of his opponents and former allies[a]—from the Bolsheviks to the Kadets—but would spend the next half a century relentlessly defending his eight-month record in the Provisional Government. Indeed, it was a task for which he spared no effort, answering each and every accusation, serious or trivial, for he must have believed that these charges, if left unanswered, would perpetuate. The result of this unrelenting pursuit, assembled as if it were a carefully prepared defense, was an unmatched memoir testimony of a thousand pages, written between 1918 and 1964. Kerenskii further supported his memoirs with three hefty volumes of an additional 1,800 pages of documents on the Provisional Government that he compiled in the late 1950s with assistance of an American scholar. To this day, it remains the single largest collection of documents on "Kerenskii in power."[b]

---

[a] The only contemporary politician, though not really an opponent or a vocal critic of Kerenskii's, who outlived Kerenskii—by six years—was the moderate nationalist Duma deputy and the Duma Committee member V. V. Shul'gin, who from 1956 on lived under virtual house arrest in the Soviet provincial city of Vladimir, outside of Moscow.

[b] See A. F. Kerenskii, *Delo Kornilova* (Moscow: Zadruga, 1918); *Izdaleka: sbornik statei, 1920–1921* (Paris: Russkoe izdatel'stvo Ia. Povolotskogo, 1922); "Fevral' i Oktiabr'," *Sovremennye zapiski* 9

These writings served as an important source for several scholarly biographies and a plethora of biographical sketches and political portraits.[c] Historians of 1917 have studied or at the very least commented upon every major decision Kerenskii made while in office. For better or for worse, his place in history is firmly secured as the leading personality in the short-lived Provisional Government, under whose watch Russia was taken over by the Bolsheviks. At the same time, his role during the February Days has received considerably less attention, both from Kerenskii himself and from subsequent historians.[d] This is especially striking in view of his unparalleled contribution to the overthrow of the old regime and his long since acknowledged role as "the central figure of the 'February Days'."[e]

(Paris, 1922): 269–93; "Gatchina," *Sovremennye zapiski* 10 (1922): 147–80; *Catastrophe: Kerensky's Own Story of the Russian Revolution* (New York: D. Appleton, 1927); "Iz vospominanii," *Sovremennye zapiski* 37 (1928): 295–309; 38–9 (1929): 230–73; *The Crucifixion of Liberty* (New York: John Day, 1934); "Soiuzniki i Vremennoe pravitel'stvo," *Sovremennye zapiski* 55 (1934): 271–89; "O revoliutsii," *Novyi zhurnal* 15 (1947); "Dva Oktiabria," *Novyi zhurnal* 17 (1947); "Kak eto sluchilos'," *Novyi zhurnal* 24 (1950); "Moia zhizn' v podpol'e," *Novyi zhurnal* 84 (1966); *The Kerensky Memoirs: Russia and History's Turning Point* (New York: Duell, Sloan & Pearce, 1965; London: Cassell, 1966); *The Russian Provisional Government, 1917: Documents*, 3 vols. Selected and ed. Robert Paul Browder and Alexander F. Kerensky (Stanford: Stanford University Press, 1961).

[c] Richard Abraham, *Alexander Kerensky, the First Love of the Revolution* (New York: Columbia University Press, 1987); M. I. Basmanov, V. A. Dines, G. A. Gerasimenko, V. G. Gusev, *Aleksandr Fedorovich Kerenskii* (Saratov: Izdatel'skii tsentr SGEA, 1996); V. L. Strongin, *Aleksandr Kerenskii. Demokrat vo glave Rossii* (Moscow and Vladimir: AST: Zebra EVKT, 2010). See also D. Sverchkov, *Kerenskii* (Leningrad: Priboi, 1927); V. I. Startsev, *Krakh Kerenshchiny* (Leningrad: Nauka, 1982); Startsev, "Vzlet i padenie Aleksandra Kerenskogo," *Vstrechi s istoriei* (Moscow: Molodaia gvardiia, 1987); M. J. Fontemont, "Symbolism in Persuasion: The Influence of the Merezhkovskii Circle on the Rhetoric of Aleksandr Fedorovich Kerenskii," *Canadian-American Slavic Studies* 26, 1–3 (1992): 241–65; V. P. Blokhin, S. P. Kolpakova, "A. F. Kerenskii. Paradoksy politiki: demokrat i diktator," *Istoriia otechestva v portretakh politicheskikh i gosudarstvennykh deiatelei* (Briansk: Grani, 1993); M. M. Gorinov, "Kerenskii, Aleksandr Fedorovich," *Politicheskie deiateli Rossii 1917 g. Biograficheskii slovar'* (Moscow: BRE, 1993), 143–9; G. L. Sobolev, *Aleksandr Kerenskii: liubov' i nenavist' revoliutsii. Dnevniki, stat'i, ocherki i vospominaniia sovremennikov* (Cheboksary: izdatel'stvo Chuvashskogo universiteta, 1993).

[d] A most welcome reversal of this trend, which avoids the dismissive clichés of previous generations, is beginning to take hold in more recent Russian historiography. See, for example, B. I. Kolonitskii, "Kerensky," in Edward Acton et al., eds., *Critical Companion to the Russian Revolution, 1914–1921* (Bloomington and Indianapolis: Indiana University Press, 1997), 138–49; Kolonitskii, "A. F. Kerenskii i krug Merezhkovskikh. 1917 god.," *Petrogradskaia intelligentsia v 1917 godu*, ed. O. N. Znamenskii (Moscow and Leningrad: Institut istorii SSSR AN SSSR, 1990); A. B. Nikolaev, "A. F. Kerenskii o Fevral'skoi revoliutsii," *Klio: zhurnal dlia uchenykh* 3, 26 (2004): 100–11.

[e] Richard Abraham, "Kerenskii, Aleksandr Fedorovich (1881–1970)," 330, in Harold Shukman, ed., *The Blackwell Encyclopedia of the Russian Revolution* (Oxford: Blackwell, 1994). See also his *Alexander Kerensky. The First Love of the Revolution*.

Nowhere is this contribution more apparent than in his May 31, 1917 interview with the Polievktov Commission. Recorded shortly after the events it describes, with his popularity nearly at its height and a record of accomplishments that any revolutionary could proudly call his own, the interview represents Kerenskii's earliest, most expansive, and most reliable testimony on the February Revolution. Here he has yet to defend his policies as a cabinet minister or answer his soon to be swelling ranks of critics. He was assured by the interviewers that his testimony would be locked away in an archive and remain inaccessible for decades. He thus spoke "for history" (as he himself emphasized at the end of the interview), displayed no obvious agenda, and apparently had no grudges to grind or scores to settle. Considering his balanced narrative, his measured tone, and the few remarks made in passing, he did not attribute every success to himself or blame every failure on others. He gave credit where it was due, and commended (or criticized) his friends and foes alike. In sharp contrast to his later memoir accounts, he comes across as a forgiving and generous politician of the kind that earned him a well-known contemporary reputation as "the true and beloved leader of the February Revolution."[f]

To be sure, Kerenskii was a radical, fully committed to a revolutionary (not evolutionary or constitutional) change. For him, the February Revolution, that is the overthrow of the old regime, was not an end but only the beginning of a long transition to a socially just and democratic order. Yet he was no doctrinarian. The Kerenskii of the February Days demonstrated a rare ability among politicians of his day and background to adjust to the fast changing revolutionary whirlwind and to lead or, if the circumstance afforded no better alternative, to be led by the revolutionary crowds. He also comes across as a revolutionary leader of enormous ability, boundless energy, and inspiration, someone with acute political instincts who could act swiftly and decisively. Under the extreme circumstances of the moment, these qualities served him well. Small wonder, then, that his rise to power was so meteoric or that he commanded such authority among the insurgents and secured a considerable following among broad segments of the population. In short, his interview should go a long way toward explaining his early successes, thereby modifying the traditional, though not entirely unjustified, image of his later days as a weak leader and a meandering and hysterical politician.

Kerenskii was born to a noble family in the city of Simbirsk on the Volga, where his father was director of a male gymnasium (among the Kerenskii *père*'s earlier students were Aleksandr Ul'ianov and his younger brother Vladimir, who would later become the Bolshevik leader V. I. Lenin). When Kerenskii was eight years old, the family moved to Tashkent following his father's appointment as chief school district superintendent of the Turkestan region. In 1899, Kerenskii graduated with a gold medal from the Tashkent classical gymnasium, and in the fall of the same year

---

[f] As cited in Kolonitskii, "Kerensky," in *Critical Companion,* 148.

matriculated at St. Petersburg University. During his first year he studied in the historico-philological faculty, but soon his interests changed and he transferred to the faculty of law. Among his most influential teachers at the time were the liberal jurist (and future Kadet) L. I. Petrazhitskii, who had just developed his psychological theory of law, and the young neo-Kantian philosopher intuitionist N. O. Losskii. Following graduation, Kerenskii joined the St. Petersburg bar in 1904; a year later, he formalized his political affiliation by becoming a member of the Socialist Revolutionary party. For the next seven years—notwithstanding brief imprisonment and administrative exile—he successfully combined political activism (editing the SR newspaper *Stormy Petrel*) with the practice of law, specializing in political cases.

In the fall of 1912, in the wake of his much-publicized role in the public investigation of the tragic shooting of workers at the Lena goldfields, he was elected deputy to the last Imperial Duma from Saratov province. There he quickly emerged as a leader of the small but vocal Labor Group (faction), which was but a more politically palatable name for the SRs. In 1913 he served as the group's deputy chairman, and from 1914 to 1917 as its chairman and representative on the Duma Council of Elders. His fiery, if not very substantive or eloquent, speeches on mostly political issues (he rarely spoke on routine legislative business) were widely circulated and soon gained him a reputation as one of the most outspoken "legal" critics of the government. By 1915 his radical speeches in the Duma, combined with his growing fame as a highly successful lawyer specializing in political trials, made him a "household name" in a variety of radical and moderate opposition circles in the country. His friendship with the members of the Merezhkovskii–Gippius circle and close involvement with other popular left-leaning cultural figures of the day further assured him a following among the educated public and bohemian elites in the two capitals.

But perhaps just as significant for his quick rise to prominence was his relative nonpartisanship and an ideological flexibility which led him to recognize the need to coordinate activities among divergent radical and opposition groups committed to the destruction of the old regime. It was this realization that in 1912 brought him into the ranks of the recently revived political Masonry. In the clandestine meetings of the Duma-based lodges, sometimes camouflaged with traditional Masonic rituals, Kerenskii's organizational skills were rightly matched with his often-cited penchant for mysticism and theatrics. As in the Duma and the legal-political arena, here too Kerenskii quickly climbed up the ladder of the Masonic hierarchy, and by the summer of 1916 he succeeded his political friend N. V. Nekrasov as the secretary-general of the Supreme Council of the Grand Orient of the Peoples of Russia.

The significance of these loose political associations in organizing the anti-government forces, before and especially during the February Days, should not be overestimated. Yet the lodges did provide an important and otherwise unavailable medium for a motley collection of like-minded individuals to meet and discuss political matters without fear of being watched by the ubiquitous Russian political police, who were apparently unable to penetrate the multilayered conspiratorial structure of the Masonic network. It was in these lodges where Kerenskii grew closer to his Duma colleagues and future revolutionary comrades-in-arms: the Social Democrats Chkheidze and Skobelev, the Progressists Konovalov and Rzhevskii, and the Left Kadets Nekrasov and Volkov, among others.

When discussing Kerenskii's role during the February Days, historians usually focus on his leadership position in both institutions of revolutionary authority, the Duma Committee and the Petrograd Soviet. His later inclusion in the Provisional Government is also explained by this dual membership that guaranteed a "vital link" between the liberal cabinet and the Socialist leadership of the Petrograd Soviet.[g] While his interview clarifies some of the aspects of this unique position "in between the two camps," it also underscores two additional aspects of his role in defeating the old regime. First, he was the organizer and first commander of the revolutionary headquarters at Tauride Palace, known as the Duma Military Commission, which brought under its command the insurgent soldiers, sympathetic officers, and left-leaning politicians and activists. On Kerenskii's orders, the commission seized key government buildings, carried out the first arrests of tsarist officials, and successfully neutralized or fought loyal government forces. Kerenskii's other pivotal contribution was to end the monarchical form of government in Russia. Supported by Nekrasov, Konovalov, and Tereshchenko, it was Kerenskii who on March 3 played the single most important role in convincing Grand Duke Mikhail to renounce the throne, thereby ending the three-hundred-year reign of the Romanov dynasty and effectively eliminating any realistic prospects for its restoration.

However, Kerenskii's subsequent performance as a statesman—minister of justice from March 2–May 5; minister of war and navy from May 5–September 1; Minister-President starting on July 8; head of the Directorate September 1–25; Supreme Commander-in-Chief of the armed forces starting on September 1—was far less successful. His tenure in power was marred by a succession of blunders and political crises that led to the Provisional Government's eventual demise in October.

Kerenskii fled Russia in June 1918. He spent the rest of his long and colorful life first in Paris and Berlin, and after 1940 in the United States and London, writing, lecturing, and teaching university students about how "his Russia" was betrayed by the obstinate Right and destroyed by the radical Left. During all his years in exile he remained a staunch anti-Bolshevik. He apparently never forgave Lenin for forcing him out of power and into a perpetual exile. Still, in the late 1960s he briefly entertained a thought of visiting his homeland, and even inquired with Soviet dip-

[g] See, for example, Tsuyoshi Hasegawa, "The February Revolution," in *Critical Companion*, 59; Hasegawa, *The February Revolution, Petrograd, 1917* (Seattle and London: University of Washington Press, 1981), 528.

lomatic representatives abroad about the possibility of repatriating. But nothing came of it.[h] During the last decade of his life he practically lost his sight and had to rely on others to read and write for him. Yet he never lost his feistiness or the will to defend his political record, and devoted his remaining energies to dictating a final version of his memoirs, which came out in the mid-1960s under the characteristically grandiose title, *The Kerensky Memoirs: Russia and History's Turning Point*. He died in New York at the age of 89, but was buried in London where his two sons, Gleb and Oleg, resided.

The text of the Kerenskii interview is reproduced on the basis of a master version compiled by Rusudana Nikoladze-Polievktova, with minor stylistic corrections also in her hand; and a draft transcript written in shorthand by Tamara Nikoladze (a great admirer of Kerenskii's at the time), who also conducted the interview.

★ ★ ★ ★ ★ ★

War and Navy Minister A. F. Kerenskii. May 31, 1917

I did not keep a day-by-day chronology. For me, it was one long day. My adjutants[1] kept a very detailed diary starting on February 28. Each evening, the two of them recalled and summarized events.

On the eve of the events, there was a meeting in my apartment. It must be said that these meetings had begun taking place sometime before the events, and among the permanent participants were myself, N. D. Sokolov, Skobelev, and I don't remember who else.[2] We wanted to reach an agreement between parties; we engaged in the organization of various agreements and the formation of unifying blocks of SRs, SDs, and P[opular] S[ocialist]s. We thought that the events were inevitable, the dispersal of forces was undesirable, and that it was necessary to form a core group. However, this was not going well because the majority did not think that the events were imminent. The organizational bureau consisted of representatives from two [Duma] factions (Skobelev and Chkheidze, and myself); Bolsheviks, Mensheviks, the Interdistrict Group,[3] SRs and PSs. We met fairly regularly. By the way, in anticipation of disturbances on February 14 we organized an observation post in the City Duma and set up a meeting of representatives from various public groups to maintain contact with the population. But

---

[h] "'Vozmozhnosti ne predstavilos' (O popytke A. F. Kerenskogo vernut'sia v Rossiiu)," *Rodina* 5 (1992): 56–7.

nothing came of this, and skepticism increased. Many started taunting us. The organizational bureau subsequently held meetings.

Bread riots erupted. On the eve of the events, I hosted the last meeting with the representatives of the parties (Peshekhonov,[4] Gor'kii, and others). Tellingly, those who are now the most uncompromising hotheaded revolutionaries were then very pessimistic in their analysis of the troops' moods (this was exactly at the time when the news of the Pavlovskii soldiers came in);[5] they were very skeptical about the possibility of a soldiers' uprising and pointed to the declining mood. They thought it necessary to concentrate their attention on propaganda, on literature. Representatives of the Inter-regional Group, exactly those who would soon adopt the most radical attitudes, were very poorly oriented in what was happening. Those of us who remembered 1905 came away from this meeting quite discouraged by their narrow parochialism and their inability to analyze the situation or to understand events. This took place in my flat on the evening of the 26th.

I want to say that a majority of those who later claimed that they had prepared the revolution and created it acted haphazardly during the days preceding the events of February 27. In order to understand the events, it is quite telling, very enlightening, and helpful to recognize the extent to which everything was consciously prepared by those elements that were later destined to play a role. I am not saying that there were no other elements. Organization proceeded, but not in those circles. We shared no common language with them. They were totally green and had no continuity with revolutionary traditions, mostly because of ceaseless persecution. In other words, they were very primitive, elementary, and politically illiterate. I heatedly disputed their prognosis together with Nikolai Dmitrievich Sokolov and someone else whom I can't recall. We argued instead that the events were unavoidable because of all the developments, the warning signs among the troops…but our opinion is well known.

The disturbances continued for three to four days in a row. At the State Duma, everything changed suddenly—deputies on the Right fell silent and disappeared, the [Progressive] Bloc lost all status and clout, and attitudes toward our wing changed radically. We were taken seriously, and some of our directives started to be heard and followed. All came to the realization that the events were unavoidable and wanted to survive them with minimal damage to the war effort. There were a great many conferences and consultations; Duma deputies planned trips and meetings for the purpose of persuasion [uveshchaniia]. Members of the [Progressive] Bloc (blokisty) were meeting in perpetual session. Five days earlier, we had been approached by sizeable groups of Bloc members (Shul'gin and others) in the lobbies, who asked what might be "enough." We responded with: immediate promulgation of a [new] course, amnesty, and liberties.[6]

On the 27th, I was awakened at 8:00 in the morning and told that the Duma had received the decree of prorogation; I was also informed of the uprising of the Volynskii Regiment and two murdered officers. Nekrasov told me about the prorogation. We had been, and stayed, in continuous contact with him. It was decided to go to the Duma at once. I got dressed and ran, and didn't return home for the next five days. On my way, there were a lot of people; Volynskii solders stood nearby. In the Duma there were relatively few people, and they were anxious. We took measures to summon more people. Rodzianko showed up quickly. That morning, the deputies who were there met in Rodzianko's office. I was constantly running in and out of this meeting—I had to be in twelve to fifteen places at the same time. The leadership of events fell de facto to us, that is: to me, Chkheidze, Skobelev, Nekrasov, Rzhevskii[7]—partly to the left-wing [of the Duma], and partly to the left-faction of the [Progressive] Bloc.

Shul'gin, the Temporary Committee, and the Progressive Bloc discussed everything together. As more and more news came in—that the Volynskii soldiers were joined by soldiers from the Preobrazhenskii, the Engineers, the Lithuanians, and so on—their spirits and mood darkened.

Troops were coming to the Duma, creating a mood of anticipation which was exhausting and torturous for some and invigorating for others. Different rumors were coming in, suggesting that troops had not gone to the Duma but rather to the ministry of the interior to catch Protopopov. Personally, I thought it necessary for them to come to the Duma as soon as possible to shake the Duma out of its indecision. I called a friend, asking him to send troops to the Duma quickly (he lives not far from the Volynskii barracks).[8] When I arrived at the Duma, I myself had been asked to go to the Volynskii soldiers. At the time, I thought it was impossible for me to leave the Duma before it was internally organized and prepared. In the Duma, there were continuous meetings in Rodzianko's office. Under the influence of events, the direction was quickly becoming more and more radical. Our group insisted on the creation of the Temporary Committee, which would take administration and organization into its hands; we had not yet thought in terms of a cabinet. Everyone was waiting for the moment when troops would arrive at the Duma. The most interesting thing was that the people had searched for a focal point and intuitively turned the Duma into such a center.

Troops were wandering the streets during the first [few] hours of the day, but they did not go to the Duma. Later, all-too-familiar faces—all our radicals [*vsia nasha radikal'shchina*]—started to show up. Without passes, of course: Charnolusskii...Shnitnikov (people from the street). Then a sharp exchange took place between Charnolusskii and Rodzianko which made a big impression.[9] Charnolusskii declared...but about that, Charnolusskii can tell you better himself.[10]

A rumor spread that troops were moving toward the Duma. At that time, a meeting started in the semicircular hall.[11] I was very busy. I was torn in multiple directions. Two officers were brought in who had been arrested at the water tower.[12] From then on—and I cannot understand how it happened—people began to turn to me for everything. I signed permission for the Committee of Duma Journalists to publish *Izvestiia*.[13] It was counter-signed by Chkheidze. The arrested officers were also brought to me, and I had to assume responsibility. Troops came. They stood, indecisively, for some time; I was also indecisive. Finally, I ran out and greeted them. In 4–5 minutes, Chkheidze ran up. I declared that they should follow me and act as if they were the first revolutionary guard of the Duma. Then, a comical scene occurred. I did not know how to avoid it, so I had to set them on post myself. Even though the old guard did not leave, the guardroom was taken without a fight. The old guard ended up on our side.

When troops appeared in the Duma,[14] doubts disappeared. In the upper echelons of the Duma, and at the Council of Elders, it became clear that decisive action was unavoidable: either to cut ties with the movement and look for support against it; or to merge with it. In fairness, historically speaking, we should give credit where credit is due: it should be said that among the leaders of the Duma nobody even made an attempt to resist. All felt that this was the only way out of the situation.

In the preceding days, there had been a long series of negotiations involving Duma circles, military leadership, and public organizations, which together intended a different type of outcome—a palace coup. There were negotiations with representatives of the fronts, and some agreed. But those who were supposed to act (some of us participated) in the end did not have the nerve. By their indecision, they precipitated the movement. A coup had been planned expressly to avoid such an outcome, and a palace coup had to be carried out in the interests of the war. All realized that the war effort could not be risked; the war had to be brought to a successful conclusion.

That approach did not yield satisfactory results, but they accepted the outcome that was least desirable for them. Change was in the air; people were prepared for the new order of things. They knew that it was unavoidable and acquiesced. Before the events began there were many consultations about a possible type of supreme authority—regency or a new tsar, guardianship or regency with a [ruling] council. Reliable military elements were considered, and the mood of various segments of society was studied. Work undoubtedly went on.

Certain groups of people set before themselves the task of merging bourgeois-revolutionary and democratic-revolutionary elements into a unified strike force. Leading elements (if it is even possible to speak of leading) strove to join all that were creative and active into one fist. This approach was later borrowed by the Provisional Government; the same impetus was also acknowledged when the Provisional Government was reorganized—to preserve at all costs the unity of the country.

With the lack of preparedness shown by the real revolutionary and local democratic elements, it was difficult to count on them; they could not start anything. That is why the organization of the Soviet of Workers' Deputies began *post factum*.

It should be admitted that the events began outside of organized democracy. The historical authority of the Duma arose before the emergence of the Soviet of Workers' Deputies. At the end of the day [27th] there was a significant moment—the creation of what would later become the Military Commission—but that is a long story. The military uprising happened without any participation by the officers. During February 27–8, we had at our disposal only a few ensigns and colonels (they now have appropriate positions), who stayed with us throughout.[15] The officers did not arrive before the situation clarified, but they showed up *en masse* on the third and fourth day.

A peculiar kind of organization had already coalesced on the first day (it was put in room 42 of the State Duma) from the few officers who happened to be there—those who sympathized with us in a real sense and came to us on their own. This was the future Military Commission. I was there as well. I had to set this whole enterprise up: to dispatch the guard, to decide on the movement of forces against the enemy, to send automobiles with machine-guns, and so on. There was a lot to do. Officers participated in my work. Later, the work was continued by Colonel Engel'gardt.

This Commission was under the Executive Committee[16] of the State Duma. Its work began and continued independently of the Soviet of Soldiers' and Workers' Deputies. I say this for the sake of history, for the correct understanding of the events. Toward the evening of the 27th—at 3:00–4:00 [in the afternoon], rather—after the release of the politicals, when the war industrial group appeared (Gvoz'dev and others), I was asked to assign the [Duma] Budget Committee's room[17] to the Soviet of Workers' Deputies, which started organizing there. I was almost never there. Late at night on the first day, I was told that the presidium had been elected: Chkheidze, Skobelev, and myself. My work during those days went a little bit outside of what would later become the Soviet of Soldiers' and Workers' Deputies. I had to act on both sides. Chkheidze and I were elected from the Temporary Committee, which we in fact represented [in the Soviet]. Chkheidze often presided. I was more in the center, rather in the very center. In the meetings that I chaired, in the name of democracy, I applied all pressure toward the Right. We mainly worked at night from twelve until six in the morning, when the stream of people to the Duma slowed to a trickle. There was one additional moment when the liquidation of the old authority started—the arrest of Shcheglovitov.

The Executive Committee of the State Duma was created around three in the afternoon.[18] Rodzianko agreed to assume power only in the evening. During the day of the 27th, the new authority de facto began to give orders without yet being organized, mainly acting at its own risk and without having a clear awareness of the correlation of forces.

Historically speaking, one has to acknowledge that many conservative and liberal Duma elements were risking much more at that time than those who joined us later. There was a sense of uncertainty among the main leaders.

It's worth mentioning the shameful panic that occurred on the second day, the 28th. In the afternoon, a rooftop machine-gun accidentally opened fire toward the main entrance of the Duma.[19] A great panic occurred. Mirrored glass windows were broken in the Catherine Hall when people jumped into the street. Despite the fact that machine-guns were all over the small courtyard, people rushed through it to escape. I had to stick my head out through a small opening windowpane and shout: "Comrades, this is embarrassing!" The complete uncertainty of the situation explains this behavior. A great many rumors were coming in. The telegraph was idle.

By assuming responsibility, we—just as Rodzianko, Shul'gin, and others —showed revolutionary risk. Unfortunately, this was soon forgotten. Many people from Right and Left sat out and waited for the events to end so that they would not be asked, "Where were you during the first days?" Among them, many did not believe in a revolution, or that democracy should intervene in the revolution. I've come across many who are now in the most radical ranks, but whom I was not able to involve in revolutionary work over the course of the preceding two years. Radicalism of demands in the subsequent period of the revolution is in inverse proportion to the intensity of the revolutionary activity during the first moments. I can prove this with a few names.

I did not spend much time in the Soviet of Workers' and Soldiers' Deputies because we were carrying out a struggle with the supreme authority. On our orders, the engineer Bublikov took over the ministry of transportation and the direct wire.[20] That seizure played an enormous role. We sent telegrams everywhere, saying that the old authority had been removed. The telegraph gave me a free hand to organize the cordoning off and detention of the sovereign. None of his moves or actions remained unknown.

Then tragicomic nights began; actually there wasn't much that was comical, just the tragic. The nights were filled with tension; we played cat and mouse. We intercepted several panicked telegrams and used them to conduct searches and arrests. Throughout, we followed and undertook measures. Nicholas's train sped to Tsarskoe Selo. We blocked his path. He attempted a detour and then gave up. All the time, we conducted negotiations via Rodzianko with the pertinent elements at the court—Voeikov[21] and Fredericks.[22] Some of the demands made in the name of the Duma were conveyed by Rodzianko in the well-known telegrams to the front commanders.[23] Our position, given that we did not know the mood there, was significantly strengthened by the answers from some of them. This was on February 28.[24] On the 2nd [March], Guchkov and Shul'gin departed. Our plans did not include the project with Mikhail Aleksandrovich. The combination with Mikhail was a surprise: it was not acceptable, but it freed our hands.

On the evening of the 27th I was asked whom to arrest (the initiative came from the mob, several from the military as well as civilians). I named several addresses: Shcheglovitov, because he was closer than anyone else at

Tavricheskaia [Street] number 7, Protopopov, and others…Shcheglovitov was brought in.[25] At that time, the mood was not yet certain, much remained unknown, and Shcheglovitov's arrest made a stunning impression on the Duma's Council of Elders. Demands to release him began; Rodzianko wanted to invite him to his office as a guest. I did not allow that, and said that he belonged to me. At that time, many thought that the house of peoples' representatives should not be turned into a jailhouse. I pointed to the ministerial pavilion. The government pavilion was not considered our territory. Shcheglovitov was put there. He was alone. I turned to him with a proposition. I argued that everything was irrevocably lost, and that if he had any love left for his motherland and if he wanted to redeem his past, then he would call on the phone—where to call he knew better than I did—and ask them to surrender. He refused. Overall, Shcheglovitov conducted himself with real dignity. He did not panic and he was not a coward.

After that, the Duma became an encampment. Ministers, government officials, and innocents were brought in *en masse*. People poured in. My current adjutants were in charge of military transports, and were passing them on to Znamenskii.[26] At that time, the Peter and Paul Fortress was captured on our orders. Detailed telegrams were dispatched about the uprising.

The defense of Sukhomlinov. I was compelled to defend Sukhomlinov. I did not really want to defend this bastard myself, but in order to prevent the development of a disgusting scene, I had to literally put myself in front of him and stop the mob.[27] If someone wanted to, it would have been possible to arrange for a shocking scene of lynching. In general, I have to say that at that time the soldiery and workers really contained themselves—there were no insults or swearing. There were exceptions: Nikolai Maklakov was brought in with a head wound which was bleeding, but that happened at his home.[28] Beatings took place when arrests occurred in homes. The rules which we imposed at the [ministerial] pavilion were very humane; we were thanked. Another department, which was upstairs, was for plebes, precinct policemen, gendarmes, and people from the street.[29] On the side of the pavilion there was another department, the Expedition of the State Duma. There, people who had been torn to pieces were brought from the street—agents of the political police accused of espionage, etc. The work was intense. Everything had to be decided, mediated, assigned. The Duma investigative commission was established.[30]

There was an interesting episode connected with Goremykin's appearance.[31] Goremykin showed up and sat in Rodzianko's office wearing a house coat and a big chain of the Order of St. Andrew the First Called.[32] Peasant Duma deputies, priests, and deputies from the Right looked at it with awe: would I dare to arrest St. Andrew? When I called the guard in to take Goremykin away, the scene was stunning—authority had finally been confirmed.

On the other side, intense work was under way—organizing and delineating the direction of the Soviet of Workers' Deputies. Negotiations about a government began on the basis of well-known conditions. Chkheidze, myself, Steklov, Skobelev, and Sukhanov were set up as designated contacts. Negotiations about the composition of the cabinet were ongoing. I did not participate in them. The Soviet representatives took the position that the distribution of ministerial portfolios was not their affair. They would not join the Provisional Government. The organization of authority was entirely in the hands of the Duma Committee. It was already organized, whereas the Soviet was only searching for its policies. They later offered us two seats: one to me as minister of justice; the other to Chkheidze as minister of labor. We only had the right to reject candidates.

The organization of authority was entirely within the power of the propertied [*tsenzovye*] elements. At that time, the Executive Committee of the Soviet of Workers' Deputies could not pretend to organize any new authority. The propertied elements still felt strong, and offered us two seats; they did not want to make further concessions. I stand by my opinion that, at that time, the Executive Committee [of the Soviet] made a profound blunder— they unanimously resolved not to join the cabinet. The organization of authority could have happened earlier. The cabinet in its present form could have been easier to arrange. The Executive Committee was in the hands of absolutely rudimentary, primitive, naïve, and entirely uncompromising elements who just happened to be there. Now, they have faded away and been forgotten. Once or twice I had to go there and help. Right away (on the afternoon of the 28th) an absolutely intolerable literature appeared, which I confiscated.[33] During the first two months of the revolution the organization of democracy was still a work in progress.

Only Rodzianko was categorically rejected, no one accepted him into the cabinet. The propertied group opposed including him in the cabinet; his wisdom as a statesman did not inspire sufficient confidence. It must be said that, from the moment he acquiesced, his behavior was impeccable. He was crossing the Rubicon. He understood the full risk of his position. He was saying that he was old—that he was in his twilight. His vacillations were entirely human. He conducted himself impeccably after the decision (for as long as he and the Provisional Government were together). During the famous scandal with Guchkov and Miliukov at Mikhail Aleksandrovich's, when they were trying to convince him not to follow the people who were influenced by the street (pointing to us), Rodzianko played a different and noble role. When the revolution was purely political and radical, without the character that it later assumed, his behavior was impeccable. The reason why Rodzianko was excluded from the cabinet was not any consideration that he had to stay at the head of the Duma, that the Duma was needed as a reserve. Rather, this was a motive for him. At that time, the theory emerged that we [the Provisional Government] were only an emanation of the Duma. The Duma, Rodzianko, and the Executive Committee of the State Duma are the father and mother of the new authority, and we are only their progeny. Later, and for a long time, he could not reconcile himself with the idea that after Mikhail Aleksandrovich's abdication, we were the only sovereign authority in the country.[34] During the reorganization of the Provisional Government, there was a tendency on their part to endorse the new government.

If I had turned down the ministry of justice, it would have been given to one of the Kadets. Maklakov was minister of justice for one hour. The cabinet was already formed and they were just waiting for my acquiescence, but I couldn't do so because the Soviet Executive Committee had decided unanimously that none of its representatives could enter the Provisional Government. My nomination to the post of minister of justice was discussed in the Executive Committee [of the Soviet] on March 1. Mikhail Aleksandrovich abdicated on March 3. Miliukov delivered his speech on regency at about four in the afternoon [on March 2], after the cabinet had already been formed and I had agreed to join it...At one point, I thought that I would not be in the cabinet. Some on the Executive Committee tried to persuade me to join the cabinet and leave the Executive Committee of the Soviet of Soldiers' and Workers' Deputies. I could not accept this, of course. In the morning, after sleeping for two hours, I woke up (on the 2nd [March] there was supposed to be a meeting of the Provisional Government). Actually, I was lying in a state of semi-consciousness. It was then that I categorically made up my mind to join. One of my motives was that I could not abandon the detainees under the circumstances. Someone else (the other candidate was leaning toward the Right) could have adopted a very soft approach, which might have provoked the movement into unwanted excesses.

This was more of an instinctive reaction than a conscious one. Because I was so involved with the events and the organization of [new] authority, I could not have made this decision rationally; I acted intuitively. It would have been difficult to expect judicious action in those days, which we will probably never live through again. So I decided to accept and then go and explain my position. I knew the position of the Executive Committee [of the Soviet], but it didn't seem to me that it reflected the opinion of the St. Petersburg working masses. I was not impressed by those politically near-illiterate people who had dominated the Executive Committee during the preceding days of revolutionary work. For his part, Nikolai Semenovich Chkheidze did not think it was possible for me to accept. My situation was somewhat different. I resolved to accept, communicate my decision by telegraph, and then go directly to the members of the Soviet to explain my decision. I argued that if I did not join the government, the responsibility would rest with the democratic masses. While I was on my way there, my friends on the Executive Committee warned me and began to mourn me, saying that I would have to endure very difficult things. Everything turned out to be the opposite.

The night of the 3rd [March] was the most interesting. The question of the monarchy was being decided. In the Soviet of Workers' Deputies, it was felt that no one wanted to accept regency and that it would be difficult to establish. We were preparing something different and did not know how the Temporary Committee would react to a regency. However, they felt that it would be difficult to introduce a regency—that the moment for that had passed. If the sovereign had abdicated earlier, and if he had given his answer right away on the 28th,[35] there might have been hope for them to preserve the situation to some degree. The delay played into our hands. The events ripened into the final and most correct outcome.

Guchkov and Shul'gin left to obtain an abdication in favor of the heir. They had appropriate instructions [from the Temporary Committee]. The introduction of Mikhail Aleksandrovich [as an alternative] was unexpected. We received a telegram about the regency, and not about a new sovereign. This caught us unprepared. Guchkov and Shul'gin did not provide an explanation. We were only going for the minimum. The thesis was the abdication of the tsar—at that time, we did not know the mood in Russia and in Pskov. We did not present the possibility of Alexei with a regent to the democratic public in Petrograd. This might have sparked a new movement. During the negotiations [between the Soviet and the Provisional Government], this point was overlooked. None of the nine points of the agreement mentioned regency.[36] And I don't remember this either, since I didn't attach any significance to it at that time. I thought that, despite all the solemnity surrounding the question of regency, it had little significance. In revolutionary periods, these arguments about words are extraordinary…In subsequent conflicts during the changeover in cabinets, I didn't pay much attention to the arguments about the texts of this or that declaration. I was right. Later, when the Provisional Government was attacked, the text of those points was so forgotten that the implementation of the declaration was viewed as counterrevolution.

At the time, the question of war aims was not touched upon. Miliukov was accepted *in toto*; Guchkov, that great organizer of counterrevolution, was accepted as well. There was also no talk about revisiting treaties—something that was used later to reprimand those who represented democracy. Everything was clear and understood at the time. We understood that the main task was the struggle against the old regime, and that presented no controversy. The logic of events was not yet sufficiently developed. All were united; no one predicted the events that would follow. The agreement was concluded without *"postol'ku, poskol'ku."*[37] That came later. The speech about the Provisional Government that Nakhamkes–Steklov, born as Nakhamkes, gave at the All-Russian Conference[38] consisted of one set of misrepresentations and insinuations after another, from A to Z! I really cannot understand what forced this man to depart so far from the truth.

There were no arguments about the form of government. The thesis put forward was that the form of government should not be predetermined before the Constituent Assembly. We did not want to recognize any authority except the one we were talking to. I remember on the second day I went to the Executive Committee of the Soviet to answer the accusations against the Duma Committee regarding the tsar's abdication. The train episode triggered the accusations. They assumed that the train had been sent for the sovereign. Steklov's idea was to send a detachment to arrest the sovereign.[39] But only we, the future Provisional Government, had access to the direct wire. It was very difficult for others to accomplish anything.

The pre-dawn discussions on March 3 were decisive. The majority of those opposing Miliukov wanted Mikhail Aleksandrovich to refuse. I thought that they had one and a half votes (Miliukov and Shingarev, who always supported him decidedly). Later, when Guchkov arrived, they had two and a half. The mood of the rest was unanimous. But Miliukov was unbending. He did not even want to come with us. "I will come along if you give me an opportunity to present the opinion of the minority." We pointed out to him that this was not a minority opinion, but rather his personal opinion. He replied that Guchkov's and Shul'gin's positions were still unknown, and then he said, "There are people here with me who share my views, like Andrei Ivanovich [Shingarev]..."

That night, I had to speak with Mikhail Aleksandrovich on the phone. His adjutant said that he was asleep. In view of the urgency of the matter, I asked that he be woken up. I conveyed the news to him that the abdication had occurred, and that we would like to see him. From the other end of the line, we heard a voice that was not that of a pretender to the throne. It appears that he truly did not know anything; he had been asleep. He had been awakened. Actually, I don't know, perhaps he knew something. I didn't tell him that he was the sovereign, but said that now the matter "concerns you." At that time, he was staying at Millionnaia 12, at the private apartment of his close friends the Putiatins.[40]

We wanted to finish everything by the time the next crowd burst into the Duma, so that we could announce that the decision had already been made. We did not hear a damn thing from Guchkov and Shul'gin. We worried, fearing that Mikhail would be proclaimed sovereign, that the troops would take the oath, and that a scandal would break out. At 6:00 or 7:00 in the morning, we set out without any guards—without anything. And we were also received without any guard—or any fear. Only I was accompanied by my adjutants, who at that time were already inseparable from me.

The discussion started. Rodzianko gave a speech about the state of things. "We think that, given the circumstances of the moment, the role which has fallen to him is beyond his strength. For the well-being of the family, and in the interests of the homeland, he should refuse." Rodzianko spoke in his usual style. [Prince] L'vov spoke after him—very well. They were both on a high plane. Mikhail Aleksandrovich asked if we wanted to say anything. The atmosphere was extremely tense. As soon as Rodzianko had received the abdication, he sent telegrams to the front commanders urging them not to announce the sovereign's abdication and not to say anything about Mikhail until further clarification (and this was a brave move on Rodzianko's part). This was one of the indirect causes for Nepinin's death. It became known that the telegram had been received but withheld. Rodzianko was not trusted within the navy—they were afraid of counterrevolution. They did not understand why there was a delay even though we were demanding the abdication. This was typical of mass psychology.

We already had a unanimous decision when we arrived.

After that, Miliukov's presentation took place, for which history is unlikely to forgive him. He urged and tried to persuade Mikhail for over half an hour. His speech was a lecture on constitutional law. It was torture for everyone. He began to speak before Guchkov's arrival and spoke excessively lengthily in order to delay the meeting until Guchkov arrived. When Guchkov got there, he took Miliukov's side. Our position took Shul'gin by surprise, but he had the tact to submit to the majority and did not take part in the discussions. Miliukov's argumentation was quite *ad hominem*; he played on feelings and on instincts for power. This man was saying that one must not follow the people influenced by the street, that one has to listen to sober people who think in terms of the interests of the state. The consequences could be frightening, but the road must be traveled.

This was apparently the way that the tsar's old ministers always talked about the senseless dreams of a tiny group of intelligentsia who claimed to represent the will of the people. It was assumed that we were dealing with the mindset of someone who wanted power and was only looking for a pretext to hold onto it. Mikhail Aleksandrovich was worried and on edge— the long speech was intolerable to him. Guchkov spoke much more tactfully. He did not play on instincts for power but insisted passionately that the throne not be rejected, reasoning that Russia should not be thrown into an unknown future. He quite accurately portrayed several phenomena that we had lived through. He did not have faith in democracy and the ability of the people themselves...

After that, we spoke quite a bit. There was no unanimity among the representatives of the nation. The scene which unfolded in front of Mikhail Aleksandrovich turned out to be quite undesirable for the prestige of the people's power. I had to intervene. I spoke as I speak, rather forcefully, appealing to Mikhail Aleksandrovich's conscience. He asked for the opportunity to take consultation and to consider by himself. He wished to speak with two of us. We got scared. We thought that meant Guchkov and Miliukov, but he named others—it turned out that he meant L'vov and Rodzianko. Then, it became absolutely clear that the battle with the *Kabardinians* had been won completely.[41] I think Rodzianko said that we were bound by mutual responsibility and could only talk to him in the presence of all. I said that if this was Mikhail Aleksandrovich's wish, we could not refuse such a request. There should not be any hint of distrust toward one another. The three of them left, and then he was left on his own. He came out and said that he agreed, and that he considered it his duty to refuse for the well-being of the country. After that, we went away for a while. L'vov stayed, along with Shul'gin and someone else. I think it was Nabokov who came to compile the manifesto of abdication. During the second meeting, someone else came.[42] I am certain that there were some people, but I cannot remember who they were. During that day Mikhail behaved like a gentleman, especially after the speeches by our two heroes. He felt certain responsibilities.

When there was talk about a coup before the revolution, Mikhail Aleksandrovich was considered a candidate among possible regents. After the tsar's manifesto, Mikhail Aleksandrovich had made up his mind, and it was difficult for him to listen to Miliukov. Miliukov pursued his own personal line, defending it as an utter doctrinaire and speaking about the necessity of a monarch, but not necessarily Mikhail. Guchkov spoke firmly that if Mikhail refused, he would leave the cabinet. Miliukov declared that he would do the same, but did not carry out his threat. Guchkov agreed to stay after he was persuaded that this was the majority's decision, and because we could not let him go. Our objection was that we did not want to introduce one more unknown when there were already so many unknowns in the cabinet. We took his ties with the Octobrists and his stature among the generals into account. Later, when a complete reevaluation of all considerations took place, it became clear that this special popularity of Guchkov among the officers was a myth. Nowadays, he has completely disappeared from the scene. Perhaps he will again have a role to play if our friends on the Left create an opening for a counterrevolution. Back then, he said that he would only remain for three days until his successor was found. Later, things calmed down. He did not bring it up, and we did not raise the matter either. He left not after three days, but two months.

Miliukov put it bluntly. He declared that if Mikhail Aleksandrovich refused, he, Miliukov, would leave—and that this would have enormous significance for Russia and history. Guchkov did not talk about himself in his speech, but during the break he told us the same thing. Mikhail, while asking questions, kept repeating, "I see ... if that is the case ... right." He was apparently very worried. It was difficult for him to retain his composure. Later, it became clear he had already made the decision to abdicate before the meeting. It was hard for him to listen to Miliukov's long speech, which contained lengthy historical segments—a popular lecture on constitutional law. None of us could imagine the possibility of giving such a speech on that morning. If we had told the Duma about it right away, not even his cat-like moustache [*koshach'i usy*] would have been left to him. I was rebuked for covering it up, but I considered it impossible to do otherwise; two months were needed for Europe to learn that Russia's foreign policy did not rest entirely on P. N. Miliukov—that Russia would survive without him.

Foreign policy questions were avoided in the beginning, because it would not have been easy to free ourselves from Miliukov too early. The Soviet of Workers' and Soldiers' Deputies' only uncompromising position was on breaking with the dynasty. We were told, "Why are you even considering regents when we have recognized you as the authority?" Miliukov and Steklov maintained friendly relations with each other. The question of foreign policy was only raised later, artificially, during the epoch of so-called dual power. I don't think there was ever such a thing as an epoch of dual power. The Soviet didn't have the ammunition to attack the Provisional Government. Steklov himself was never able to point out where, exactly, the terms of the agreement had been violated. This was already a struggle against individuals. In the sphere of domestic policy, everything went exceptionally well. The program was made public and was moving forward. Everything that has been done was outlined and begun during the first two months. It was a colossal job to dismantle the old institutions and create new ones. History will appreciate it all. We are now building upon the foundation that was laid during the first two months. Foreign policy questions were also raised at that time. The state of international affairs did not change. We concentrated on domestic organization, speedy democratization, and the destruction of the old regime. During that month and a half, the Provisional Government had the patience to listen to that same Steklov,[43] and gave him an opportunity to express himself. This was an intolerable situation, but we endured it. He would come and throw his feet on the table, but Chkheidze, given his tolerant nature, put up with him. Later, the Siberians and émigrés came back (Tsereteli and others)—the sober minds of the revolution.

April 21st and 22nd were the psychological turning point. It was natural that the process of anarchy and disintegration continued. This was unavoidable, but it had to be endured. For our part, we only wanted to stop excesses; inside the cabinet, the majority supported this point of view. In no way would we react like the old regime. Instead, we would trust the organizing force of the people and our democracy. An authority that rules otherwise disconnects itself from the people. We were not powerless—our strength is in the appeal to the people's consciousness. If we were to rule mechanically, as was suggested by some, the catastrophe would have been significant. I, Shingarev, Miliukov, Nekrasov, and Trubetskoi went to General Headquarters for the first time.[44] On the way there, we talked among ourselves.

I, Tereshchenko, and others raised the question of a new course in foreign policy. This was also raised in the Provisional Government (the question of a new declaration), but it was delayed because we were traveling and the wave from the Soviet of Workers' Deputies caught us up. The blame was put on Pavel Nikolaevich [Miliukov]. He did not understand the situation. Inside the Provisional Government, we led an intense struggle against him.

Historical events should only be narrated from a distance. I do not want to pass judgment on the front. Order Number One was the greatest crime, which under certain conditions could have exploded the entire army. It contributes to the disorganization of the army and is equal to the current Bolshevik propaganda: it allows people's behavior to be dictated by their base instincts. It is clear to me from touring the front that one can paint a telling picture that the success of Bolshevik propaganda is inversely proportional to the unit's intelligence. This most often applies to all the backward, cowardly, illiterate soldiers who have spent two years in the trenches—those who cannot be organized and can be shaken up only by knocking them on the head [*obukhom po golove*]. Their internationalism is defined by: "I don't care; anyway, the Germans won't reach Tambov Province."

Order Number One might have been understandable for the Petrograd Garrison, and even justified to some extent. But at the front, things were different. Here in Petrograd, the officers were absent. It might have been psychologically possible to suspect them, to introduce elections, etc. But at the front, the revolution was greeted unanimously. This was an enormously uplifting time. Order Number One was the creation of a profoundly civilian mind, and it was an absurdity. They did not understand what the army is all about. It was the height of irresponsibility and thoughtlessness—to any individual with the state's interests at heart, it was a crime. This is terrible. All the work of the army soviets, committees, and other functioning organizations which we rely on for the introduction of sensible discipline are struggling with the consequences of this disorganization. I will keep the name of the author of Order Number One secret—even from history.[45]

NOTES

1 Kerenskii probably refers to his then self-appointed adjutants, the colonels of the general staff G. N. Tumanov and G. A. Iakubovich. His brother-in-law, Lieutenant Colonel (colonel after July 1917) Vladimir L'vovich Baranovskii (1882–1931), would become his "inseparable" adjutant after the February Revolution.

2 The meeting at the Kerenskiis' took place on February 26. See the Skobelev interview (Chapter 10).

3 Or the so-called *Mezhraionka* (formally the Interdistrict Committee of the Russian Social Democratic Workers' Party), a small group of radical intellectuals standing between the Bolsheviks and left Mensheviks. The *Mezhraionka* was formed in St. Petersburg in November 1913 in an effort to reconcile various Bolshevik and Menshevik groupings. By the fall of 1917, most of the Interdistrict Group joined the Bolshevik party.

4 Aleksei Vasil'evich Peshekhonov (1862–1933) was a founding member of the moderate Popular Socialist party and a well-known publicist. During the February Revolution, he was one of the organizers of the Petrograd Soviet and served as the Soviet/Duma Committee commissar in charge of the important Petrograd District; he later became a member of the Soviet EC and from May 5 to August 31, 1917 served as minister of food supply in the Provisional Government.

5 This refers to the mutiny of the 4th Company of the Pavlovskii Regiment's reserve battalion on February 26. See the interview with P. V. Gerasimov (Chapter 5). By "the most uncompromising hotheaded revolutionaries" Kerenskii probably refers, among others, to the representatives of various underground workers' organizations, the SR Maximalist Aleksandrovich, and the leading *Mezhraionets* (and future Bolshevik) I. Iurenev (K. K. Krotovskii). According to another participant in that meeting, Iurenev "poisoned us all with his skepticism and disbelief. 'There is no revolution, nor will there be,' he reiterated stubbornly." V. Zenzinov, "Fevral'skie dni," *Novyi zhurnal* 34 (1953): 209 as quoted in George Katkov, *Russia 1917: The February Revolution* (New York: Harper & Row, 1967), 255. See also Hasegawa, *The February Revolution*, 325.

6 Kerenskii's account finds corroboration in the minutes of the Kadet faction meeting on February 25, 1917: N. K. Volkov reported that Kerenskii replied to Shul'gin that a government of bureaucrats was no longer acceptable, censorship should be relaxed, and the right to form workers' committees should be promulgated. According to the minutes, Kerenskii also emphasized the enormous significance of the Duma, which could become a magnet for striking workers. See GARF, f. 579, op. 1, d. 147.

7 Vladimir Alekseevich Rzhevskii (1865–after 1917) was a Moscow astronomer, engineer, zemstvo activist, and the leader (from August 1915) of the Progressists' faction in the fourth Duma. From June 1913 to February 27, 1917, he also served as senior deputy to the Duma Secretary. He was a member of both the Council of Elders and the leadership of the Progressive Bloc. During his tenure as a Duma deputy, he also joined the Duma lodge of the Grand Orient of the Peoples of Russia, led at the time by Kerenskii, Nekrasov, and Chkheidze. On February 27, 1917, he joined

the Duma Committee and also took part in the work of the MC. At the end of March, he was sent to Moscow as the Provisional Government's commissar.

8 Kerenskii's "friend" may have been N. I. Iordanskii, who lived on nearby Furazhnyi Lane (no. 4). See the Skobelev interview. The barracks of the Volynskii Regiment's reserve battalion, including the 2nd company (which started the soldiers' uprising on the morning of February 27), were located along the intersection of Vilenskii Lane (no. 15) and Paradnaia Street (nos. 3, 5, 7), around the corner from the Preobrazhenskii barracks and Furazhnyi Lane, and only a short walk from the Tauride Palace.

9 See the interviews with Nekrasov and Gerasimov (Chapters 8 and 5).

10 Charnoluskii waited for ten years to recount this often-cited episode. V. Charnoluskii, "Desiat' let nazad. Vospominaniia o pervykh momentakh Fevral'skoi revoliutsii," *Izvestiia TsIK*, March 12, 1927, 6.

11 That is, the private meeting of the Duma deputies.

12 This may have been the main Petrograd water pump and tower, located just across from the Tauride Palace on Shpalernaia Street no. 56. It was taken over in the early afternoon of February 27 by a detachment of insurgents under the command of Charnoluskii, who apparently acted on Kerenskii's orders. See A. B. Nikolaev, *Revoliutsiia i vlast': IV Gosudarstvennaia duma, 27 fevralia–3 marta 1917 goda* (St. Petersburg: RGPU, 2005), 191–2.

13 The reference is to the *Izvestiia* of the Committee of the Petrograd Journalists, see n. 27 to the Skobelev interview.

14 This occurred between 1:00 and 2:00 in the afternoon.

15 See n. 27 to the interview with Chikolini (Chapter 4).

16 That is, the Temporary Committee of the State Duma.

17 That is, Room 13 of the Tauride Palace. The members of the CWIC's Labor group who were released, including Gvozdev, came to the Duma shortly after 2:00 in the afternoon on February 27.

18 Kerenskii left the private meeting around 3:00 in the afternoon. Thus, in his mind, the decision to form the Duma Committee must have been made by that time. However, it took approximately two more hours to finalize the process and make the announcement.

19 This incident took place around 3:00 in the afternoon on February 28.

20 Bublikov served as the Duma Committee's commissar to the ministry of transportation from February 28 to March 2, 1917. In his memoirs, he claimed that during the day on February 27 he repeatedly asked Kerenskii, Nekrasov, and Chkheidze to authorize the seizure of the ministry of transportation, which had its own telegraph station, but that he finally received permission from Rodzianko in the early morning hours of February 28. A. A. Bublikov, *Russkaia Revoliutsiia (ee nachalo, arest Tsaria, perspektivy). Vpechatleniia i mysli ochevidtsa i uchastnika* (New York, 1918), 20–1.

21 Vladimir Nikolaevich Voeikov (1868–1942) was a major general of his majesty's imperial suite and the palace commandant (from December 1913); he was also Count Frederiks's son-in-law (see n. 22). He witnessed the act of abdication on March 2, 1917; five days later, he was arrested by the Provisional Government and confined to the Peter and Paul Fortress until September. In his first interrogation by the Provisional Government on the day of his arrest, Voeikov mentioned a telegraphic exchange with Rodzianko about his plans to meet the tsar at Dno on March 1 or 2. When the Duma President informed the tsar that he had to cancel his trip, Nicholas II, who was already in Pskov, wanted to reply with a telegram granting a responsible ministry. However, neither Voeikov nor Frederiks were in a position to communicate this to Rodzianko because General Ruzskii had insisted that all correspondence with the Duma leaders be handled through him. See GARF, f. 1467, op. 1, d. 1038, l. 2–20b.

22 Count Vladimir Borisovich Frederiks (Fredericks) (1838–1927), baron (until 1913), was general adjutant, general of the cavalry, member of the State Council, minister of the imperial court and domain (1897–1917), and one of Nicholas's most trusted courtiers. As minister of the imperial court, he countersigned the abdication manifesto and other of the last acts of Nicholas as emperor. Frederiks was arrested on March 9, but soon released. Rodzianko and Frederiks had known each other for a long time, and remained on friendly terms. Their ties go back to the period of 1877–82, when Rodzianko served as a young officer in the Cavalry Guards' Regiment under the command of then Major General Frederiks.

23 The reference is to the telegram sent by Rodzianko to General Alekseev (in General Headquarters) and the front commanders at 21:53 on February 26, urging them to support his appeal to the tsar to appoint a new premier who would form a government that could be trusted by the population as a whole. "Fevral'skaia revoliutsiia...," *KA* 21, 2 (1927): 5–6; *Kak sovershilas' Velikaia russkaia revoliutsiia. Podrobnoe opisanie istoricheskikh sobytii za period vremeni s 23 fevralia po 4 marta 1917 goda* (Petrograd: Narodopravnaia Rossiia, 1917), 8.

24 Rodzianko received replies to his telegram of February 26 (see the previous note) from Generals Ruzskii and Brusilov on February 27, not on the 28th.

25 This is Kerenskii's first and only known admission that the arrests of some of the "most dangerous" high-ranking tsarist officials on February 27 were carried out on his orders, which is also corroborated by at least one other contemporary account (M. Merzon, "A. F. Kerenskii v Moskve (pis'mo iz Moskvy)," *Nizhegorodskii listok*, June 1, 1917, as cited in Nikolaev, "Kerenskii o Fevral'skoi revoliutsii," 110). Shcheglovitov was arrested at his residence and brought to the Tauride Palace at 5:30 in the evening on February 27.

26 This may have been Sergei Filimonovich Znamenskii (1878–after May 1929), who during the night of February 27–8 acted as commander of the Tauride Palace's revolutionary guards. He came to the Duma on the evening of the 27th; on the morning of the 28th he reportedly put himself in charge of the Ministerial Pavilion, and for the next several days served in the Duma Military Commission. In mid-March he was co-opted to the Soviet EC. Znamenskii was a graduate of the historico-philological faculty of Petrograd University and an active member of the SR party, later of the Labor group. Before the First World War he worked as a history teacher in several Petersburg gymnasia. He was mobilized in the summer of 1915, and from April 1916 to February 27, 1917 served as an ensign in the 1st infantry reserve regiment in Petrograd.

27 Sukhomlinov was arrested on March 1, and brought to the Tauride Palace at 10:30 at night by an ensign and two sailors. Later that night he was transferred to the Peter and Paul Fortress.

28 N. A. Maklakov was brought to the Tauride Palace shortly after 8:00 in the evening on March 1.

29 The reference is to the so-called Lower Investigative Commission (LIC), which operated from February 27 to the middle of March 1917; it was organized to receive, question, and determine grounds for possible further detainment of low-ranking police officials, officers, precinct cops, and gendarmes who were being brought to the Duma during the February Days. The Commission occupied room 45 and held the detainees in rooms 43 and 44. It is estimated that 479 persons were questioned by the LIC during the two weeks of its operation.

30 The reference is probably to the Higher Investigative Commission. See n. 19 to the Gerasimov interview.

31 Ivan Loginovich Goremykin (1839–1917) was one of the longest serving high-ranking officials of his day; he began his career in 1860 in the Senate and Ministry of Justice, and later served as Minister of Internal Affairs (1895–1899) and chairman of the Council of Ministers (1906, 1914–16). Arrested on the afternoon of March 1, 1917, he was transferred to the Peter and Paul Fortress where he was kept March 1–13.

32 The Order of St. Andrew the First Called (*Orden sviatogo Apostola Andreia Pervozvannogo*) was the first and highest decoration for service in Imperial Russia. Goremykin received the honor for his loyal service to three tsars and in recognition of his rank of Acting Privy Councilor, 1st

class—the first rank of the Table of Ranks. He was one of only thirteen recipients ever to receive this rank before 1917.

33 Kerenskii might be referring to the order written by the *Mezhraionets* Iurenev and the SR Maximalist Aleksandrovich, inciting the soldiers to act against their officers and to disobey the orders of the Duma Committee. Kerenskii, reportedly supported by Sukhanov and Steklov, was indignant about the order and demanded its confiscation. On March 2, he succeeded in convincing the majority of the EC to authorize confiscation of all copies (Hasegawa, *The February Revolution*, 535). On the same day Kerenskii (as minister of justice) and Chkheidze (as chairman of the Petrograd Soviet) issued a proclamation calling any such orders "a malicious provocation." *Kak sovershilas' Velikaia russkaia revoliutsiia*, 54–5; *Velikie dni rossiiskoi revoliutsii 1917 g. Fevral': 27 i 28-go. Mart: 1, 2, 3 i 4-go* (Petrograd: Biuro rossiiskoi pressy, 1917), 49.

34 See, for example, the Rodzianko interview (Chapter 6) and his remarks to the meeting of members of all pre-revolutionary Dumas on April 27, 1917 in *Stenograficheskii otchet zasedaniia chlenov Gosudarstvennoi dumy pervogo, vtorogo, tret'ego i chetvertogo sozyvov. Chetverg, 27 aprelia 1917 g.* (Petrograd: Gos.Tipografiia, 1917), 2–3; and Rodzianko's note to Prince L'vov, April 28, 1917 in RGIA, f. 1278, op. 10, d. 9, l. 123.

35 That is, if Nicholas had answered Rodzianko's appeals of February 26–7, or complied with his younger brother's recommendation on the night of February 27 to fire his cabinet and appoint Prince L'vov to head a new ministry of confidence, or granted a constitutional monarchy as requested by Rodzianko and the Grand Dukes Pavel, Kirill, and Mikhail on February 28 and March 1.

36 See n. 13 to the Chkheidze interview (Chapter 9).

37 That is, without the well-known Soviet EC formula of conditional support for the Provisional Government, "only insofar as."

38 The reference is to Iu. M. Steklov's speech "On the Petrograd Soviet's attitude toward the Provisional Government," which was delivered at an evening session on March 30 of the (first) All-Russian Conference (not to be confused with the first Congress) of Soviets of Workers' and Soldiers' Deputies (March 29–April 3, 1917), and debated over the course of the next three sessions, held on March 31 and April 1. See *Vserossiiskoe soveshchanie sovetov rabochikh i soldatskikh deputatov. Stenograficheskii otchet* (Moscow and Leningrad: Gosizdat, 1927), 106–24, 125–88. In his speech, Steklov attacked his former allies from the Duma Committee for their allegedly reactionary politics and counterrevolutionary policies, and reiterated the centrality of the dual power arrangement to the relations between the Soviet and the "bourgeois" government. As Kerenskii notes, the speech was filled with misrepresentations of some of the well-known facts on the timing and circumstances of the creation of the Duma Committee and the Petrograd Soviet. In a sense, the speech represented a more aggressive (and much longer) version of Steklov's address to the Petrograd Soviet on the afternoon of March 2, in which he retrospectively defended the EC's negotiations with the Duma Committee on the creation of the Provisional Government (*Petrogradskii Sovet rabochikh i soldatskikh deputatov v 1917 g. Dokumenty i materialy*. Vol. I: *27 fevralia–31 marta 1917 g.* (Leningrad: Nauka, 1991), 61–6). Steklov may also have wanted to reassure the increasingly radicalized representatives of local soviets that the leadership of the Petrograd Soviet could be trusted to monitor the "bourgeois" government, and that it stood ready to withdraw its conditional support, when necessary.

39 See n. 49 to the Tugan-Baranovskii interview and *Petrogradskii sovet*, I: 218–21.

40 The reference is to Prince Pavel Pavlovich Putiatin (1872–1943), a colonel of the Cavalry Guards' Regiment and equerry of the imperial court; and to his wife, Princess Ol'ga Pavlovna née Zelenaia (1877–1967).

41 The allusion is to a once very popular lowbrow novel in Russia, *The Battle of the Russians with the Kabardinians, Or the Beautiful Muslim Woman, Dying on Her Husband's Coffin* (1840), by the long since forgotten writer Nikolai Il'ich Zriakhov.

42 This must have been Boris Emmanuilovich Nol'de, another prominent Kadet jurist. See n. 23 to the Nekrasov interview.

43 "Steklov" was crossed out in Rusudana Polievktova-Nikoladze's hand and replaced with "Nakhamkis."

44 This may have been Prince Grigorii Nikolaevich Trubetskoi (1873–1930), a former diplomatic representative to Serbia and a senior official in the foreign ministry's near eastern department. In the middle of March 1917, he was appointed chief of the diplomatic chancellery at General Headquarters. Kerenskii, Miliukov, Nekrasov, and Shingarev visited General Headquarters on March 18, 1917.

45 For some reason, Kerenskii decided not to name his longtime political friend and Masonic "brother" N. D. Sokolov, whose identity as the author of Order Number One was reportedly already an open secret by April 1917. See Sokolov's deposition to B. I. Nikolaevskii, 13 [?] January 1927, Nicolaevskii Collection, box 525-3, notebook 1, p. 113, HIA.

12

Mikhail Ivanovich Tereshchenko

Mikhail Ivanovich Tereshchenko (1886–1956) served in every cabinet of the Provisional Government, from March 2 to October 25, 1917, and throughout his tenure remained Kerenskii's most loyal and unwavering ally. He was minister of finance in the first Provisional Government (March 2–May 5, 1917), and after May 5 held the foreign ministry portfolio in all three coalition cabinets. He was a member of the five-man Directory (September 1–27) set up by Kerenskii as an interim cabinet in the aftermath of the Kornilov Affair, and served as deputy prime minister beginning on September 5.

Both memoirists and historians have raised questions regarding his inclusion in the first Provisional Government. His participation has been variously ascribed to his supposed Masonic ties with Kerenskii and Nekrasov, to his senior position in the Central War Industry Committee (CWIC), and to the need to include representatives of big business.[a] For the most part, his role in the February Revolution also remains obscure, and the same can be said of his brief political career, which began and ended with the ill-fated Provisional Government. Tereshchenko himself is the main contributor to this ambiguity. He did not write memoirs, avoided publicity, and in general during his post-revolutionary life preferred to stay away from anything and anyone connected to his past.[b]

---

[a] See the discussions in George Katkov, *Russia 1917: The February Revolution* (London: Fontana, 1969), 379–82 and in Tsuyoshi Hasegawa, *The February Revolution, Petrograd, 1917* (Seattle and London: University of Washington Press, 1981), 527–9. See also Richard Pipes, *The Russian Revolution, 1899–1919* (London: Collins Harvill, 1990), 406; Hasegawa, "The February Revolution," in Edward Acton et al., eds., *Critical Companion to the Russian Revolution, 1914–1921* (Bloomington and Indianapolis: Indiana University Press, 1997), 59; Richard Abraham, "Kerenskii, Aleksandr Fedorovich (1881–1970)," in Harold Shukman, ed., *The Blackwell Encyclopedia of the Russian Revolution* (Oxford: Blackwell, 1994), 330; Howard White, "The Provisional Government," ibid., 125; White, "The Provisional Government," in Acton et al., eds., *Critical Companion*, 392; *Politicheskie deiateli Rossii 1917 g. Biograficheskii slovar'* (Moscow: BRE, 1993), 313.

[b] There is one short biographical sketch on Tereshchenko in English (Rex Wade, "M.I. Tereshchenko," *Modern Encyclopedia of Russian and Soviet History*, Joseph L. Wieczynski, ed., 39 (1985): 7–9), and only a handful of mostly unreliable recent biographical entries in Russian. See,

His interview for the Polievktov Commission, recorded only three months after the fall of the old regime, thus represents his only known testimony. With its focus on the first day of the February Revolution and the preceding developments, this interview sheds new light on such usually taboo topics as the preparations of a plot to remove Nicholas II. It also helps explain Tereshchenko's appointment to the first revolutionary government.

Mikhail Ivanovich Tereshchenko was heir apparent to one of the richest families in pre-revolutionary Russia. He was born in Kiev where his father (Ivan Nikolaevich) and grandfather (Nikolai Artemovich)—themselves descendants of a Cossack trader—were prominent sugar, coal mine, land, and railway magnates that literally owned a good chunk of the city. Tereshchenko's personal wealth, most of which he inherited at the age of 17, was estimated at a staggering 70 million rubles. From his early childhood, he often accompanied his mother and two sisters on frequent trips abroad and lived for months and sometimes years at a time in France, Germany, and England. His education was superb. He studied at Eton College, and by the time he entered the 1st Kiev classical gymnasium, he was already fluent in several modern European languages and could comfortably read Latin and Ancient Greek. He also studied music (and was said to have been an accomplished pianist) and acquired exquisite social manners (invariably noted by contemporaries). He studied law at Kiev's St. Vladimir University and economics at the University of Leipzig (1905–8) with Karl Bücher, the leading German economist of his day and a founder of non-market economics.

During one of his long stays in France, Tereshchenko met and came under the influence of Maksim Maksimovich Kovalevskii, the famed Russian scholar and liberal activist. Apparently, it was Kovalevskii who convinced his young millionaire admirer to return to Russia to complete his law studies and to dedicate his talents and wealth to the liberal cause. In 1909, Tereshchenko went back to Russia. Later that year he passed external examinations and received a law degree at Moscow University. For the next year and a half, he taught in the Roman and Civil law department, but in 1911 joined the mass resignation of the Moscow University faculty in protest against the violation of university autonomy by the notorious minister of popular enlightenment, L. A. Kasso.

Unlike many of his former colleagues who now had to look for new employment, Tereshchenko decided on a "career change" and took up the role of patron of the arts. He hired Kovalevskii's old friend, the prominent Moscow zemstvo liberal and constitutionalist Dmitrii Nikolaevich Shipov, to manage his enormous assets and devoted the next several years to the promotion and advancement of the performing arts. While perfecting his own artistic skills—he was said to have been

for example, A. I. Serkov, *Russkoe masonstvo, 1731–2000. Entsiklopedicheskii slovar'* (Moscow: ROSSPEN, 2001), 1143. While in emigration, he only occasionally and for a very brief period corresponded with Nicholas Basily and V. A. Maklakov. See Collection N. A Basily, box 8; A. F. Kerenskii to V. A. Maklakov, September 16, 1955, Collection V. A. Maklakov, box. 8-27, HIA.

taking acting lessons from the famed Moscow theater director K. S. Stanislavskii—he also volunteered his services to the director of the imperial theaters, V. A. Teliakovskii. In 1911–12, he worked without pay as Teliakovskii's assistant for special tasks, using his new official position to bring noted European opera singers and theater companies to Russia and obtain permits and secure funding for the construction of the conservatory for music in Kiev, which opened its doors in 1913. In what retrospectively might appear counterintuitive for an admirer of Kovalevskii and a minister in the future revolutionary government, Tereshchenko also used his position in the state service to obtain hereditary nobility, which came with his newly conferred court rank of Kammerjunker, or gentleman of the bedchamber, who traditionally oversaw the tsar's entertainment. In the archaic world of Russian social estates, this was a privilege money alone could not buy.

A similarly revealing episode occurred not long after his interview in June 1917. Tereshchenko and his Provisional Government colleague Irakli Tsereteli, now ministers of foreign affairs and post and telegraph respectively, rode together in the former tsar's private railroad car to Kiev in an attempt to dissuade the Ukrainian Central Rada from declaring national and territorial autonomy from Russia. They left Petrograd on June 27 and arrived in Kiev the following day with a few free hours to idle away. According to Tsereteli, at one point Tereshchenko turned to him and, with what one might speculate was a flare of pride and satisfaction, remarked: "In the past [before the revolution] I could afford anything money could buy, except for my own private railroad car. I had thought about that a lot, and really wanted [it], but it was not permitted. The Revolution gave it to me."[c]

There is no reason to doubt Tsereteli's account. He had never been a gossiper and always enjoyed the impeccable reputation of an honest and decent man. He and Tereshchenko had never been political or personal enemies and were generally on good terms. Tsereteli recounted the episode to his old and trusted friend, B. I. Nikolaevskii, who himself had no reason to undermine Tereshchenko and apparently never intended to make the account public. Tereshchenko's deference to social status and his acutely manifested "bourgeois mentality" are quite revealing, though these two incidents should hardly be taken as the sole explanation of why this *über* wealthy, talented, and energetic person joined the revolution. Even so, they do reveal that it would also be misleading to describe Tereshchenko as a "repentant capitalist"[d] who dedicated himself to the service of the people.

Returning to 1912, Tereshchenko, still in his role as patron of the arts, now found himself increasingly involved with the leading Symbolist writers in St. Petersburg, among them his new close friend, the poet Alexander Blok. With his two sisters,

---

[c] See the handwritten transcript of Tsereteli's conversation with B. I. Nikolaevskii, August 16, 1928, Paris. Notebook 1, 29. B. I. Nicolaevskii Collection, box 525, f. 3, HIA.

[d] As cited in Ziva Galili, "The April Crisis," in Acton et al., eds., *Critical Companion*, 67.

also known for their patronage of artists and writers, Tereshchenko set up and bank-rolled a publishing house, called "Sirin," which between 1912 and 1914 printed the works of major Symbolist figures, including Andrei Belyi's celebrated novel *Petersburg* (in 1913).

The outbreak of the First World War brought new opportunities for self-fulfill-ment. Tereshchenko could now focus his energies and apply his wealth, organiza-tional talents, government connections, and newly acquired patriotic fervor to the arena of national defense. With his usual dedication, Tereshchenko threw himself completely into this new field. He began by setting up and paying for a large mili-tary hospital in his native Kiev, and by organizing one of the first front-line medical detachments, which in 1914–early 1915 operated under his leadership on the south-western front.[e] There he met and befriended many senior army officers, including the front commander General N. I. Ivanov—the future "dictator" of Petrograd and commander of the failed punitive expedition on February 27–March 1, 1917. Ivanov invited Tereshchenko to accompany him as Russian forces triumphantly entered L'vov in late August 1914.

In July of 1915, Tereshchenko became one of the organizers and chairman of the Kiev War Industry Committee and soon after was elected deputy chairman of the all-Russian CWIC under A. I. Guchkov. The Moscow industrialist and Duma Progressist deputy A. I. Konovalov was also elected a deputy chairman. At the same time, Tereshchenko's wide-ranging activities and recognition of his administrative talents extended beyond the nationwide network of war industry committees. He was asked to join the main ruling committee of the joint Union of Towns and the Zemstvo. Beginning in the second half of 1915, he participated in the work of the Special Council on Defense under the minister of war. There, he regularly inter-acted with many of his future revolutionary colleagues and would-be co-conspira-tors from the government, the Duma, and the wartime public organizations, including Rodzianko, B. A. Engel'gardt, Miliukov, Guchkov, Nekrasov, and Konovalov, as well as Generals A. A. Manikovskii and A. A. Polivanov. Finally, and perhaps most significant to his subsequent entry into national politics, was his close involvement, beginning in the fall of 1916, in the Guchkov-led plot to remove Nicholas II.

It is true that in early 1917 Tereshchenko could not claim to have a history in the revolutionary movement, nor had he served in the Duma[f] or any other elected posi-tion, locally or nationally. Still, his leading role in the main conspiracy against the throne, combined with a long list of accomplishments during the first two and a half years of the war, gave him enough clout to be a serious candidate for a future public cabinet. In short, there is every reason to challenge Miliukov's famously dismissive

---

[e] V. V. Kovalinskii, *Sem'ia Tereshchenko* (Kiev: Presa Ukraïni, 2003), 329.

[f] Contrary to the claims in two recent biographical entries (Serkov, *Russkoe masonstvo*, 794; *Politicheskie deiateli Rossii*, 312), Tereshchenko was not a deputy to the fourth Duma.

(and disingenuous) remark that Tereshchenko had been virtually unknown before his name was put forward as finance minister on March 1, 1917.[g]

As Tereshchenko reveals in his interview, Miliukov was not only well aware of his role in the Guchkov plot, but raised no questions about his or his co-conspirators' participation in a future cabinet when ministerial portfolios were discussed in late January 1917 and then again on February 20–1. Of the five leaders of the Guchkov plot, four were civilians: Guchkov, Tereshchenko, Nekrasov, and Prince D. L. Viazemskii. The fifth was a cavalry officer whose name (D. V. Kossikovskii) was divulged in this interview for the first and last time. Prince Viazemskii was mortally wounded by a stray bullet on the night of March 1. However, the three who survived—Guchkov, Tereshchenko, and Nekrasov—all became ministers in the first Provisional Government.

Considering Tereshchenko's leading role in the central and most advanced known plot, and in light of prerevolutionary discussions of the plotters' roles in a future cabinet, his inclusion in the first Provisional Government should come as no surprise. Although it has been proven beyond doubt that a strong Masonic bond existed between Kerenskii, Nekrasov, and Konovalov, and that it probably helped solidify their opposition to the monarchical form of government, direct evidence that Tereshchenko ever belonged to the same Masonic organization is at best inconsistent.[h]

In any event, Tereshchenko and Kerenskii were the longest-serving members of the Provisional Government and remained in the cabinet from the first day to the last. On the night of October 26, 1917, Tereshchenko was arrested in the Winter Palace with other "bourgeois ministers" and spent the next several months confined in the Peter and Paul Fortress. His release from Bolshevik prison was secured in the spring of 1918 by his mother, who reportedly was allowed to pay a hefty ransom on the condition that she also paid for the release of another former minster, the Kadet N. M. Kishkin. She complied, and she and her son fled Russia in a common train car that took them to the Finnish border.

Tereshchenko left the bulk of his wealth behind, as well as his proclivity for political conspiracies. But he kept his risk-taking character. He also kept his love of opera and ballet as well as his financial acumen, with which he sustained a

---

[g] See the discussion in Hasegawa, *The February Revolution*, 527–9. See also V. V. Shul'gin, *Dni: zapiski* (Belgrade: M. A. Suvorin, 1925), 289; P. A. Buryshkin, *Moskva kupecheskaia* (New York: Izdatel'stvo imeni Chekhova, 1954), 316–18; Orlando Figes, *A People's Tragedy. A History of the Russian Revolution* (New York: Viking, 1996), 336. It is worth recalling that Tereshchenko had replaced Miliukov as foreign minister after the Kadet leader's forced resignation and hence had no reason to expect forgiving treatment from Miliukov, who was known to his contemporaries as tactless, vindictive, and egocentric.

[h] Even the greatest contemporary authority on Russian Masons, the Moscow historian A. I. Serkov, only tentatively identified Tereshchenko as a possible member of just a single political lodge, which was very atypical for political masons who usually belonged to at least half a dozen lodges and often rotated their memberships. See Serkov, *Russkoe masonstvo*, 1143.

respectable income for the rest of his life. During the 1920s and the early 1930s, he successfully managed Scandinavian and French banks belonging to the Wallenberg and Rothschild families, respectively. In the late 1930s, he took up the new business of managing plantations and processing coconut oil in Mozambique, and for years divided his time between Madagascar and Lisbon. By the early 1950s, he had accumulated a considerable fortune and retired in Monaco, where he died a few years later.

He was soon completely forgotten. But then in the late 1990s his extraordinary life and adventurous character attracted Alexander Piatigorskii, a leading Russian-British philosopher and scholar of Buddhism and Indian philosophy. He made Tereshchenko the central character, under the name "Mikhail Ivanovich," in his bizarre novel *Remember the Odd Man…*[i] At about the same time, he was suddenly remembered in his native (and now independent) Ukraine as a generous philanthropist, and has also been hailed as a true Ukrainian patriot—though he likely would have disapproved of this characterization.

The interview is reproduced below on the basis of a master version compiled by Rusudana Polievktova-Nikoladze and two draft transcripts written in Rusudana's hand and that of another interviewer (either T. V. Krupskaia or V. I. Pavlov) who also recorded one of the draft transcripts of the Skobelev interview.

★ ★ ★ ★ ★ ★

Transcript of Conversation with Mikhail Ivanovich Tereshchenko, Minister of Foreign Affairs, June 7, 1917

Tereshchenko is ill. He lies on his couch under a plaid blanket in a suite in his private mansion at 22 Dvortsovaia Embankment. From his window there is an exceptional view of the Neva River and of the St. Peter and Paul Fortress. June 7, 1917. Mikhail Ivanovich Tereshchenko is the minister of foreign affairs in the coalition cabinet and, since June 6, also the minister of finance. Before the revolution he was chairman of the War Industry Committee in Kiev and deputy chairman of the Central War Industry Committee (led by A. I. Guchkov) in Petrograd.

Any account of my impressions on the revolution would have to begin with a meeting that took place in the apartment of A. I. Konovalov in December [1916].[1] But rather than looking so far back, I should perhaps begin directly in February of 1917. I arrived in Petrograd on the 18th, intending to stay four days and then return to the War Industry Committee in Kiev. During

---

[i] Aleksandr Piatigorskii, *Vspomnish' strannogo cheloveka…*(Moscow: NLO, 1999).

my previous stays in Petrograd I had lost all hope in the possibility of any quick changes in the existing situation, which we felt was intolerable. I also expected little of this trip. I had been taken aback by a recent meeting with the commander in chief of the southwestern front,[2] whom I had met on February the 13th. Although I was not as close to him as I was to General Ivanov,[3] he nevertheless spoke frankly with me and asked that our conversation, devoted entirely to matters of internal politics,[4] be relayed to his Duma deputy friends in Petrograd.

After breakfast, over which we had discussed a number of technical questions, he began to question me about the situation in Petrograd. He told me that everyone in the army, from a front-line soldier to the commander in chief, was more preoccupied with the political situation in the rear than with fighting the Germans; more interested in Protopopov and his lackeys than in combat maneuvers or fresh offensives. He had concluded that poor military strategy had deeply affected the morale of the army and the people. Turning to yet another troubling topic, he complained that certain irresponsible individuals at the highest levels had interfered in matters of state administration. "They should never forget one thing," he said, "I swore an oath of allegiance to him but not to her! So let her remember that!"[5] Those were his actual words.

Before bidding farewell, Brusilov asked that I pass along a message to his friends V. A. Maklakov, Rodzianko, and others in the Duma, requesting that they visit him at his headquarters in Kamenets[6] and stay in touch.[7] Otherwise he felt that he was entirely cut off from events in the capital.

Upon arriving in Petrograd, I communicated all this to A. I. Guchkov, with whom I had daily meetings at the War Industry Committee,[8] and to several other Duma deputies. The mood in the capital was anxious and tense. Although not yet obvious on the street, we felt it strongly in our work. Aleksandr Ivanovich Guchkov worried about Protopopov-instigated repressions, which had become all too familiar, and which depressed us greatly. He mentioned the harassments to which the members of the Labor Group of the War Industry Committee—those few who still remained free—were subjected.[9]

On February the 20th and 21st there was a small meeting of individuals who had, at an earlier gathering of public figures on January 27, [1917],[10] declared it impossible to remain neutral in the event of a coup d'état. On February 20 we assembled at a restaurant called "Medved'."[11] We met again on the 21st, this time in an apartment on Troitskii Street that A. I. Guchkov had rented for this purpose. Miliukov and Shidlovskii declared that serious politicians should avoid taking an active role in any coup, waiting instead until the dust had settled, and then taking power. This reasoning was unacceptable to the rest of us and met with an unsympathetic response. We argued that we would gain nothing from an act that had been accomplished by others. A bear's killer does not permit others to share the hide. And anyway, we could never allow the mob to assume control. We stuck to this principle, and future events proved us correct. There were five of us, altogether. We decided that a coup was necessary and set out to discuss concrete measures to bring it about. Since the tsar had left for General Headquarters shortly before our meeting, our plan could not be implemented immediately.[12] We therefore set a date for the coup in early March.[13] With this date in mind, I decided to return to Kiev on the 22nd so that I could be back in the capital in time.[14] But during the day on the 22nd rumors began to spread of tensions at the munitions factories. A. I. Guchkov asked whether I was still intent on my trip, then urged me to stay in Petrograd. At the meeting of the Central Committee of the [Central] War Industry Committee, he requested that all of our staff members also stay in the office, given the gravity of the situation.

February the 23rd began with street protests and disorders, demands for "Bread!" Political demands and slogans against the government were also heard: "Down with the Tsar!" and so on. Strangely, whenever soldiers and Cossacks ran into crowds, which consisted largely of women and workers, the latter immediately began to greet the former by shouting "Hurrah!" This made a powerful impression on the men in uniform. Embarrassed, the officers and soldiers worked to disperse the crowds, but they did so as gently as possible. No one was hurt. These sporadic cries of "Hurrah!" left a powerful impression, both odd and grave.

On the 24th, a Friday, we had our regular meeting of the bureau of the Central Committee. After the meeting was over A. I. Guchkov informed us that in the evening there would be an additional session with the two remaining unarrested workers from the Central War Industry Committee, along with representatives of several cooperatives—all in all about twenty-five to twenty-six people.[15] Around the time of our meeting reports came in of substantial disturbances and unrest in the city center. On Nevskii the troops had set up barriers, secured the Nikolaevskii Railway Station, and were out patrolling the streets. There was talk of impending arrests. That evening, A. I. Guchkov had to attend an emergency session of the City

Duma and asked me to stay on to ensure that the evening meeting at the Central War Industry Committee continued as planned and without excesses. The *Okhrana* [tsarist secret police] was apparently informed that the meeting was scheduled to take place.

Returning home around 9:30 that night, after finishing my usual errands, I was almost immediately summoned to the Central War Industry Committee, where the Labor Group was already in session. A secretary there told me that a police official accompanied by marshals and a detachment of soldiers from the Volynskii Regiment, numbering about twenty-five, had just arrived at the Labor Group session and had begun detainment procedures. I immediately tried to enter the room where this was taking place, but was initially stopped by two marshals. Then the Volynskii soldiers let me in. I went downstairs to the office of the Chairman of the War Industry Committee's Central Committee and from his office proceeded upstairs to the deputy chairman of the Labor Group, who wanted to see me.

There, the chief of the police station [*pristav*] (the same one who shut down the February 14 meeting[16] and filed the report) told me that the current meeting was not permitted. He therefore had to register all those present. For that, he had to take everyone to the police station. I pointed out to him that this meeting was far from prohibited. It was not open to the public; all of its participants were known to the bureau and had been invited. But he remained firm and categorically forbade the meeting, even though his orders reflected a certain apprehension. At that time, the Duma deputy Tuliakov[17] came in. I asked him to telephone A. I. Guchkov from the next room and to ask A[leksandr]. I[vanovich]. to talk to the City Administration and Police Chief[18] about the possibility of releasing the workers after their names had been recorded.

As the marshals hurriedly rounded up the meeting's participants, I struck up a conversation with the soldiers, who seemed to look on with complete apathy. It turned out that they all came from different provinces, but a few were from the estate of one of my relatives in the Volyn' province. They continued to watch the arrests with complete indifference, oblivious to the back and forth between the workers and the police officer, as if their surroundings had failed to make any kind of impression on them. They executed their orders precisely and faithfully, though in the adjacent rooms they began to show signs of weakening discipline. I even remarked at one point that perhaps the soldiers should stand during the conversation since they were also standing guard.

In the beginning, the workers were very anxious. Eventually they calmed down a bit and the atmosphere improved. Some of them talked to me, but not about politics—about their families, about the cooperatives and ration cards; jokes were passed around. Guchkov arrived, and after informing us of the lack of progress in his negotiations, he left to meet again with Prince Golitsyn.[19] We asked him to keep us updated on further developments. Soon an officer from the Volynskii Regiment appeared. He was a Pole, and quite overbearing and boisterous. His orders were to move everyone immediately to a police station on Nadezhdinskaia Street. I implored him to wait until the outcome of negotiations between Guchkov and Prince Golitsyn, but he brushed me off, saying that any delay would mean disobeying his orders. As an officer in the Volynskii Regiment, which had always prided itself on its strict adherence to discipline, he could not disobey his commanders. "We are taking your workers to the police station," he said. "You can talk to the police if anything comes of your negotiations." The workers did not resist. The officer ordered a unit of about fifty Volynskii soldiers to surround the workers.

We all walked together. They wanted Tuliakov to walk with the rest of the detainees. However, when it became clear that he was a Duma deputy, they allowed him to walk on the sidewalk with me. The sidewalk was next to the street down the middle of which the group of twenty-eight detainees walked, tightly surrounded by soldiers. Once at the police station, the long process of registration and identification began. I drove to the Central Committee to see if Guchkov had an answer for me. Once I learned that he had been unable to resolve the matter, I drove back to the police station and stayed there until 4:00 in the morning, when they finished the list of names.

The workers were divided into two groups: one was interrogated; the other was not. The first group was released; the second group was detained. This was carried out according to a consultation between the *pristav* and an *Okhrana* official. As this was going on, I was sitting there and talking with the workers, and inadvertently learned the mechanics of "booking." The *pristav* would ask a worker his surname, then he would go behind a screen, where the *Okhrana* official sat with a notebook. They would confer. The *Okhrana* official would check the name against the list in his notebook, and depending upon whether or not the name was on it, the worker would be interrogated and released or detained without questioning. It was my impression that those who were released (fifteen people) gave the outward impression of simple folk. Those who were detained (fourteen people) had the appearance of more intelligent people.[20] The detainees gave me a list of their surnames and asked me to take care of their families. They also started passing me notes to their loved ones. As soon as the *pristav* saw this, he abruptly said that this was forbidden. However, one of the workers later managed to pass his note to me. At around four in the morning, when the registration of detainees was completed and they were officially put under arrest, I left the station without being able to find out where they would be taken. One of the arrested, named Weisman[?], as he was taken away, cheerfully remarked: "One more push and we win! Just do not give up!" It appeared strange to me that under the circumstances such a confidence in victory could exist, that in such a situation it was possible to speak of success.

The next day, Saturday the 25th, passed quietly in the city center despite the presence of troops in the streets and the occasional gunshot. Many were under the impression that Protopopov had won. On the outskirts of Petrograd, however, the picture was very different. While I was not personally involved in any of the organizational activity there, I heard repeatedly from A. I. Konovalov that an extensive groundwork was being laid inside the factories, including manifestos, calls to organize workers, to hold elections to soviets, and the like.[21]

The night from the 25th to the 26th passed calmly. On Sunday, the 26th, there was a noticeable change in the city's mood, a feeling that some turning point had been reached. Soldiers from the nearby barracks of the Pavlovskii Regiment were stationed in our Admiralty district.[22] Already on the 25th we had heard rumors that the soldiers patrolling the streets had become extremely apprehensive, even furious, about having to conduct their patrols with disguised policemen. By Sunday this situation had deteriorated. When I arrived home Sunday evening after visiting with acquaintances, where conversation had focused on the impending victory of Protopopov and his forces, my house servants informed me that the nearby Pavlovskii Regiment had mutinied and killed their commander. The rumors were numerous and contradictory, but all noted shooting in the city and Pavlovskii's soldiers being encircled and blocked off. A colonel and a popular ensign had been wounded, it was said.[23] This was at 7:00. I immediately left home to see for myself what was going on. I walked down Moshkov Lane and saw that it had indeed been encircled. I was able to cross it only by explaining to the soldiers that I lived on the Palace Embankment and had to get to the city center. Checkpoints were placed everywhere on the Moika River embankments and in Koniushennaia Square. On Nevskii there stood rows of soldiers. From time to time single shots rang out.

That evening I had dinner at the home of Mikhail Vladimirovich Rodzianko.[24] When I arrived there, all present were in a state of confusion, everyone with the same question on their mind: was the situation at last settled or was this only the beginning? I told them what I had heard about the Pavlovskii Regiment. Returning home, I saw crowds out on Millionnaia Street and felt that in the last two days a profound change had occurred. This was all deeply unsettling.

On the morning of the 27th I walked to see General Manikovskii to discuss things related to the War Industry Committee.[25] On Millionnaia Street I ran into General Adlerberg,[26] whose son[27] had married one of my relatives. He was walking and looking cheerfully up at the sun. After greeting me, he remarked: "What a disgrace that they mutinied. Soldiers are so bored that when we have disturbances, they rebel. Of course there is no great danger, but it is still a shame that these were soldiers from the Volynskii Regiment and companies from the Preobrazhenskii Regiment." He spoke amiably, apparently not realizing the significance of the events that had taken place. I continued along the embankment. On the corner of Liteinyi Avenue, near the Main Artillery Administration, I met up with General Ipat'ev,[28] and we started a conversation. I remember the time being ten minutes to ten.

As we chatted, gunfire broke out and a few bullets flew by. At that moment I saw my car and motioned to my driver to park it on Zakhar'evskaia Street. General Ipat'ev and I remained to see why gunfire had erupted. We thought that perhaps the troops were trying to clear the streets. Then the shooting intensified. We took cover and looked on to see what we could discover. Soon a crowd of soldiers, with red flags on their bayonets, were marching in the sun down Liteinyi Avenue. We understood that these were rebellious soldiers who had joined the revolution. A terrible panic set in on the streets. We quickly ran into the Main Artillery Administration. There, in Manikovskii's office upstairs, we found the general along with several other individuals, including the British military attaché Knox, and General V. I. Timiriazev.[29] Some of them were sitting, others stood by the window. I was waiting with Ipat'ev and Manikovskii to see what happened. Panic erupted. Manikovskii was informed by telephone that the commander of the artillery factory had been either killed or wounded.[30] A report came in that the troops were rebelling, taking up arms and storming the Main Artillery Administration.

Nothing could be seen from the side windows. We could only see what was happening in the front. There, we saw troops approaching. Someone started closing the gates.

Everyone in the room got very agitated. Only General Manikovskii and the British attaché remained calm. Then a bullet came through the window, quickly followed by another, then more. This terrified those in the room. Most dashed out into the corridor looking for an exit, yet finding none.

I remained standing by the central window of the general's office, opposite Zakhar'evskaia Street, and suddenly I saw soldiers marching along in ranks under the red flag. The front ranks walked in disorder and appeared to be shouting. I could not hear what they yelled, but I was shocked by the sight of them—their wide open mouths and their strained, changed faces. They had the look of drunken men. For me, coming from a professional military family on my mother's side[31] and raised in the spirit of military discipline, this was a deeply disturbing, unusually difficult thing to witness.

My first impression was that these people in the front ranks had lost their military bearing and did not understand where they were headed. I had to strain every nerve, call upon all of my past, in order to understand them and to suppress within myself a sense of disgust. There was a knock on the closed doors. I saw an automobile come under fire as it turned from the Liteinyi Bridge onto Zakhar'evskaia Street. Then a general jumped out of it, crossed the street, and hid. The soldiers began firing at the lower floor; then someone started trying to break the door down and the shooting intensified. I surmised that they would soon take over the entire building and massacre everyone inside. Knox, General Manikovskii, and I went to the corridor and stood there on the staircase. The banging on the lower door intensified, and we soon heard the door let loose. A mob of soldiers broke through the door, rushed to the coat rack, and began searching the pockets of the military coats hanging there. They were looking for weapons; they took revolvers and sabers. At that moment I bid farewell to General Manikovskii and Knox, slowly and quite calmly went downstairs, pushed my way through the soldiers, took my coat and hat, and forced my way out of the building.[32] They let me go because I was a civilian. As I was crossing Liteinyi, I heard a few bullets fly by. A soldier yelled. I walked along Zakhar'evskaia and I told my chauffeur to take the car home when he had a chance.

I headed towards the Duma. I knew that the tsar had issued a decree dissolving the Duma and that the deputies had decided to gather there at 10:00

that morning to discuss the situation.[33] The shooting continued. The bullets flew on Zakhar'evskaia as well. Small clusters of people who had been walking along Zakhar'evskaia attempted to hide themselves. A platoon of soldiers in full formation was marching from the Tauride Gardens. From a distance, I got the impression that they were heading to suppress the insurgents, but I soon noticed that they did not have an officer. More importantly, I saw red flags attached to their bayonets. Their arrival at the Main Artillery Administration caused a commotion. The soldiers looked at the newcomers, and could not figure out why they had come. When they got closer—by Voskresenskii Avenue—the soldiers who were standing by the Main Artillery Administration building understood what was happening, and all greeted them with a "Hoorah!" The approaching soldiers shouted back in kind.

The Duma was completely quiet. The private meeting of Duma deputies was in session; occasionally deputies would step out, talk among themselves, and then return to the meeting. I saw several deputies. Then I walked into the office of the President and saw V. V. Shul'gin there. V. A. Maklakov and I wandered about the enormous Catherine Hall together for quite awhile. We saw Kerenskii and Miliukov leave the meeting and go into the hall talking to each other. Later I spoke with A. I. Konovalov, who updated me on the soldiers' uprising: three companies from the Preobrazhenskii Regiment had rebelled; the Volynskii Regiment had also mutinied; and the city was divided into sections. I told him my impressions of what had happened in the Main Artillery Administration, and my assumption that General Manikovskii had been killed. Someone had called the general's residence, and he was not there. A. I. Guchkov, who was already in the Duma, started phoning the Main Artillery Administration, but there was no answer. At the same time, the private meeting was in session.[34] Since I was not a member of the Duma, I found myself moving back and forth between the office of the Duma President and the Catherine Hall.

A myriad of conflicting rumors, which later proved to be either accurate or not, began to reach the Duma. Among other things, there were reports that crowds of workers and soldiers were moving towards the Duma. Around 1:00 in the afternoon, the first big crowd of soldiers showed up; they were accompanied by armed workers and civilians who had gotten rifles from the rebellious troops. We also saw the famous revolutionary automobiles, prickling like hedgehogs with rifle barrels and bayonets [oshchetinivshiesia], which would roam the city for the next three days. The crowd stopped before the gate of the Gardens; Duma negotiators went out to the soldiers.

The crowd's demands and wishes, along with rumors of arriving soldiers, caused a lot of nervousness inside the Duma. The crowd was moving closer and closer. Around half past 1:00, it had already gotten up to the very front of the Tauride Palace, but had not yet burst inside. The negotiators from the Duma informed the crowd that the private meeting was still in session, but that it had not reached a decision. Around 2:00, they finally came out and told the impatiently waiting crowd that the Temporary Committee of the Duma had been formed.[35]

As this was happening, Konovalov informed me of a conversation between Kerenskii and Miliukov that had occurred when Kerenskii went out to greet the crowd. The crowd was made up of soldiers and clusters of people from among the intelligentsia and the lower–middle classes [*intelligentov i polu-intelligentov*]. Kerenskii and Chkheidze were trying to contain the crowd by coming out and talking to them. On his way to greet the crowd, Kerenskii turned around and asked Miliukov, "Which program should I tell them about?" "That should be obvious," Miliukov replied. "Which one?" asked Kerenskii. "The program of our [Progressive] Bloc," answered Miliukov. Kerenskii threw his arms up in despair. "What kind of program is that? We can't really stop at that now!" He exclaimed in disappointment and without asking anything further, approached the crowd.

During discussions on the creation of the Temporary [Duma] Committee, it was pointed out that officers should be represented on the Temporary Committee in order to restrain the soldiers, organize the masses of insurgent troops, and so on, since there were no officers among the insurgent troops. Rodzianko, Guchkov, Konovalov, Miliukov, Shul'gin, and I, having considered the possible choices, decided on General Manikovskii, but first needed to discover his whereabouts.[36] I telephoned his flat and he happened to be in. By the way, at this very moment before my own eyes A. I. Guchkov was writing the second of Rodzianko's telegrams to the tsar. His first telegram I had read earlier when I arrived at the Duma. Realizing that Manikovskii was alive and at home, Guchkov and I headed out on foot to see him.

We walked down Shpalernaia Street. The city already looked like it would for the next three days. Crowds of soldiers were moving down Shpalernaia Street, all in one direction. From the other direction emerged the 9th Squadron of the Reserve Cavalry Regiment, still with an officer. However, no shooting occurred. The cavalrymen dismounted, talked to the approaching soldiers, and all was resolved peacefully. Sergievskaia and Zakhar'evskaia

Streets were impassable because of the heavy shooting, some of which even came from passing cars. Therefore, we turned onto Voskresenskii Avenue and then French Embankment. On the Neva, crowds of workers were walking on the ice. On the corner of Vyborgskii Bridge, some workers stopped us and asked if we were carrying weapons. One of them subjected us to a friendly search.

Then A. I. Guchkov told him: "Equality is equality—if that is the case, I am going to search you, too." One could hear rapid gunfire in the city. At the corner of Liteinyi and Sergievskaia, we saw a dense crowd. Someone was firing machine-guns. We finally got to General Manikovskii's flat via Gagarinskaia and Mokhovaia Streets. He was at home.[37] He was calm and in good spirits. He told us how he had escaped and made his way home. When a crowd rushed into the Main Artillery Administration, Manikovskii went out to face them. They demanded that he hand over weapons, but he said that he could not, as he did not have any stores of weapons or ammunition; he told them that he had only models. Then one soldier said: "Let him go, brothers [*brattsy*], he is the lead worker for defense," so they let him go. He left for home, but was stopped once again in the street. There too, he managed to make his way through without much trouble. Another soldier stopped Manikovskii and demanded that he surrender his personal weapon. The soldier asked: "Why are you wearing tsarist epaulets?" Manikovskii replied: "I will not take off my epaulets and saber. I will fight before I will remove my St. George Honor Saber—you will have to kill me." He was let go again. While Manikovskii was telling us his story, the gunfire on Liteinyi and Sergievskaia intensified.

A. I. Guchkov and I told General Manikovskii that it was imperative that a temporary minister of war be appointed at once, and that he should assume this post. "It is very difficult to make a decision right now," he replied. Although he did not refuse to take an active role in the cause, he did not give us a definite "yes." I do not remember exactly what he said, but his response was indirect, even evasive.[38] Our negotiations were interrupted several times by telephone calls: reports that several bridges had fallen to the insurgents, etc. It was disturbing news. Manikovskii stayed calm, but became unsettled when he got the news that the chief of the artillery factory had been murdered.[39]

After we left Manikovskii, on Mokhovaia Street we ran into a group that was peculiar, considering the events of the day. Count Kokovtsov, along with his wife and their little dog, had gone out for a walk at their usual time.[40] At the corner of Sergievskaia Street, a comical scene occurred when they got caught in the machine-gun crossfire and lost each other. The countess and the little dog disappeared somewhere and the count anxiously searched for them. In short, it was a comic skit: "Interrupted Walk."

It must have been around 3:30 or 4:00 in the afternoon (as it was already getting dark) when we left Manikovskii's flat and set out, again on foot, back to the Duma. When we saw that it was impossible to get in through the main entrance, we used the entrance near Zakhar'evskaia Street. Soldiers of the Volynskii Regiment, who were standing at the entrance, asked for our names. We identified ourselves. "He is the Tereshchenko whom we saw at the police station three days ago," exclaimed one of the soldiers, and they let us through. We came in near the finance department [of the Duma] and took off our coats. Servants were bringing all the food they could find from the buffet in order to feed the hungry soldiers who had come to the Duma at the end of their long day in the streets. Oh yes! I forgot to mention that when we were walking back from Manikovskii's flat, we were quite surprised to see what appeared to be the presence of organized medical teams.[41] Several motorized ambulances staffed by nurses and male student nurses were set up near the bridge. It was all sloppily organized, in part *partie de plaisir*, but in part it was also feistiness [*otchasti partie de plaisir, no otchasti khuliganstvo*]. At least someone had thought about doing it.

Returning to the Duma we saw many trucks filled with munitions (machine-guns, rifles, bullets) being unloaded and their contents brought inside. More and more trucks were arriving. Andrei Ivanovich Shingarev and I brought up the need to organize a supply of foodstuffs, as insurgent soldiers continued to pour in *en masse*, and we had nothing to feed them. We soon heard, from all directions, many and various conflicting reports and rumors: from the rumor that all regiments had surrendered, to the report that a loyalist expeditionary force was about to reach the city. Inside the Duma, there were simultaneous feelings of optimism and anxiety.

Around 6 or 7:00 in the evening, a group separated itself and formed the Soviet of Workers' Deputies. They were given a room.[42]

A rumor circulated that Shcheglovitov had been brought in. We were sitting in the president's office. Out of curiosity, many ran out of the office to gape at Shcheglovitov. I felt uncomfortable and remained. When I was leaving for home at seven in the evening, I accidentally walked past him. He was sitting in between three students and armed soldiers at a table, looking gloomy and pale. He was wearing a frock coat. He looked exactly the same when I came back to the Duma later that night. He sat absolutely motion-less at a table between boxes.

I left the Duma and headed out on foot for home. Along the way, near Liteinyi, I saw field artillery being brought out. From home, again on foot, I went to have dinner with my friends (the Tolstoys) at the Hermitage.[43] The mood was anxious there as well, because preparations were being made for the defense of the Winter Palace. They told me about the meas-ures being taken. Machine-guns were being positioned; General Bezobrazov was gathering troops on the square.[44] General Ratiev[45] reportedly clashed with General Bezobrazov, arguing that what he was doing would lead to unnecessary confrontation with the crowds, which had to be avoided in order to save the Palace. The premises where the Tolstoys and I were dining had connecting passageways between the Hermitage and the Winter Palace. During dinner, we twice heard a patrol from the first company of the Preobrazhenskii Regiment. We heard the soldiers marching in step on their way there. But on their way back, a quarter of an hour later, they were out of formation, in disarray. Because of all this, the mood at the dinner table was really anxious.

Late that evening, I set out once more for the Duma. I walked, but then noticed a truck and asked the driver for a lift. My own automobile had been missing since the morning, and I had no idea what had happened to it. The truck driver agreed and I asked him to drop me off on Furshtatskaia Street near house number 44, where the old man Kossikovskii had just died.[46] He was the father of the cavalry guard officer who had earlier spoken in favor of involving the army in a coup. He was not home, so I continued on to the Duma.

There was a great deal of gunfire on Furshtatskaia. Entering the Tauride Palace proved difficult, but I managed to squeeze myself in among a crowd of people entering from Tavricheskaia Street. Once inside, I witnessed a scene of total chaos. A great many soldiers were wandering about, and the Catherine Hall had been reduced to a pigsty. Many deputies were deeply troubled by what had become of the building. "You could not force pigs into this place," Tuliakov complained.

I entered the office of the president where I found several Duma depu-ties, including M. I. Skobelev, whom I had not previously met, and Kuz'ma Gvozdev, an acquaintance of mine from the War Industry Committee. I sat down beside him and we talked about the latest developments. On that day all of our aspirations and intentions remained quite modest; no one at the time was thinking of the kind of radical demands that would be undertaken on March the 1st and 2nd!

NOTES

1 The reference is probably to the meeting at Konovalov's Moscow residence on December 26, 1916, which was one of several information meetings of leading opposition figures held from December 24, 1916 to January 3, 1917. These meetings were devoted to the coordination of anti-government efforts, including a palace coup, and the selection of a future public cabinet, and represented the continuation of a series of earlier meetings organized by a prominent Moscow industrialist and Kadet, M. M. Fedorov, during September–October 1916.

2 That is, General A. A. Brusilov.

3 That is, Nikolai Iudovich Ivanov, the ineffectual commander of the punitive expedition against revolutionary Petrograd during the February Days, who had been Brusilov's predecessor as the front commander until March 15, 1917. Ivanov had for a long time been on friendly terms with Guchkov, "that great conspirator" and Tereshchenko's boss at the CWIC. See N. V. Savich, "Vospominaniia. Part I. Gosudarstvennaia duma," *Grani* 37, 127 (1983): 299.

4 According to Kerenskii, members of the Tereshchenko–Guchkov conspiracy were especially active in the fall–winter months of 1916–17. During this time they established and maintained contact with General Brusilov and apparently secured his "definite agreement" to the coup, which was scheduled for March 1, 1917. See the transcript of Kerenskii's conversation with B. I. Nikolaevskii [winter 1924–5], Paris. Notebook 1, 107–8. Coll. Nicolaevskii, Box 525-3. HIA.

5 "Him" refers here to Nicholas II, "her" to his wife, the Empress Aleksandra Fedorovna. Similar words were attributed to Brusilov at a January 1917 meeting of public figures at Rodzianko's Petrograd residence, which Tereshchenko also attended. See M. V. Rodzianko, *Krushenie imperii* (New York, 1986), 208.

6 At that time, the headquarters of the southwestern front was located in Kamenets-Podol'skii, a town and railway station in the Volyn' region of western Ukraine.

7 Rodzianko, Maklakov, and Tereshchenko visited Brusilov at his previous headquarters in Berdichev in the middle of July 1916. Rodzianko, *Krushenie imperii*, 174; A. A. Brusilov, *Moi vospominaniia* (Moscow: ROSSPEN, 2001), 197.

8 Most offices of the CWIC, including its Labor Group, were located at 46 Liteinyi Avenue.

9 On January 27, 1917, the police arrested nine members of the Menshevik defensists-dominated Labor Group of the CWIC at their Liteinyi office, including its chairman K. A. Gvozdev and one of its secretaries, B. O. Bogdanov. However, one member, E. Maevskii, escaped, while the group's other secretary, L. M. Pumpianskii, had been arrested earlier. Only three members of the group avoided arrest: the police spy and Menshevik V. M. Abrosimov, the SR Ia. S. Ostapenko, and the Menshevik Ia. I. Anasovskii. The last two were arrested on February 25. See n. 20 below.

10 This may have been the meeting that took place on January 29, following the arrest of the CWIC's labor group on the 27th. According to a police report from early February 1917, Guchkov chaired the meeting in which representatives of the CWIC, Zemgor, State Council, and many Duma factions (with the exception of the nationalistic Right) participated. The report specifically mentions Konovalov, Chkheidze, Kerenskii, Bublikov, Miliukov, and Kadet M. S. Adzhemov, but not Tereshchenko, though his participation should not be ruled out. The main goal of the meeting appears to have been the creation of a conspiratorial coordinating center between the labor movement and the liberal and moderate opposition groups. See

GARF, f. 1467, op. 1, d. 782, ll. 38–38ob., 39, 51; *Burzhuaziia nakanune Fevral'skoi revoliutsii* (Moscow and Leningrad: Gosizdat, 1927), 180–4.

11 Medved' (bear) was a large brasserie-style restaurant (29 private rooms and 200 staffers) frequented by Petersburg cultural and aristocratic elites. It was located on Bol'shaia Koniushennaia Street (no. 27), between Nevskii Avenue and the Moika, and operated from 1878 to 1929.

12 Tereshchenko is probably referring to a separate meeting of the plotters, without the representatives of the Progressive Bloc or public organizations, which could have taken place only after February 21. Nicholas II was with his family in Tsarskoe Selo until early afternoon on February 22, at which time he left for General Headquarters (*Dnevnik imperatora Nikolaia II* [Moscow: Orbita, 1991], 624). Thus, the plotters could have met either in the evening of the 22nd or on the 23rd. According to the palace commandant V. N. Voeikov, Nicholas II had originally planned to stay in General Headquarters for four days, until February 28. GARF, f. 1467, op. 1, d. 1038, l. 20b. This is also consistent with Kerenskii's testimony as recorded by Nikolaevskii. See n. 4 above.

13 On September 2, 1917, two days after General A. M. Krymov committed suicide following the collapse of the Kornilov movement, Tereshchenko told Petrograd reporters that Krymov had been the only general who agreed to participate in the prerevolutionary plot against Nicholas II that included Tereshchenko and D. L. Viazemskii. The coup was to take place in early March 1917, at which time Krymov was expected to come to Petrograd from the front. ("M. I. Tereshchenko o generale Krymove," *Den'*, September 2, 1917, 2, and *Russkie vedomosti*, September 3, 1917, 5). When, years later, Guchkov was asked about Tereshchenko's statement, he repeatedly (and probably correctly) denied Krymov's direct involvement, though not his knowledge, in his plot. See A. I. Guchkov to S. P. Mel'gunov, June 2, 1930, Box 226, Papers of S. P. Mel'gunov, British Library of Political and Economic Science, Division of Archives and Rare Books (BLPES); S. Mel'gunov, *Na putiakh k dvortsovomu perevorotu. Zagovory pered revoliutsiei 1917 goda* (Paris: Knizhnoe delo "Rodnik," 1931), 149–53; S. Lyandres and A. V. Smolin, eds., *Aleksandr Ivanovich Guchkov rasskazyvaet…Vospominaniia predsedatelia Gosudarstvennoi dumy i voennogo ministra Vremennogo pravitel'stva* (Moscow: "Voprosy istorii," 1993), 23, 133–4. See also Guchkov's testimony as recorded by B. I. Nikolaevskii and B. I. El'kin in Berlin, in the late 1920s, "Zapis' vospominanii A. I. Guchkova," l. 7, in Coll. Nicolaevskii, Box 775, f. 14, HIA. Krymov, who at the time commanded the Composite Cossacks Division at the southwestern front, visited Petrograd on February 9, 1917, and participated in a meeting of oppositional figures at Rodzianko's residence during which Tereshchenko famously called for overthrow of Nicholas II. The general returned to his unit two days later than expected, on February 11. See Rodzianko, *Krushenie imperii*, 204–5, and Krymov's service record in RGVIA, f. 409, op. 1, d. 52627.

14 In the late 1920s, Tereshchenko's co-conspirator Guchkov testified in a confidential statement (solicited by his executor B. I. El'kin and the Menshevik historian B. I. Nikolaevskii) that at the end of February 1917 Tereshchenko was supposed to visit the Guards Corps deployed on the western front in order to recruit officers for the projected coup, but that "the February events" prevented him from leaving the capital. GARF, f. 5868, op. 1, d. 117, l. 6; d. 62, l. 22.

15 This may have been one of the several meetings during February 24–6 called to coordinate elections in the city workers' districts to what two days later would come to be known as the Petrograd Soviet. See also part I of the Skobelev interview (Chapter 10).

16 This may have been a meeting of the CWIC scheduled to coincide with planned workers' demonstrations and the opening of the last session of the fourth Duma (on February 14), as well as renewed demands for a responsible ministry.

17 Ivan Nikitich Tuliakov (1877–1918) was a peasant (later metalworker) from the Don region, and a Social Democratic (Menshevik) deputy to the fourth Duma from the Don Cossacks'

region. During the February Revolution he worked with the insurgent soldiers in the Tauride Palace, and on March 5, 1917 was sent to the Black Sea Fleet headquarters in Sevastopol as a commissar of the Duma Committee and the Petrograd Soviet.

18 That is, A. P. Balk, who recalled that Guchkov tried to reach him several times on the telephone during the night of February 25–6, then visited his office and after being told that the city police chief was at a meeting with Prince Golitsyn, telephoned the premier's office. Both Balk and Golitsyn suspected the reason for Guchkov's persistence and hence avoided a direct conversation. See "Gibel' tsarskogo Petrograda. Fevral'skaia revoliutsiia glazami gradonachal'-nika A.P. Balka," ed.V. G. Bortnevskii and V. Iu. Cherniaev, *Russkoe proshloe* 1 (1991): 41.

19 That is, the last premier of the tsarist government.

20 It appears that by the end of the detention saga only two of the arrested activists remained in police custody: Ia. I. Anasovskii and Ia. S. Ostapenko. These were the two members of the CWIC's Labor group who escaped arrest on January 27. See S. V. Kulikov, "Tsentral'nyi voenno-promyshlennyi komitet i Fevral'skaia revoliutsiia. K voprosu o sootnoshenii faktov organizovannosti i stikhiinosti," *Vlast', obshchestvo i reformy v Rossii: istoriia, istochnik, istoriografiia. Materialy Vserossiiskoi nauchnoi konferentsii 6–7 dekabria 2006 g.* (St. Petersburg: Olearius Press, 2007), 265.

21 Skobelev mentioned similar activities in his interview on May 29, 1917. There are also additional testimonies supporting the Konovalov–Tereshchenko information that in some Petrograd factories election of delegates to the district soviets had begun as early as February 24 and continued through the 27th. See Tsuyoshi Hasegawa, *The February Revolution, Petrograd, 1917* (Seattle and London: University of Washington Press, 1981), 326–32. Hasegawa questions the validity of those reports, but he was not able to consult the interviews with Skobelev or Tereshchenko.

22 Petrograd's Admiralty district included the area of the Winter Palace and the Palace Embankment, as well as the Field of Mars, the Moika, and Koniushennaia Square, where the barracks of the Pavlovskii's 4th company were located.

23 The colonel in question was commander of the Pavlovskii reserve battalion, A. N. Eksten, who had been killed by a group of insurgent soldiers (see n. 2 to the Gerasimov interview, Chapter 5). However, the first reports on the uprising of the battalion's 4th company indicated that Eksten had been wounded (Cherniaev, "Vosstanie Pavlovskogo polka 26 fevralia 1917 g.," *Rabochii klass Rossii, ego soiuzniki i politicheskie protivniki v 1917 godu*, (Leningrad: Nauka, 1989), 175 n. 35; *Fevral'skaia revoliutsiia 1917 goda: sbornik dokumentov i materialov* (Moscow: RGGU, 1996), 109, 206). The ensign in question, who led a small detachment of the 4th company against the mounted police near Nevskii Avenue and Catherine Canal, was wounded but was soon evacuated in someone's automobile. His identity remains unknown. See Ivan Lukash, *Pavlovtsy* (Petrograd: Osvobozhdennaia Rossiia, no. 6; 1917), 6–7; Cherniaev, "Vosstanie Pavlovskogo polka," 160–2.

24 Rodzianko resided with his family on Furshtatskaia Street (no. 20), only a short walk from the Tauride Palace.

25 In an abbreviated draft transcript of this interview, which served as a basis for the master version, the description of events of February 27 begins with a more specific note that is somewhat more revealing: "[on the] 27th [at] 9¼—Manikovskii regarding public and military matters." See Interview with Tereshchenko, June 7, 1917, transcript in either Krupskaia's or Pavlov's hand, MAPP, FA. In yet another transcript of the Tereshchenko interview, recorded by R. Nikoladze, the same description carries an even more specific connotation: "Negotiations with Gen[eral] Manik[ovskii] took place on the 27th." Ibid., l. 4.

26 A. A. Adlerberg resided on Kamennoostrovskii Avenue on the city's Petrograd Side, across the Troitskii Bridge from the Palace Embankment and Millionnaia Street.

27 This may have been Vladimir Aleksandrovich Adlerberg (d. 1966), who at the time was an officer in the Life Guards of His Majesty's Ulans Regiment.

28 Vladimir Nikolaevich Ipat'ev (1867–1952) was a prominent Russian (after 1930 American) chemist and a lieutenant general in the imperial army (1916). From 1916 to 1917, he organized and headed the chemical committee for the development and production of new explosives, incendiary, and asphyxiate materials under the Main Artillery Administration (MAA). He is considered the founder of the Russian military chemical industry. In his memoirs, Ipat'ev described the events of the morning of February 27, 1917 but did not mention Tereshchenko. V. N. Ipat'ev, *Zhizn' odnogo khimika*, vol. II: *1917–1930* (New York: Izdatel'stvo imeni Chekhova, 1945), 10–11.

29 This may have been Vladimir Ivanovich Timiriazev (1849–1919), a prominent Russian entrepreneur, sometime state official, and elected member of the State Council. From 1915 to 1917, he was a member of the Special Council on Defense and in this capacity may have come to the MAA on the morning of February 27 to discuss some business with general Manikovskii. Knox corroborates Tereshchenko's account that he and Ipat'ev came to the MAA together at around 10:00 in the morning. See Alfred W. F. Knox, *With the Russian Army, 1914–1917. Being Chiefly Extracts from the Diary of A Military Attaché*. 2 vols. (London: Hutchinson & Co., 1921), II: 553.

30 See n. 39 below.

31 Tereshchenko's mother, Elizaveta Mikhailovna née Sarancheva (d. 1921), was the daughter of lieutenant general Mikhail Andreevich Saranchev (d. 1885); her uncle, Vasilii Andreevich, was a colonel in the army; her brother, Andrei Mikhailovich Saranchev (1862–1935), was also a career military officer with the rank of lieutenant general (1911).

32 Knox confirmed in his memoirs that Tereshchenko was the first to leave the building by way of a rear exit. After that, the British military attaché and Ipat'ev went to pick up their coats near the main entrance. Knox then walked one floor up to Manikovskii's office, but the general was not there. Knox, *With the Russian Army, 1914–1917*, II: 555.

33 There apparently had been several meetings scheduled for the morning of the 27th (between 9:30 and 11:00), including conferences of the Progressive Bloc leadership and the Council of Elders. See GARF, f. 9026, op. 1, d. 3, l. 191; RGIA, f. 1276, op. 8, d. 12, ll. 110–11, S. P. Mansyrev, "Moi vospominaniia o Gosudarstvennoi dume," *Istorik i sovremennik* 3 (1922): 24.

34 The private meeting of the Duma members lasted, with interruptions, from about 2:30 to 4:00 or 4:30 in the afternoon on February 27. Tereshchenko may have been referring to the meeting of the Council of Elders, scheduled the previous day for the morning of the 27th, which was still in session around noon and possibly lasted until 1:00 in the afternoon.

35 In actuality, it was Rodzianko who informed "the impatiently waiting crowd" that the question of the new Duma authority was being decided by the deputies at that very moment. The Temporary Duma Committee (or the Duma Committee) was formed and an announcement made closer to 5:00 that afternoon.

36 Tereshchenko's testimony is most valuable in naming the persons involved in the decision to choose General Manikovskii as the most senior military figure to work with the new Duma authority. Yet it is also quite misleading, for it was Tereshchenko who went to see the general on the morning of the soldiers' uprising (February 27), and it was also his close ally Nekrasov who suggested Manikovskii's candidacy to become a temporary military dictator at the start of the private meeting, about 2:30 that afternoon and again in the evening, during the meeting with Grand Duke Mikhail. See *Fevral'skaia revoliutsiia 1917 goda*, 113, 146; Lyandres, "Protokol'naia zapis' 'chastnogo' soveshchaniia chlenov Gosudarstvennoi dumy 27 fevralia 1917 g. kak istochnik po istorii parlamentarizma v Rossii," in V. I. Startsev, ed., *Istoriia parlamentarizma v Rossii (k 90-letiiu I Gosudarstvennoi dumy). Sbornik nauchnykh statei* (St. Petersburg, 1996), II: 30–1.

37 Manikovskii resided on Mokhovaia Street (no. 1).

38 Countess L. L. Vasil'chikova, whose brother D. L. Viazemskii was a leading member of the Guchkov–Tereshchenko plot, supported the general accuracy of this interpretation. According to her memoirs, her brother and her husband, the Octobrist deputy Prince I. S. Vasil'chikov, accompanied Tereshchenko on his visit to Manikovskii (*Ischeznuvshaia Rossiia. Vospominaniia kniagini Lidii Leonidovny Vasil'chikovoi (1886–1919)* (St. Petersburg: Peterburgskie sezony, 1995), 358). She did not mention Guchkov, but his presence was confirmed by V. N. Kokovtsov, who had run into Guchkov and Tereshchenko on Mokhovaia Street, not far from the MAA. See V. N. Kokovtsov, *Iz moego proshlogo. Vospominaniia (1903–1919 gg)* 2 vols. (Moscow: Nauka, 1992, 2nd edn), II: 341.

39 This may have been major general Nikolai Ivanovich Matafanov (1865–1917), who was a member of the artillery committee under the MAA, and chief (*nachal'nik*) of the Petrograd artillery factory from May 13, 1916.

40 Count Vladimir Nikolaevich Kokovtsov (1853–1943) was a minister of finance (1904–5, 1906–14), an appointed member of the State Council (1906–17), and Russia's prime minister from September 1911 to January 1914. After the February Revolution he was briefly detained by the Provisional Government, then released and stayed in Russia until November 1918. He later lived in Paris. Countess Anna Fedorovna née Oom (1860–1950) was V. N. Kokovtsov's wife. In February 1917, the couple resided on Mokhovaia Street (no. 27).

41 These may have been groups of several dozens of medical cadets from the Military Medical Academy, organized by Professor Colonel V. A. Oppel' and one of his senior cadets, A. S. Maksimovich. See A. B. Nikolaev, *Revoliutsiia i vlast': IV Gosudarstvennaia duma, 27 fevralia–3 marta 1917 goda* (St. Petersburg: RGPU, 2005), 169; "Mediko-sanitarnaia organizatsiia Tavricheskogo dvortsa v dni revoliutsii," *IVKGD* 3 (May 4, 1917): 8.

42 This was room no. 13, previously used by the Duma Budget Commission. It was reportedly secured for the nascent Petrograd Soviet by the Socialist deputies Kerenskii, Chkheidze, and Skobelev on the afternoon of February 27.

43 Count Dmitrii Ivanovich Tolstoi (1860–1941) was a prominent art collector and connoisseur; from 1909 to 1917 he was director of the Hermitage Museum and deputy director of the Museum of Alexander III (The Russian Museum). On March 3, 1917, he was appointed commissar in charge of the temporary administration of museums (RGIA, f. 1278, op. 5, d. 1245, ll. 12–120b.). Countess Elena Mikhailovna née Chertkova (1865–1955) was the wife of D. I. Tolstoi. At the time, the couple resided in the Old Hermitage Pavilion on the Palace Embankment.

44 Vladimir Mikhailovich Bezobrazov (1857–1932) was the general of the cavalry, and the disgraced commander of the Guards Corps (until August 24, 1915) and of the Special Army (in July 1916). He subsequently held no position of responsibility, but in February 1917 he succeeded in securing personal audiences with the tsar and Aleksandra Fedorovna, who appealed to her husband "to remember" the old loyal warrior when a suitable position became available (*Skorbnyi put' Romanovykh, 1917–1918 gg. Gibel' tsarskoi sem'i. Sb. dokumentov i materialov*, ed. V. M. Khrustalev (Moscow: ROSSPEN, 2001), 28; *Dnevnik imperatora Nikolaia II*, 623). The February uprising presented an opportunity for the idle general to prove his worthiness to his emperor. Bezobrazov's Petrograd flat was on Millionnaia Street (no. 38), next to the Palace Square and the barracks of the first company of Preobrazhenskii's reserve battalion on Millionnaia (no. 33). Although there are no independently confirmed reports that Bezobrazov "was gathering troops on the square," he did offer his services to General Khabalov, the commander of the Petrograd military district. On the night of February 27, he visited the government headquarters in the Admiralty and presented his plan for capturing the Tauride Palace, arresting the Duma leaders, and thus defeating the uprising. His advice was ignored. (N. F.

Akaemov, "Agoniia starogo rezhima (po pristavskim doneseniiam i pokazaniiam svidetelei," *Istoricheskii vestnik* 148: xxvi–xxvii; "Gibel' tsarskogo Petrograda," *Russkoe proshloe* 1 (1991): 53). In his diary, Bezobrazov confirmed his presence in the Winter Palace that night, and that he was advising the commander of the Preobrazhenskii reserve battalion, Colonel K. S. Argutinskii-Dolgorukov, on measures to defend the palace (Vladimir Mikhailovich Bezobrazov, *Diary of the Commander of the Russian Imperial Guard, 1914–1917*, ed. Marvin Lyons (Boynton Beach, FL: Dramco Publishers, 1994), D.123–5).

45 Prince Ivan Dmitrievich Ratiev (Ratishvili) (1868–1958) was a retired cavalry officer of Georgian extraction, who in 1913 was appointed acting chief of the Winter Palace police and lieutenant colonel of the Imperial Guard cavalry. He was promoted to colonel in 1916, but never reached the rank of general. During both the February Revolution and the Bolshevik assault on the Winter Palace in October, he was widely credited with saving the palace treasures from being looted and destroyed by the mob. In recognition of his efforts to protect "the people's treasures," the Provisional Government appointed him deputy commandant of the Winter Palace in April 1917, while in November the Bolshevik government appointed him commandant of the Winter Palace and of all state museums and palaces of the Petrograd District.

46 This and the next sentence refer to the jurist and mid-level official (actual state councilor) Vladimir Vladimirovich Kossikovskii and to his son, Dmitrii Vladimirovich Kossikovskii (1882–1944). The latter was a *rotmistr* (cavalry captain) in the Cavalry Guards Regiment of the 1st Cavalry Guards Division, where he served following his graduation from the Imperial Law College in 1903 and the Nicholas Cavalry School shortly thereafter. From 1911 to 1914 Kossikovskii also served (without formally leaving his unit) as a personal adjutant to the liberal Grand Duke Nikolai Mikhailovich, who was known for his criticism of court camarilla and his tacit approval of the idea of a palace coup. During the February Revolution, Kossikovskii belonged to the core officers' group of the MC (along with other would-be conspirators Engel'gardt, Polovtsov, V. P. Gil'bikh, and Balabin). See GARF, f. 3348, op. 1, d. 141, l. 270, Engel'gardt's interview; RGVIA, f. 3545, op. 4, d. 1398; ibid, f. 400, op. 11, d. 128; ibid., f. 409, d.7467; OR RGB, f. 218, f. 306–3, l. 94 (308). Kossikovskii's subsequent fate deserves a comment here. Not long after the February Revolution he reportedly turned into a committed monarchist; in 1918 he belonged to a small group of officers that contemplated rescuing the former tsar from Bolshevik custody in Ekaterinburg; during the civil war he fought against the Reds in the South, then emigrated to Serbia, pledged allegiance to Grand Duke Kirill Vladimirovich, and was active in various monarchist organizations in emigration. In 1941 he joined the so-called Russkii okhrannyi korpus or Russisches Schutzkorps Serbien, organized by the German army to fight against Tito's communist guerrilla force in Yugoslavia. Curiously, his older sister, Aleksandra Vladimirovna (1875–1923) was a longtime lady-in-waiting to the tsar's younger sister Ol'ga and, from 1904 to 1907, the presumed fiancée of Grand Duke Mikhail Aleksandrovich. During the war years, she served as a nurse in the Duma's Frontline Detachment of the Red Cross, organized by her friend and fellow Kadet I. P. Demidov. See I. Demidov, "A.V.," *Poslednie novosti*, April 21, 1923: 2; Rosemary and Donald Crawford, *Michael and Natasha. The Life and Love of Michael II, the Last of the Romanov Tsars* (New York: Avalon Books, 2000), 6, 10–12, 16; OR RGB, f. 218, f. 306–3, l. 94 (308); S. V. Volkov, *Entsiklopediia Grazhdanskoi voiny. Beloe dvizhenie* (St. Petersburg: "Neva," Moscow: Olma-Press, 2002), 268–9.

13

The Interviews: An Interpretation

THE INTERVIEWS IN this volume take the contemporary reader to the heart of the February Days. They present wide-ranging perspectives on the revolution's politics and rapidly shifting dynamics from its leading participants—men of varying ages, experiences, and temperaments, and from diverse political, social, and cultural backgrounds. Not yet overwhelmed by post-1917 labels and quarrels over "who lost Russia," the interviews capture both the intensity and the details of the unfolding revolutionary drama with a fresher, less partisan, and more discerning eye than subsequent memoir accounts. The interviews provide crucial new evidence that challenges, modifies, or confirms aspects of the traditional interpretation. They are particularly useful in illuminating the nature and workings of the so-called dual power arrangement between the Duma Committee and the Petrograd Soviet during the first days of the February Revolution, the origins of the Petrograd Soviet, and the role of the Duma Military Commission in neutralizing and defeating the forces of the old regime.

Contrary to the dominant view that allegedly wavering liberal and moderate Duma politicians were forced to become revolutionaries by either the insurgents or their more radical Socialist colleagues, the interviews show that the Duma President M. V. Rodzianko, the Chairman of the Central War Industry Committee A. I. Guchkov, and other "reluctant revolutionaries" acted independently of any such pressure. In fact, they often preempted their Socialist colleagues, setting the pace for subsequent actions by the Petrograd Soviet. Actions that have traditionally been presented as examples of the liberals' "paralyzing indecisiveness" or attributed to their inherent fear of popular revolt can actually be explained in the context of institutional interests, competing visions and strategies, personal ambitions, and unforeseen circumstances that required instant readjustments of previously determined courses of action. The formation of the Duma Committee on the first day of the revolution, that is, Rodzianko's decision to commit the Duma to a revolutionary course, as well as his support for the abdications of Nicholas II and his brother, Grand Duke Mikhail Aleksandrovich—the final and arguably most consequential acts of the February Revolution—are cases in point.

No single interview is likely to settle the dominant historiographical debates on whether spontaneity or leadership played a larger role in the February Revolution, or whether it was more political, social, cultural, or regional in character.[1] Taken together, however, these previously untold stories do add credence to the "leadership" and political interpretations, bringing us a tangible step closer to a more comprehensive and balanced understanding of 1917. Indeed, the interviews introduce so many new details on events, personalities, relationships, and motivations that the political history of the February Revolution needs to be rewritten to integrate all that is contained in this volume.

---

[1] For the most useful recent discussion of these and related debates in the English-language literature of the last two decades, see Rex A. Wade, "The Revolution at Ninety-(One): Anglo-American Historiography of the Russian Revolution of 1917," *Journal of Modern Russian History and Historiography* (*JMRHH*) 1 (2008): 1–42; Steve A. Smith, "Writing the History of the Russian Revolution After the Fall of Communism," *Europe–Asia Studies* 46 (1994): 563–78; Stephen Kotkin, "1991 and the Russian Revolution: Sources, Conceptual Categories, Analytical Frameworks," *Journal of Modern History* 70 (1998): 384–425. See also Daniel Orlovsky, "A Survey of Documents Published Since 1991 on Governance in 1917," *JMRHH* 1 (2008): 43–5. For an informed discussion of recent research that has "shifted its focus away from the capitals and political elites," see Sarah Badcock, "The Russian Revolution: Broadening Understandings of 1917," *History and Compass* 6, 1 (2008): 243–6. Useful discussions of mostly pre-1991 historiography are in Edward Acton, "The Revolutions and its Historians. The Critical Companion in Context," in Acton et al., eds., *Critical Companion to the Russian Revolution, 1914–1921* (Bloomington and Indianapolis: Indiana University Press, 1997), 3–11; Tsuyoshi Hasegawa, "The February Revolution," in Acton et al., eds., *Critical Companion*, 48–54; Ronald Grigor Suny, "Revision and Retreat in the Historiography of 1917: Social History and Its Critics," *Russian Review* 53 (1994): 155–82. For the most recent discussion of the question of spontaneity and leadership, see S. V. Kulikov, "Tsentral'nyi Voenno-promyshlennyi komitet nakanune i v khode Fevral'skoi revoliutsii 1917 g.," *Rossiiskaia istoriia* 1 (2012): 69–71. See also David Longley, "Iakovlev's Question, Or the Historiography of the Problem of Spontaneity and Leadership in the Russian Revolution of February 1917," in Edith Rogovin Frankel, Jonathan Frankel, and Baruch Knei-Paz, eds., *Revolution in Russia: Reassessments of 1917* (Cambridge: Cambridge University Press, 1992), 365–87; Michael Melancon, *Rethinking Russia's February Revolution: Anonymous Spontaneity or Socialist Agency?* (University of Pittsburg: Carl Beck Papers in Russian and East European studies, 2000); V. I. Startsev, "Stikhiinost' i organizovannost' v Fevral'skom vosstanii 1917 goda v Petrograde," *80 let revoliutsii 1917 g. v Rossii* (St. Petersburg, 1997), 24–7.

This revision cannot, of course, be accomplished in a single interpretive chapter. But by examining just one relatively little-studied question—that of prerevolutionary conspiracies to overthrow Nicholas II—we can demonstrate the interviews' factual value as well as their broad interpretive implications.

Over the past eight decades, ever since the publication of S. P. Mel'gunov's seminal study of prerevolutionary conspiracies,[2] historians have tried to determine how seriously they should regard the Guchkov-led and other known plots to depose Nicholas II.[3] Answering this question depended largely on establishing whether any of the conspiracies progressed "beyond salon talk" or, as Guchkov put it in an often quoted phrase, "beyond the embryonic phase."[4] Here, however, the historians' efforts have been seriously handicapped by two factors: the paucity of direct and reliable evidence, and the assumption that, preempted by a popular revolt, "no conspiracy was actually put into effect."[5] Unable to reach definitive conclusions, historians more recently have shifted their focus to the role of palace coup conspiracies in shaping political conditions on the eve of the revolution. Here the results

[2] S. P. Mel'gunov, *Na putiakh k dvortsovomu perevorotu. Zagovory pered revoliutsiei 1917 goda* (Paris: Knizhnoe delo "Rodnik," 1931).

[3] See, for example, Bernard Pares, *The Fall of the Russian Monarchy. A Study of the Evidence* (London: Jonathan Cape, 1939), 429–31; V. S. Diakin, *Russkaia burzhuaziia i tsarizm v gody pervoi mirovoi voiny, 1914–1917* (Leningrad: Nauka, 1967), 298–310; V. Ia. Laverychev, *Po tu storonu barrikad* (Moscow: Nauka, 1968), 159; V. I. Startsev, *Russkaia burzhuaziia i samoderzhavie v 1905–1917 gg.* (Leningrad: Nauka, 1977), 189–90, 206–10, 237–40, 248–50; Startsev, *Russkoe politicheskoe masonstvo nachala XX veka* (St. Petersburg: Tret'ia Rossiia, 1996), 132–61; E. D. Chermenskii, *IV Duma i sverzhenie tsarizma v Rossii* (Moscow: Mysl', 1976), 238–45; George Katkov, *Russia 1917: The February Revolution* (New York: Harper & Row, 1969), 173–7, 181–7, 427–8; Richard Pipes, *The Russian Revolution, 1899–1919* (London: Collins Harvill, 1990), 269–70; Orlando Figes, *A People's Tragedy. A History of the Russian Revolution* (New York: Viking, 1996), 288–9. For a useful summary in English, see Tsuyoshi Hasegawa, *The February Revolution, Petrograd, 1917* (Seattle and London: University of Washington Press, 1981), 186–90; Hasegawa, "The February Revolution," in *Critical Companion*, 48–9; O. R. Airapetov, *Generaly, liberaly i predprinimateli. Rabota na front i na revoliutsiiu (1907–1917)* (Moscow: "Tri kvadrata," 2003), 191–204; S. V. Kulikov, "Fevral'skaia 'revoliutsiia sverkhu' ili fiasko 'generalov dlia pronunsiamento,'" *Rossiia XXI vek* 4 (2004): 134–79. For a recent discussion, see Semion Lyandres, "O dvortsovom perevorote ia vpervye uslyshal posle revoliutsiii ...," *Russian History/Histoire Russe* 32, 2 (Summer 2005): 216–18.

[4] The phrase "embryonic phase" or "embryonic plot" belongs to Guchkov, who, as far as we can establish, first used it during his conversations with B. I. Nikolaevskii in the late 1920s and in correspondence with Mel'gunov in 1930 ("Zapis' vospominanii A. I. Guchkova," typescript, p. 7, Coll. Nicolaevskii, Box 775, f. 14, HIA; A. I. Guchkov to S. P. Mel'gunov, June 16, 1930, Box 226, Papers of S. P. Mel'gunov, British Library of Political and Economic Science, Division of Archives and Rare Books [BLPES]).

[5] Hasegawa, *The February Revolution*, 185, 188, 190.

have proven to be more fruitful. It has been credibly argued that by the end of 1916 many among the political and military elites, including the aristocracy, had come to recognize that "only such a drastic move" as Nicholas's removal from the throne "could improve the government's ability to prosecute the war, head off a popular revolt and save the Russian state."[6]

This observation is important to our understanding of prevailing reactions to the tsar's near complete isolation on the eve of the revolution, but it tells us little about the plots themselves (their membership and plans), or whether any of them, particularly Guchkov's, had been set in motion by the start of the February uprising. Also obscured has been the degree to which Rodzianko and Miliukov, the leaders of the Duma Committee and two of the most recognizable public figures in the country, accepted the idea of a palace coup generally and embraced the Guchkov plot specifically.

The interviews go a long way toward answering these important questions. They reveal previously unknown details of the Guchkov-led plot, including the name of a key participant. By suggesting a direct connection between the plotters' plans and their attempts to establish a new authority on February 27, 1917, the interviews take debates about the existence and significance of prerevolutionary conspiracies to a new interpretive level. In turn, this highlights the importance of prerevolutionary plans and attitudes in explaining key political decisions that Duma leaders took during the decisive first days of the revolution.

The Guchkov Plot: Membership, Prerevolutionary Plans, and Attempts at Implementation during the February Days

The interviews confirm that the Guchkov plot was the most advanced of the known conspiracies and that four of its five leaders were Guchkov, Prince Viazemskii, Nekrasov, and Tereshchenko.[7] In his interview, Tereshchenko also disclosed for the first time the name of the fifth and leading military participant, the cavalry guards' captain (*rotmistr*) Dmitrii

---

[6] Rex A. Wade, *The Russian Revolution, 1917*, 2nd edn (Cambridge: Cambridge University Press, 2005), 22.

[7] These were not the same four that have appeared in the literature over the years. The names of A. I. Konovalov, Kerenskii, and most frequently that of General Krymov have been listed in various combinations as members of the core group. See, for example, Hasegawa, *The February Revolution*, 191, 195–6; Airapetov, *Generaly, liberaly i predprinimateli*, 203–4; and n. 13 to the Tereshchenko interview (Chapter 12).

Vladimirovich Kossikovskii, whose role and identity were corroborated, albeit indirectly, by Engel'gardt.[8] This information challenges Guchkov's later "confession" that he "could not succeed in involving [in the plot] anyone from the military."[9] But the significance of Tereshchenko's testimony goes beyond discrediting Guchkov's deliberate effort to distort the historical record. By naming Kossikovskii, Tereshchenko in fact casts doubt on the long-held view that the conspirators failed to recruit energetic and capable officers, as a result of which the military side of the plot was prepared by amateurs, and was thus doomed from the beginning.[10]

We know little about Kossikovskii's reasons for joining the conspiracy against Nicholas II or, for that matter, what led this passionate officer "of the most prestigious regiment of the Russian army" less than a year later to become a staunch monarchist and a leading participant in the officers' plot to rescue the former tsar from Bolshevik custody in Ekaterinburg.[11] The interviews suggest that he was assigned a key role in the Guchkov plot, and that its success depended in large measure on Kossikovskii's swift and decisive actions.

He joined the conspiracy at the end of 1916, sometime after October. Years later Engel'gardt recalled that Kossikovskii had first approached him, and that he in turn introduced the cavalry officer to Guchkov. The two met in the quarters of the State Council (of which Guchkov was then an elected member) in the Mariinskii Palace and apparently agreed to collaborate.[12] Kossikovskii became the fifth and to this day the least known member of the "ruling five." But it was only in his May 1917 interview that Engel'gardt— never explicitly identifying his own involvement in the Guchkov plot, yet providing just enough details to make such a conclusion inescapable— revealed Kossikovskii's role. He was, "with the squadron from the 1st Cavalry

---

[8]   See n. 46 to the Tereshchenko interview, and n. 12 to the Engel'gardt interview (Chapter 3).

[9]   See Mel'gunov, *Na putiakh*, 149; Hasegawa, *The February Revolution*, 191.

[10]   Tugan-Baranovskii's remarks are a good example of this attitude. See his interview (Chapter 7).

[11]   OR RGB, f. 218 [Engel'gardt], f. 306–3, l. 94 (305); n. 46 to the Tereshchenko interview.

[12]   OR RGB, f. 218, f. 306–3, l. 94 (305). In his memoirs, Engel'gardt did not identify Kossikovskii by name, referring to him instead as "an officer from the most prestigious aristocratic regiment of the Russian army and former adjutant of one of the grand dukes." Guchkov was similarly elusive during his conversations with N. A. Basily, calling Kossikovskii "a very valuable participant in the plot" who joined it at a later stage, presumably after Viazemskii. (S. Lyandres and A.V. Smolin, eds., *Aleksandr Ivanovich Guchkov rasskazyvaet…Vospominaniia predsedatelia Gosudarstvennoi dumy i voennogo ministra Vremennogo pravitel'stva* [Moscow: "Voprosy istorii," 1993], 20.)

Guard [Reserve] Regiment [of the 1st Cavalry Guards Division], [to] march
on Tsarskoe [Selo] and carry out a coup."[13]

The available evidence suggests that this was one of the three possible
plans which in the end had to be abandoned for fear of risking a clash with
a local garrison. The final plan envisioned capturing the tsar's train along the
railway line somewhere in Novgorod province, not far from the so-called
Arakcheev barracks in Krechevitsy—the home of the 1st Cavalry Guard
Reserve Regiment—and forcing him to abdicate.[14] Kossikovskii was to
lead a small cavalry unit from this regiment to seize the tsar on his return
from General Headquarters on March 1, 1917, as had been originally anticipated.[15] Kossikovskii thus emerges as the key military figure in the plot,
which, considering the involvement of only one small mobile cavalry unit,
could be easily adjusted to the circumstances as they unfolded. This also suggests that what is known as the Guchkov plot had a sound plan of action,
and a better organized and more committed military force than many well-
informed contemporaries knew about or were willing to acknowledge.
What makes this conclusion even more plausible is that the execution of the
plot's military component was entrusted to an accomplished and extremely
well-connected cavalry guards' officer. Indeed, Kossikovskii had previously
served as personal adjutant to the liberal Grand Duke Nikolai Mikhailovich
and his older sister, Aleksandra Vladimirovna Kossikovskaia, was a lady-in-
waiting to Grand Duchess Ol'ga (the tsar's younger sister) as well as the
ex-fiancée of Grand Duke Mikhail Aleksandrovich.[16]

---

[13] See the Engel'gardt interview. Compare what he says in the interview to his unpublished
memoirs, in OR RGB, f. 218, f. 306-3, l. 94 (308).

[14] "Zapis' vospominanii A. I. Guchkova," p. 4, Coll. Nicolaevskii, Box 775, f. 14, HIA; Lyandres and
Smolin, eds., *Guchkov rasskazyvaet*, 18. Different stations have been named, but all are located within a
short distance of each other and along the imperial train's route between General Headquarters and
Tsarskoe Selo. In his interrogation by the Soviet secret police, Nekrasov named the village and train
station Medved', southwest of Novgorod, not far from the main railway line connecting Pskov, Staraia
Russa and Dno. Guchkov mentioned Chudovo, a railway hub just north of Novgorod. "Iz sledstvennykh del N. V. Nekrasova 1921, 1931 i 1939 godov," *Voprosy istorii* 11–12 (1998): 19–20; Lyandres and
Smolin, eds., *Guchkov rasskazyvaet*, 18. For Krechevytsy's location, see the Map of Railways (Map 2).

[15] Nicholas's initial plan was to leave General Headquarters on February 28, which would have
placed him in Tsarskoe Selo on the morning of March 1. See the Tereshchenko interview;
V. N. Voeikov's March 7, 1917 interrogation in GARF, f. 1467, op. 1, d. 1038, l. 1–10b.; and handwritten records of B. I. Nikolaevskii's conversation with Kerenskii in Paris [winter 1924–5] (Notebook 1,
pp. 107–8. Coll. Nicolaevskii, Box 525-3. HIA) and of Mel'gunov's with Kerenskii in 1930 (Papers of
S. P. Mel'gunov, Box 226, f. "Fevral'–Mart 1917 g. Besedy i pis'ma," l. 16, BLPES). See also GARF, f.
3348, op. 1, d. 132, l. 17.

[16] See n. 46 to the Tereshchenko interview and Kossikovskii's service record in RGVIA, f. 3545,
op. 4, d. 1398; ibid., f. 400, op. 11, d. 128; ibid., f. 409, d. 7467.

The fact that the coup envisioned by the plotters never took place does not mean that no part of their original plan was put into effect at the time of the February uprising.[17] In fact, a comparison of the new evidence from the interviews with the records of the Duma Military Commission makes it clear that at least some aspects of the Guchkov conspiracy were set in motion on February 27, 1917. Prior to the revolution, the plotters had intended to bring a "loyal force," selected from the guards' cavalry units stationed in the Arakcheev barracks, to Petrograd close to the time of the coup in late February 1917. Just as their plan called for, during the night of February 26–7, several hours *before* the outbreak of the soldiers' uprising, a detachment consisting of two squadrons (the 6th and the 9th, about two hundred cavalrymen altogether) from the Krechevitsy-based Guards' Reserve Cavalry Regiment of the 1st Cavalry Guards Division, did come to Petrograd.[18] Upon their arrival, the two squadrons were given temporary quarters in the barracks of the Life Guards Cavalry Regiment (located very close to the Duma, between Voskresenskii Avenue and Zakhar'evskaia and Shpalernaia Streets), but four hours later (by 8:00 in the morning) they had already begun patrolling a small area between the intersections of Nevskii with Liteinyi Avenue and Sadovaia Street in the heart of the city. In contrast to numerous other units stationed in Petrograd that day, the cavalrymen did not join the insurgency, maintaining discipline and cohesiveness during the rest of their twenty-four hour deployment in the capital.[19]

It remains unknown whether anyone from the two squadrons made contact with the plotters while the cavalrymen were stationed in Petrograd. But we can surmise from an oblique reference in Tereshchenko's interview that he and Guchkov (and possibly Viazemskii[20]) "accidentally" came upon the 9th squadron of the Guards' Reserve Cavalry Regiment and saw their accompanying officer around 2:30 that afternoon. The encounter took place on Shpalernaia Street, somewhere between the Tauride Palace and Liteinyi

---

[17] As has been argued, for example, by Hasegawa, *The February Revolution*, 188, 190, 197. See also Wade, *The Russian Revolution, 1917*, 23.

[18] See the record of Mel'gunov's conversation with Guchkov, Papers of S. P. Mel'gunov, Box 226, f. "Fevral'–Mart 1917 g. Besedy i pis'ma," l. 36ob., BLPES; Lyandres and Smolin, eds., *Guchkov rasskazyvaet*, 18, 20; RGIA, f. 1278, op. 5, d. 1353, l. 71. I thank Professor A. B. Nikolaev for providing this reference, upon request. Krechevitsy (now part of Novgorod) was the home for two Arakcheev barracks, named after military settlements established in the beginning of the nineteenth century by Alexander I's notorious adviser A. A. Arakcheev. See also Mel'gunov, *Na putiakh*, 148–54, and Hasegawa, *The February Revolution*, 187.

[19] RGIA, f. 1278, op. 5, d. 1353, l. 71–2.

[20] According to his sister's memoirs, [L. L. Vasil'chikova] *Ischeznuvshaia Rossiia. Vospominaniia kniagini Lidii Leonidovny Vasil'chikovoi (1886–1919)* (St. Petersburg: Peterburgskie sezony, 1995), 358.

Avenue—not exactly in the area that the cavalrymen were originally assigned to patrol but very close to their temporary barracks. We cannot be certain that the officer in question was Kossikovskii, but events over the next fourteen hours would prove that this supposition is not improbable.

By 4:00 in the afternoon, when dusk descended on the tumultuous northern city, both squadrons returned to their barracks only to receive new deployment orders early the next morning. The orders are noteworthy for their origins as well as their substance. First, they were issued by the Duma Military Commission in the name of the Duma Committee even though available sources provide no evidence that the cavalrymen had pledged allegiance to or formally placed themselves under the new authority. Second, it was none other than *rotmistr* Kossikovskii (now also working with the Military Commission) who was asked to deliver the new deployment orders and see to it that the squadrons "return to their home barracks in Krechevitsy and await further orders from the Duma Committee."[21] Finally, and perhaps most intriguingly, the orders were originally issued at about 2:00 in the morning on February 28 but then changed to 5:00.[22] This change appears to reflect the time of Nicholas's departure from General Headquarters.

Shortly after midnight on February 28, the Duma Committee commissar A. A. Bublikov, assisted by railway engineer Iu. V. Lomonosov and others, took control of the Transportation Ministry, which had its own telegraph station extending across the national railway system, and began supplying the Duma leaders with hourly updates on the movement of Nicholas's train.[23] In his interview Nekrasov, who monitored the tsar's whereabouts for the Duma Committee, recalled that he had been notified either at 2:00 or at 3:00 that the imperial trains had left General Headquarters for Tsarskoe Selo, which was around the time indicated on the initial deployment orders. But the trains were then delayed and did not leave the station until about 5:00, a change duly reflected in the orders.[24]

---

[21] A copy of the order's delivery slip (*otpusk*) is preserved in RGIA, f. 1278, op. 10, d. 60, l. 2. The document bears no signature, which was typical of the night of February 27–8. Many similar orders were issued by the Military Commission in the name of the Duma Committee during the first days of the revolution, and were usually signed by Nekrasov, Engel'gardt, or Rodzianko. On Kossikovskii's connection to the MC, see GARF, f. 3348, op. 1, d. 141, l. 270.

[22] RGIA, f. 1278, op. 10, d. 60, l. 2.

[23] Hasegawa, *The February Revolution*, 437. See also GARF, f. 3348, op. 1, d. 132, l. 17 and the Nekrasov interview. Nicholas left General Headquarters at 5:00 in the morning on February 28 (*Dnevnik imperatora Nikolaia II* [Moscow: Orbita, 1991], 625).

[24] See the Nekrasov interview (Chapter 8); *Dnevnik imperatora Nikolaia II*, 625.

Later that morning, as per their orders, the two squadrons arrived at the Nikolaevskii Railway Station and boarded the train after a brief skirmish with the soldiers guarding the station.[25] The cavalry units, however, did not proceed to their home barracks in Krechevitsy. Three days later they were still sitting at Chudovo, a railway hub some 26 miles (42 km) northeast of Krechevitsy.[26] The significance of this sudden delay is not difficult to ascertain. Considering its relatively short distance from Petrograd, only 71 miles (115 km) on a direct line, the force should have reached Chudovo the same day they departed Petrograd. In other words, they would have arrived there in time to disembark and prepare to prevent the passage of the tsar's train through that station to Tosno and from there to Tsarskoe Selo, as Nicholas had originally intended before reaching Malaia Vishera around 2:00 in the morning on March 1.[27] He was expected in Chudovo in less than two hours.

But then, as Hasegawa has demonstrated, Lieutenant K. F. Grekov, the revolutionary commandant of Nikolaevskii Railway Station, along with Nekrasov's contacts in the Transportation Ministry, deliberately deceived the tsar's entourage by reporting that the next two stations en route to Tsarskoe Selo, Liuban' and Tosno, "had been captured by the revolutionaries."[28] Apparently "the seizure of Liuban' and Tosno by the revolutionaries had not taken place," but because this was unknown to Nicholas's aides at the time, the imperial trains never reached Chudovo.[29] Instead, they were redirected to Bologoe and from there proceeded to Dno and Pskov, where Nicholas abdicated the next day. Considering, however, that the tsar could have attempted to get through to Tsarskoe Selo anyway (either ignoring the information from Petrograd or realizing that it was false), the presence of a reliable and mobile cavalry force strategically located at Chudovo should be viewed as a necessary precaution by the competent and well-organized plotters-cum-revolutionaries. That this force consisted of the same squadrons (and under the command of the same able and decisive officer) that were originally designated to carry out the coup suggests that a key part of

[25] RGIA, f. 1278, op. 5, d. 1353, l. 71–2.

[26] Ibid., l. 72.

[27] Hasegawa, *The February Revolution*, 438, 448–9; *Dnevnik imperatora Nikolaia II*, 625.

[28] Hasegawa, *The February Revolution*, 448–9; *Dnevnik imperatora Nikolaia II*, 625. On Grekov, see the interviews with Tugan-Baranovskii and Chikolini (Chapters 7 and 4).

[29] Hasegawa, *The February Revolution*, 449.

the plotters' plan, including Nicholas's arrest, could still have been implemented almost forty-eight hours into the revolution.[30]

More to the point, the fact that the two squadrons remained in Chudovo as late as midnight on March 2, that is, at about the time of Nicholas's abdication, adds credence to the idea that the cavalrymen were sent there to ensure his abdication. Had things gone badly in Pskov and Nicholas refused to give up the throne, any attempt to reach Tsarskoe Selo or Petrograd by way of either Staraia Russa–Novgorod–Chudovo or Bologoe–Chudovo could have been blocked by the cavalry force deployed in Chudovo, which was standing ready for "orders from the Duma Committee."[31]

Attempts to Establish Temporary Military Dictatorship on February 27, 1917

As the cavalry squadrons were patrolling the streets in the center of the capital, Kossikovskii's co-conspirators in the Tauride Palace moved ahead with the "political" component of the plot, aimed at establishing a temporary authority in the form of military rule. The interviews suggest that while both the military and political parts of the plan were closely interconnected and required coordination, the events of the first days demonstrated that they could be enacted independently of one another. Put otherwise, the establishment of the temporary authority did not need to wait until Nicholas's abdication. The role of military dictator was to be delegated to General A. A. Manikovskii, the chief of the Main Artillery Administration (MAA), who was popular with many leading opposition figures including Guchkov, Tereshchenko, and Engel'gardt, and who was rumored to have sympathized with the idea of a palace coup.[32]

On the morning of February 27, the first of Tereshchenko's many tasks for the day was to see A. A. Manikovskii in his office in the MAA, on the corner of

---

[30] On the Military Commission's order to arrest Nicholas on February 28, see the Chikolini interview, n. 17; the Tugan-Baranovskii interview, n. 48; and Hasegawa, *The February Revolution*, 438, 447–9.

[31] RGIA, f. 1278, op. 5, d. 1353, l. 72.

[32] See Mel'gunov, *Na putiakh*, 107, 193; Hasegawa, *The February Revolution*, 186; E. E. Petrov and K. O. Bitiukov, *Velikokniazheskaia oppozitsiia v Rossii 1915–1917 gg.* (St. Petersburg: Asterion, 2009), 75, 97, 181. See also V. V. Polikarpov, "22–23 fevralia 1917 goda v Petrograde," *Padenie imperii, revoliutsiia i grazhdanskaia voina v Rossii* (Moscow: Sotsial'no-politicheskaia mysl', 2010), 13.

Liteinyi and Shpalernaia.[33] It is unknown whether he was aware of the soldiers' revolt before he left his mansion on the Palace Embankment at around 9:00 in the morning. By the time he walked into the MAA building less than an hour later, however, he could see the full extent of the uprising with his own eyes. The MAA, already under attack, was soon taken over by the insurgents. Tereshchenko gave his interviewers (and posterity) a vivid, if self-serving, description of what happened. Everyone inside was either running for cover or busy trying to escape the building. Tereshchenko was among the latter, though he granted himself a dignified getaway in his recollection of this episode. He acted "slowly and calmly," and even had the fortitude (and the time) to "bid farewell to General Manikovskii."[34] It is highly unlikely, however, that the two had any time to discuss serious matters, which might explain why he and Guchkov had to make another attempt to see the general a few hours later.

From the MAA Tereshchenko rushed to the Duma (three long blocks down along Shpalernaia Street) to inform his co-conspirators of what he just witnessed on Liteinyi and to share his fears that Manikovskii was trapped inside and had possibly been massacred in the attack.[35] At least three of the other four leaders of the plot were already in the Duma, taking steps to form a new authority. Guchkov was in Rodzianko's office, helping him to compose his "second telegram to the tsar," in which he reiterated the previous day's call to name a popular figure who could form a cabinet that would enjoy the country's trust. (Viazemskii, who accompanied Guchkov everywhere during the first days, was also by his side.) In the meantime, Nekrasov convened a meeting of the leaders of several Duma factions to discuss the situation and ways to organize a temporary authority.[36]

---

[33] Tereshchenko's attempt to portray his visit to Manikovskii as unrelated and routine—after four days of unprecedented popular unrest and on the first morning of the soldiers' uprising—is hardly convincing. The general's other visitors that morning did not pretend to have come to the MAA for "business as usual," but did so precisely because of what was happening in the streets. See, for example, V. N. Ipat'ev, *Zhizn' odnogo khimika. Vospominaniia*, vol. II: *1917–1930* (New York, 1945), 10, 21, 23.

[34] See the Tereshchenko interview.

[35] See the interviews with Tereshchenko, Skobelev, and Nekrasov in this volume.

[36] Rodzianko's second telegram was compiled before noon, but sent to General Headquareters only at 12:40. See A. B. Nikolaev, *Revoliutsiia i vlast': IV Gosudarstvennaia duma, 27 fevralia–3 marta 1917 goda* (St. Petersburg: RGPU, 2005), 125; *Fevral'skaia Revoliutsiia 1917 goda. Sb. dokumentov i materialov* (Moscow: RGGU, 1996), 110–11; Chermenskii, *IV Duma*, 282; the interviews with Gerasimov and Skobelev; and Hasegawa, *The February Revolution*, 150. See also Guchkov to Mel'gunov, September 23, 1930, Mel'gunov Papers, Box 185, BLPES; Rodzianko's deposition, "Dopros M. V. Rodzianko, 4 September 1917," in *Padenie tsarskogo rezhima. Stenograficheskie otchety doprosov i pokazanii, dannykh v 1917 g. Chrezvychainoi Sledstvennoi komissii Vremennogo pravitel'stva*, vol. 6 (Moscow and Leningrad: Gosizdat, 1926), 262.

According to Skobelev, who participated in this meeting, which lasted from 11:00 to shortly after 12:00 noon, "Nekrasov burst in and reported" that the MAA had been taken over by the insurgents. "Reacting to that, Shingarev nervously exclaimed, 'Only Germans could have done this!'" Then "Nekrasov came in again and reported that General Manikovskii had apparently been killed in the Artillery Administration." This report was depressing."[37] Guchkov's reaction to the same information, which undoubtedly came from Tereshchenko, was apparently less dramatic yet more revealing. He showed an unusual concern for the general's fate. Though busy with numerous and presumably more urgent tasks, Guchkov appeared to have pushed all other matters aside and took it upon himself to find out if Manikovskii had survived the attack.[38]

It took the conspirators quite some time, somewhere between one to two hours, to locate the general. According to Tereshchenko, who helped Guchkov with the task by telephoning various places and people, they found him at home, alive and unharmed. Tereshchenko then arranged a meeting with the general in short order. Tereshchenko also told his interviewers that *before* he and Guchkov "headed out on foot to see" Manikovskii, the general's candidacy for the proposed role of military dictator was endorsed by several Duma leaders, among them Rodzianko, Konovalov, Miliukov, and Shul'gin. It was around 2:30 in the afternoon when the plotters embarked on their short journey—just as the Duma deputies gathered in the semicircular hall for their famous private meeting to decide on the form of the new authority.[39]

Manikovskii's selection as the preferred candidate did not come as a surprise to the Duma leaders or to the general himself. Although we have no direct evidence that Manikovskii was consulted about his prospective role prior to February 27, it is hard to imagine that a position of such significance and prominence would be offered to him at the spur of the moment, even if that moment was a revolution.[40] He was one of the most reputable senior generals, respected for his professionalism and moderate political views, and was widely credited for improving the flow of military supplies

[37] See the Skobelev interview (Chapter 10).
[38] See the Tereshchenko interview.
[39] See nn. 34, 36 to the Tereshchenko interview, n. 24 to the Engel'gardt interview, and nn. 8, 9 to the Gerasimov interview (Chapter 5).
[40] See Mel'gunov, *Na putiakh*, 107, 193.

in the wake of catastrophic shortages of the 1915 campaign.[41] He was also on record criticizing the government for its organization of the war effort. In the spring of 1916, he proposed his own far-reaching measures to overhaul the entire system of civilian and military administration of the home front. His plan called for the creation of a wartime military dictatorship under the Supreme Minister of State Defense (he reportedly considered himself an obvious front-runner) to oversee all civilian and military agencies, except in matters of strategy and warfare.[42] In many respects, what Guchkov and Tereshchenko were about to offer Manikovskii was akin to his own proposal, which had been shelved by the tsar in the summer of 1916. The plotters thus had good reason to expect a favorable response.

It must have been this belief that explained Nekrasov's famous proposal, which he made at the very start of the private meeting, to form a temporary military dictatorship under Manikovskii with "a committee of representatives from the Duma."[43] According to the meeting's minutes, a brief discussion ensued but the idea received little support. Different combinations as well as different candidates for the position of a military ruler were suggested, but in the end Nekrasov's proposal was not included in the list of several options put to a final vote at around 4:00 in the afternoon. It was decided to entrust the leaders of the Duma factions to appoint, from among the Duma deputies, a special committee that would become the temporary authority. Then, in another hour, close to 5:00 in the afternoon, Rodzianko announced the decision to form the "Temporary Duma Committee of the members of the State Duma for the restoration of order in the capital and the establishment of relations with public organizations and institutions," or the Duma Committee.[44] By the time the decision was announced, Guchkov

[41] See, for example, the memoirs of N. A. Rostovtsev, a leading Octobrist in the fourth Duma, in GARF, f. 9026, op. 1, d. 3, l. 184; and a copy of the January 18, 1917 police report to the minister of interior, in GARF, f. 1467, op. 1, d. 578, l. 46.

[42] See S. V. Kulikov, *Biurokraticheskaia elita Rossiiskoi imperii nakanune padeniia starogo poriadka, 1914–1917* (Riazan': NRIID, 2004), 214–18; A. A. Manikovskii, *Boevoe snabzhenie russkoi armii v mirovuiu voinu*, 2nd edn (Moscow and Leningrad: Gosizdat, 1930), II: 345.

[43] See the two published versions of the minutes and commentary in Lyandres, "Zur Errichtung der revolutionären Macht in Petrograd: Neue Dokumente über die inoffizielle Beratung von Mitgliedern der Staatsduma am 27.2.1917," *Berliner Jahrbuch für osteuropäische Geschichte* (1997): 312, 319, and Nikolaev, *Revoliutsiia i vlast'*, 142–3. According to a Duma-based journalist who reported from inside the Tauride Palace, Nekrasov told his colleagues that such a committee should consist of *five* members, the same number that formed the core of the plot. See RGIA, f. 1278, op. 10, d. 66, l. 2.

[44] See n. 24 to the Engel'gardt interview.

and Tereshchenko had already returned to the Duma and reported on their failure to persuade Manikovskii. Whether this information affected the outcome of the deputies' deliberations or simply delayed Rodzianko's announcement is impossible to tell at the present state of our knowledge. Unless new evidence emerges, any definitive conclusion should probably be avoided. Yet given the time correlation between the two events, such a connection should not be ruled out.

Manikovskii's refusal to accept the plotters' proposition was, by all indications, ambiguous. While it is undeniable that he declined the role of temporary dictator, his rejection was most likely conditional. He appears to have left the door open to revisit his decision if circumstances became more favorable. This, at least, is how Nekrasov and his co-conspirators seem to have understood his position. When later that evening members of the Duma Presidium, including Rodzianko and Nekrasov, drove to the Mariinskii Palace to persuade Grand Duke Mikhail Aleksandrovich to replace his reigning brother, Nekrasov again raised the question of appointing "a popular general devoted to a constitution" who would head "a provisional government of public figures [read: leading Duma deputies] to administer the country."[45]

In considering possible explanations for Nekrasov's persistence in establishing a temporary military dictatorship (and on Manikovskii as the plotters' preferred candidate), we should probably rule out fear of popular unrest, pressure from below, and similar class-based causes. If anything, his well-deserved reputation for shrewdness, keen political instincts, and sensitivity to popular needs and aspirations were well known and beyond question. More likely, his and his co-conspirators' actions can be understood in the context of their continued adherence to the prerevolutionary plans that shaped their thinking and informed their behavior during the first part of the February Days.

Astonishingly, Nekrasov and his co-conspirators operated as if what was happening on the streets was not an unprecedented political and social upheaval in the making but a localized unrest that afforded a unique opportunity to realize their plans for a palace coup. One could argue that they did not fully grasp the immensity of the change until after the emperor's abdication on the fourth night of the revolution, that is, only when the conspiracy's ultimate goal was finally achieved. In retrospect, this might seem (and probably was) counterintuitive, short-sighted, and self-destructive, but it

---

[45] See the Nekrasov interview.

also undermines the traditional narrative that the Guchkov-led plot did not develop much "beyond the embryonic phase," was poorly organized, or that no part of it was ever implemented. Even if one still prefers to treat the plotters' actions, as evidenced in the interviews and interpreted here, as a series of mere coincidences, the presence of so many of them—from personalities to military units to times and locations—can no longer be dismissed without a thorough and open-minded reexamination of all available evidence considered in the context of the plotters' prerevolutionary plans and their behavior during the first days of the February Revolution.

The Duma Committee Leaders' Attitudes toward a Palace Coup and the Question of Nicholas II's Abdication

The significance of the interviews extends beyond their value in introducing new details and establishing previously unknown connections pertaining to the most advanced of the prerevolutionary plots. Equally important, they shed new light on the attitudes toward a palace coup held by Rodzianko and Miliukov, the two leaders of the Duma Committee. In doing so, the interviews challenge the traditional explanation of their support for the central event of the February drama—the abdication of the reigning monarch.

Neither Rodzianko nor Miliukov was directly involved in any of the known plots to depose Nicholas II, and both repeatedly emphasized this point in their postrevolutionary memoirs. Not only did they express their unequivocal opposition to the very idea of a coup, but they explicitly denied any specific knowledge of the plotters' plans. In the absence of direct evidence to the contrary, historians have had little choice but to accept these claims. Some scholars have gone further and weaved them into the familiar social narrative of the revolution. For instance, Hasegawa, who seemed to have accepted the basic premises of their denials, has argued that the reason why "the majority of the [Duma] liberals led by P. N. Miliukov" stayed away from the Guchkov plot was their fear that a palace coup "might provoke a mass uprising from below which…would sweep away not only the state but also society."[46] But if Miliukov's supposed disapproval of a coup derived from fear of "a mass uprising from below," what can be said about the

---

[46] Hasegawa, "The February Revolution," in *Critical Companion*, 49.

considerably more conservative Rodzianko, who repeatedly insisted that he had rejected the idea and stopped its proponents from discussing it in his presence?[47]

The interviews discredit these assertions as products of hindsight that did not accurately reflect Rodzianko's and Miliukov's position at the time. As Tereshchenko revealed in his interview, Miliukov was not only well aware of the Guchkov plot through his participation in a series of prerevolutionary meetings of leading opposition figures in Moscow and Petrograd, but had also been kept abreast of its preparations by leaders of the group.[48] His endorsement of the nomination of General Manikovskii as temporary military ruler also implies a deeper level of involvement than previously believed. Years later, in a private conversation with B. I. Nikolaevskii, Miliukov acknowledged that he had possessed more than a cursory knowledge of the impending coup. He admitted this primarily to undermine Kerenskii's allegation that he had tried to postpone it in hopes of finding political accommodation with the regime.[49] None of this, of course, directly implicates Miliukov in the coup or makes him a participant. At the same time, his detailed knowledge of the plot and at least tacit support can no longer be in doubt.

As to Rodzianko, who prided himself on being a lifelong monarchist and the chamberlain of his majesty's court, his interview demonstrates in no uncertain terms that he in fact was a strong proponent, not an opponent, of a palace coup. The interview makes it clear that, contrary to his later writings

---

[47] See, for example, Diakin, *Russkaia burzhuaziia*, 302; Hasegawa, *The February Revolution*, 189–90, citing [M. V. Rodzianko], *The Reign of Rasputin: An Empire's Collapse. Memoirs of M. V. Rodzianko* (New York: A. M. Philpot Ltd, 1927), 244–5; Rodzianko, *Krushenie imperii. IV Gosudarstvennaia Duma i Fevral'skaia 1917 goda revoliutsii. Pervoe polnoe izdanie zapisok predsedatelia G[osudarstvennoi]. Dumy. S dopolneniiami E. F. Rodzianko* (New York: n.p., 1986), 208, 210, 280–1; Mel'gunov, *Na putiakh*, 151–2; Airapetov, *Generaly, liberaly i predprinimateli*, 195.

[48] See the Tereshchenko interview, and also S. A. Smirnov's testimony as recorded by Mel'gunov, in which he confirmed that Miliukov was well aware of the preparations for the plot (Papers of S. P. Mel'gunov, Box 226, f. "Fevral'–Mart 1917 g. Besedy i pis'ma," l. 6, BLPES). During 1916–17, Smirnov served as Konovalov's deputy at the Moscow WIC and later as state comptroller in the third coalition of the Provisional Government. In December 1916 he participated (along with Miliukov) in the meeting of opposition figures held at Konovalov's Moscow residence during which preparations for the plot were discussed. See n. 1 to the Tereshchenko interview.

[49] See a handwritten record of Nikolaevskii's conversation with P. N. Miliukov in the presence of B. I. El'kin, January 8, 1927, Nikolaevskii Collection, Box 525-3, l. 132, HIA; B. I. Nikolaevskii, *Russkie masony i revoliutsiia* (Moscow: Terra, 1990), 93.

as well as the prevailing historiographical narrative, the conservative Duma President was committed to deposing Nicholas. Indeed, as his unusually expansive interview illustrates, he became so frustrated by the political impasse with the imperial regime that "a political coup" appeared to him as the only feasible way out. Though known for his verbosity and a proclivity to dramatize, Rodzianko nevertheless appeared to have spoken candidly when he acknowledged that he "could not envision the salvation of Russia without a coup." [50] This was hardly a slip of the tongue or a misstatement, but an unprecedented admission repeated several times during his interview.

More broadly, Rodzianko's attitude toward a coup helps explain his generally misinterpreted position regarding Nicholas's abdication. Simply put, by endorsing the idea of a coup Rodzianko also implicitly accepted the necessity of replacing the reigning monarch, which of course was the central element of any palace coup. Thus, contrary to the conventional view that the Duma President resisted the abdication for "as long as he could" (until the night of March 1) or that the decision was forced on him by the "course of [revolutionary] events," and that he finally acquiesced only after much wavering and soul searching,[51] Rodzianko, in fact, had concluded well *before* the revolution that (his) Russia could not be saved without replacing "the obstinate tsar."

Rodzianko's Decision to Support the Abdication of Grand Duke Mikhail Aleksandrovich

This brings us to the last subject of this chapter which is, fittingly, also the closing episode of the February Revolution—the abdication of Grand Duke Mikhail Aleksandrovich and Rodzianko's controversial, if little understood, role in supporting this decision. It was this role that so dismayed his

[50] See the Rodzianko interview (Chapter 6). Rodzianko's knowledge of the plot as well as his tacit support was also confirmed by Guchkov. See a summary of his conversation with Mel'gunov, in Box 226, folder "Fevral'–Mart 1917 g. Besedy i pis'ma," l. 36ob. BLPES.

[51] As argued, for example, by Hasegawa, *The February Revolution*, 450–4, and Katkov, *Russia 1917*, 295–300. In his posthumously published work, V. I. Startsev, the last great Soviet historian of the revolution, suggested that Rodzianko made up his mind about the necessity of removing Nicholas from the throne shortly after his last official audience with the tsar on February 10, 1917. (V. Startsev, "Tshchetnye usiliia Rodzianko," *Mezhdu dvukh revoliutsii 1905–1917. Istochniki, issledovaniia, istoriografiia* (St. Petersburg: Nestor, 2004 [2005]), 201).

loyal supporters at the time and has puzzled historians ever since.[52] And while Rodzianko stopped short of discussing it in his interview, he did offer valuable insights on how he perceived his position as the Duma President and chairman of the revolutionary Duma Committee. When examined in conjunction with the other interviews, his motives become evident.

Historians of the Russian Revolution have long recognized the far-reaching implications of the grand duke's decision and the crucial role Rodzianko played in persuading "the last of the Romanovs" to renounce the throne.[53] Hasegawa expressed this point most recently and forcefully when he defined Mikhail's abdication as "the final act of the February Revolution," which "drove the last nail into the coffin of the monarchical system in Russia," and reiterated the view that "the role played by Rodzianko was decisive."[54] Yet his assertion that Rodzianko's support for the abdication was unexpected and represented "a 180-degree turnaround" is less convincing. Among the likely reasons that led the conservative Duma President to make his dramatic volte-face, Hasegawa argued, were the fear of "popular resentment to the monarchy," his desire to take revenge on Miliukov (the strongest opponent of Mikhail's abdication), whom he believed responsible for removing his name from the list of the Provisional Government, and his hopes "to bolster" his and the Duma's prestige by siding with "the radical wing" of the Duma Committee (led by Kerenskii and Nekrasov) in opposing Mikhail's acceptance of the throne.[55] Likewise, George Katkov, who rejected broad social explanations and focused instead on the role of character and personality traits, was all too ready to explain the conservative Duma President's presumed change of heart as a momentary aberration, bordering on madness.[56] It seems that the reason for these and similar excur-

---

[52] See, for example, V. A. Maklakov to A. F. Kerenskii, April 12, and May 14, [1951], Collection Maklakov, Box 8–13, HIA, and his preface to J. Polonsky and L. Polonsky, eds., *La Chute du Régime Tsariste—Interrogatoires. Collection de memoires pour server a l'histoire de la guerre mondiale (comptes rendus sténographiques)* (Paris, 1927); N.V. Savich, *Vospominaniia* (St. Petersburg: Logos, 1993), 205–8; Mel'gunov, *Martovskie dni 1917 goda* (Paris: Éditeurs réunis, 1961), 223; Katkov, *Russia, 1917*, 411, 415; Hasegawa, *The February Revolution*, 547–9; Leonard Schapiro, "The Importance of Law in the Study of Politics and History," in Leonard Schapiro, *Russian Studies*, ed. Ellen Dahrendorf, introduced Harry Willetts (New York: Penguin Books, 1988), 43.

[53] See, for example, Pares, *The Fall of the Russian Monarchy*, 468–70; Katkov, *Russia, 1917*; Hasegawa, "The February Revolution," in Acton et al., eds., *Critical Companion*, 59; Pipes, *The Russian Revolution*, 317–19.

[54] Hasegawa, "The February Revolution," in Acton et al., eds., *Critical Companion*, 59.

[55] Hasegawa, *The February Revolution*, 547–8; Hasegawa, "The February Revolution," in Acton et al., eds., *Critical Companion*, 59–60.

[56] According to Katkov, Rodzianko "practically lost his head." Katkov, *Russia, 1917*, 410.

sions into the unpredictable territory of collective behavior and the murky world of human personality is the historians' apparent inability to reconcile Rodzianko's "paradoxical" support for ending the monarchical form of government with his long-cultivated and ostensibly unassailable reputation as a devoted monarchist.

The interviews refute some of the most enduring of these explanations. They suggest instead less transient reasons for Rodzianko's position that are more consistent with his long-term strategy as head of the national legislature. To begin with, Miliukov was not alone in resisting Rodzianko's inclusion in the cabinet. It is true that Miliukov bears primary responsibility for making certain that the Duma as an institution of the old regime was kept out of the new power arrangement. But it is also true that "No one proposed Rodzianko for anything."[57] Or as Kerenskii recalled: "Only Rodzianko was categorically rejected, no one accepted him into the cabinet."[58] Though there was no love lost between the ambitious Duma President and the determined Kadet leader, it is improbable that such a seasoned politician (and the longest-served Duma President) would act primarily on the basis of a personal vendetta when the future of the monarchical system was at stake. (His many years of political coexistence with S. I. Shidlovskii, his principal rival and *bête noir* in the Octobrist party, is a case in point.)

"Bolstering the image of the Duma" or "recovering" Rodzianko's own prestige, which was supposedly tarnished in the opening days of the revolution, should also be excluded from among his likely motivations. As a superb recent study demonstrated, the Duma's status was still very high during March 2–3 and had in fact been considerably strengthened as a result of Nicholas's abdication.[59] Finally, Rodzianko's alleged fear of "the spectre of the further popular unrest which the preservation of the monarchy might have unleashed"[60] cannot be sustained as an acceptable explanation for what was probably the most controversial and consequential decision of his political life and—in the absence of reliable evidence—remains an untested hypothesis.

While on the face of it, Rodzianko's "180-degree turnaround" may have seemed unexpected, it was much more consistent with his actions during the first revolutionary days than historians have been willing to

---

[57] See the Chkheidze interview (Chapter 9).
[58] See the Kerenskii interview (Chapter 11).
[59] Nikolaev, *Revoliutsiia i vlast'*, 554.
[60] Hasegawa, "The February Revolution," in Acton et al., eds., *Critical Companion*, 60.

recognize. It was evidently his consistency in supporting the revolutionary course that his noticeably more radical colleagues Kerenskii and Nekrasov found so commendable, especially in contrast with the "intransigent Miliukov" and some of the Petrograd Socialist leaders on the far Left. Nekrasov expressed this sentiment well when he told his interviewers that from the moment he agreed to assume authority on the evening of February 27 and "until the end of the revolutionary days, Rodzianko behaved admirably, firmly, without wavering—in a word, this was a man at his very best."[61]

Disappointingly, Nekrasov never elaborated on what motivated Rodzianko's "admirable" behavior, but his close ally Kerenskii did. This is how he put it to his interviewers on May 31, 1917:

> When the revolution was purely political and radical, without the character that it later assumed, his behavior was impeccable. The reason why Rodzianko was excluded from the cabinet was not any consideration that he had to stay at the head of the Duma, that the Duma was needed as a reserve. Rather, this was a motive for him. At that time, the theory emerged that we [the Provisional Government] were only an emanation of the Duma. The Duma, Rodzianko, and the Executive Committee of the State Duma [the Duma Committee] are the father and mother of the new authority, and we are only their progeny. Later, and for a long time, he could not reconcile himself with the idea that after Mikhail Aleksandrovich's abdication, we were the only sovereign authority in the country.

What Kerenskii seemed to suggest here is that, as Duma President, Rodzianko's principal concern and political motivation had been to preserve and advance the standing and expand the powers of the representative legislative assembly over which he presided. When forced to choose between the monarchy and the Duma, Rodzianko followed his interests and chose the latter. And he relentlessly pursued this strategy in the favorable circumstances of the February Days, sparing no effort to transform the Duma under his leadership, now in the form of its surrogate, the Duma Committee, into the supreme authority. For Rodzianko, this promised to be a much bigger and more worthwhile undertaking than presiding over a Duma-appointed "responsible cabinet," as generally assumed.

---

[61] See the Nekrasov interview. Significantly, this was said on May 26, 1917, when Rodzianko and his former deputy speaker were no longer allies or even on good terms.

Thus, when the time came to decide the fate of Nicholas's reign, Rodzianko supported his removal, hoping that Grand Duke Mikhail Aleksandrovich would become a constitutional monarch (as regent for Nicholas's young son) and rule in agreement with the Duma. Nicholas's unexpected abdication in favor of his brother brought with it an unparalleled opportunity to elevate the Duma Committee to the status of supreme authority—the Supreme Committee, as Rodzianko famously remarked to General Alekseev on the morning of March 3, shortly *before* the fateful meeting with Mikhail.[62] With only the reluctant grand duke standing between the speaker of the (now prorogued) legislature and his aspiration of becoming the de facto ruler of the Russian state, the choice was obvious. Rodzianko sided with the Kerenskii group and went out of his way to persuade Grand Duke Mikhail Aleksandrovich to renounce the throne. This is the real reason for his decision—the pivotal choice that proved decisive in ending the three-hundred-year rule of the Romanov dynasty and effectively abolishing the monarchical form of government in Russia.

That his aspirations were not shared, indeed were opposed, by his Duma Committee colleagues and the just-formed Provisional Government, who saw to it that the new revolutionary government was to be "vested with all the plenitude of power," was an eventuality for which he found himself utterly unprepared and from which he never recovered. Rodzianko would spend his three remaining years in Russia trying to resurrect the very institution he had inadvertently helped turn into a relic of the loathed past. He was supported by only a handful of his former Duma colleagues, including "that great conspirator" Guchkov and "the smartest and most moderate of the [Duma] Kadets" V. A. Maklakov.

This discussion of the interviews does not aim to present the final word on any of the selected topics and is by no means exhaustive. It will take many years and more than a few historians to make sense of these newly discovered "untold stories of the February Revolution," let alone to fully comprehend their significance and wide-ranging implications. In choosing to concentrate on such a seemingly peripheral issue as the conspiracy to depose the reigning monarch, we did not wish to revive the old myths or to imply that conspiracies can adequately explain revolutionary politics or suggest that they alone can be sufficient to rewrite the political history of the February Revolution. At the same time, by focusing on this once

---

[62] "Fevral'skaia revoliutsiia 1917 goda (Dokumenty Stavki)," *KA* 3,22 (1927): 26.

hotly debated but now largely abandoned historical topic, we have tried
to emphasize the importance of prerevolutionary plans and visions in
explaining some of the most pivotal decisions that led to the fall of
tsarism—from establishing the new authority in the form of the Duma
Committee to securing the abdications of Nicholas II and his brother,
Grand Duke Mikhail.

Select Bibliography

Acton, Edward, et al., eds., *Critical Companion to the Russian Revolution, 1914–1921* (Bloomington and Indianapolis: Indiana University Press, 1997).

Burdzhalov, E. N., *Russia's Second Revolution. The February 1917 Uprising in Petrograd*, trans. and ed. Donald J. Raleigh (Bloomington and Indianapolis: Indiana University Press, 1987).

Figes, Orlando, *A Peoples' Tragedy. A History of the Russian Revolution* (New York: Viking, 1997).

Hasegawa, Tsuyoshi, *The February Revolution, Petrograd, 1917* (Seattle and London: University of Washington Press, 1981).

Katkov, George, *Russia, 1917: The February Revolution* (New York: Harper & Row 1967).

Melancon, Michael S., "Who Wrote What and When? Proclamations of the February Revolution in Petrograd, 23 February–1 March 1917," *Soviet Studies* 42, 3 (1988): 479–500.

Mel'gunov, S. P., *Martovskie dni 1917 goda* (Paris: Éditeurs réunis, 1961).

Nikolaev, A. B., *Revoliutsiia i vlast': IV Gosudarstvennaia duma, 27 fevralia–3 marta 1917 goda* (St. Petersburg: RGPU, 2005).

Pipes, Richard, *The Russian Revolution* (New York: Knopf, 1990).

Read, Christopher, *From Tsar to Soviets. The Russian People and their Revolution, 1917–21* (New York: Oxford University Press, 1996).

Service, Robert, *The Russian Revolution, 1900–1927*, 3rd edn (New York: St. Martin's Press, 1999).

Shukman, Harold, ed., *The Blackwell Encyclopedia of the Russian Revolution*, 2nd edn, rev. and updated (Oxford and Cambridge, MA: Blackwell, 1994).

Smith, S. A., *The Russian Revolution. A Very Short Introduction* (Oxford and New York: Oxford University Press, 2002).

Steinberg, Mark D., and Khrustalev, Vladimir M., *The Fall of the Romanovs. Political Dreams and Personal Struggles in a Time of Revolution*, Russian documents, trans. Elizabeth Tucker (New Haven: Yale University Press, 1995).

Sukhanov, N. N., *The Russian Revolution, 1917. A Personal Record*, trans. Joel Carmichael (London and New York: Oxford University Press, 1955).

Wade, Rex A., *The Russian Search for Peace, February–October 1917* (Stanford: Stanford University Press, 1969).

——— *The Russian Revolution, 1917*, 2nd edn (Cambridge: Cambridge University Press, 2005).

White, James D., *The Russian Revolution, 1917–1921. A Short History* (London, New York: Edward Arnold, 1994).

Wildman, Allan, *The End of the Russian Imperial Army*, vol. I: *The Old Army and the Soldiers' Revolt* (March–April 1917) (Princeton: Princeton University Press, 1980).

Index

Note: Page numbers in italics indicate maps and illustrations.

Printed in the USA/Agawam, MA
July 13, 2023

812964.004